PSYCHOLOGICAL PERSPECTIVES ON POLITICS

Carol Barner-Barry
University of Maryland

Robert Rosenwein
Lehigh University

WAVELAND PRESS, INC.

Prospect Heights, Illinois

For information about this book, write or call:

Waveland Press, Inc.
P.O. Box 400
Prospect Heights, Illinois 60070
(708) 634-0081

For Linda—with love and admiration
And to the memory of Phillip Brickman and Jeanne Knutson

CONTENTS

PREFACE

In the academic world, discontent often breeds textbooks. We are no exception. As teachers of courses in political psychology, we discovered that there were relatively few books on the market that approached comprehensiveness, and even fewer that were written collaboratively by persons with advanced training in *both* psychology and political science. The existing array of books—in spite of their many virtues—seemed to be either too narrow in focus or deficient in some degree in the skill with which either political or psychological concepts were handled. This book is our attempt to combine the backgrounds of a psychologist (R.R.) and a political scientist (C.B.B.) to produce the kind of relatively comprehensive textbook we would use in our classes.

The title of this book, *Psychological Perspectives on Politics*, promises many things. So that there will be no confusion, we wish to make clear what we intend by this title. *First,* to say that this book is reasonably comprehensive implies certain conscious choices to include some things and exclude others. Our criteria for doing so arose out of our struggle to synthesize a vast literature that reaches across at least two major disciplines. We came to realize that much of what we found in psychology came together in a way that illuminated the nature of the political process itself. Our book is organized around our model of political process in a way described in Chapter 1 and elaborated in Chapter 10. This model dictated, in part, our choice of material included in the book. *Second,* we do not claim that psychology is *superior* to any other discipline for the analysis of political behavior. Thus we offer no argument against the use of other frameworks for analysis, but simply try to indicate what psychology has to offer in illuminating political behavior. It follows from this belief that we see psychological perspectives as *complementary* to those of sociology, anthropology, economics, and the like. We ask: What does psychology have to offer in illuminating political behavior in ways that complement the insights of other disciplines?

This point leads to another that is central to our enterprise. We do not think it possible to conceptualize political behavior in terms of any one factor, such as power. Modern psychology and biology have more than adequately demonstrated (though there remain many unanswered questions) that human behavior is the result of a complex interaction of many factors—some coming from within the individual and some stemming from factors in both the proximate and wider environment. Political behavior is the outcome of a complex and as yet inadequately understood interaction among many such factors, operating through time and within historic contexts. We assert that our approach is interactionist (see Chapter 1 for more detail on this term).

Finally, this work is not a handbook. It does not pretend to collect and summarize every study that could be called "political psychology," nor does it pretend to present every bit of the vast material in psychology that applies to political phenomena. However, the reader will find a more than representative array of materials drawn from many subareas of psychology and should, in reading the text, find our treatment reasonably comprehensive.

As is usual in projects of this scope, any listing of those to whom we are intellectually indebted would far exceed our page limitations. A glimpse at the references at the end of the book will identify some of the more obvious people to whom we are indebted, but will not exhaust the list. It is much easier to acknowledge those who have in some way been of direct help to us. Primary mention should go to Stan Wakefield, our editor at Prentice-Hall, who was willing to take a chance on a book in an emerging field—and in these tough economic times, that takes courage. We are also indebted to Audrey Marshall, his assistant, and Marjorie Borden, our production editor, for their unfailing willingness to help in any way possible.

Special mention is also due to those brave souls who were willing to read the entire manuscript and who gave us the benefit of their comments and suggestions: Louise Kidder, Bill Kitchin, Steve Peterson, and Marc Ross. We owe a special debt of gratitude to Thomas Blank of Lehigh University for an extremely comprehensive reading of the text and for comments that were of particular value in helping to shape the book in its final stages of preparation. The measure of support and encouragement given both of us went far beyond our expectations. Others who have helped in various ways in the preparation of one or more sections of this book include: Donald Barry, Connie Bowers, Louis Cantori, Phil Henderson, Stanley Renshon, and Linda Rosenwein. Deborah Auger, Dennis Muniak, and John Gatewood were most helpful in supplying illustrations. We would also like to thank the staffs of the libraries at Lehigh University and the University of Maryland, Baltimore County, and the secretarial staffs of the Social Relations Department and Political Science Departments at Lehigh and the Political Science Department at the University of Maryland, Baltimore County. Special mention should be made of the reference librarians at both institutions who cheerfully complied with many difficult and unusual requests for information.

Finally, we would like to acknowledge the environment of intense political discussion and thinking in which we grew up. We have no doubt that our formative history of interaction with our parents about politics through our early years led to our lifelong interests in politics and, ultimately, to this book.

1

THE MANY FACETS
OF POLITICAL PSYCHOLOGY

HARRY'S STORY

"Where do you want this box, Congressman?"

Harry Cackalari looked up from the desk drawer into which he was trying to fit too many pens, pencils, and yellow pads.

"Oh, just stick it up on top of the others in that corner." He gestured with a ballpoint. The mover wrestled the box on top of the pile, turned, and went out the door.

Cackalari leaned back in his swivel chair, shut the drawer, and put his feet up on the desk. Through the window of his new office, he could just barely see the Capitol dome.

He smiled.

"So I'm finally here," he thought. "Unbelievable!" Heaving a great sigh of satisfaction, he began to reminisce about his campaign and his unexpected victory over a supposedly invincible opponent. Donald True-hart was a six-term congressman, considered by many to be a real power in Congress. Harry remembered the first conversations that led to his candidacy. A reasonably successful banker, Harry had always enjoyed office politics. He saw politics as a game that was fun to play. As he had become more skilled his pleasure in playing the game had increased. And there was always the satisfaction of emerging victorious. Unlike many of

1

his colleagues, however, he did not see office politics as an end in itself. It was a way of furthering certain values he held and certain beliefs he had about the way the banking industry ought to be run.

People frequently commented that Harry "expanded into the opportunities." Indeed, as his influence on his bank's policies grew, many of his colleagues and friends noticed that he was becoming restless. He looked as if there was something more he wanted to be doing.

The idea that he run for Congress first came from the Banker's Roundtable, that group of "old boys" who met Friday afternoons down at the Oak Bar, a favorite watering hole of the corporate elite. Harry remembered the shiver of excitement that ran up his spine when someone broached the idea. Suddenly, he saw that it might be possible to influence the banking industry on a much larger scale than simply by being the first vice-president of his bank. A seat in Congress might allow him to develop his political skills to the point where he could make a contribution to cleaning up the economic mess the country was in and to building a strong economy. The excitement of that prospect was overwhelming.

"How about it, Harry?" someone had said. "You're a good looking boy, and God knows you like to talk. What about it?"

The opportunity and the challenge were irresistible. So that was the beginning. The next few months had been a whirl of events and activities, so many and so new that Harry could hardly sort them out, even now. He remembered the rigors of fund raising and dealing with the problem of the Political Action Committees (PACs), which the "old boys" had set up. He remembered the Walk Across the County, a technique everybody seemed to be using but effective nonetheless and great for media exposure. He remembered the time he'd used the issue of busing effectively against Truehart during their one debate. Harry had to admit—a little guiltily—that he had been less than kind to Truehart on that issue. Truehart's position had probably gotten slightly distorted, but after all, that was the way the game was played. He remembered the polls that had Truehart winning 2 to 1; those polls may have kept enough Truehart voters home to make a Cackalari victory (narrow as it was) possible.

Anyway, that was history. He was here. Now where to start?

His reverie was broken by a knock on the door.

"Harry, my boy, nice to see you with us!"

At the door was the man Harry had more or less expected to show up immediately. Philip Bluster, senior congressional representative in the state, the man you'd least want to trust but a man who knew what buttons to press to get what you wanted.

"Philip, good to see you again!" Harry exclaimed. "I expected to see you sooner."

"Well, you know, my boy, I've got quite a few irons in the fire right now, but you were on my list!" He laughed.

They talked about trivial matters for a while, and then Harry asked the question.

"So, Phil, what are the chances of my ending up on the banking subcommittee?"

"Well, Harry," Bluster said, looking serious, "I think it's a real possibility, a real possibility. Tell me, is there something I can do for you?"

"Well, Phil," said Harry, looking equally serious, "I wonder if you could put in a good word with the Speaker."

"I think that's a real possibility, a real possibility," Bluster replied (indulging his well-known tendency to repeat himself). "I'm seeing him this afternoon, and I'll keep it in mind."

The conversation moved to other matters, and then Bluster popped *his* question.

"Tell me, Harry, have you given any thought to the position you're going to take on that abortion question we're all so concerned about?"

Harry knew this was a loaded one. He said carefully, "Well, Phil, I made my position reasonably clear during the campaign, but I think you know me well enough to know I always have an open mind."

"So you really don't know how you'll vote, then?" Bluster said, his eyebrows arching.

"Phil," Harry said, looking right into his eyes, "I'm prepared to listen to all reasonable arguments."

Brightening, Bluster said, "Well, that's fine, Harry, just fine; knew I could count on you to keep an open mind. Well, don't want to keep the Speaker waiting. Take care of yourself and say hello to that lovely family of yours."

"Oh, I will, Phil, and thanks," he said to Bluster's back as Phil Bluster left.

Harry leaned back again. Well, he thought, that's one that will be difficult to handle. Bluster had taken a position on the upcoming abortion legislation that was not entirely different from Harry's. It was, however, different enough so that certain powerful constituents of his would be likely to raise a fuss if he voted along with Bluster. On the other hand, it was clear that getting that place on the banking subcommittee required Bluster's influence, and Bluster was not being subtle about the price he wanted from Harry. Perhaps he could vote along with Bluster without doing real disservice to his own views. After all, a position on the banking subcommittee was essential if Harry was to accomplish the goals that had made the hard work and risks of the campaign worthwhile. It was a tough decision. He would have to think long and hard about what he should do and how he should do it. This initial step could make a big difference in the long haul.

The long haul, Harry thought, smiling. This political life agreed with him. Yes, he thought, as the mover returned with more boxes, I am definitely here for the long haul.

DONNA'S STORY

When Donna Franklin drove up to City Hall, she could see that the planned action was developing fast—maybe too fast. Hundreds of East Town residents were milling around in front of the building, camera trucks were arriving, the picket line was already moving, and Donna's assistant, Gene, was leading the chants: "Clean up the stores or clean out City Hall! Power for the people! Health for our children! No more rats! No more fat cats!" She parked the car hurriedly and rushed over to Gene.

"What's happening?" she said.

"They're getting ready to go into the mayor's office right now— better get in there!" he replied.

"You bet," she said over her shoulder as she pushed through the crowds on the steps and into the main lobby of the building.

Inside she quickly made her way to the second floor and saw about twenty-five East Town Organization (ETO) members crowding around the door to Mayor Smith's office. June, Greg, and Reverend Michael, ETO's steering committee, were arguing strenuously with an aide to the mayor. Donna acknowledged their greetings as she came up to the group.

"What's the problem?" she said. "Did you tell them why we're here?"

Reverend Michael turned his level gaze to her. "We have indeed, Donna; we have told them about the telegram and they claim never to have seen it. And this gentleman has the nerve to say we have no appointment with the mayor today!" He winked at her.

The wink said a lot, as Donna well knew. The problem of the unclean supermarket on South Grand Street had long been a thorn in the side of the largely poor, largely black and Hispanic population of the area. Since many people could not afford cars, and since mass transportation was a joke, the supermarket was almost the only place to shop. But like too many stores in poor areas, this one had been allowed to deteriorate. Complaints had been ignored, and the issue had gotten heated after rats were seen in the storeroom by the stock clerks. Donna had been in the neighborhood for a couple of months as a community organizer and had been instrumental in beefing up the ETO. Trained in the use of confrontation tactics, she had been successful in helping the group to initiate several successful "actions." It had not been easy to teach people confrontation tactics; fortunately, she had an ally in Reverend Michael, the activist minister of the local church. He shared her views about the value of these actions, as she liked to call them. Indeed, Reverend Michael had a real zest for them, and his willingness to get involved had certainly encouraged others to join in. She remembered very well that quiet Eva Gomez had agreed to make a presentation at a city council meeting, and how she had schooled Eva, making sure that the woman would shout down stock speeches and soothing platitudes. Keeping a tense atmosphere had its advantages. And she remembered how nervous Eva had been before the presentation. But Eva had done it and had felt her shyness and fear drop away behind the role. Donna would never forget what Eva said later: "You really learn a lot about your potential."

Now they were here trying to move Mayor Smith to put pressure on the company to clean up the store. They'd sent him a telegram asking for an appointment on a certain date, and when he failed to reply, they came anyway.

"Well," said Donna, turning to the mayor's aide, "we've got an appointment and we're going in."

"But, but, the Mayor's not here; I've tried to explain that!" He looked very annoyed as he moved toward the door to the office.

"We can wait," said June, and she turned to walk into the office.

"No, no, you can't!" The aide's voice rose suddenly, and with a look of panic, he pushed June aside roughly, rushed into the office, and slammed the door.

For a moment there was silence. Then an outraged babble of cries and angry words broke out. Thinking quickly, Donna turned to Reverend Michael.

"Reverend Michael, I think that gentleman owes June an apology, don't you?"

"Donna, my dear, you have a good point there. I would even go so far as to say that an apology is *demanded*."

Turning, he pounded loudly on the door. "I'm a minister; open up."

The door opened. Quickly Reverend Michael pushed inside along with several other members of the steering committee. The door closed.

Donna smiled as the supporters in the hall began to chant again. The TV cameras had got most of it, she thought, including the scuffle. The mayor was going to have to take some action now, and if he was smart, he would not try to label a minister as an agitator. This group really had it together. She probably wouldn't be needed in East Town much longer.

Making her way out to the steps, she was stopped by Chet Forbes, Channel 3's ace investigative reporter, whom Donna knew from other actions.

"Donna Franklin," he said, shoving a microphone into her face and motioning his cameraman to move in more closely, "do you think this protest today is going to have any effect?"

"Chet," Donna said, "I think the East Town community is finally beginning to realize its own power to change the conditions in which it lives." She went on talking, but inside she realized how tired she really was. You tried to work through the system, you wrote polite letters, you petitioned, you voted, and what did you get? The same old thing: nothing, no change, no improvement. Saul Alinsky was right; to move the system, you've got to confront the people in power, embarrass them, do what is necessary to get them to move. People know life is unjust; they know it's not equitable, but they need to know that they have the power to change it, if they move *together* and are not afraid to take risks.

She finished the interview with Chet and walked off. Her spirits lifted a little as she began to anticipate the next challenge. This was her life, she thought—getting the losers moving, making them feel like winners, making things happen for those on the bottom. That was where it was at. As she walked back to her car, she tried hard not to hear that little voice with its continually nagging question:

"What kind of society is it that has to have winners and losers?"

"It's an egalitarian society; that's what politics is all about," she said aloud. A passing couple gave her a curious look.

"Oh," said the little voice, "is it?"

Donna thought about the rats in the storeroom of the East Town supermarket and tried to ignore the little voice.

OVERVIEW: HOW THIS BOOK IS ORGANIZED

The stories of Harry Cackalari and Donna Franklin are rich in the stuff of political psychology. Here we see two individuals acting within or upon institutions which are formally charged with the responsibility for making decisions that can be regarded as political. What we intend to do in this book is to look at the process by which political policy is made and explore some of the psychological dynamics of that process.

The first thing we need to do, then, is delineate the sorts of decisions that can be fairly regarded as political. Many scholars have attempted to define and delineate the political (e.g., Dahl 1976, p. 3; Eckstein and Gurr 1975, p. 22; Isaak 1969, 15-17). We have chosen as our focus for political inquiry the formulation suggested by David Easton, who asserts that politics involves all the activities in a society which are "involved in the formulation and execution of social policy" (Easton 1971, p. 129). Political science, then, would be "the study of the authoritative allocation of values for a society" (ibid.). These values may be formally embodied in a law or in a political institution or they may merely be "lodged in the consequences of a practice" (ibid., p. 131). In any case, what we have is a public process which culminates in some sort of outcome—usually an authoritative decision (or, perhaps, failure to act). This is what we will regard as the political component. But where do we begin as political *psychologists*?

The casual reader can see immediately that there are many personal differences between Donna and Harry. Harry seems to relish the political game, and one senses in him what could be called ambition. "Wheeling and dealing" in the congressional environment not only is attractive to him, it is an activity consonant with the kind of person he is. Donna, too, takes pleasure in her competence and her ability to set up a situation that has certain consequences. But we also get a strong feeling for her concern about injustice. More than Harry, she seems genuinely interested in those at the bottom and their problems. The extraordinarily difficult job of community organizer seems as consonant for Donna as a person as is the job of congressman for Harry. Thus, we arrive at the psychology part of our formulation. People acting in the political realm have unique qualities which they bring to their tasks; they are also embedded in an environment which has some relationship (good or bad) to their personal qualities. Thus, political psychology can be seen as the study of people who are doing the authoritative decision making for a society, as well as of others who are trying to influence those decisions. In short, political psychology is the study of politically relevant activity in relation to the environment within which it takes place.

This raises the question of the extent to which it makes sense to compare people like Donna and Harry. It may be unfair to ascribe personal qualities to Harry and Donna when we are not comparing them within the same environment or situation. How would Donna behave if she were the newly elected member of Congress? What kind of community organizer would Harry be? Of course, we imply above that people tend to gravitate, if possible, toward environments that suit their personal qualities. But this does not invalidate the point about making comparisons between individuals. Therefore, in focusing on individual characteristics, it is important that we remember that differences in behavior between and among individuals may result from a number of factors; and that these factors include the obligations and pressures felt by people because they are situated in positions that carry with them certain responsibilities and expectations on the part of other people. For example, Harry and Donna both have constituencies. But here, Donna is working directly with her constituents while Harry's contact is much less direct. If we are going to make any progress in understanding the behavior of people like Harry and Donna and its effects on the direction and outcome of the political process, we will have to understand not only who they are, but also the environments in which they act.

When we look across the broad array of frameworks, theories, and concepts that psychologists have brought to bear on the understanding of political behavior, we find that there frequently has been a stress either on factors residing "inside" the person (e.g., a need for power) or on factors residing in the environment or situation (e.g., social class). The rest of this chapter is devoted in part to a brief introduction to frequently used concepts in both categories. The concepts noted here will be more fully developed later in the book. But, as the two previous paragraphs clearly imply, a person's behavior is influenced by the properties of both the person and the situation. This *interaction* perspective has characterized much of the work of social psychologists over the past thirty years, and is therefore a dominant theme in this book. That is, we will always be asking ourselves: Given any particular political behavior or class of political behaviors, how do the properties of the person and the properties of the situation interact to influence behavior?

The concept of interaction, however, is not as simple as it may sound. For example, whether a concept is "in the person" or "in the environment" is often not easy to specify. Further, through behavior, an individual may modify the situation that is influencing her. The influence which the situation then exerts on the individual may change. At the end of this chapter we spend some time exploring some of the complicated nuances involved in understanding what is meant by "interaction."

As is true for so many political psychologists, our formulations about person, situation, and interaction owe much to the programmatic framework of the relationship of personality and political behavior developed by M. Brewster Smith (1968). As an "intellectual strategy" (Smith 1968, p. 16), his approach has been pervasive in the work of political psychologists during the past 15 years (see, for example, Bonham and Shapiro, 1967; Etheredge, 1978; Falkowski, 1979; George, 1979; Greenstein, 1971; Hermann, 1980; Hermann and Hermann, 1982; Holsti, 1976; Jervis, 1976; Stone, 1974; Walker, 1977; Walker and Falkowski, 1982; Winter, 1973). It should be noted, however, that Smith has a particular perspective on the personal and situational elements. He asserts that any individual's political behavior fulfills one or more of three functions for the person: (1) relating things in the world to a person's motives, interests and values; (2) mediating the relationship between the person and other people; and (3) resolving inner conflict. Smith sees environmental factors as being related to the fulfillment of these functions. Although we see virtue in this approach, we feel that there are many other possible ways of talking about the linkages between person and situation (some of which are reviewed later in this book). The central task, however, is clear for Smith and for us: *How do personal and environmental factors, taken together, act jointly to influence political behavior?*

Let's return to Harry Cackalari and Donna Franklin. In reading their stories, and in thinking about political behavior generally, three themes predominate—the conflictual nature of political behavior; winning and losing; and the perception of justice. *First,* while we freely acknowledge that cooperation has been central in humanity's past and current political behavior (Deutsch 1973; Barner-Barry, in preparation), we agree with Dan Nimmo that political behavior is more accurately characterized as "the activity of people collectively regulating their conduct under conditions of social conflict" (1978, p. 6, italics omitted). We see relationships in political life as usually asymmetrical in nature. At any particular time or place and with reference to any specific issue or value, some people tend to exercise more political influence than others. It therefore seems that conflict is inherent in any situation involving the authoritative allocation of public resources.

Second, we feel that the conflictual nature of politics creates a dynamic in which some individuals—or groups of individuals—end up having more or less resources than others. The extent to which a person or group of persons ends up perceiving themselves as winner or loser in this sense is a function of many elements associated with the personal characteristics of the individual and the situation. Winning and losing is a matter of interpretation and degree. By and large, in relatively stable political systems, everyone gets something, but not everything they may have hoped to get. And some people consistently get more or less than others.

Third, people tend to judge the outcomes of political processes in normative terms. Were they treated fairly? Did they get justice? Are they reasonably satisfied with how they were treated in a particular instance? Over time? Thus, along with judgments about winning and losing, people tend to draw conclusions as to the fairness or justice of both the political process and the outcomes of particular political conflicts.

We believe that these three themes are linked together in ways that describe a model of the political process. We have used this model as a device for organizing the major portions of this book (Chapters 3 through 9). Although the model is considered in more detail in Chapter 10, we will review it briefly here, indicating how the structure of the book is related to it. As we do so, we will make certain assertions without fully justifying them, leaving that task for Chapter 10.

To begin with, the political process is activated when authorities or partisans perceive that there is a public resource allocation problem that needs to be resolved. Will authorities or partisans get involved in solving the problem? If so, what tactics and strategies will they choose to employ? In Chapter 3, we consider the question of political involvement. What are the ways in which people can become active in political life? How does the way in which they become active influence what they accomplish? Does political involvement bring individual rewards that are less obvious than the accomplishment of political policy objectives? Does the role one plays in the political process have an impact on one's view of the process itself? Trying to answer such questions impels one to look backward. Chapter 4 therefore considers the problem of political socialization. Politically active adults were once adolescents; before that, children; before that, infants. They were raised in families and spent much of their youth in schools. Parents, teachers, peers, the media—all taught them what it means to be a person in their society and culture, including what it means to be a politically active person (Doob 1983, p. 39–43, 45–48).

The choice of tactics and strategies for involvement is not only mediated by political socialization and the political culture in which one is embedded, but is also filtered by the degree of structure in the conflict situation itself. The question of conflict structure is discussed more fully in Chapter 8. In particular, the nature of political institutions is seen to have a significant influence on how much structure (or lack thereof) characterizes the conflict situation. Given a certain degree of structure, people choose mechanisms for regulating or resolving the conflict over public resource allocation. Chapters 5 through 8 consider four familiar mechanisms: leadership, persuasion, bargaining, and force. Ultimately, some decision needs to be made about the allocation problem. But how are such decisions made? What factors influence both the process and the outcome of decision-making? These matters are considered in Chapter 9.

TABLE 1-1   Representative factors political psychologists have called on to understand and explain political behavior

Personal Factors	Habits
Motives	simple
	complex
needs	
drives	Environmental Factors
impulses	Microenvironment: eyeball to eyeball
	relationships
Emotions	normative structure
anxiety	norms
guilt	sanctions
depression	roles
	interpersonal structure
Cognitions	personal style
attributions	
personality	Microenvironment: immediate but imaginary
motivations	reference groups
relationships	
categories	Macroenvironment
stereotypes	
implicit theories	Organizational structure
codes (schemas)	position
cognitive maps	division of labor
perceptual screens	
ethnocentrism	Economic
	class
Hybrids	mode of production
beliefs	
attitude	The Sea
value	history
ideology	culture
self-esteem	
identity	
Faculties	
skills	
abilities	

Once a decision is made, affected individuals evaluate whether they are winners or losers. Although these terms seem pejorative, we simply intend them to mean that some people get more and some people get less as a result of most political decisions. A major source of dynamics in the political process comes when people evaluate their winner/loser status in terms of its fairness. Was justice done? Was the process itself fair? If people feel that justice was served, then further action is unlikely. If, however, people perceive that justice was not served, people may or may not act on this perception. For example, suppose poor people who rely on food stamps find that the government has cut back on food stamp availability. Many may feel that this decision is unfair. Will they take action to rectify this perceived injustice? If so, what will this action be—write letters to their congressional representative, stage a rally in front of the local welfare office, organize a sit-in at congressional offices, try to elect more sympathetic congressional representatives? Clearly, each of these decisions (or the decision to do nothing) will condition the scope, direction, and intensity with which political goals are pursued. If action is taken by losers to change the status quo, it is likely that winners will act to maintain outcomes favorable to them. Thus, the process may or may not be reactivated, depending on the ability of losers or winners to move the process toward another round of decisionmaking activity, or to repress such activity. The question of justice from a psychological point of view is discussed in detail in Chapter 10.

As mentioned earlier, political psychologists have evoked a multitude of concepts or facts, both personal and situational, in attempting to understand and explain a wide variety of political behavior. Since one of our tasks in this book is to provide a reasonably comprehensive review of these attempts, we begin by briefly defining and discussing some of the more popular and enduring concepts. We will not attempt in this chapter to review the diversity of perspectives on the way in which personal and situational factors interact. Instead, we will limit ourselves to a discussion of some of the nuances and subtleties involved in using an interaction approach. Table 1-1 lists the factors we will be describing and discussing here.

PERSONAL FACTORS IN POLITICAL BEHAVIOR

We begin by reviewing the concepts that are based on the idea that there are things "inside" individuals which are somehow connected to, have a relationship with, even "cause," a person's political behavior. Two points need to be made. First, we must distinguish between things "inside" individuals that are shared by all or most humans and things "inside" that clearly differentiate individuals. For example, people in Western culture have a shared tendency to be attracted to individuals whom they perceive to be like themselves, particularly when the similarity is based on beliefs or values (Byrne 1969; Rokeach 1979). However, in this connection, we might want to talk about an individual's "need to be liked." The need to be liked is a property which varies considerably from one individual to another. Indeed, when a person consistently seems to need to be liked, we talk about their personality or their personality *trait*.

Second, two strategies have been employed by psychologists in focusing on those things inside individuals which we call "personality." On the one hand, we may look at particular individuals and try to discover how their personalities developed and how they affect behavior. Alternatively, we may try to discover how they are representatives of a more general class of individuals who have similar characteristics. In the first instance, we might do a thorough inventory of Harry and Donna, employing a battery of sophisticated tests as well as an examination of their life histories. This clinical or psychobiographical approach typifies much of what has been called political psychology in the past (Glad 1973). In the second instance, we might try to find other political actors whose behavior is like that of Donna or Harry and see whether they share some set of similar characteristics. This is the delineation of political types which has a venerable and important place in modern political psychology (e.g. Barber 1972).

Political psychologists have focused on one or more of the following five categories: motives, emotions, cognitions, faculties, and habits.

Motives. The word motive comes from the Greek, *movere*, literally "to move." If we can think metaphorically for a moment, the idea is that there are things inside a person that move or impel him or her into action. Different words are used for the term "motive"—need, impulse, drive. Different writers use these terms in different ways. Needs, for example, imply a deficit, something the person lacks and then tries to make up for through his behavior. The concept of a "need for power" proposed by Joseph Veroff (1957) and later expanded considerably by David Winter (1973) is an example of this kind of concept. The person lacks the gratification that is derived from the exercise of power. Hence, he or she may be drawn to situations in which influence and control can be exerted, i.e., certain political roles. For example, is Harry Cackalari high in the need for power? He certainly enjoys the trappings of his office and looks forward to being on a committee that will allow him to influence financial legislation. In any event, one can imagine the need for power concept being invoked to explain Harry's behavior. On the other hand, the need concept has also been used to refer to behavior oriented toward growth, as opposed to behavior oriented to making up a deficit (e.g., Maslow 1954). The terms "impulse" and "drive" both imply certain forces inside a person that push her in a certain direction. These terms are often linked to a metaphor of the personality as "energy" channeled and directed by factors such as learning. The name Sigmund Freud is historically associated with this sort of approach.

Emotions. The realm of feelings or emotions is equally complex. Of the many different perspectives on the nature and origin of emotions, the ones most associated with political behavior focus on those emotions that seem related to interpersonal relationships. A prime candidate for an important emotion in the study of political behavior is *anxiety*. There are two general perspectives on anxiety. The first sees anxiety as a kind of signal to an individual of some impending harm or of some vulnerability he or she may have. This perspective is central to Freud's theory of the personality. A second perspective sees anxiety as a learned response to certain environmental events. In particular, it is seen to arise from the association of feeling with the occurrence of some stimuli. This process is called conditioning. The significance of anxiety in both perspectives is that it may trigger action by the individual to reduce the anxiety. These actions may be called defenses or learned defensive maneuvers: In either case, they may lead to certain patterns of political behavior (Lasswell 1950). For instance, some political psychologists have speculated that when people are anxious, they are much more prone to make scapegoats of others and much more susceptible to the influence of a leader who is adept at discovering "enemies" as the "cause" of people's anxieties. The theory of the authoritarian personality has this kind of concept at its core, as does Erich Fromm's notion of the anxiety associated with democratic freedoms, an anxiety leading to a desire to "escape from freedom" (1941).

Two other emotions with interpersonal implications have been discussed by political psychologists. The first of these is *guilt,* the emotion one feels when internal standards for behavior are violated (or are perceived to have been violated). For example, the analysis by George and George (1956) of Woodrow Wilson's personality focuses on the role that low self-esteem and guilt played in decisions Wilson made as president. The other emotion is *depression.* Depression centers on one's inability to control events in the environment. Again, depression may be considered to arise out of internal personality dynamics, or it may be seen as a form of "learned helplessness" (Seligman 1975). However it is conceptualized, depression as fate control or effectance (the ability to affect the environment in desired ways) has frequently been invoked to account for the degree of an individual's involvement in the political system. Harry is anything but depressed. Donna, on the other hand, leaves with some sense of her lack of control over situations she would like to change.

Cognition. The third category of internal things considered to affect political behavior is cognition, the realm of understanding and knowing about the world. Of great interest is "social cognition," the way we come to know about other people, who they are, and why they act the way they do. The modern study of social cognition has tended increasingly to focus on the way in which individuals handle information. Information consists of stimuli that are perceived by the individual, give one clues to the nature of the world, and help one to reduce uncertainty about it. In the most general sense, we can say that individuals select information, generate new information to supplement the information already selected, organize this information, and combine it in various ways (Wegner and Vallacher 1977). This "information processing" perspective (Neisser 1976) has yielded some concepts that have become important to political psychologists. These concepts are attribution, categories, implicit theories, operational codes, cognitive maps, and perceptual screens.

Attributions refer to complex and sophisticated guesses, interpretations, or inferences about the nature of other human beings (Wegner and Vallacher 1977). First, one can make trait attributions. Read Donna's story again. Do you think she is shy, extroverted, devious, honest, cunning, power-hungry? If pressed, you could probably come up with a list of traits which you would expect her to exhibit consistently over long periods of time.

Second, people make guesses about the causes of other people's behavior. Do you think Harry agreed to run for Congress because he wants to be the center of attention? Or do you think he is attracted to positions from which he can influence the lives of others? In either case, you are making an attribution about *why* Harry behaves the way he does. As we shall see later in the book, we may attribute any behavior to personal or situational factors, or some combination of the two (an interesting parallel to the structure of this chapter).

Third, we may also make attributions about relationships between others. For example, what is the relationship between Gene and Donna? Gene is Donna's assistant, so it is likely that one relationship you will infer between the two is that they are linked through their work in the ETO. Do these two like each other? Is there greater involvement? If pressed, it is likely that you would have some ideas about these matters. In politics, these relationship inferences may be of particular importance, since (at least in our view) knowing who is on whose side in a dispute, being aware of the likely coalitions that may form and so on, are of central importance in the regulation and resolution of conflict (see Chapter 7, and Heider 1958).

Why are attributions important to political psychologists? The answer may seem obvious, but it seems worthwhile to be explicit about the answer. Consider the discussion between Harry Cackalari and Phil Bluster. Harry clearly attributes certain traits to Bluster, i.e., that he is pompous and not particularly direct or open in dealing with others. He also apparently has decided that Bluster is there to solicit support from Harry on the abortion issue. Finally, he attributes Bluster's arrival at his office and Bluster's behavior therein to their roles in Congress. Taking all this into account, Harry takes action. In short, Harry's *behavior is predicated on the attributions* he makes to Bluster (and probably to himself as well). The relationship between something "inside" a person, like an attribution, and that person's subsequent behavior, is not a simple one (see Chapter 2). But most modern psychology has taken it as a general assumption that in order to understand any behavior (including political behavior), we must understand something about the attribution process.

Are attributions simply made up on the spot? Surely this is not the case. Through accumulated experiences, we develop a set of ideas about who people are, why they do the things they do, and how they are related to each other. Wegner and Vallacher call these ideas *implicit theories*. For example, if we attribute a relationship of liking to exist between Donna and Gene, we may make this attribution on the basis of an implicit theory which says that if two people appear to work well together, they also probably like each other. Similarly, if we attribute certain traits to Donna, it is likely that we will view some traits as more important than others. Moreover, these traits will tend to be related to each other in systematic ways (Asch 1946; Nelson and Vivekanathan 1968).

Implicit theories are important because they help us to select, organize, generate, and combine information. One of the more important aspects of implicit theories is that they consist in part of categories of information. For example, if I know that a person is a "conservative Republican," I am likely to think that this person is against government spending for social programs, supports a bigger defense budget, and votes for conservative candidates. I am also likely to think that this person places a high value on free enterprise, the sanctity of the nuclear family, and government incentives for business and agricultural enterprise. This set of attributes may not be true for every conservative Republican, of course. The point is, however, that when I know that someone is a conservative Republican, it triggers a set of related attributions.

There are two extensions of the concept of a category that have been particularly of interest to political psychologists. The first is the notion of a *stereotype,* a category in which we ascribe a particular pattern of characteristics to a group of persons. We usually are aware of stereotyping when the word "all" is affixed to the beginning of a sentence about a group, as in "all Scots are thrifty" or "all Jews are greedy." Stereotypes typically imply greater rigidity in thinking about individuals than would otherwise be the case. For example, although my category of conservative Republican is based on considerable experience with conservative Republicans, I am willing to "change my mind" (i.e., modify my category) on the basis of new information. Stereotypes are less susceptible to modification. Indeed, when confronted with information that runs contrary to the stereotype, one is likely to try to maintain it through some other device, for example: "This person's behavior is the exception that proves the rule that all Scots are thrifty."

A second extension of the category concept is based to some extent on the idea of a stereotype. We not only categorize groups as different, we also place a value on this difference. In particular, we may say that the group to which we belong is better than a group to which others belong. This notion, *ethnocentrism,* may affect conflict situations which in turn generate winners and losers. If either winners or losers perceive the category of individuals to which they belong as fundamentally better than the other group, then the issue of the perceived justice of the decision is likely to become all the more complicated. It has been suggested that the decision to contest the outcome of public resource allocation decisions (an important component of our model of political process) may be premised on the development of some degree of ethnocentrism. The perception that one's own group is better, stronger, and more deserving may make the group more unified and thus more willing to mobilize for change (Kidder & Stewart 1975, p. 29).

Finally, let us note that political psychologists have come up with other terms for implicit theory, category, and attribution. The most popular in recent years has been the term *operational code,* used to refer to the way people organize information in their minds for use in adapting to the world (e.g., George, 1969; Leites, 1951). As we shall see in Chapters 5 and 9, this concept has been used in understanding individual decision making and patterns of leadership. The term *cognitive map* refers to an organized internal representation of the physical or social world (see Chapter 9 particularly). Last but not least, the term *perceptual screen* is sometimes used to mean the processes by which individuals select and organize incoming information.

Hybrids.   The astute reader will have detected two inconsistencies in this discussion about "things in the person." *First,* the categories are not really that neatly separated from each other. For instance, when we talked about the "need for power," we said the individual may be "drawn to situations" in which influence and control can be exerted. This sounds suspiciously like attributions about the social environment, which we said was a cognitive, not a motivational, concept. Similarly, we related the emotions of anxiety, guilt, and depression to perceptions of the environment and the relationship of the self to that perceived environment.

Second, you may have also noticed that while focusing on the personal factors, we have completely ignored the fact that the person in whom these personal factors are lodged moves through environments that have obvious effects on behavior. Any individual, for instance, moves through an environment of other people. In fact, some personality theorists maintain that personality is not a "thing" lodged in a person at all, but is rather a property of the relationships one has with others. Thus, consistencies in the behavior of a set of individuals may reflect the effects of similar environments.

A number of important concepts (some students of the field would say *the* most important) are "hybrids" in the sense just described—that is, seeming to fall into two or more concept categories or having a strong situational component. Concepts of this sort which have been most beloved of political scientists have been belief, attitude, value, and ideology. What makes these hybrid concepts is that they not only combine elements of different conceptual categories, but are usually seen as being organized in relation to one another (Bem 1970).

Let us begin with *belief.* Bem defines belief as any understanding about ourselves or the environment. In this sense, it would seem to be close to the concept of attribution, and, indeed, the latter term has come to be used by psychologists in place of belief. However, belief has the important connotation of something experienced by a person as an aspect of reality (Doob 1983, p. 74). For instance, Harry knows that Bluster is a person. If you were to ask him how he knows, he would say, "Because I can see and hear him." In other words, many of our beliefs about the world are experienced as real because we have access to the world through our senses. Other beliefs about things are those which are experienced more indirectly. For example, a hypothetical person, when asked about the Senate of the United States, might reply that it is composed of 100 senators who are elected to help make laws for the country. If we ask this person how she knows, she will probably say that she has read about it or has seen television reports about it. If you press her, she will have to confess (like most of us) that she has no first-hand knowledge such a body exists but that she trusts the books or newspapers or TV when they report such a body does indeed exist. Thus, many of our beliefs are based on shared social agreement or upon our willingness to trust what certain individuals or groups tell us. We can therefore see that belief has a situational component (and, of course, a similar argument might be made for attributions).

If our hypothetical person goes on to express her feeling that those 100 senators constitute the sorriest bunch of do-nothings she's ever had the displeasure to observe, we would say that she is expressing an *attitude*. This venerable and important concept is discussed in more detail in Chapter 2, but we can note here that an attitude combines both an emotion and a belief. The term values moves us to a higher level of organization. A *value* describes a direction as perceived by the individual. It refers to "ultimate" endstates, that is, those ends to which all other goals of the individual are coordinated. A value therefore organizes some set of attitudes and associated beliefs. For example, Donna strongly values equality. All the other strategic goals she has regarding her work with the ETO reflect this basic direction in her life. This value-direction also is a kind of theme which then organizes her attitudes toward the political system and her beliefs about politics. Finally, we can move to an even higher level of organization. An *ideology* is an organization of beliefs, attitudes, and values. Thus, a democratic ideology (probably shared by Donna and Harry) includes values of freedom and equality, as well as beliefs about the nature of the democratic process and attitudes toward that process.

As we have indicated, belief, attitude, value, and ideology are all concepts that political scientists have found of particular interest in their approaches to the study of political behavior. As psychologists have begun to bring their perspectives to bear on politics, other hybrid concepts have come to take on increasing importance.

A hybrid concept currently favored by many political psychologists is *self-esteem*—that is, the degree to which one does or does not have positive feelings about oneself. The Georges' biography of Woodrow Wilson (George and George, 1956) develops the theme that Wilson's behavior as president can be explained in part by the low self-esteem he acquired in his early childhood. Lloyd Etheredge (1979) has also used the concept of low or "damaged" self-esteem in describing practitioners of "hard-ball" politics (see Chapter 9).

A very complex hybrid is the concept of *identity*. Identity expresses the individual's perception of her own continuity through time as well as her perception of aspects of continuity that she shares with members of her social groupings. Identity is seen, therefore, to be connected with values, particularly as these are experienced as special or unique compared to others. Obviously, this is a highly complicated concept, but one which can be clearly seen to be a hybrid par excellence. It is intended to express the organization of concepts from all conceptual categories discussed so far and to be a concept linking person with situation (Erikson 1950; 1959; 1971).

Faculties.   Imagine a person with a very high need for power who perceives political office as a route to satisfying this need. Would you conclude from this fact that the person has a good chance of getting elected or appointed? Probably not. Why? Because desire is not enough; a person needs *skills and abilities* to be able to pull off the enormously complicated task of gaining political office. Delivering an effective speech, persuading people to give you money, and making the hundred and one decisions necessary in the course of a campaign require a certain level of stamina, communication skill, persuasive ability, and intelligence. We do not mean to imply that muddle-headed, inept, tongue-tied, and dull people don't get elected; they do. But the question of how or why people get selected for public office is not our present concern. We are interested in the range of faculties—skills and abilities—that a person can use to obtain political influence or that might affect his or her actions. It is important to note that faculties arise as a result of unique combinations of biological predispositions and past learning experiences. We will be talking about specific faculties as they become relevant to the topics we consider later in the book.

Habits.   The final element in this grab bag of elements we label personal factors or personality is habit, a well-learned pattern of behavior that is unique to an individual. Habits are established through learning and, once established, are partially or completely unconscious. Thus, they can vary in complexity from the most simple (saying hello when you see a friend) to much more complex chains. Certain personality theorists have focused their attention on the concept of habit and have elaborated it into sophisticated analyses of political processes, such as relationships to authority (e.g., Homans 1961).

Two final notes.   Let us briefly remind you of the intent of this chapter. The book is dominated by our concern for the importance of looking at the interaction of personal and environmental factors in understanding political behavior. We are therefore briefly reviewing some of the major concepts which psychologists and political scientists have developed, both personal and environmental, to provide us with a vocabulary for discussing the nature of person-situation interactions. The individual concepts presented here will be discussed more fully in later chapters as they become relevant to specific bodies of material.

No discussion of personal factors, however, can be complete without consideration of the relationship of any personal factor to behavior. The whole question of things "inside" individuals that somehow are responsible for their behavior raises important philosophical questions that one needs to be aware of in order to think clearly about the connection between personality and political behavior. Not the least of these questions is one the answer for which many political scientists treat as an unquestioned assumption: Is there a direct connection between an internal process (such as an attitude) and political behavior? Endless survey studies of political attitudes have been done with the implied assumption that, indeed, there is such a simple connection and that knowing the political attitudes of individuals will tell us something very directly about their behavior. Twenty-five years of studying the process of attitude formation and change, however, have led psychologists to the realization that the attitude-behavior relation is extremely complicated.

Harry, for example, has some pretty firm ideas about the abortion issue. Yet here we see him anticipating having to make a deal with Congressman Bluster that will lead Harry to vote in a way not completely congruent with his ideas. Of course, we are not surprised by this; it is exactly this kind of horse trading that is the essence of the legislative process. On the other hand, it calls into question the notion that there is some simple relationship between a stated attitude and our ability to predict the political behaviors that will characterize a person holding that attitude. (See Chapter 2.)

ENVIRONMENTAL FACTORS IN POLITICAL BEHAVIOR

In the early 1960s, psychologists interested in the effects of heredity and environment on behavior had come to realize that the question "Is behavior determined by heredity or environment?" was entirely misleading—every behavior occurs within an environment (that is, some set of external circumstances in which the behavior is situated in different ways), and no behavior exists independent of a person who contains a "heredity." Translated into our terms: No political behavior exists in a vacuum; it occurs in some environment, and no political behavior exists independent of a person. We have already suggested some set of elements that we point to when we try to understand the *person* part of this question. What are we pointing to when we talk about a political environment?

The microenvironment: eyeball to eyeball.   If we look at both Donna and Harry, we can see most clearly the part of their environment that directly impinges on them and that they immediately apprehend. Most notable about this "up close" environment is the fact of other people and the relationships Donna and Harry have to them. In Harry's case we see him interact with the man moving his materials into his office and with Congressman Bluster. Donna relates to a much wider circle of individuals—Gene, the Reverend Michael, the Mayor's aide, Eva, June, the other members of the ETO, and Chet Forbes. How can we characterize these relationships?

The first and most obvious thing is that these relationships exhibit *structure*. That is, there is a certain degree of predictability in the sequence of behaviors, which characterizes them. Bluster, for example, first knocks on Harry's door and then gives him an effusive greeting. Harry responds with an equally effusive greeting, to which Bluster responds with an expression of the importance he attributes to having Harry in Congress, and so on. Even if Bluster had responded in some other, uncharacteristic way, Harry would probably have some behavior in his repertoire to handle it. In short, sequences of behaviors exchanged between individuals exhibit a patterned or predictable quality. How can we characterize this patterning or structure?

Let's distinguish two types of structure in relationships: the normative structure and the interpersonal structure. The *normative structure* is made up of rules or ideas about how people should or should not behave in specific situations. As J. Eugene Haas and Thomas Drabek (1973) point out, norms are categorical, that is, they apply to a specific class of persons (e.g., members of Congress, presidents, precinct captains). Norms are also situational, applying to certain situations rather than to all. Norms may be narrow and specific in their application (e.g., it is expected that all congressional representatives will show up for the first day of their first session of Congress) or may be more broad and vague in their application (whether representatives will get involved in initiating legislation).

Norms may be formal or legal, that is, written down and associated with specified sanctions, or they may be informal—not written down but generally accepted by members of a group. The latter are typically learned through the process of interacting with others. In a sense, it might be said that informal norms are sent from one person to another. That is, persons who have already learned the norms communicate through their behavior what the norms are to others. Often this is done by the responses of others to the violation of norms by the "new recruit." These responses, called sanctions, are frequently subtle. A glance or a movement of the body may be enough to communicate that the newcomer has violated the rule. Of course, sanctions may be more direct, such as an informal "that's not the way we do things here" or a sterner reprimand for violating a formal norm. Sanctions may be positive as well as negative. When Bluster acts grateful and happy after Harry promises to reconsider the abortion issue, Harry clearly experiences a good feeling, a sense that he is "learning to play the game."

The fact that informal norms arise through a process of sending and receiving messages from others (Rommetweit 1955) makes us aware that norms are not static entities but rather are always in a process of development and change. Thus the actions of Donna's ETO group in confronting the mayor certainly violate norms of politeness and civility; and in this instance these actions come close to violating certain legal or formal norms (disturbing the peace). These behaviors, however, may represent changing concepts of what is appropriate in a given situation. Thus the members of ETO may be learning that democracy as a concept makes it "all right" to protest, march, carry signs, speak out at council meetings, and so on.

In a sense a norm is a kind of expectation for behavior. That is, we expect people will behave in certain ways by virtue of their membership in a category of individuals (e.g., being a man or a woman) or by virtue of their position in a social structure (e.g., disadvantaged minority). The behavior of individuals in these positions and the expectations for their behavior are called roles. The kind of role expectations people hold for themselves and others form a significant part of social relationships. The role concept (e.g., Biddle & Thomas 1966; Van Maanen 1976) has been a favorite of many social scientists and, more recently, of political psychologists (e.g., Paige 1977).

There is no space here to do real justice to the many subtleties of the concept, but five points are of particular usefulness. First, expectations are understood by people through a process of communication in which other individuals send messages to a "focal person."

The focal person then may or may not choose to act out the role implied by their expectations. Role "senders" (Rommetweit 1955) are therefore exerting a form of influence (or attempting to exert a form of influence) over some other person. For example, one could say that the ETO was trying to communicate a certain set of expectations to Mayor Smith by their action (see Chapter 6).

Second, this process is often two-way. In other words, all individuals involved in the relationship can be seen as enacting roles and having expectations for others and are therefore both role senders and role receivers. For example, Donna is the community organizer. People look to her for certain kinds of behaviors that they expect from a community organizer. Similarly, Donna has certain expectations of her steering committee and the members of the ETO. Thus people are typically in role relationships in which sets of expectations are being exchanged or communicated.

Third, people tend to be involved in more than one role relationship at a time. Harry is in a role relationship with Bluster and other colleagues, but he is also in a role relationship with his constituents. Assuming that he is married, he is in a role relationship with his wife. In short, political actors, like most people, find themselves in role-sets, that is, sets of role relationships with a variety of other people. This fact creates the possibility of role conflict. For example, at times Harry may find himself cross pressured by the demands of his constituents, his colleagues, and those interests who financed his campaign. Donna may find herself coping with the demands of different groups within her constituency as well as the demands of the steering committee. The Mayor's aide no doubt wants to please his boss by keeping the ETO out; yet at the same time it is expected that he will provide satisfactory liaison between the community and the Mayor. Virtually every figure in public life must contend with a certain amount of conflict between roles played in the political arena and roles played in family and personal life. How a political actor copes with the reality of role conflict may account for a significant part of his political behavior.

Fourth, it follows that the way people understand their roles may differ, depending on such things as the clarity of the messages they are receiving, their prior understanding of what they will be expected to do, and the nature of others' expectations. For example, Harry already seems to have a good sense of what will be expected of him as a member of Congress, and his interaction with Bluster in some sense represents a trial run for Harry. Moreover, the messages he receives from Bluster would seem to indicate that Bluster feels Harry is fulfilling those expectations.

Fifth, an important aspect of role relationships is that they exist independent of the specific individuals who play the roles. Thus Donna is a community organizer. When she leaves the situation, another community organizer may take her place. Of course, this new person may play the role in a much different way than Donna does. Nonetheless, the role of organizer would be more or less the same, and the expectations others would have for the behavior of the person in that position would be more or less the same.

Norms and roles, then, are forms of environmental constraints that affect the behavior of individuals in political situations. But note the following. Harry is a member of Congress and so is Bluster. Yet the style or manner in which each enacts this role is much different. Bluster is a blusterer; Harry is smooth and ingratiating. Of course, we might attribute these behaviors to personality or to differing concepts of what it means to play the role of member of Congress. Whatever the reason for this style difference, it too operates as a constraint on behavior. In other words, there is another structure in the relationship—the personal style of the individuals involved. We will call this the *interpersonal structure*.

Numerous authors have attempted to categorize interpersonal style in terms of dimensions of interpersonal behavior. (For review see Bales & Cohen 1979; Hare 1976.) Two dimensions seem to recur in this literature. One is a dimension of liking-disliking, the degree of positive or negative feeling projected toward the other. The second dimension is sometimes called dominance-submission and reflects the degree to which one attempts to control the behavior of the other. As Leary (1958) points out, there are many degrees of intensity in these dimensions. Thus one may seek to simply teach another or, alternatively, to dominate the other's behavior. Similarly, one may express mild disagreement or hostile sarcasm.

In the "up close" environment we are describing both structures— normative and interpersonal—are confronted simultaneously and affect each other. For example, high agreement or consensus on the normative structure may lead to more positive interpersonal feeling. On the other hand, if positive feeling already exists, much greater latitude may be allowed on the normative level: "Yes, we disagree on the appropriate role of a member of Congress in determining foreign policy, but I'm not going to criticize you because we like each other."

The microenvironment: immediate but imaginary. You will have noticed that the "up close" environment as we have so far described it is the "eyeball-to-eyeball" environment; people have immediate sensory awareness of the presence of others. But there are invisible presences floating through Donna's and Harry's environments. For Harry there are his constituents. Whatever Harry does will have some effect on the relationship between him and the voters; indeed, his continued stay in office will depend on the nature of this relationship. Donna too has her constituency. On a day-to-day basis she is more likely to have direct contact with them. Still, in some sense the ETO itself seeks to represent a larger constituency of poor and disadvantaged persons. One might imagine that Donna is looking over her shoulder at this group. These groups are obviously a potent factor in the political behavior of Donna and Harry.

Still other "ghosts" float through the air for Donna and Harry. They both have ways of judging and evaluating their own behavior. One way they may do this is by modeling their behavior on some group or individual whose values or standards can serve as guides for behavior. These reference groups or individuals have been shown to significantly affect behavior, particularly when the immediate situation seems relevant to the values and standards they represent (Hyman & Sheatsley, 1954). In Donna's case, one might imagine that Saul Alinsky, the famous and innovative community organizer, whose *Reveille for Radicals* (1969) has been a standard text for organizers, might very well be a reference person. Harry's reference group is likely to be influential members of Congress, especially at this early stage of his career. In fact, although we've used examples of individuals with whom Donna and Harry may not be directly acquainted, reference groups are often real groups with whom the individual identifies emotionally—with respect, admiration and/or liking (Ridgeway 1983). Ethnic-group membership, for example, has been shown to be a powerful factor in determining behavior (Gordon 1978). In short, the reference group or figure may be someone with whom the individual has (or can have) direct contact; but often the reference group or figure is large and distant from the individual, as when a voter identifies strongly with a particular political party (Katz & Kahn 1978).

Thus besides the normative and interpersonal structures in which the political actor is situated, she carries with her one or more sets of groups whose imagined responses to her behavior will have significant consequences for that behavior. We can understand why Gordon Allport defined the field of social psychology as "an attempt to understand and explain how the thought, feelings and behavior of individuals are influenced by the actual, imagined or implied presence of other human beings" (1954, p. 5). In short, Donna and Harry are each embedded in a network or structure of relationships, both actual and imagined, with other people. This constitutes the *microenvironment* of political behavior.

The macroenvironment: organizational context.   Microenvironmental factors are those that are more immediate and personal. The macroenvironment, in contrast, refers to those factors that are not immediately present but which surround the individual in larger frameworks. The individual, it is sometimes said, is embedded in these frameworks, but is not directly in touch with all of their aspects. For example, if you are a student in a university, your life is affected in some way by all the parts of university structure. However, only some parts of this structure are immediately accessible to you at a given time. For example, when you are in class, you are not interacting with the Dean of Students. And, of course, some parts of university structure—such as the budgetary process—may never be accessible to you.

Earlier we defined the concept "role" as expectations others have about the behavior of individuals occupying certain positions or having membership in a certain category of individuals. In general, human relationships are characterized by predictability, patterning, or structure. Another way to say this is that relationships are organized or exhibit forms of *organization*. When we say "positions," then, we mean positions within some form of organization. We can point to certain forms of organization fairly easily. A stamp club, the Young Democrats group on campus, a university, a small business, and the federal government are all forms of organization.

Although it seems like a far cry from the stamp club to the federal government, both are organized in the sense of predictability or patterning of behavior. What makes them different? One is more *complex* than the other. Political activities typically occur in complex organizational settings or in groups that are evolving toward more complex organizational forms, such as Donna's ETO group.* What does "complex" mean? It means that there is a division of labor within the organization that has both vertical and horizontal components. In other words, the many tasks, jobs, things that need to be done, the "labor," is organized into a number of levels, each of which has some degree of control over levels further down. In addition, within a given level there is a further subdivision of tasks into positions all sharing similar influence and relationships to other levels. Exactly how patterns of control are exercised in organizations is not germane here nor are discussions about horizontal complexity as in the growth of bureaucracy (March & Simon 1958; Katz & Kahn 1978). What is important is that the positions in which people find themselves in political organizations vary greatly in demands and expectations for behavior and in the problems posed by carrying out the tasks.

*It is not uncharacteristic of protest movements to evolve toward more complex organization, as Max Weber the German sociologist pointed out many years ago and Zald and Ash (1966) have substantiated more recently.

Katz (1973) has given a good illustration of the way in which one's position in a political organization may affect one's behavior. Consider that any political organization, whether it be a political party or the federal government, assumes a three-level structure in the form of a pyramid in which the lowest level participates least in decision making. For example, the precinct captain or ward boss in a political party has a highly circumscribed area of influence. The task is given and so are most of the procedures for carrying it out. Individuals in this position are expected to have certain technical expertise (e.g., how to get the vote out) as well as knowledge of their constituency and its normative and interpersonal structures. Certain skills may make a person more or less successful in such a position (e.g., the ability to get volunteers working hard). Thus while individuals in these positions are not given the task of modifying or elaborating the system, they are expected to make use of the existing structure.

At the intermediate level the requirements of the position go beyond the completion of a given job and "take the form of developing the organizational structure itself" (ibid., p. 211). The skills prized here have to do with taking initiative and with innovation. Being able to compromise, bargain, negotiate are all relevant abilities as well as requirements for successfully occupying an intermediate position. In this "in-between" level position occupants experience cross-pressures from above and below. Harry, for example, must be representative of those who support him (the voters, interest groups) but must learn to adapt to, and be accepted by, the congressional leadership. His conversation with Bluster is instructive in this regard. Bluster has seniority in Congress. He is head of an important committee. It is therefore important for Harry to find ways of being accepted by Bluster while at the same time maintaining an orientation toward those "below" in which he can be seen as effective and "doing things" for them.

At the top level (for example, the executive level in government) there is much greater latitude for policy formulation and the exercise of influence. Of course, as Katz points out, this statement is redundant in an authoritarian system. In a democratic system, where authority can be changed by the electorate, the degree of influence is much more severely circumscribed. Nonetheless, it is clear that the role expectations for these positions do focus more on innovation, creativity, and policy formulation.

Individuals in these positions are often required to take a system perspective, that is, to orient to the organization as a whole and to its problems more generally. The faculties that might make a person effective in these positions are clearly more conceptual and intellectual (or at least this should be true of the advisory staff). This is consistent with the ability to "see, conceptualize, apprise, predict, and understand the demands and opportunities posed to the organization by its environment" (ibid., p. 214).

This discussion leads us to the most important point about the influence of the organizational environment, namely, that the political actor is constrained by the demands of the organization to carry out the tasks associated with a given position in the structure. Thus another element in understanding the behavior of the individual in terms of the macroenvironment is to recognize that the political actor is also embedded within this larger organizational framework.

The macroenvironment: market and state.   We have defined the realm of political psychology as the study of individuals or groups acting within or upon institutions that are formally charged with responsibility for making authoritative decisions concerning the allocation of society's human and material resources. But if we are all actors within the state system in this sense, then we are also actors within the alternative "instrument" for allocation of resources, namely, the economic system or the market (Lane 1979). To put it another way, the market allocates goods and services through transactions and price mechanisms, the state through central decisions, "sometimes by transfer payments, sometimes by direct command, sometimes by producing goods either for individual fees or for collective use" (ibid., p. 11). What then is the relationship between market and state, if they are both instruments for allocating human and material resources? How does one's role as an economic actor help us to understand one's behavior as a political actor?

Harry is a member of the banking community; in other words, he is a member of that group which controls some portion of the financial resources of the society. Although we don't have any information on Donna, let's assume she comes from groups that do not control significant financial or industrial resources. One way to express this is to say that Donna and Harry come from different *social classes*. To understand this idea we must encroach on the domain of political sociologists who concern themselves with the problem of *stratification*, the ways in which a society divides itself into segments based on different criteria, one of which is economic.

Class is a term used to describe stratification that is vertical, that is, where one segment or group has more of something, such as control over economic resources. Class as a concept is, at its core, based on economic control, but this does not entirely define what is meant by the concept. Class membership also brings with it an array of beliefs, attitudes, values, and approaches to the world, including political life. Some theorists like to speak of a class consciousness, that is, a central awareness of oneself as belonging to a particular class. This approach to defining class is very controversial and complicated. More common and less controversial is a definition of class based on three things—education, occupation, and income.

Recent data show Americans to be keenly aware of the notion of class and of their own class membership. In the analysis of a national survey conducted by the Institute for Social Research at the University of

Michigan in 1975 Mary and Robert Jackman (1983) found that 97 percent of their sample identified themselves with one of the named classes: 8 percent identified with the poor, 37 percent with the working class, 43 percent with the middle class, and 8 percent with the upper middle class, while an additional 1 percent claimed membership in the upper class. Moreover, this subjective judgment was surprisingly consistent with the objective measures of class noted above. Perhaps most interesting was the discovery that class rivals race or ethnicity as a source of group identity. The strength of this identification was particularly marked for those who called themselves members of the lower classes (poor or working class). Overall these people, both black and white, expressed stronger emotional bonds to their own class, were more likely to interpret class differences as being caused by biased opportunities, and were more likely to see their own and other class interests as mutually opposed. Thus class functions in part as a reference group but one in which a person's role as an economic actor (particularly one's degree of control over economic resources) is central.

One answer then to the question of the effect of one's position in the economic system on one's behavior as a political actor is that class may have some influence. But can the concept of class also help us to understand the relationship between market and state more generally? One who thought so was the nineteenth-century philosopher Karl Marx, whose ideas have influenced much of world history during the last century. Marx strongly asserted the primacy of market over state. To him the state was clearly a servant of those who had the greatest accumulation of material resources and who controlled the means of production and finance. He was particularly fascinated by the capitalist mode of economic activity because, in his view, it set up a conflict between those who accumulated profits and those who generated them through their work. Marx's view was that the class that owned and managed the productive forces (financial and industrial) in the economy was in effect a ruling class, which put its enormous economic power to use making sure that the political system did nothing, in terms of resource allocation, that would undercut this economic power.

During the last twenty years many researchers have attempted to test the validity of Marx's proposition about the relationship of market and state. Miliband (1969), for example, found a close relationship between those who control economic resources and the political elite. He noted that since 1889 the largest single occupational group in the cabinets of the United States has been businessmen and that since 1961 businessmen have composed over 60 percent of each cabinet, whether a Republican or Democrat was in power. Domhoff (1967, 1978) demonstrated how those who sit "on top" of the financial and manufacturing branches of the economy "attend the same schools, marry into one another's families, vacation at the same resorts, and appoint one another to high-level decision-making positions at all sectors of American life: the media, government, business, banking, education. . . . " (Chambliss & Seidman 1982, p. 301). Moreover, there is a strong relationship between the amount of money a candidate has available and the likelihood of getting elected (Chambliss 1978). This fact would seem to suggest that those who control economic resources tend also to control the operation of the state.

Is the state as rigid an agent of "ruling-class interests" as Marx suggested? Is this macroenvironmental element of class membership so powerful? There is additional evidence that market and state are somewhat more independent than Marx suggested. Marx's theory does not account well, for example, for large segments of legislation passed by the U.S. Congress. Mollenkopf (1975) makes this point in regard to the great bulk of legislation passed during the New Deal period, legislation that was strenuously opposed by powerful capitalists. One might also point to the strong consumer and affirmative-action legislation passed during the 1970s. Moreover, the notion of a common consensus in the ruling class does not hold up to close scrutiny. Domhoff, while maintaining that there is high consensus within the economically powerful elite, recognizes that there is a split between ultraconservatives and moderates (Domhoff 1978, pp. 64–87). Other researchers (e.g., Offe 1974; Poulantzas 1969) have demonstrated similar splits in the so-called consensus.

If the state is at least relatively autonomous from the market in its operation, then is there some alternative to Marx's formulation? Max Weber, a German sociologist, made the following proposal in "Class, Status, Party" (Gerth & Mills 1946, pp. 180–95). Economic factors do not operate in a vacuum; rather they function within a particular political and community power context, which they in turn condition. Since these factors are associated with particular occupational specializations, they have the effect over time of producing a status order, which in turn plays a role in determining economic rewards. Different economic rewards make for different life styles, which in turn lead to further divisions between groups or classes. All of these phenomena, set in motion by the economic system, in turn affect its operation. This perspective, while not necessarily contradictory to that of Marx, nonetheless asks us to look at market and state as two different sets of allocative factors, which are interwoven in complex ways, thus making the relationship between market and state much more flexible. Such a view allows us to consider the way in which personal factors may operate to determine political behavior as well. We are, therefore, acknowledging the extraordinary importance of economic factors in determining political behavior but at the same time allowing for *interactions* between economic and other factors—but this gets us ahead of our story.

Before leaving this consideration of economic factors, one additional point is in order. Robert Lane (1979), who holds that market and state are relatively autonomous (talking specifically about the capitalist market and the democratic state), asks: What individual motives must be mobilized for market and state to function effectively? He notes that in certain cases these motives may be in conflict. For example, the capitalist market favors equity in relationships (people should get resources proportional to their investments), while the democratic state favors equality in relationships (resources should be distributed in a more equal fashion). The complicated question of justice is discussed more fully in Chapter 10, but we should note here the interesting point that economic factors have some very important implications for personal functioning.

The macroenvironment: history and culture.   There is yet a final area with which a political psychologist must come to grips. There are two things Donna and Harry share in common that we have not mentioned. In fact, there is no way to show them although they suffuse and inform every aspect of the lives of these two people. The first of these is *history*. The particular historical moment in which they are living their lives is characterized by momentous events. Not the least of these is a dramatic change in the thrust of the American government's relationship to its citizenry. Also, there has never been a time when all of humankind seemed so close to annihilation. It is a different world from that of fifty years ago, when the world was in the throes of the most severe economic depression ever. Surely such events must have some impact, however indirect, on the political behavior of Donna and Harry. How are we to understand what this impact might be? This is again a task for a political psychology worthy of its name. As we shall see, the role of historical events will emerge at a number of points in this narrative.

The concern with history also has a more subtle aspect to it. As we study political psychology, we are immersed in a particular set of historical circumstances. These circumstances change over time. Thus what seems to us to be true about the political behavior of people now is, to some extent, an expression of a particular set of historic circumstances. Why, for example, in 1981 was Prentice-Hall interested enough in political psychology to give us a contract to write a book about it? Why was an international society for the study of political psychology founded in 1978? Why is there a new journal called *Political Psychology,* or a book called *Preventing Nuclear War: A Psychological Perspective* (White 1984)? Why are government agencies hiring political psychologists or encouraging their employees to get training in various aspects of political psychology? Why, in short, is political psychology itself suddenly becoming a "hot item"?

This phenomenon is not just a random event or even a necessary outgrowth of attempts to understand the political system. Rather, the current interest in political psychology arises at least in part from the historical circumstance that political power (and other forms of control and influence as well) seems to be concentrated in fewer and fewer hands (Horowitz 1979; Mills 1959). Indeed, in a nuclear age the fact that the power of life and death for the human race may lie at the fingertips of small groups of people, or even of individuals, inevitably leads us to an interest in, a worry about, a concern with, the mental processes of the persons in those positions. In short, the way we think about political psychology may be an outgrowth of our current historical concerns.

The other thing Donna and Harry have in common is more obvious—they are both Americans, operating within an American political context. Would they behave similarly in other Western democracies, not to mention other systems of government? Is the way in which we account for their behavior also appropriate in other contexts? Here we begin to intrude on the province of the political anthropologist. The anthropologist professes to study a concept he or she calls "culture." This term has been as variously defined as the term "personality"; indeed, there are some people who see little difference between the two concepts. For our purposes let us say that culture is the total range of behavioral and mental patterns that characterize a people. Anthropology pays a great deal of attention to comparisons—of patterns of political leadership or of patterns of political socialization, for instance. Underlying much of the anthropologist's work is a fundamental interest in the nature of human nature. How much of what we call being human, the anthropologist asks, comes from growing up in a given culture, and how much transcends culture? As some anthropologists have put it: In what ways are we like all other humans, like some other humans, and like no other humans? In summary, history and culture are to human beings what the sea is to fish. Until a fish is caught and lifted out of the sea, it undoubtedly has no concept of water, never having experienced its absence. Similarly, we "swim" through our history and culture, although unlike the fish we can perform the mental act of "stepping back" and becoming aware of the effects our historical place and our degree of acculturation have on our political behavior.

A final word: objective and subjective environments.   We have reviewed a number of concepts often used by those who have applied psychological perspectives to politics. The last task in this chapter is to discuss the concept of interaction and consider some of the subtleties of that approach. Before proceeding, however, we need to consider one final issue.

In discussing environmental factors, you may have noticed that many concepts are quite subjective or personal in nature. For instance, when we talked about role as an environmental factor, we talked about how people come to know their role. In discussing the concept of norms, we pointed out that norms are communicated or sent by one or more persons and received by others. For example, social scientists have relatively sophisticated ways of estimating the social class of any particular individual; they base their determination on formulas combining education, occupation, and income. Ordinary people also see themselves as being of one or another social class, but their determination is usually subjective and might not be the same as that yielded by a social scientist's formula.

Political psychologists are interested in the way people come to understand the environments through which they move. On the other hand, they assume that there is a "reality" about which objective social scientists can agree. Thus, we might all concur that there is a normative structure in a government agency (for example) while also realizing that specific political actors may have different ideas—ideas that may change over time—about what the normative structure is. The question of objectivity is therefore partly a question of measurement. Similarly, social scientists can generally agree that there is a physical environment "out there," at the same time understanding that people may respond quite differently to that environment, attaching different interpretations to it.

There is yet another slant on this particular problem. While in general there may be shared agreement about many aspects of social life, as indicated in the previous example, the agreement is rarely 100%. Thus many psychologists—particularly those who work in politics—take the view that, insofar as there is a shared social reality, this reality is continually being constructed through the behaviors and interactions of individuals. Some people view this as a process of negotiation (e.g., Goffman, 1955). Others see it as an influence process (e.g., Berger and Luckman, 1966). There are even those who argue that while individuals may construct their worlds, there is no logical need for agreement, as long as all parties are satisfied with their outcomes (e.g., Wallace, 1971). In any case, the reader should be aware that these ideas form a basic set of assumptions underlying many psychological perspectives on politics.

AN INTERACTION PERSPECTIVE

In trying to understand the individual and his or her political behavior we are faced with a curious situation. We are tempted, on the one hand, to act as if political behavior were the result of something "inside" the individual. On the other hand, we are also tempted to explain political behavior by reference to the environment, whether immediate or more distant, whether objective or subjective. Let us consider, however, that there is an *interaction* between the properties of the person and the properties of the environment. It is this interaction that results in political behavior (Davies 1973, p. 251; Smith, 1968).

The meaning of the term "interaction" is not completely obvious. Figure 1-1 illustrates some of the most common forms of the notion of interaction. In diagram 1a political behavior (B) is caused by some aspects of the person (P) and some aspects of the environment (E). The problem with this approach is that it ignores the relationship between the person and her environment. Diagram 1b says that there is an interaction between the subjective and objective environment. That is, the individual acts on the environment by interpreting it and giving it meaning, and the environment in turn acts on the person by offering her opportunities for

From J. Howard, "Person-situation interaction models,"*Personality and Social Psychology Bulletin*, 1979, 5, p. 192. Used with permission.

FIGURE 1-1   Models of the Interaction between Person, Environment, and Behavior

making these interpretations. But this model too is not sufficient, since it does not specify how this interaction in turn is related to behavior. Diagram 1c remedies this defect in part by introducing behavior into the interaction. Here the objective and subjective environments interact with each other, and both in turn affect behavior.

But this is still not enough, and for a reason thus far not addressed. In the previous discussion we acted as if a person's political behavior flowed out of his or her personality, the objective environment, and the subjective environment. But this ignores the real possibility that a person's behavior in turn changes those environments. Thus when Harry implies that Bluster has his support, this act changes, if ever so slightly, the nature of the relationship between the two men. It also changes the way in which Harry now perceives Bluster, that is, the psychological meanings the senior member of Congress has for Harry. All this in turn will affect Harry's subsequent behavior. So a more appropriate interaction model, we believe, is the one represented in diagram 1d. In this model there is reciprocal influence between the person, the environment, and the person's behavior. Thus all of the elements we thought important in understanding political behavior plus the behavior itself now become part of the larger explanatory framework. Environments can influence persons; persons can influence environments; and both persons and environments can influence behavior, which in turn can influence both persons and environments.

This model has a number of interesting properties, some of which are obvious, and some of which are more subtle. First, the model is dynamic; that is, it doesn't take for granted that any element in the model is necessarily fixed. As different elements affect one another and vice versa, they change, so that in subsequent interactions the elements are now different. Consider, for example, what happens in a general election for Congress. People vote; votes are tabulated; some persons who were in office remain there; others lose and are replaced. Sometimes the shifts are dramatic. At other times they may be minor. In every case, however, the election has changed the nature of the Congress. Members of Congress now orient, albeit sometimes only slightly, in a different way to each other and to their constituents. The fact that there ordinarily appears to be relative stability in Congress is not the point. The point is that as any new component is added it inevitably changes some element in the vast set of elements we think are important in understanding political behavior. This change in turn increases the probability of further changes in everything else.

Further, because this is a change-oriented, or dynamic, model, it provides us with a vehicle for developing a more sophisticated model for understanding the psychology of political behavior. Let's explore this thought a little further. So far, we have discussed the interaction between person and situation as if we could clearly distinguish between these two entities. But consider the following quote from Raush:

> The glasses I wear are an object apart from me; I am not quite me without them; my beard is even more borderline between me and not-me; a pimple, a pain, a cold are "not-me." Are they then situations? [1977, p. 290]

In a similar vein, Nuttin says:

> Personality is a mode of functioning that, essentially and intrinsically, implies an object or world. In other words, the psychological or behavioral functions constituting personality, such as perceiving, imagining, thinking, planning, doing something, all imply and are an active reference to, and deal with, an "object." Therefore, personality as a whole . . . is a mode of being actively or virtually related to a world. [1977, p. 51]

Both Nuttin and Raush are drawing attention to the curious fact that not only are the boundaries between person and situation fuzzy but in fact the whole approach that sees them as clearly separate and relatively fixed does violence to the nature of the relationship of persons to situations.

The fluidity of the boundaries between persons, situations, and behavior can also be seen if we consider some examples. We said earlier that our model assumes that individuals are active in seeking out the environments or situations that are meaningful for them. But situations themselves can be seen to be selective. For example, it is hard to imagine a Hitler coming to political power except in a situation of extreme crisis. Thus both persons and situations select each other in a variety of complicated ways, and it may be difficult to distinguish between the selective processes in any given instance (see particularly Chapter 5, on leadership).

Similarly, consider the following example from primate interaction noted by Bateson (1972). An ape who makes a dominance display has a high probability of receiving a submissive display in return. In some proportion of cases a dominance display will evoke a dominance response; we refer to this as a *struggle for power*. Submissive behavior, however, always evokes some form of dominance. Therefore, submissive behavior is more likely than dominance behavior to determine the other individual's behavior. This seeming paradox can be resolved if we treat the relationship between person, situation, and behavior as the unit of analysis rather than taking each component separately.

Finally, it needs to be explicitly noted that one person can be part of the situation or environment of another person. The relationship between two human beings seems to be a unit of analysis that exists somewhere "in between" the individuals involved. This means that, while each of the individuals in a relationship can be treated as a separate unit of analysis, the relationship itself must also be considered as something separate from the individuals involved. In fact, a relationship between two or more people is, in and of itself, a unit of analysis.

Taking all these examples together, we can see that the model of interaction in diagram 1d needs to be revised. We can't say at this point exactly what this revision would look like. We can say, however, that it needs to be a model that can treat the E, P, and B of figure 1-1 as a single unit of analysis. Also it needs to be a model that allows for a much greater openness between elements so that we can shift comfortably between a focus on the individual, as if she were clearly bounded and separate from the environment, to a focus on the person-environment relationship as a single "thing." Finally, it needs to be a model that allows us to deal with relationships between E-P-B elements as they relate to other E-P-B elements (Simon 1961).

What we have said so far about the interaction model is not limited to those behaviors that are the concern of political psychologists. Rather, it is applicable to the entire domain of social behavior. Figure 1-2 attempts to illustrate and summarize these points graphically. Each of the circles in the Venn diagram represents one of the three components: personality, microenvironment, and macroenvironment. The fact that it is sometimes difficult to draw a precise boundary between the personality and the situation (i.e., the microenvironment and the macroenvironment) is illustrated by the fact that the lines which trace the boundaries of the circles are permeable.

The relationship between each set of components is represented by an overlay between the circles and behavior is shown in the center where all three of the circles overlap. This indicates our conviction that each action taken by any political (or social) actor is the outgrowth of a complex set of forces which emanate from all three sources of influence. Also, any change in any of the components reverberates throughout the entire domain. To illustrate this, Figure 1-2 shows a change taking place in the macroenvironment. This change has a direct effect on the macroenvironment. The directional arrows show the reverberations which this change has throughout the domain and the fact that the effects of the change "bounce back" as well as "ripple out."

SUMMARY

With Harry and Donna's stories we have been privy to small scenes from the lives of two people who have chosen classical, but different, ways of being part of the political system: 1) office-seeking and holding, and 2)

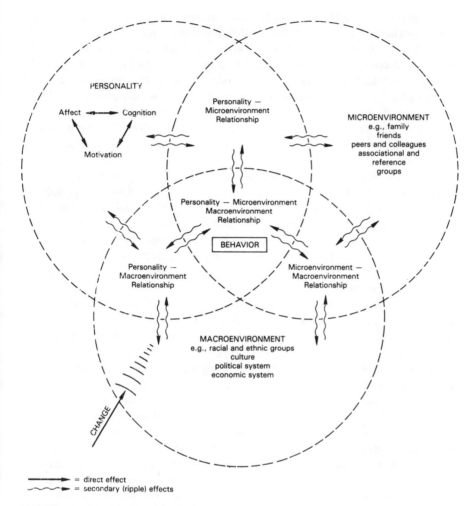

PERSONALITY

Affect ◄──► Cognition

Motivation

Personality —
Microenvironment
Relationship

MICROENVIRONMENT
e.g., family
friends
peers and colleagues
associational and
reference
groups

Personality — Microenvironment
Macroenvironment
Relationship

BEHAVIOR

Personality —
Macroenvironment
Relationship

Microenvironment —
Macroenvironment
Relationship

MACROENVIRONMENT
e.g., racial and ethnic groups
culture
political system
economic system

CHANGE

──────► = direct effect
∿∿∿► = secondary (ripple) effects

FIGURE 1-2 The Domain of Social Behavior

policy-oriented agitation from outside the governmental apparatus. In considering the psychological dynamics of political activity, it is important to take into account both the personality of the individual and the environment within which that person is acting. The former includes emotions, cognitions, faculties and habits. The latter includes the immediate environment, the organizational context, the market, the state, history and culture. Also, environments may be conceptualized in terms that are both objective and subjective.

A central theme in political life is conflict. Harry's focus is on winning and the fact that "winners" are in a position to effect changes they perceive to be needed. Donna's focus is on changing the "losers" of society into "winners" by means of political activism on their own behalf. In both cases, power and influence are on the line and each protagonist is exhilarated by the challenge of battle in the political arena.

Any individual's behavior in any particular political conflict is the result of a complex interaction between that person's personality and the characteristics of both the microenvironment and the macroenvironment within which that person is pursuing his or her political objectives. These three aspects of the situation are not sharply delineated, but shade into and influence each other in complex and dynamic ways. This complicated interaction can be thought of as a separate unit of analysis, a relationship which has properties not found in any of its subcomponents.

In the next chapter we will focus on the fact that political psychology is beset with any number of philosophical and methodological problems. In part, this is attributable to the fact that it is a relatively new and interdisciplinary field of study with all of the attendant growing pains to be expected in such a case. To a larger extent, however, these problems stem from the inherent nature of the subject matter and the fact that it is being analyzed by human beings who are fallible—especially when they are trying to understand themselves. We have selected three sets of problems to discuss at some length, focusing on their implications for the growth and development of political psychology—the use of language, implicit ideology in political psychology, and the relationship of attitude to behavior. While there is a very large (some might say interminable) number of problems with which an emerging discipline like political psychology must necessarily deal, these three seem to us to be most urgent. Language is the vehicle of communication among human beings. It forms the basis for our mutual understanding of ourselves and the world around us, including the phenomena which we might want to study. What problems does language present to political psychologists? Social scientists generally have come to realize that no science is value-free, that ideology (as defined in this chapter) plays a role in the selection of research problems, the way we think about these problems, and the way we do research. What particular traps lie in wait for the political psychologist? Finally, as mentioned earlier in the chapter, things "inside" the person bear no simple relationship to overt behavior, although this connection is often taken for granted. What factors affect the relationship between personal factors and behavior? We examine in detail *one* formulation for thinking about the relationship between attitude and behavior, using this as an example to illustrate some of the complexities.

2

CONFUSIONS, MUDDLES, AND CONCERNS:
Some Problems of the Political Psychologist

PROBLEM 1: LANGUAGE AS TRICKSTER

All of us try to make sense of the things we see in the world around us. For example, we may see a person pointing at a pile of rocks, and another person, seemingly in response, picking them up and putting them somewhere else. Subsequently, we might observe someone standing in front of a group of others, throwing her arms around and saying many loud words; the others listen, apparently in fascination and periodically applauding. Next, there may be a group of little children. One of them starts to run and then stands on one foot; the others follow suit. As all of these impressions sink into our conscious minds, we may suddenly see a similarity that blends them all together. The label we choose to describe this basic similarity might be "leadership."

By calling these observed behaviors leadership, then, we have done nothing more than apply a label to them. We have not discovered some magical new property of the world or some new explanation for events. Rather, we have made our lives much easier because we have reduced and classified a tremendous amount of information (the large number of observed behaviors) so that we may more easily cope with it. Notice, of course, that the *word* "leadership" is completely arbitrary. We could have said "birdfoot" or "fingerbath" or "snickelfritz," and it would have done as well—assuming we were starting from scratch and making up a word.

You, of course, are trying to make sense of what you observe in the world. You see some of the same things we do, but you also see a number of other things. Suppose you now decide to use the same label, leadership, for your collection. If we were to have a conversation together about leadership, the difference in our collections of observations might lead to confusion or misunderstanding. We might even start to argue about what observables deserve to be lumped together as sharing this quality, leadership. Such words are like little mental file cabinets; we are, in effect, arguing about what ought to go into the file cabinet "leadership." If we agree, then it can be said that we have engaged in the process of communication, and we can therefore get on with working together on related problems of mutual interest.

So at the level of observables (the denotations of language) our task as political psychologists is to reach *agreement* on the observables for which we will use certain words as labels. One way to do this is by trying to use other words to define a word (in this case, *leadership*) in which we are interested. The problem of definition is a tricky one. Obviously, if our definition sticks fairly close to the concrete nature of the things we have observed, we are much more likely to make ourselves understood to others and to reach agreement.

On the other hand, here is a definition of leadership that is fairly far from observables:

> Leadership is the reciprocal process of mobilizing, by persons with certain motives and values, various economic, political, and other resources, in a context of competition and conflict, in order to realize goals independently or mutually held by both leaders and followers. [Burns 1978, p. 425] *

For our purposes this definition is fascinating, and we will return to it later on. At this point, though, you can see that the words that Burns uses to define the word we are interested in (leadership) are themselves labeling fairly complicated chunks of the world of observables. The definition itself seems to contain little that is "close to" things we can actually observe. Of course, demanding that definitions stick close to observables is pretty confining. If Burns had to specify just what he meant by "political" or "economic" or "motives" or "values", he would not have gotten much further. After all, there is a general agreement about the nature of these terms, isn't there? Well, maybe yes and maybe no. The point is that, whether or not we have some agreement on all the words in the definition, the further we are from observables, the more dangers arise.

One of the dangers inherent in the use of words as labels is the problem of the *connotation* of words. Words are very powerful for human beings. A single word can set off a wide variety of thoughts and feelings. Many of these are shared; some are not. The problem is that many of these connotations can strongly bias attempts to figure out what the phe-

*From J.M. Burns, *Leadership* (New York: Harper & Row, 1978).

nomenon is we are trying to label. For instance, in the early 1980s the words "political leadership" evoked powerful feelings among Americans. People were saying that they wanted their elected officials to display more of it. It—political leadership—conjured up images of strength, of being tough, of being in control, of not being pushed around. As a contrast, consider the connotations evoked by the term political leadership just five or six years earlier. Then connotations would have centered on images of honesty, of conciliation, of the ability to bring groups together to form more coherent communities, and so on. Connotations are often called "surplus meanings," in the sense that they burden a label with many extraneous properties, making it difficult to explore whatever it is the word labels.

There is a more sinister problem lurking here as well. Because of the power words have to evoke thoughts, feelings and beliefs, words are often used as *tools* for the formulation and implementation of policy decisions. Because of their power to create or dissipate anxiety, words are a resource that politicians and administrators use to mobilize individuals and groups as well as to control their behavior. For instance, Murray Edelman has analyzed the way the words "crisis" and "public opinion" function in the service of groups of individuals who stand to profit or lose from the outcomes of certain social events (Edelman 1977).

This can all be very discouraging, since words are our primary means of communication with other human beings. If they are so slippery and have so many potential pitfalls, what recourse do we have? The answer, of course, is that we have very little choice. Inasmuch as language is such an important means of communication, people who care about communicating precisely are forced continually to be aware of words— what they denote and what they connote. It is only with great care and thought on the part of people using the language that the worst of the potential pitfalls can be avoided.

As if these problems with language weren't enough, consider the following: Leadership does not exist. It never has, and it never will. All that exists is a certain set of events, things, relationships, or outcomes that we have observed (at best, together and in agreement) and to which we have affixed a label. The more technical term for words used in this way is to say they are *concepts*. Earl Babbie defines concepts in a way quite close to our sense of the term:

> Concepts are mental images we use as summary devices for bringing to-gether observations and experiences that seem to have something in common. [1983, p. 119]

Babbie also has a nice way of talking about the process by which we make labels into real things. (See figure 2-1.) In presuming to think that the concept actually exists, as opposed to being a way of referring to several concrete observations in the world, we commit the error called *reification*.

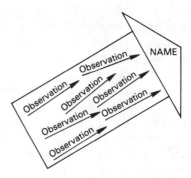

1. Many of our observations in life seem to have something in common. We get the sense that they represent something more general than the simple content of any single observation. We find it useful, moreover, to communicate about the general concept.

2. It is inconvenient to keep describing all the specific observations whenever we want to communicate about the general concept they seem to have in common, so we give a name to the general concept — to stand for whatever it is the specific observations have in common.

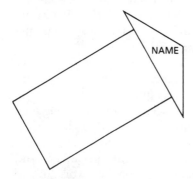

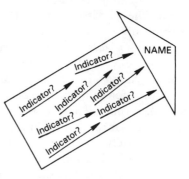

3. As we communicate about the general concept, using its term, we begin to think that the concept is *something* that really exists, not just a summary reference for several concrete observations in the world.

4. The belief that the concept itself is real results in irony. We now begin discussing and debating whether specific observations are "really" sufficient *indicators* of the concept.

From *The Practice of Social Research*, 3rd ed., by Earl Babbie. ©1983 by Wadsworth, Inc. Reprinted by permission of Wadsworth Publishing Co., Belmont, Calif. 94002.

FIGURE 2-1 The Process of Reification

We treat an abstraction as though it were something concrete, as if it had existence in the real world.

The error is compounded when we begin to use the label as if it were an explanation. An example: We see one person make a suggestion to another; it is carried out. We say "leadership" has occurred. It is all too easy to slip into saying that what we observed was leadership *causing* orders to be carried out. That is, we can very easily begin to think that "leadership" is a property the leader had that in some way caused the other person to act on the leader's suggestion.

There are, of course, ways in which a term like leadership could be used to explain something in which we were interested. For example, the explanations social scientists give for events do not always involve phenomena that can be directly observed. Sometimes, we observe individuals who have a tendency in many situations to try to control or dominate whatever is going on. These individuals are always looking for ways to get themselves into positions of influence and appear to be unhappy when they cannot do so. We often laughingly refer to people like these as "politicians." Now what we can do is to try to explain this behavior by inferring that these persons have a very high "need for power," which propels or pushes them to attempt to gain control of situations. This is an attractive idea and one that has been pursued in any number of forms and ways for a long time (e.g., Lasswell 1948). But since the need is not directly observed, it remains only one possible explanation for what is happening. Indeed, many of the theories we will be considering in this book rely heavily on a whole range of inferences about things going on both "inside" and "outside" human beings.

But is this example reification? Not necessarily. We can get around this problem *by specifying as precisely as possible what it is about this concept* (e.g., the need for power) *that makes it work the way it does*. For example, we should be able to delineate as clearly as possible what kinds of situations will trigger off this need for power or what properties such situations must have.

We should also be able to specify the kinds of training in the family or the kinds of experiences that give rise to this need. We should then be able to *predict* when it is that we will see the need for power motivating behavior (or not motivating behavior). Actually, we may find that in trying to specify how the concept works, we may need to invent or bring in other concepts that are linked to the original concepts. Systematic statements about relationships between concepts and between concepts and observables are called *theories*. Actually, theories are just complicated networks of inferences.

The idea of inference and the use of concepts to explain and predict things and events is far from falling into the trap of reifying words. In the latter case we have simply confused a description (that is, a label for observed similarities between things) with some property of the world. In the case of inference we are fully aware that the thing we think is going on does not in fact really exist but is made up by us to explain and predict things and events. When inferences are used in this manner, they have a very nice property: They can be shown not to work. To put it another way, a concept can vary in its usefulness, both for explaining and predicting. This is enormously important since it allows us to make use of our minds to come up with new or better alternatives when a given concept no longer seems useful. In other words, the fact that inferences can be shown not to be useful forces us to try to come up with a better solution—one that helps us to explain and predict events and things more satisfactorily.

PROBLEM 2: MAKING TOO MUCH OF THE PSYCHOLOGY OF POLITICAL PSYCHOLOGY

This book explores the contributions of psychology, broadly conceived, to the study of political behavior. We stand in a long historic line of persons who think that explaining politics requires that we take the individual (however we define this term) into account. But consider the following. If various aspects of politics can be explained by the nature of individuals and their relationships with others, as many political psychologists would like to argue, it then follows that the onus of responsibility for public policy and political change will have to lie with individuals. If individuals are to be blamed, i.e., given responsibility for the state of the political world, then clearly we don't need to look at the operation of institutions or social structures very closely, even though it may be more appropriate to explain political behavior in these terms.

Taken to its extreme, this tendency can result in "blaming the victim." For instance, we ask ourselves, "Why do so few people vote in elections anymore? It must be that people are irresponsible or not smart enough to understand the issues." Or if we are more sophisticated we say, "They don't see the connection between the political act of voting and their own lives." We blame lack of voting on individual psychological properties, not on the properties of a political system that by its very structure may be unable or unwilling to respond to the needs of much of the electorate. So to develop a political psychology that is insensitive to the fact that individual psychology is only one element in the larger explanatory framework for understanding politics becomes a commitment to a certain kind of *ideology*. This ideology would clearly be one that supports the social status quo and opts for changes in individual psychologies to bring about the amelioration of problems.

Numerous authors have made similar points not only about political psychology but about the social sciences in general. For instance, Herbert Kelman suggests,

> to the extent that we engage in an analysis at the psychological level there is a tendency, a danger that we may be placing the problem on the shoulders of those whom we are studying, and they very often represent the powerless element of the society. . . . If we define the problem as the psychological problem of a certain group of people, then we're more likely to develop policies that involve changing these people, rather than policies that involve changing the social structures that help sustain their powerlessness. [1979b, pp. 101–2]

Barbara Ringwald analyzed themes in sixteen years of social psychological research. She found that during periods when liberal politics were in the ascendancy in this country, researchers tended to support the values of equality in resource distribution decisions. During more conservative times, however, she found that researchers seemed to favor more unequal distributions of social resources (her work is contained in an unpublished doctoral dissertation, 1974).

Is it possible to do political psychology without giving implicit support to one political ideology or another? Is it possible to have a political psychology, in short, that does not contain *prescriptive* elements (i.e., those that give directions or issue injunctions)? The problem is complicated and troubles all the disciplines that deal with human behavior. Perhaps it can be addressed if we discriminate more carefully between what are really two questions. First, in what ways does ideology *determine* the kinds of research being done, the sorts of research questions being asked, the way data are interpreted? Second, to what extent should researchers be concerned with the *uses* to which their research is put?

Kinds of research.   In relation to the first question, psychology and political science during the past century (and particularly the last fifty years) have tried hard to model themselves after the natural sciences. It was felt that the approaches of the "harder" sciences, with their emphasis on the careful control of sources of error, including the bias of the experimenter, offered a way to understand human behavior free of subjective judgments and ideological predispositions. Yet numerous commentators over the last two decades have noted that ideological stances do unintentionally color all aspects of the research process. For instance, Kenneth Gergen, in his influential article "Social Psychology as History" (1973) notes many examples of the ways in which the kinds of results obtained from social psychological experiments conform closely to cultural stereotypes. For example, he points out that "treatises on conformity often treat the conformer as a second-class citizen, a social sheep who foregoes personal conviction to agree with the erroneous position of others" (p. 311). Further, he notes that the closer the subject is to the researcher in education, socioeconomic background, sex, race, and personal values, the more favorably the subject appears on a variety of psychological measures. For example, well-educated persons usually end up having low scores on authoritarianism and high scores on open-mindedness. In short, people who share our view of the world tend to end up looking "good."

The problem also turns up in a more subtle way. Social scientists have often assumed that certain "facts" established through research and the psychological or political principles based on those "facts" were stable over time and across cultures (as would be true for, say, principles of physics). But in fact many of these "facts" and principles may be expressions of the particular period in cultural and social history during which the research on them was done. For example, a popular and influential theory that attempts to explain much of human social behavior is the theory of social comparison (Festinger 1957). It assumes that people wish to evaluate themselves accurately and in order to do so compare themselves with others. This theory is based on assumptions characteristic of American society at this point in its history. One can imagine other societies where such assumptions would not hold and, in fact, many social commentators are critical of our common tendency to define ourselves through the opinions of others. Similarly, under the influence of the writings of Max Weber and America's love affair with machines and technology, early twentieth-century ideas about public administration took a highly mechanistic view of behavior in organizations (e.g., Taylor 1911; Follett 1951; Willoughby 1927; Fayol 1930; Gulick & Urwich 1937). Now under the influence of the computer revolution, there is a tendency to see organizations as cybernetic systems (e.g., Katz & Kahn 1978). Thus the job of the political psychologist requires great sensitivity to the assumptions and biases that arise out of the historical context in which research work is done.

Uses of research.   The second problem under the rubric of ideology is the problem of the use to which research is put. There are two aspects to this problem. First, even to acknowledge this problem propels us into murky moral waters through which scientists, both natural and social, have struggled since there was such a thing as "science." For the physical scientists, in modern times, it has been the use of new discoveries and theories to create ever more deadly weapons of destruction. For the biological scientists it lies in the area of genetic manipulation and recombinant DNA technology (Teich & Thornton 1982; Blank 1982). For the social and behavioral sciences it centers on concerns about the control and manipulation of behavior. Interestingly, certain political psychologists, for example, Erich Fromm (1955) and Robert Lifton (1971), have seen the goal of political psychology to unmask and expose the uses of psychology for these ends. As Irving Louis Horowitz puts it, political psychology of this sort can be seen as

> an exposé of the machinations of psychiatry, psychology or psychoanalysis as it bears on the political process; having, as its essential mission, exposure of mind abuse and making clear the manipulations of behavior for the purposes of prearranged political goals. [1979, pp. 99–100]

This specter loomed large in 1971 when many social scientists became upset over the following statement made by Dr. Kenneth Clark in a presidential address to the American Psychological Association:

> It would seem logical that a requirement imposed upon all power-controlling leaders and those who aspire to such leadership would be that they accept and use the earliest perfected form of psychotechnological biochemical intervention which would assure their positive use of power and reduce or block the possibility of their using power destructively. [1971, p. 1056]

Clearly, Dr. Clark intended that we use our knowledge in the fields of psychology and psychophysiology to benefit humankind. Others, however, did not share his value system and called attention to its vulnerability or pointed out that other values might well override the values expressed by Dr. Clark.

This brings us to the second aspect of the problem of the use to which research is put: Should political psychology attempt to be value free? The question was first raised in the discipline of sociology by Max Weber (Gerth & Mills 1946). Weber felt that there were grave hazards in the expression of value judgments by sociologists, particularly since their "expertise" might give them unwarranted influence and also might play into the hands of those with political goals, a possibility that Weber saw as dangerous. Ultimately, he concluded that sociologists could speak out if they clearly separated what was a statement of value from the "scientific" statement of fact. In the 1950s and 60s the idea of a "value-free" sociology (as well as psychology and political science) was taken up by American academic social scientists. It conformed nicely to the idea that the social sciences would be most effective if modeled after the natural sciences. But as Alvin Gouldner pointed out in an influential article (1963), the idea of a value-free social science was, and is, a myth. To oversimplify Gouldner: While the idea of a value-free social science may have helped people to move ahead and establish the credibility of the social and behavioral sciences, it also had the unfortunate effect of relieving people from contemplating the moral and ethical significance of their work and the problems of society to which the results of their work might be applicable.

Now to the extent that one is involved in developing a political psychology, which in fact has as one of its goals that of being critical of political and social systems, the problem of value-free social science will be less troublesome, if only because one is dealing "up front" with questions that are clearly questions of value. But for those political psychologists who seek a more neutral stance in order to evaluate the role of, say, personality factors in decision making, who, in short, wish to take a more "scientific" stance, the problem is greater.

Since the authors of this book regard themselves in the latter tradition, we urge readers to keep a watchful eye on the material we will be presenting. In particular, the intelligent reader should ask: What value assumptions are the authors making? How sensitive to historical circumstance are the results, the "facts," the theories they present?

PROBLEM 3: THE RELATIONSHIP BETWEEN ATTITUDES AND BEHAVIOR

In 1930 a sociologist named Richard LaPiere and a young Chinese couple began two years of travel throughout the United States. During the two years they patronized 251 hotels, auto camps, restaurants, and the like. Only once—at a California auto camp—were they turned away.

LaPiere found this surprising because he had previously been under the impression that American prejudice against Orientals was both widespread and intense. Since his experience with the Chinese couple seemed to contradict this perception, he decided to explore the issue further by sending questionnaires to the establishments they had patronized. The key question was, "Will you accept members of the Chinese race [sic] as guests in your establishment?" He got replies from 128 of the businesses; only *one* answered the question with an unequivocal yes, and over 90 percent answered with a flat no. From these responses LaPiere concluded that people do not always do what they say they are going to do (LaPiere 1934–35). This raises the important issue of whether attitudes are very good predictors of behavior.

To explain why this issue is an important one in the study of psychology and political behavior we must go back approximately a quarter of a century to the 1950s when a small group of political scientists were criticizing what they thought was the unscientific state of political research. Basically, they were calling on political scientists to begin trying harder to live up to the term "science" in political science. Their call for more rigorous development of theory and more sophisticated analysis of empirical data was soon taken up by others, some of whom began to try to practice what they preached. The result is now usually referred to as "a shift from the institutional to the behavioral approach" (Irish 1968, p. 17). This approach places emphasis on the theoretical basis of research, the collection of empirical data, accurate measurement, and systematic, usually quantitative, analysis. In short, the approach to political research became more sophisticated, with research in the natural sciences serving as the model.

This "behavioral" approach to political research now dominates the discipline. In 1978 John Wahlke, then president of the American Political Science Association, decided to take a closer look at the impact of the "behavioral revolution" on contemporary political science. He was very critical of what he found and concluded that "political behavior research remains 'pre-behavioral' " (Wahlke 1979, p. 9). While his whole argument need not be summarized here, one part of it is directly relevant. To indicate the state of research in the discipline, he analyzed all of the articles and research notes in the *American Political Science Review* (the major research journal in political science) during 1968–77. He found 180 that could be classified as political-behavior studies. Of these, 131 analyses rested partly or entirely on survey data. The overwhelming majority of the variables analyzed were either attitudinal or self-reports of actions performed or intended.

Implicit in much of this research is the assumption that self-reported attitudes and behavioral intentions are reasonable surrogates for actual behavior. In other words, behavioral researchers tend to assume (usually without discussing it in their publications) that it is possible to learn something useful about actual political behavior by asking people about their attitudes, past behaviors, and behavioral intentions. Well, maybe it is and, then again, maybe it isn't. The point is that we don't really know. As Wahlke points out, there is a whole tradition of research, including La-Piere's study, that demonstrates that the relationships between attitudes, behavioral intentions, and actual behavior are extremely problematical. Thus any assumptions about the attitude-behavior relationship should be made with extreme caution and an explicit recognition that this relationship is highly complex and currently not well understood by social scientists. Certainly the assumption that the behavior of responding to a survey or a questionnaire predicts any other political behavior is, as we shall see, highly problematic.

In the discussion that follows, we will present one approach to understanding the complexities of attitude-behavior relationships, the "Theory of Reasoned Action" (Ajzen & Fishbein 1980). We are fully aware that there are other approaches to this issue (for a review see Deutscher 1973). However, our feeling is that this particular approach makes many of the issues involved in thinking about the problem quite clear.

The attitude concept.   Our discussion begins with a closer look at the complexities of the attitude concept itself.

There is a fair amount of conceptual agreement among scholars on the definition of the term, attitude, though the exact words used vary somewhat from author to author. Here are some examples:

> Attitudes are likes and dislikes. They are our affinities for and our aversions to situations, objects, persons, groups, or any other identifiable aspects of our environment, including abstract ideas and social policies. [Bem 1970, p. 14]

> [An attitude is] a learned *predisposition* to *respond* to an object in a consistently favorable or unfavorable manner. [Fishbein & Ajzen 1975, p. 336; italics in the original]

> Attitudes have generally been regarded as either mental readinesses or implicit predispositions which exert some general and consistent influence on a fairly large class of evaluative responses. These responses are usually directed toward some object, person, or group. [They] are learned rather than innate. [Zimbardo & Ebbesen 1970, p. 6]

> We can define an *attitude* as a predisposition to respond to a particular stimulus in a particular manner. [Manheim 1975, p. 7; italics in the original]

The first component involved here is *cognition*. It is by cognition that "a living creature obtains knowledge of some object or becomes aware of its environment" (Eysenck 1972, p. 177). So in order to have an attitude there must be a perceived something that serves as the focus of the attitude. It can be as concrete as an object, person, or group; it can be as abstract as a situation, an idea, or a social policy. In any case, functions such as comprehension, judgment, memory, and reasoning are involved in cognition.

The second component is *affect,* which is generally synonymous with emotion. By using words such as "likes and dislikes", "favorable or unfavorable", and "evaluative responses", most definitions of "attitude" indicate that a person's emotional responses are evoked by the perception of phenomena that are the focus of his or her attitudes.

The affective dimension of attitudes is also characterized by *direction, intensity,* and *centrality.* Affect-indicating words tend to come in pairs. You either like something or dislike it. You feel an affinity for one person and an aversion to another. Attitudes have a positive or negative direction, except perhaps when the attitude is one of ambivalence. This situation, though, calls attention to the phenomenon of intensity. Donna, for example, feels very strongly about the supermarket situation which is the principal grievance of the ETO. But how does she feel about Chet asking her questions on the front steps of City Hall? We can guess that at that moment, while she appreciates the publicity and thus feels mildly positive about being interviewed, she also is somewhat tired and depressed. Thus, we might say that she is *ambivalent* about being interviewed, meaning that her intensity of emotion is weak enough so that the positive has a tendency to shade into the negative, or vice-versa. Thus, attitudes have a generally positive or negative direction which can vary in intensity from very strong to very weak.

Centrality is closely related to intensity. Everyone has many, many attitudes, which vary in their importance to the individual holding them. The ones that are most central are those that are most basic to a person's self-concept. For a politically active person raised in a politically active family, the attitude that Republicans are more intelligent than Democrats (or vice versa) might be quite central. If he sees Republicans as more intelligent, and he is a Republican, then his self-concept as an intelligent person is enhanced. A politically apathetic person, on the other hand, might also think Republicans are more intelligent but hold this attitude quite peripherally. When we express surprise that long-time politicians like John Connolly or Strom Thurmond were able to switch from the Democratic party to the Republican party in midcareer, we are tacitly acknowledging the importance of centrality in individuals' attitude systems.

The term, attitude system, is appropriate because attitudes do not generally exist in mental space side by side without touching. They are interrelated and mutually influential in ways that are often obscure to the researcher and unexamined by the person holding them. Attitudes may be consistent, such as "I like the Democratic party" and "I always vote for candidate X (who is a Democrat)." There is no reason, however, why they have to be consistent. In fact, in real life it is common for persons to have mutually contradictory attitudes. Most legislators' nomination for the classic example would go to those interest-group representatives who come to legislative hearings to ask for lower taxes and more government services or benefits for their supporters. They neatly overlook the issue of where the money will come from—or make wildly unrealistic suggestions.

We have an image, then, of multiple clusters of attitudes centered on certain objects. Each cluster is organized in terms of core-peripheral attitudes, and these attitudes are interrelated and mutually influential in various ways. But the clusters themselves are also organized in terms of the core-peripheral distinction and are also interrelated and mutually influential. Figure 2-2 gives us a simplified visual picture of such an attitude system. In the figure, the cluster concerning attitudes toward energy is blown up in size to illustrate that both clusters and attitudes within clusters are interrelated in different ways. For example, in this person's attitude system, attitudes toward energy are more peripheral. That is, for this person, the whole issue is of less concern than her attitudes toward the economic system. However, within the energy policy cluster itself, certain attitudes are more and less peripheral. Thus, she is strongly against nuclear energy and this is a core attitude. More peripherally, she is in favor of conservation but is mildly negative toward solar energy. Her attitudes toward conservation and solar energy seem inconsistent although it is likely that, if we were to question her about this inconsistency, she would find a way to justify it (Chapter 6). What would we predict about this person's behavior if she were asked to sign an anti-nuclear petition? Although her opposition to nuclear energy is central to this cluster, in her attitude system as a whole the whole energy question is rather peripheral. Moreover, we know that she has what appears to an outsider to be somewhat inconsistent attitudes about the energy situation. Thus, the connection between her "attitudes" about energy and the behavior of signing the petition is somewhat problematic, a judgment based on the nature of her attitude system alone. If we were to take into account the situation in which she was asked to sign (e.g., whether other people were around, how she felt about the person circulating the petition) a prediction about her behavior based on her "attitudes" would become even more difficult to make.

Most researchers do not devote as much care to defining *behavior* (Ajzen & Fishbein 1980, p. 27). In fact, many do not define it at all; they simply assume that everyone will automatically know what they mean. While this approach is not entirely without justification, it does tend to underrate the subtleties involved in drawing the line between behavior and nonbehavior. For example, is "having an attitude" a form of behavior? In order to sidestep such quandaries, we will give "behavior" a very basic definition here. For purposes of this discussion "behavior" will be defined as observable actions, which can be studied in their own right (adapted from Fishbein & Ajzen 1975, p. 335). This can also be (and often is) referred to as "overt behavior".

The path between attitudes and overt behavior is an intellectual no man's land where the outlines of the process are blurred and imperfectly understood. One component that is there in reasonably clear outline,

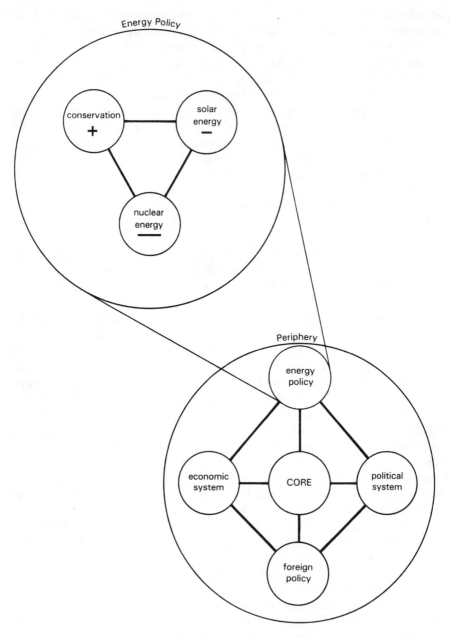

FIGURE 2-2 Simplified diagram of a hypothetical person's attitude system with enlarged view of one attitude cluster

though, is what can be called a "behavioral intention" (Ajzen *et al.* 1982). This can be viewed as an attitude but is probably—for our purposes at least—better considered as a phenomenon intermediate between an attitude and a behavior. It is a readiness to act, which grows out of a process usually referred to as *conation*—the "evaluation of the potential conse-quences or the potential impact of the behavior" (Manheim 1975, p. 23).

Thus we have the following components that can be identified with some certainty as playing a role in the attitude-behavior relationship:

1. **Cognition** (e.g., "There is an election next Tuesday and I have to decide whether to vote.")
2. **Affect** (e.g., "I feel guilty and unpatriotic when I don't vote—especially when my shop steward asks me if I did.")
3. **Conation** (e.g., "I have to do a job with my shop steward next Wednesday, and I'm sure he'll ask me if I voted. I'll be embarrassed to tell him I didn't.")
4. **Behavioral intent** (e.g., "I'd better plan to vote on Tuesday.")
5. **Overt behavior** (e.g., The worker actually goes to the polls and votes.)

While this set of illustrations is somewhat oversimplified, it does convey the flavor of the process. Suppose, though, that on Monday our hypothetical worker finds out that his shop steward has been temporarily reassigned to another part of the factory and that he probably won't see the steward for a month? Suppose, in addition, that our worker's car breaks down on Tuesday and he has to find some other means of trans-portation to the polls? Or, alternatively, one of his coworkers becomes a father and he is invited to join the celebration in a nearby bar after work on Tuesday? The situation in which a person finds himself or herself may have a great deal of influence on the rather fragile link between attitude and behavior. Given such changes in our hypothetical worker's situation, he might reconsider, size things up differently, and arrive at the conclu-sion that he has too many important things to do on Tuesday and conse-quently cannot vote. "After all," he might say, "what difference can one vote make anyway? You don't have to vote every time to be a good citizen."

This is a relatively trivial example (though not an uncommon type of situation) in the sense that the worker's vote or nonvote probably will have relatively little impact on the political system or on his own life. Other situations in which a person finds himself or herself, however, may have a more profound effect. Gandhi, having been born into a well-off Indian family and having studied law in England, traveled to South Africa to work. In South Africa he found himself in a situation of intense discrimi-nation against nonwhites. Neither his family's status nor his education mattered. He was treated as just another "coolie" by persons considerably his inferior by almost any measure other than skin color. In reaction, he developed a strategy of civil disobedience, which started him on a career of political leadership that occupied the rest of his life. Had he not gone to South Africa, he might have pursued a comfortable but uneventful career as a prosperous barrister.

According to Donald T. Campbell (1963, pp. 159–62), much of the apparent inconsistency between attitudes and behavior can be resolved if one considers situational thresholds. The underlying notion here is that situations differ as to the ease with which a person can act according to their expressed attitudes. Returning to the LaPiere study, he points out that "it is very hard to refuse a well-dressed Chinese couple traveling with a European in a face-to-face setting, and very easy to refuse the Chinese as a race [sic] in a mailed questionnaire" (p. 160). Thus he sees this as evidence not of inconsistency but of the fact that the proprietors held an attitude of Sinophobia with sufficient intensity to record it on a questionnaire but not with sufficient intensity to express it to LaPiere and his friends. To Campbell a true inconsistency would have been the failure to express it on the questionnaire and the willingness to express it in the face-to-face situation. Thus attitudinal factors, such as intensity, can interact with situational factors to influence whether a person acts in accordance with his or her expressed attitudes.

Recent research has indicated that other individual differences affect the extent to which situational factors influence behavior (Snyder & Kendzierski 1982). For example, in order for attitudes to influence behavior in some concrete way, a person must be aware of his or her relevant attitudes and define them as being important potential influencers of behavior in a particular situation. It is at this point that other factors may enter into the equation. For example, peer-group pressures may "overrule" the promptings of one's attitudes. One's position in an organization may seem to dictate certain lines of behavior that diverge from those one might take purely on the basis of personal attitudes: "I don't like to do this, but I have to enforce the rules." The point is that there are occasions on which a person's actions may more clearly reflect the situation than that individual's personal attitudes.

And to further complicate things, it seems that some people are more susceptible to situational effects than other people. For example, if an individual is very confident about his or her attitude, the attitude is more likely to be reflected in behavior (Fazio & Zanna 1978). Also, some people are more instrumental with regard to social behavior and interpersonal relationships than others and are thus more likely to adjust their behavior on the basis of what seems appropriate to the situation—personal attitudes to the contrary notwithstanding (Ajzen et al. 1982; Snyder & Kendzierski 1982). Other factors that may break or strengthen the link between attitude and behavior include a person's level of self-awareness, whether or not the attitude has been formed as a result of direct experience, and the influence of extraneous events.

Situation can also be important in a much more subtle way. There is a body of research evidence that suggests that behavior can influence attitudes. That is, if a person finds herself in a situation in which she is behaving in a way contrary to her relevant attitudes, she may adjust her attitudes to be more consistent with her behavior, rather than vice versa.

In 1959 there was a clash between Yale students and the New Haven police. The students accused the police of brutality, and most of the uninvolved Yale students agreed with the anti-police interpretation of the event. Yale psychologist Arthur Cohen decided to use this situation for research on the relationship between attitudes and behavior. He and his students walked around the campus picking Yale students at random and asking them to write an essay called "Why the New Haven Police Actions Were Justified." As an inducement, the students were offered payment for writing the essay. The pay offered was at four different levels: 50¢, $1, $5, and $10. Reluctant students were pressured by the experimenters to cooperate. Upon finishing the essay, each student was asked to fill out a questionnaire that would indicate his actual opinion of the police. Cohen wanted to find out whether the students would persuade themselves of the merits of the police position while writing the essay. He also wanted to know if the amount of money the student was being paid would make a difference.

The students who were paid $10 or $5 ended up with opinions not much different from those of a control group of students who did not write essays. Those who were paid less, however, did become significantly more sympathetic to the police. In fact, the less the individual was paid, the more favorable his attitude toward the police became (Brehm & Cohen 1962, pp. 73–77). Subsequently, other researchers have gotten similar results using various types of experiments, so Cohen's research cannot be dismissed as a fluke or chance result.

There is more than one way of interpreting this. Cohen explained it on the basis of the theory of cognitive dissonance. This theory, formulated by Leon Festinger in 1957, is based on the assumption that human beings try to eliminate or reduce psychological inconsistency because it creates an unpleasant tension within them. Dissonance is present whenever the person is aware of conflicts between or among attitudes, opinions, beliefs, or behaviors. Cognitive dissonance theory holds that the individual experiencing the tension will try to reduce it by changing one component to bring it more comfortably in line with the other and thus reduce the tension.

So if you take a student who thinks that the police actions were unjustified and you induce her to write an essay that says they were justified, you are creating cognitive dissonance within her. Giving her a large sum of money ($10 or $5 was worth more then than it is now) allows her to reduce the tension by reasoning that she was just doing it for the money. On the other hand, this is a weak justification if the sum is small (50¢ or $1 was a small amount even in the 1950s). Therefore, the tension of the dissonance is not reduced by the payment, and the student has to change her attitudes to make them more consistent with her behaviors.

Another interpretation can be based on Daryl Bem's self-perception theory. According to Bem:

> To us, as observers, the most important cues to an individual's inner states are found in his behavior. When we want to know how a person feels, we look to see how he acts. Accordingly, my theory about the origins of an individual's self-knowledge predicts that he might also infer his own internal states by observing his own overt behavior. [Bem 1970, p. 57]

Thus according to Bem, a person observes himself and uses the money payment as a signal to tell *himself* whether or not he believes what he has written in the essay. A student getting a large sum of money could see the act of writing the pro-police essay as stemming strictly from pecuniary motives. It would not be an indicator of his true attitudes. A person getting little or no money, however, "could look at his behavior and infer from it (nonconsciously) that he must be somewhat favorable toward the police actions. ("Why else would I have written the essay?") (ibid., p. 59).

For our purposes it does not matter which interpretation you find more persuasive. The important point is that it cannot be simply assumed that the line of influence necessarily always runs from attitudes to behavior. Under some conditions behavior can influence attitudes. The reasons why this happens are a matter about which reasonable persons can differ.

In what is perhaps the most ambitious effort to date to illuminate the relationship between attitudes and behavior, Ajzen and Fishbein (1980, pp. 1–91) have generated a theory of reasoned action. Underlying the theory is the assumption that "human beings are usually quite rational and make systematic use of the information available to them" (ibid., p. 5). The most immediate determinant of action and consequently the most important variable to be used in predicting action is behavioral intention. This is "a measure of the likelihood that a person will engage in a given behavior" (ibid., p. 42). Thus if you accost a voter on her way to the voting booth and ask her how she intends to vote, her answer will be an expression of her behavioral intention.

Ajzen and Fishbein are careful to emphasize that behavioral intention cannot be diffuse but the person must know *exactly* what she intends to do in order for behavioral intention to be a good predictor of subsequent behavior. In order to be this specific, the behavioral intent must be expressed in terms of action, target, context, and time. To return to our hypothetical voter, the action would be pulling the lever beside the name of a particular candidate. The target is the set of candidates running for office and, in this example, the candidate for whom the voter says she will vote. The context is the particular election in which she is voting. For example, it could be an election for mayor in her home town or it could be an election for president of the United States. The time is the particular moment in which she will vote.

While the specification of these elements may seem a trivial emphasis on the obvious, the omission of one of them can make a crucial difference. For example, if you knock on the door of a registered voter in Massachusetts and ask her if she would vote for Teddy Kennedy, you might get one answer if she assumes you mean a senatorial race and quite another if she assumes you mean a presidential race. Correspondingly, she might be willing to vote for him in 1988, but would consider him "too old" to be president or senator in 1992. Even the nature of the action must be clear. If you ask her whether she supports Teddy Kennedy, her yes might indicate a willingness to vote for him but not to contribute to his campaign. The importance of being perfectly clear about the target of the behavioral intention was proven by the many elections during the 1960s in which candidates named Kennedy rode to public office on the crest of popular enthusiasm for John F. Kennedy. Thus in order to be a good predictor of behavior, any statement of behavioral intent must be quite specific with regard to all four behavioral elements: action, target, context, and time. Further, information on behavioral intent must be gathered at a point in time close to the projected behavior.

While a knowledge of behavioral intention is crucial for predicting behavior, it is necessary to dig deeper to understand that relationship. A behavioral intention is a function of two basic determinants: the attitudinal factor and the normative factor. The attitudinal factor is the individual's judgment that the action contemplated is good or bad, that she is in favor of, or against, performing the action. For example, people might differ as to whether or not they should take part in an antinuclear demonstration. One person might oppose such participation because he fears possible arrest and imprisonment. Another might be in favor of participation because he fears the personal consequences of nuclear war.

The other determinant, the normative factor, is the individual's perception of the social pressures placed upon her to perform the action in question. To go back to our previous example, a person might be reluctant to participate in an antinuclear demonstration because of a fear that her boss, who is pronuclear, might hear about it—even though she is strongly opposed to the use of nuclear energy for both military and peaceful purposes. On the other hand, her brother, who is not terribly interested in the nuclear issue, might decide to participate because all of his closest friends are going to participate. Thus, "generally speaking, individuals will intend to perform a behavior when they evaluate it positively and when they believe that important others think they should perform it" (ibid., p. 6).

Because of the possibility that attitudinal factors and normative factors might contradict each other it is necessary to determine the relative importance of a person's attitudinal and normative considerations. In the case of the woman with the pronuclear boss, her concern with her relationship to her boss outweighed her conviction that something has to be done about the growth of nuclear power. If the issue were different, however, the weights assigned the two types of considerations might also be different. For example, the knowledge that her boss prefers brown to blue is less likely to cause her to form an intent to buy a brown suit when she perceives a blue suit to be much more attractive and practical.

Behavioral beliefs in turn underlie attitudes toward behavior, and normative beliefs underlie subjective norms. Beliefs represent the information people have about themselves and the world around them.

> In the course of a person's life his experiences lead to the formation of many different beliefs about various objects, actions, and events. These beliefs may be the result of direct observation, they may be acquired indirectly by accepting information from outside sources, or they are self-generated through inference processes. Some beliefs may persist over time, others may be forgotten, and new beliefs may be formed. [Ajzen & Fishbein 1980, p. 63]

Although an individual may have many beliefs about something, he or she can take into account only a limited number at any one time. The beliefs actually taken into consideration in the formation of a behavioral attitude or subjective norm are salient beliefs. They are the immediate determinants of a person's attitude or norm. Among them are a set of beliefs that are particularly important in the formation of subjective norms. These are beliefs about whether that individual's "important others" think that he or she should (or should not) perform the action in question. For example, our hypothetical demonstrator might hold the salient belief that the proliferation of nuclear weapons will lead inevitably to the extinction of the human race. She might also believe that her friends will think her a hypocrite if she refuses to participate in the demonstration.

Finally, it should be noted that Ajzen and Fishbein's theory of reasoned action does not attempt to explain behavior by reference to such factors as personality, attitudes toward groups, or demographic variables. They acknowledge that such phenomena may sometimes influence behavior, but they assert that this influence is not only indirect, but is mediated by all the steps we have previously considered. They call such variables "external variables" and assert that they "will be related to behavior only if they are related to one or more of the variables [previously] specified" (ibid., p. 82). Thus the higher one's self-esteem, the more likely one might be to participate in an antinuclear demonstration in the face of the disapproval of the boss. Ajzen and Fishbein would probably argue, though, that the decision to participate would be based not on self-esteem itself but on self-esteem as mediated by one of the elements of the model. For example, a person might perceive herself as being good enough in her job performance that her boss will be unwilling to lose her contribution, even though he may not agree with her politics. Or, she might have the strong belief that she can easily find another job, if necessary.

Figure 2-3 graphically sets forth the theory of reasoned action. Through this theory the relationship of attitudes to behavior is explained in terms of a relatively limited number of factors. Ajzen and Fishbein have demonstrated how these factors can be studied in order to enhance our understanding of the precursors of behavior for such events as presidential elections (ibid.). Aside from pointing out interesting and potentially useful new lines of research, their theory demonstrates that the very notion of an attitude-behavior relationship is an oversimplification of an extremely complex and variable phenomenon.

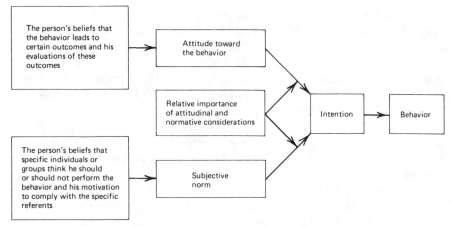

Note: Arrows indicate the direction of influence.

Icek Ajzen, Martin Fishbein, *Understanding Attitudes and Predicting Social Behavior*, © 1980, p. 8. Reprinted by permission of Prentice-Hall, Inc., Englewood Cliffs, N.J.

FIGURE 2-3   Factors determining a person's behavior

SUMMARY

It would be impossible in the small amount of space that can be allotted to any single chapter to even touch on all of the confusions, muddles, and concerns that beset the political psychologist. It might not even be possible within the scope of a single book. What we have tried to do here is to call attention to the fact that such problems exist and give some examples. We have chosen those that seem to us to be most in need of discussion at this point in time: 1) the problems inherent in the fact that political psychologists usually think and communicate using the written or spoken word; 2) the danger of letting psychology "take over" our thinking about problems and issues in the political sphere; and 3) the elusiveness of the relationship between attitudes and behavior. Others might (and probably would) have made different selections. This is one of the ways in which we betray some of the value assumptions which underlie our work.

In its essence, language is arbitrary. A language is simply a tradition within a certain group of people which specifies that definite clusters of vocal sounds and written symbols will represent specific objects or concepts. These can be combined according to certain grammatical rules yielding more complex thought patterns. Using this vehicle, human beings make sense of their world and attempt to convey this understanding to others. In creating language, we have given it great power over ourselves. What words denote usually changes relatively slowly, although the mass media may be accelerating this process (e.g., the rapidity with which the use of the word "gay" to denote "happy" has been supplanted by its use to denote "homosexual"). What words connote, however, can change rapidly and can vary greatly from person to person at the same point in time. Also, words can mobilize and control behavior. Finally, we can confuse real objects and events with the labels we use to identify them or with the words we use to understand how they might be related. The abstract and the concrete can become confused—as can labels and causes. Thus, it is important that words be used as carefully and precisely as possible and that their limits be firmly kept in mind.

The way in which we relate psychological concepts to political phenomena can be an ideological statement. Thus, it is important to remember that psychological constructs are only one element in a larger explanatory framework and that too much emphasis on psychology can result in too much emphasis on individual responsibility for political problems. In turn, this can lead to an underestimation of the contribution of other factors, such as institutional structures.

There are two ways in which this lack of balance can have a troublesome influence. It can distort the way in which research on political phenomena is done and it can influence the way in which research is translated into policy proposals. Values inevitably inform both the process of research and the ways in which research is utilized by actors in the political system. It is imperative that all instances of this process should be comprehended and consciously evaluated with respect to their implications.

Finally, there is a tendency—especially among political scientists—to "assume away" the problematical nature of the relationship between attitudes and behavior. Attitudes tend to be the focus of much research because of their amenability to study by survey research techniques which yield attractively high "N's" and data that can be statistically manipulated in relatively sophisticated ways. Attitudes, however, have relatively little meaning in the political arena if they are never translated into behavior. Political behavior is less well researched than political attitudes and the relationship between the two is a subject causing considerable controversy among psychologists while being virtually ignored by political scientists.

In this chapter, we have not tried to advance a single widely accepted version of the attitude/behavior relationship. Rather, we have tried to explore the complex nature of the problem and to present the outlines of a few of the more plausible models that have been advanced by psychologists studying the topic. The key seems to be the relationship between the individual and the situation in which she finds herself. There is, however, no general agreement about the exact mechanism by which attitudes are translated into overt behavior.

Now we would like to turn to a consideration of political behavior in a more concrete sense. What are the ways in which a person can become involved in politics? What relationships do people have within and with their political systems? Why do some people participate actively in political life while others do not? How does the nature of one's participation affect one's perspective on political issues?

3

INVOLVEMENT:
The Active Support
of Political Continuity or Change

Democratic values are in essence participatory values. At the heart of democratic theory is the notion that people should get involved in the process of governing themselves. Their relative failure to do so is ritually decried both before and after every major election in the United States. Political commentators point to statistics showing low voter turnout and bewail voter apathy. Underlying such observations is the sense that citizen participation not only gives an aura of legitimacy to a particular regime but also demonstrates and reinforces support for the existing system of government. Thus even in a country such as the Soviet Union where election ballots contain only one choice for each office, there is considerable emphasis on getting out the vote (Friedgut 1979). In fact, although there is less opportunity for the kind of participation that has a significant impact on policy, there is considerable pressure on Soviet citizens to participate in a wide variety of political activities (Kozhokaŕ & Markiman 1973, p. 7).

Much of the participation required of Soviet citizens is ritualistic or symbolic in value. The intent of those who encourage such participation seems to be to take advantage of some of the persuasive effects of self-perception (e.g., Brehm & Cohen 1962; Bem 1970) discussed in chapter 2 (p. 53). In general, demonstrations of loyalty to regime and nation are fostered in virtually all countries on the as yet unproven premise that they have some value. That is not, however, the type of political involvement with which this chapter will mainly be concerned. Even the most politically apathetic will get up and sing the national anthem before a ball game, but that is hardly the *active* support of political continuity or change.

Sometimes the line between participation that is purely ritualistic and participation that is intended to influence policy is sharp and clear to all. Often, however, the distinction is somewhat blurred. Some forms of participation may be undertaken for either ritualistic reasons or in an attempt to influence policy. The difference can be regarded as a function of intent (Shingles 1981, p. 79). Alternatively, participation may hinge on the probability or hope that the given act or activity will have an effect on the policy-making process. Voting is a case in point. For some the act of voting means supporting a candidate or policy position about which they have strong beliefs. For others it is a patriotic gesture or a way of demonstrating to others that they are good citizens. In either case a single vote is likely to have very little effect, if any, on the outcome of an election— except, perhaps, in some local elections. At any rate, the focus here will be on activities that have some reasonable potential for influencing the policy-making process.

The second dimension is the conventional/unconventional dimension. In other words, does an individual's involvement take place within the limits that are placed on citizen participation by the constitutional arrangements and laws of the particular political system? Or is the participation outside that framework and perhaps even subject to legal sanctions? For some people the distinction may not be entirely clear. An example would be the many people who, at least initially, assumed that the sit-ins and peaceful demonstrations that swept the United States in the 1960s were illegal rather than legitimate expressions of First Amendment freedoms.

Traditional studies of political participation have tended to focus on conventional types, especially the act of voting (LaPalombara 1974, pp. 53, 420–62). From this point of view, then, political participation can be defined as "those legal activities by private citizens which are more or less directly aimed at influencing the selection of governmental personnel and/or the action they take" (Nie & Verba 1975, p. 1; Verba & Nie 1972, p.2; Verba, Nie, & Kim 1978, p. 1). Studies of extralegal attempts to influence the political system have been considered a separate topic, of primary interest to scholars of political conflict and violence.

It is our considered opinion, however, that the traditional distinction between legal and extralegal forms of political involvement is, in some ways, an artificial one* and that while there are important differences

---

*Most obviously in cases where a particular act, such as peacefully demonstrating in opposition to a government policy, may be illegal in one country and perfectly legal in another.

between them in any given political system, they are most profitably studied with reference to each other (see, e.g., Barnes, Kaase et al. 1979). Thus we would prefer a definition that unlike Nie and Verba's does not limit participation to legal activities. This calls for a broader definition, such as that of Marc Howard Ross's (1980, p. 2): "efforts on the part of members of a community to influence either directly or indirectly the authoritative allocation of values in their society." (See also Milbrath 1981, p. 198). Such a definition makes no assumptions about the structural arrangements in the political system or the legality of the efforts at influence. The merit of such an approach has been increasingly recognized in recent years (Langton 1980, p. 99; Milbrath 1981, pp. 206–7; Smith et al. 1980, pp. 81–82; Hunt & Goel 1980, pp. 133–52; and Barnes, Kaase et al. 1979, pp. 149–57).

One of the problems with dividing political participation into conventional and unconventional categories is that there is no clear agreement as to the kinds of acts covered by these labels. As indicated above, Nie and Verba define participation to include only *legal* activity, yet they exclude consideration of political protests, some of which surely would be legal, at least in the United States and Western Europe. Milbrath includes in unconventional activity both legal acts, e.g., some kinds of street demonstrations, and presumably illegal activity, e.g., riots (1981, pp. 206–7). Hunt and Goel suggest a broader range of political participation, including assassinations, military coups, and revolutions (1980, p. 134). This lack of agreement is to some extent a function of the fact that unconventional political involvement has received relatively little attention from students of political participation. For purposes of this book and in keeping with the Ross definition, we will consider all forms of involvement in efforts to influence the authoritative allocation of values in a society. This chapter, however, will focus almost exclusively on conventional forms of participation. A later chapter will deal with the use of force in politics—a topic that includes (but is not limited to) many unconventional forms of participation.

Finally, there is what might be termed the intense/casual dimension. Not all persons who are involved in political activities are involved to the same degree. For some, politics may be a central preoccupation in their lives—perhaps even *the* central preoccupation. For others, politics may be a vaguely interesting pastime that they enjoy dabbling in from time to time when the spirit moves them or when something unusual is going on. There are, of course, all gradations in between these extremes. In fact, some people might consider total political inactivity a more appropriate criterion as the extreme for such a dimension than occasional casual activity. Nevertheless, intensity does set a tone to political involvement, and it may be expressed in a number of ways, such as the amount of time one spends in political activities, the duration of involvement in particular activities, and the vigor of one's involvement (a factor that assumes its greatest importance in unconventional political behavior).

THE INDIVIDUAL AND THE POLITICAL SYSTEM

In order to be involved an individual must have some sort of relationship with a political system. This relationship is conditioned by the extent to which the individual accepts the influence of the political system over her behavior. Kelman (1958) has suggested that there are three different processes of influence: compliance, identification, and internalization.

Compliance occurs when a person accepts influence emanating from political or government leaders because she hopes to achieve a favorable reaction or avoid a punishment. Whether or not the individual actually "believes in" what she is doing is irrelevant; she is motivated by the expectation of approval or rewards and the avoidance of disapproval or punishments. Thus people who object strongly to the inequities of our tax system or the uses to which tax dollars are put usually pay their taxes because they fear the sanctions the Internal Revenue Service can wield. Another example is the Soviet government, which commands a large and intricate system of rewards for system-supportive behavior and punishments for dissidence (Barry and Barner-Barry 1982, pp. 54–58). Often these rewards and punishments are two sides of the same coin. Become a devoted and active leisure-time participant in the agitation and propaganda system and you may reap enhanced opportunities for career advancement; apply for a visa to emigrate and you may find yourself out of a job.

Identification occurs when a person accepts the influence of political or governmental officials because he wishes to establish or maintain a satisfying relationship with the political system. Here the individual does believe in what he is doing. He does so, however, because the specific beliefs are associated with the desired relationship, not because of their inherent merit. For example, a person may attend a political rally because he admires and respects the person organizing the rally and who asked him to attend. Going to the rally, then, becomes a way of maintaining a positive relationship with this person.

Finally, *internalization* occurs when a person accepts the influence of political or governmental officials because "it is congruent with his value system" (Kelman 1958, p. 53). The behaviors involved are undertaken because they are intrinsically rewarding, are useful for solving a problem, or are congenial to the person's needs. The satisfaction comes from acting in a fashion one believes in because of the perceived merits of the behavior. Thus many people signed up to fight in World War II because they thought the Nazis and Italian Fascists represented an evil force that had to be stopped. Many of those who did not qualify for reasons of age or physical defect felt an acute sense of frustration at not being allowed to serve their country in such a situation.

It is easy to find isolated instances of political behavior that can serve as relatively pure examples of each of these three types of relationship to the political system. The reactions of individual human beings to the political systems in their countries, however, are more likely to be "mixed" than "pure." For example, the attitude of a person toward the values expressed in the Bill of Rights of the Constitution might be characterized by internalization. On the other hand, she might identify with a particular political party or leader and comply with the demands of the local tax collector or traffic police.

The one overarching reality is that in any case the political system is salient to the individual. Even in cases of extreme political alienation the political system is important in that it provides a focus, something to be alienated from. It may even provide an object for one's hostility, something to fight against. Thus alienation or "estrangement between the self and the polity" (Schwartz 1973, p. 8) can also provide the impetus for political involvement—albeit usually involvement of an unconventional sort. Correspondingly, the compliance, identification, or internalization of an actively alienated individual would be a response to the influence of individuals or groups struggling against the political status quo.

On the other hand, apathy that is essentially a non-response to politics (Gilmour & Lamb 1975, p. 95) is a relationship to the political system that is highly unlikely to lead to any useful political participation. Thus for the approximately one-third of Americans who can be characterized as apathetic (Milbrath 1965, pp. 16–21; Gilmour & Lamb, 1975, p. 96; Milbrath & Goel, 1977, p. 11) minimal compliance with the most imperative demands placed upon them by political authorities probably constitutes the extent of their participation. People who identify with the political system or have internalized its values are more likely to become involved in the true sense of trying to influence the choice of leaders or policies for that system.

POLITICAL EFFICACY

Aside from ritualized or socially motivated behavior, people are unlikely to become politically active unless they think that their participation has at least minimal potential for making a difference. Quite obviously, this involves one's perceptions of how the political world functions. On a deeper level, however, a person's perceptions of how the political arena functions may be premised on more basic beliefs about their own relationship to the world. For example, one of the most influential early formulations in political psychology was Lasswell's assertion that, for the "political personality," the search for political power is an effort to overcome a low estimate of the self (Lasswell 1948). Also, one of the most basic beliefs about how the political world functions has to do with the potential for individual action and effect (Renshon 1974, p. 69).

On the balance, does a given individual believe that his own efforts and personal characteristics have a substantial influence on what happens to him, or does he regard life as a lottery in which chance or luck plays the major role? Relatively few people, if any, believe that life is totally governed by fate or chance. Correspondingly, the notion that anyone has complete control over what happens in his or her life is probably equally rare. What we have then is a continuum or dimension along which people can be placed with reference to their personal beliefs regarding the relative importance to their lives of factors they can or cannot control (Phares 1973, p. 3). An individual who thinks that luck, fate, or chance plays a predominant role in his life is said to perceive an external locus of control, while a person who thinks that she plays the predominant role is said to perceive an internal locus of control (Rotter 1966, p. 1).

Thus human behavior, political participation included, can be said to be motivated by two main factors (Phares 1973, p. 3). First, there are the goals toward which one is striving. If the political system is not seen as relevant to one's important concerns in life, one is not likely to formulate goals that involve political participation or even to think much about politics (Renshon 1974, pp. 75–81). If one does see politics as important, and if one has definite preferences regarding what should be happening in some part of the political world, the second factor comes into play. To what extent is it reasonable to expect that one's political activity will, as a matter of fact, result in the achievement of one's goals or at least in some progress toward them? If one thinks that life is basically a lottery, there would seem to be no particular incentive to expend the time and energy required to become politically active (Gore & Rotter 1963; Phares 1965; Strickland 1965).

Up to this point we have been dealing with locus of control almost exclusively as a personality characteristic: How does the individual perceive the world? There is, however, a situational aspect. The situation in which a person finds herself may realistically permit more or less individual influence (Langton 1980). A friend of one of the authors once lost an election to local office by one vote. While she might be willing to give fervent testimonials to the importance of each individual vote, it is still true in most elections that one vote does not make an absolute difference.

Thus voting is a situation in which even a person with a relatively high opinion of her efficacy in other situations might feel relatively powerless to effect change personally. On the other hand, the chairperson of a key congressional committee might, with considerable justification, feel able to significantly influence the course of events—at least with reference to questions coming before that committee. Thus locus of control can be regarded "both as a specific expectancy arising from a specific situation and as a relatively stable, generalized perception of events" (Phares 1973, p. 6).

As a personality attribute, the concept of locus of control is closely related to the concept of self-esteem.* A person with high self-esteem is more confident than the person with low self-esteem about her ability to

---

*In this discussion of self-esteem, we have drawn heavily on Sniderman 1975.

cope with the problems of life. Compared to individuals with high self-esteem, those with low self-esteem are much more likely to exhibit feelings of political impotence, lack a sense of political efficacy, and, possibly, have a sense of helplessness. Because one's sense of confidence and competence are likely to be influenced by one's record of success, it is important to look at the characteristics of persons with low self-esteem that can influence their chances for success in politics. Generally, persons with low self-esteem are thin-skinned; they have trouble dealing with criticism. This is a dysfunctional characteristic in politics, where the conflictual and essentially adversarial nature of the enterprise means that criticism, whether justified or unjustified, is not only inevitable but is an integral part of the process. A person with low self-esteem is reluctant to strike up conversations, tense in unfamiliar situations, and hesitant about expressing his views. All of these are critical handicaps in an activity that is intensely social and centered around the expression of contrasting and conflicting points of view. On the other hand, high self-esteem encourages the social confidence and competence that make the tasks of political involvement less demanding and stressful. This in turn contributes to a higher probability of success in politics among those with high self-esteem who choose to become politically active. In short, compared to persons with high self-esteem, persons with low self-esteem are likely to find political activity more punishing both in terms of the intrinsic stressfulness of the task and in terms of the likelihood of success (Milbrath 1981, pp. 220–21).

All of this seems to contradict Lasswell's assertion that for the "political personality" the search for political power is an attempt to overcome a low estimate of the self (Lasswell 1948). On the other hand, we all know that political life is not devoid of persons who exhibit some of the characteristics of low self-esteem. On the basis of his research Sniderman hypothesizes that such exceptions to the rule are the result of a kind of compulsive dynamism that leads to an obsessive determination to succeed in politics. This determination can lead to an incessant striving that, for some at least, eventually ends in success. We see this pattern in David Abrahamsen's description of Richard Nixon's reaction to law school:

> Nixon felt threatened by his new, strange, and competitive environment; he was afraid of the new surroundings, fearful of being outdone by his peers. His response, however, was hard work. . . . [1978, pp. 97–98]

One of Nixon's professors recalled that "he was what today we'd call uptight—there was the suggestion of an intellectual inferiority complex" (Abrahamsen 1978, p. 98). Thus early in his adult life Nixon manifested the obsessive determination that took him to the presidency as well as the insecurity that led him to condone—at least tacitly—activities that eventually resulted in his loss of that office.

The concepts of locus of control and self-esteem are in turn closely related to the concept of political efficacy. The traditional view of political

Low self-esteem	High self-esteem
(e.g., Nixon)	(e.g., Roosevelt)
External locus	Internal locus
of control	of control
leads to:	leads to:
political participation	political participation
driven, success leads to	instrumental, significant
feeling of political	preexisting feeling of
efficacy.	political efficacy enhanced by success.

FIGURE 3-1   Self-esteem, locus of control, political efficacy, and political participation: the Nixon and Roosevelt examples

efficacy is that it is a perception one has about one's self and one's ability to influence political outcomes in any particular situation. The politically efficacious person sees himself as capable of influencing the political process. Thus he participates in order to accomplish some goal. The motivation for participating is the desire to realize some political end, buttressed by a reasonable amount of confidence that the goal is, as a matter of fact, achievable. This view of political efficacy, then, seems implicitly grounded in some notion of an internal locus of control combined with a relatively high level of self-esteem. The more efficacious one perceives oneself to be, the more likely one is to become politically active (see Figure 3-1).

An alternative view of political efficacy has been advanced by Stanley Renshon (1974). He sees the basic underlying personality dynamic as the need of people "to have some control over the people, events, and processes that impact upon and shape [their] lives" (Renshon 1974, p. 1). This need translates into a corresponding motive to influence the political process—if politics is perceived as an important factor in the life of the individual. Under this interpretation, then, people do not participate in political life because their personalities include a component that can be labeled political efficacy. Rather, they participate in order to fill a basic need for personal control. If their participation is reasonably successful either in particular instances or, on the balance, over time, the feeling of political efficacy that results is, in and of itself, the motivating force. Thus one reward for success is a feeling of political efficacy.

This interpretation is important because it suggests something quite different with regard to the relationship between locus of control, self-esteem, and political efficacy. The traditional view of political efficacy assumes a sort of rational calculus approach to political participation. The individual calculates the importance of the political system to his life. If politics is deemed important enough to justify the expenditure of energy in the attempt to achieve certain goals, actual participation becomes a function of a decision by the individual as to the probability of success and the psychological difficulty involved in carrying out the necessary activities. The Renshon interpretation taps a deeper level of motivation that is not rational in quite the same sense.

Here again there is a determination that the political system is sufficiently relevant to be the object of some expenditure of effort. The driving force behind political participation, however, becomes the need to reduce the anxiety attendant upon an unfulfilled need for personal control over salient aspects of the environment. This would suggest that the imperative to political participation might be the individual's perceptions regarding the importance of politics to his life. (See Goel 1980, pp. 125–26 and the sources cited therein.) If politics are seen as sufficiently important, there will be a motivational push toward political participation, *regardless of* the individual's locus of control or level of self-esteem. A person with an internal locus of control and a high level of self-esteem might find the task easier and more congenial. But up to a certain point (which would differ from individual to individual), the person with an external locus of control and low self-esteem would not be seriously deterred by the difficulty and unpleasantness of the job because these considerations would be secondary to the important need for increased personal control.

The picture Lasswell (1948) paints of the political personality seems to be one of a person with low self-esteem and an external locus of control who sees politics as important enough to justify a concerted and often painful struggle to achieve enhanced control. For example, Richard Nixon's political writings emphasize themes of control, will power, struggle, and the necessity to undergo pain in order to achieve goals (e.g., Nixon 1981). We also find hints in other persons' perceptions of Nixon. For example:

> Considering that Nixon was withdrawn, hostile, and unable to get along with others, it might seem remarkable that he sought a career in politics. Even Kissinger, who has known Nixon for a long time, has said, "I have never understood how he became a politician." [Abrahamsen 1978, p. 126]

Similarly Phares has observed:

> A simple prediction that internals will always be more action-oriented than externals does not appear to hold. In the realm of political-social activity, it is often the external who is more active. [1973, p. 126]

Thus persons with both high and low self-esteem, as well as internal and external loci of control, can be accommodated within the Renshon model. Those with internal loci of control and high self-esteem also fit within the framework of the traditional model. Although they undoubtedly have the same need for personal control as others, the need has evidently been less acute—probably owing to an early and continual satisfaction of the need (Renshon, personal communication). This implies a lower chronic-anxiety level and less intensity in the striving to meet the need for personal control. Because of their lower anxiety level and the ease born of their higher confidence of success at less personal cost, they are psychologically free to focus their primary attention on the goals for which they strive and to take an approach to political participation that is based more on a "rational" calculus than on an obsessive drive for personal control and self-esteem-enhancing experiences. This description is reminiscent of the affable and confident Franklin Delano Roosevelt, who at an early age could say of his relationships with his playmates: "But Mummie, if I didn't give the orders, nothing would happen!" (Beschloss 1980, p. 34).

Up to this point we mainly have been discussing individual level variables with only a passing nod at the fact that the individual is interacting with a microenvironment and a macroenvironment. Although neither of these can be dealt with in any great detail here, it should be noted that one of the best-documented findings in the literature on political participation involves the relationship between socio-economic status (SES) and participation. The conclusion that higher-SES persons are more likely to engage in political activities than lower-SES persons has been confirmed by countless studies covering a number of countries (Milbrath and Goel 1977, p. 92). Even in socialist Yugoslavia, there is a close correlation between SES and workers' political activity level (Pateman 1980, p. 90).

Without going into the details of various definitions, SES is usually calculated on the basis of occupational, educational and economic data about individuals. These three variables are usually highly intercorrelated, especially the first two. Renshon (1974, p. 238) describes SES as a "summative variable, an indicator of the effects of traversing a certain life path." It can also be regarded as a good indicator of some important characteristics of the microenvironment and the macroenvironment within which an individual is embedded. Thus, SES is a "shorthand way of describing the psychological effects of one's life experiences and the way in which what we think is shaped by the life experiences we have been through" (Renshon 1974, p. 238).

The situationalist orientation of much of the research on political participation has led to a neglect or discounting of the potential importance of personality factors in a political activity. From a situationalist point of view, belief that one has or can have political influence depends on the situation. After considering the effects of this on scholarly views of participation, Langton (1980) emphasizes the importance of the interaction between personality and situation. He cautions us to avoid treating political efficacy as a "global psychological disposition" and calls attention to indicators that it can vary from situation to situation (Langton 1980, p. 128).

What we are trying to suggest, in short, is that the relationship of political involvement to both personal and situational factors is a complex and as yet imperfectly understood one. While it may be possible to place political activists along a spectrum ranging from the obsessive striving of a Richard Nixon to the calm confidence of a Franklin D. Roosevelt, it is also necessary to remember that they were acting within very different micro- and macroenvironments. Thus, neither the traditional nor the Renshon models of political efficacy and political participation is necessarily right or wrong, and neither is a complete explanation. They differ in their usefulness for the analysis of any particular political activist or event depending on both personality and situational factors.

LEVELS AND TYPES OF POLITICAL INVOLVEMENT

From the foregoing we can see that the importance of politics to the individual is, not surprisingly, a major factor in political involvement (Milbrath 1981, pp. 213–14). In order to trace the different types and levels of political involvement, then, it is appropriate to start with the questions: Is politics perceived as relevant to a given individual? Does it loom large in her life space? If the answers to these questions are no, then it is highly probable that the individual is more or less apathetic with regard to the political system. Since it is difficult to withdraw completely, however, such a person's relationship to the political system would probably be characterized most often by minimal compliance. Politics, and especially government, tends to be intrusive. It encroaches on people's lives and makes behavioral demands upon them. Failure to comply with these demands can result in the imposition of sanctions or the withdrawal of privileges or benefits. Thus, for example, those who fail to pay their taxes may find themselves the object of some unpleasant forms of attention from the Internal Revenue Service. Similarly, people who refuse to salute the flag or to treat it with respect may experience hostile comments or glances from those around them. Whether they like it or not and whether they care or not, most people comply with the most unavoidable political or governmental demands—at least on a minimal level. If the answers to the questions above are yes, then we are likely to find a more intense level of involvement than simple compliance.

The influence of any situation, including political situations, depends to a large extent on the kind and amount of relevant stimuli received by an individual. "The more stimuli about politics a person receives, the greater the likelihood that he or she will participate in politics and the greater the depth of that participation" (Milbrath 1981, p. 209). In order to affect our behavior, however, a stimulus has, at least, to be apprehended and considered by us. This means that it has to get past our perceptual screens. We all have perceptual screens, psychological mechanisms that control what we attend to and what we ignore. A person is exposed to political stimuli, not just as a function of its availability but as a function of the person's interest or receptiveness. Increasing exposure can in turn build greater interest and a greater tendency to interact with persons holding similar interests. Attention can peak during an election (especially a U.S. presidential election) when the amount of available political stimuli also peaks. There is also the possibility of stimulus overload. The amount of stimuli can be so great that everything is garbled or the intensity of the stimulus can be so great that the senses are dulled (ibid., p. 211). Both of these effects can be seen operating in a country like the Soviet Union, where the amount and intensity of political propaganda greatly exceed that in the United States. Putting aside subliminal effects (which are not at issue here), all of these political stimuli seem to breed in most Soviet citizens a profound disinterest in political information except to the extent that any particular message might be directly and practically relevant to some facet of their own lives.*

Perceptual screens have another important function. They can protect a person against political messages that are, for some reason, threatening. If a particular political message is unpleasant or threatening, it can be either blocked completely from the consciousness or distorted in order to make it easier to deal with. During World War II information about the slaughter of the Jews that filtered out of the territories controlled by Nazi Germany was widely ignored or discounted by Western leaders, because the implications of such messages were too profoundly disturbing. In their case the mechanism operated to keep them from feeling impelled to get involved. In other situations perceptual screens can allow us to get involved in matters better avoided, as when a political candidate invests an enormous amount of time and energy in an election that a detached observer could assure him he will lose.

To return to the issue posed at the beginning of this section, if politics is perceived as relevant to a given individual, then we are likely to find a more permeable perceptual screen and a more intense level of involvement than simple compliance. Other questions then arise. Does the individual identify with the political system? Has he internalized its values? If an individual does not identify with the political system, then his relationship to it can be said to be characterized by estrangement or alienation.

Alienation can take many forms, most notably the rejection of a particular regime or constitutional order and, possibly, identification with, or internalization of, the values of some alternative. Thus while there may be such a thing as diffuse political alienation, more probably the individual is withdrawing from something relatively specific (Labaw & Rappeport 1975) and may be, at the same time, embracing something else (Yinger 1973, p. 178). This raises the possibility of unconventional political involvement (Schwartz 1972). Thus the question should not be whether a person is politically alienated but whether he is alienated from some specific political person, group, or institution and whether he has formed compensating political attachments (Yinger 1973, pp. 189–202).

If an individual does identify with a political system, then we can be sure that she is, at the very least, likely to be involved in some ritualized or

---

*This generalization is based on the personal impressions of one of the authors, who has lived in the Soviet Union.

symbolic political activity. Active involvement probably indicates that there is some internalization of the values and attitudes prevailing in the political system—at least the participating ones. Having said this, however, we hasten to add that it is extremely difficult to trace the pattern of interaction between personality, belief, attitude, microenvironment, and macroenvironment that leads to active, conventional political involvement (Browning 1968, p. 93; Milbrath 1981, p. 219). We will limit ourselves to a brief consideration of those factors that seem—at this time—to be significant variables in this complex interaction.

Very little good research has been done that explores the relationship between personality traits and political involvement. Among those that seem to be important is ease in social interactions (Goel 1980, p. 122; Milbrath 1981, p. 219). In representative democracies, where politicians are required to "sell" themselves to the public, it can be an advantage if this ease shades over into extraversion and gregariousness. Related to these is self-confidence, which is especially important in active participation, where the conflictual nature of the process requires people to continually risk failure.

In order to become actively involved, a person must have relatively high needs for achievement or power (Browning 1968, pp. 97–100). Otherwise, there is little incentive to play a game that may involve an absolute win or an absolute loss (at least in the case of persons running for political office and in many other political conflicts as well) under conditions of public scrutiny. Correspondingly, a politically active person's need for affiliation cannot be unduly high for the very reason that political life centers on conflict rather than cooperation. Finally, from the perspective of Maslow's hierarchy of needs,* Knutson's research (1972) reminds us that the politically active tend to be those for whom the lower-level needs (i.e., for physiological satisfaction, safety, and security) have been met.

So far we have been talking about personality characteristics. Another aspect of the individual level in the interaction model discussed in Chapter 1 (pp. 11–19) involves attitude. It is possible to speak with much more confidence about attitudinal variables in political participation since much research in political science has been directed at this issue. Party identification has perhaps gotten more attention from researchers on political participation than any other attitudinal variable. What the research seems to suggest is that the higher the intensity of a person's party identification, the more likely that person is to be politically active. This also seems true of candidate and issue preferences (Goel 1980, p. 131). Persons with strong feelings in these areas are more likely to engage in voting and campaign-related activities than in any other form of active political involvement (Milbrath 1981, p. 216).

Another example of what seems pretty conclusively to be an impor-

*For a discussion of this concept see chapter 5.

tant attitudinal variable is a sense of civic obligation* or duty to participate. This has sometimes been related to citizen competence. Education
and upper socioeconomic status seem to be important here because of the
tendency of the more highly educated and more economically comfortable to socialize their children to place a high value on civic participation.
The fact that this seems to be a socialization phenomenon, however,
means that it can vary from country to country and within countries
because of differences in the prevailing political culture (ibid., p. 215).

Up to this point we have been talking primarily about individual-
level variables. The influence of situations, however, should not be neglected, since the situation (both microenvironmental and macroenvironmental) mediates the impact of individual characteristics in any decision
to become politically active (Petrocik 1980). The classic illustration of situational effects on political participation is the tendency for restrictive
voting laws to depress turnout. On the other hand, party officials in the
Soviet Union are judged by their success in getting out the vote and
consequently strive to create a situation that will maximize the tendency of
Soviet citizens to vote regardless of personality and attitudinal characteristics (Barry & Barner-Barry 1982, p. 95).

As was the case in our consideration of attitudinal variables, space
constraints force us to limit our consideration of situational variables to
two illustrative examples—one macroenvironmental, the other microenvironmental. The first is the type of party system prevailing in a given
country (Petrocik 1980). The more closely party identification is tied to
other loyalties or reference groups, the greater the probability of active
involvement. Incentives to participate are reinforced by religious, ethnic,
class, and regional identification and organizational memberships. This
effect can be seen in the case of black Americans, who have become
increasingly involved in conventional politics since the 1960s and have
made significant political gains, working primarily through the Democratic party (Shingles 1981).

Prevailing party systems and the political culture accompanying
them can be regarded as macroenvironmental phenomena; stages in the
life cycle of human beings and their relationship to political behavior are
microenvironmental phenomena (Post 1980). Levinson (1978) identifies
three critical points in the life cycle: (1) early adult (ca. 17–22 years of
age), (2) midlife transition (ca. 40–45 years of age), and (3) late adult (ca.
60–65 years of age). Various types of political involvement can be the
result of an interplay between the internal impact of being at a particular
stage and the external impact of whatever is going on in the environment
at that time.

Lenin was seventeen when his brother, Alexander, was hanged for
involvement in revolutionary activities (Wolfe 1964, pp. 70–71). Because

*While this has been treated as an attitude by political scientists (Milbrath 1981), we
feel constrained to point out that "sense of civic obligation" is more clearly a value in terms
of our definition (see Chapter 1).

of Alexander's political activities Lenin could not pursue his education in the normal way. He was unjustly arrested and expelled from the University of Kazan. "Thus did tsarism tend to drive young men into the profession of revolutionary by closing all other professions to them" (ibid., p. 79). Also, Stalin's consolidation of power took place during his midlife transition (Tucker 1973, pp. 292–93). And a few years ago we saw the Soviet Union stagnate under the gerentocracy of a Brezhnev increasingly incapacitated by the infirmities and illness of old age but typically unwilling to retire from his rewarding and enormously successful career (Post 1980, p. 42).

Finally, because people vary in their perceptions concerning the relevance of politics, their political participation also varies in level of intensity and mode of expression. At the lowest level of intensity is the simple act of voting, which is largely an expressive gesture. The voter is giving generalized support to the government and political system at the same time that he or she is giving a tiny amount of specific support to one or more candidates. Although the most active almost invariably vote, the average voter is only minimally interested in politics and tends to be a spectator in the political arena. Although voter turnout is relatively small compared to what it might be if all who were eligible voted, it is still quite large compared to the turnout for other forms of political involvement.

More demanding forms of political involvement can generally be divided into two modes (Verba & Nie 1972). The first is the electoral mode, which encompasses both voting and campaign activity. The second is the nonelectoral mode, which encompasses communal or group-based activities and particularized activities, such as writing one's senator or representative about a particular policy issue. Returning to the stories in chapter 1, Harry has chosen the electoral mode of political involvement, while Donna has chosen the nonelectoral mode. Such choices are related to the individual's beliefs about government and politics, especially with reference to what they expect to get from their political participation. Also it should be noted that political activists tend to specialize in one or another mode.

AUTHORITIES AND PARTISANS

Another way of looking at such distinctions is in terms of the overall role an individual tends to play in political life. Gamson (1968) suggests that political actors tend—at any particular time—to function as either authorities or partisans.

Authorities are those in the political system whose decisions about the allocation of valued public resources are binding on others. They are people who play such roles as judge, legislator, and chief executive. For our purposes, authority will be assumed to be *effective* authority rather than merely formal or legal authority. Thus the mere possession of a position or title of authority will not be sufficient. An individual will be considered an authority only if the potential authority conferred by the position or title is actually converted into the exercise of political influence. Harry, for example, has acquired a position of political authority. He still has before him the task of establishing himself as a member of Congress who can get things done.

The basis for the effective use of political influence is usually considered to be a perception on the part of those subject to the authority that the exercise of authority by that individual is, as a matter of fact, legitimate. In some cases mere legitimacy is sufficient; in others the ability to impose sanctions is a crucial adjunct. In the latter case authority begins to shade over into power. Thus one may make a distinction between a political actor whose influence rests on a special relationship between the ruler and the ruled and a power wielder who governs because he has the ability to punish those who do not obey him (Burns 1978).

In most real-world cases, political leadership is some blend of these pure types. American judges are perhaps the best example of a relatively clear-cut case in which influence is based almost completely on legitimacy. Aside from their ability to command marshalls to maintain order in their courtrooms and to enforce other rulings directly related to the actual conduct of a trial, judges have virtually no ability directly to enforce their orders, sentences, or rulings. They must depend for enforcement on other governmental authorities. A chief executive, on the other hand, is usually directly in command of police or military forces and therefore can impose sanctions at will—limited only by rules of law and prevailing custom.

It is perhaps the fact that most political influence is based on some mixture of legitimacy and the ability to wield power that makes government possible in the face of the normal vicissitudes of societal life. Let us take an example close to home: the authority of university administrators to govern student behavior on their campuses (Gamson 1968, pp. 22–23). In the mid-1960s, various conflicts occurred between students and administrators at campuses across the United States. At the University of Michigan the office of the vice-president for student affairs issued a ruling that sit-ins at private offices were a violation of university rules. The students challenged this pronouncement, not on the basis of its content but because of the way in which it was made. In fact, the student government council held that the ruling did not have to be obeyed because it was not properly issued.

Was the decision by the university administrators authoritative? In this case it could be argued that it didn't matter. Whether or not the students liked it, the ruling could have been enforced by sanctions. That is, if the ruling had been violated, the administration could have taken punitive action against the students. They could have been expelled, prevented from registering for courses, and otherwise denied the right (or privilege, depending on your point of view) of being a student at the University of Michigan. This case, however, also illustrates the limitations of powerwielding. In point of fact, the ruling was never enforced since the administration concluded that the costs of doing so would have been prohibitive. Also it might be pointed out that to have resorted to the brute use of sanctions in this case might have severely compromised the legitimacy of the university officials when they tried to act authoritatively with reference to other matters for which they were responsible. While it is nice to have some power in reserve for use in emergencies, legitimacy is still the key to authority.

Partisans, on the other hand, are any set of actors who are affected in some significant way by a given decision concerning the allocation of valued resources. It is important to note that most partisans are *potential* partisans. They do not become active partisans until they perceive that political activity is necessary and they are mobilized in some way to protect or achieve certain values. It should be noted that authorities can be partisans. Since authorities are themselves affected (or can be affected) by any decision, they are likely to attempt to make sure that outcomes are favorable to themselves. Moreover, partisans can make an outcome of an authoritative decision affect the authorities. Thus in the example above enforcement of the rule about sit-ins could have led to (or authorities might have believed it would lead to) a general strike by the students, riots, and massive disruption of the operation of the university.

Just as authorities tend to be organized (into boards, committees, administrations, legislatures, courts, and so on), so partisans are more than just random collections of dissatisfied or potentially dissatisfied individuals. Rather, they are typically organized into groups (Key 1958; Latham 1956; Verba 1961; Golembiewski & Miller 1981). Various writers have come up with different ideas about what constitutes a partisan group. For instance, we can speak of interest groups, bound together by a common interest in the achievement of certain political goals. Or we can speak of a *quasi-group* (Dahrendorf 1959), people whose latent interests make it likely that they will eventually come together in some organized fashion to influence resource-allocation decisions. Lasswell & Kaplan (1950) define another order of partisan groups, which they call solidarity groups. These groups are psychological groups in which "egos are emotionally bound together in relation to demands in the name of identified groups" (p. 11). In more ordinary language, individuals in solidarity groups feel an attachment to each other because they think in terms of the effects of political decisions on the group and feel in some way personally affected by what happens to that group. Examples might be ethnic groups and religious groups. During the 1982 session of Congress, congressional partisans battling over the federal budget were called a variety of entomological names—gypsy moths, yellow jackets, and boll weevils—each of which presumably represented a set of interests in the American electorate.

Authorities and partisans have somewhat different perspectives on conflict. Partisans will generally be concerned with the effects of conflict on the allocation of public resources in which they are interested. They will, by definition, focus on only some of the actors and events in the system rather than the entire system. In other words, they want to exert influence to achieve goals they perceive to be in their best interest.

Authorities, on the other hand, will be concerned not just with "who gets what" but also with the state of the whole system. They will feel concerned about the integrity and maintenance of the system and the effects of discontent on the capacity of the system to function effectively. What will be the effect of discontent on public perceptions of the legitimacy of authority itself? What will be the effect of resource-allocation decisions on the capacity of the system to attain collective goals as well as individual ones? Hence authority will be concerned with the regulation of conflict as well as with allocation decisions in conflict situations. Gamson (1968) calls this the social-control perspective for exactly this reason—that is, authority treats conflict resolution as the management or control of the use of influence.

It is immediately apparent that this distinction between influence and social control reflects two sides of the same coin. We are talking, in essence, about individual or system orientations toward the resolution of conflict. It is not surprising, therefore, that "partisans" are often concerned with the effects on the integrity of the system of attempts at influencing resource-allocation decisions. Martin Luther King, for example, championed the use of nonviolent tactics of influence not only because he felt they were particularly effective but also because of his own concern for maintaining the integrity of American democracy while, in his view, making that democracy more fully representative (Tucker 1981).*

Further, as we have noted, authorities are always potential partisans, and therefore may often act in ways that seem more characteristic of individuals pursuing individual interests, as opposed to the collective good. Indeed, both partisans and authorities may rationalize their orientations to resource allocation *in the name of* the collective good. Perhaps it is best to say that all actors in the political system may display a mix of personal interests and concern with the integrity of the whole system.†

SUMMARY

There are variations from political system to political system in the extent to which people become actively involved in political life. Within any political system the level and type of political participation varies greatly from individual to individual. Several dimensions can be used as analytic tools to assess these variations. They include a range from participation that is purely ritualistic to participation that is thoughtfully intended to

---

*Late in his life this reformist leader began to consider that the system was in need of more "revolutionary" change.

†This extended discussion of authorities and partisans is particularly relevant to our model of the political process discussed in more detail in Chapter 10.

have a real influence. Second, there are more and less conventional types of political activity. Finally, participation can range from intense to casual. These are not the only dimensions, but we consider them three of the most important from a psychological point of view.

People also vary in the nature of their relationship to their political systems. This variation occurs over time and from situation to situation. The three main types of relationships are compliance, identification, and internalization. It is probably safe to assume that most people exhibit all three of these in varying mixes. They may also display apathy, which is essentially a nonresponse to much that goes on within the political arena, as well as alienation, which is a more hostile reaction. It seems that most people's involvement is more often characterized by apathy and simple compliance than by high levels of identification and internalization.

Unless people think that their participation can "make a difference," they are unlikely to become politically active. The belief that one can be politically efficacious is related to some other basic personality characteristics, such as internal versus external locus of control, high versus low relevance of politics, high versus low self-esteem, and a need for control over the events that affect one's life. There is no one profile of a politically active "type." Rather, these and other personality and situational factors can interact in a myriad of ways to produce relatively high or low levels of active political involvement from person to person.

The extent to which situational factors come into play is a function of the kind and amount of relevant stimuli perceived by the individual. This, in turn, depends on the absolute amount and type of stimuli available in the environment, as well as the perceptual screens of the individual. The more relevant politics is believed to be, the more permeable an individual's perceptual screen is likely to be. In turn, such factors lead naturally to a more intense level of political interest and activity. Personality factors that seem to be important in this process include a relatively high need for achievement, ease in social interaction, self-confidence, relatively low need for affiliation, and satisfied lower-level Maslowian needs. Important attitudinal variables seem to be intense party identification, strong candidate or issue preferences, and a sense of civic obligation. Finally, three significant situational factors are the nature of the electoral system, the extent to which participation is valued by reference persons or groups, and events that can impel an individual to a level or type of political activity not previously contemplated.

Political involvement can also be influenced by the role an individual is currently playing within the political system. A person may be an authority, making public policy decisions binding on others. Or one may be a partisan, a person affected by political decisions who may or may not presently be trying to influence public decision makers. Individuals playing such roles are frequently organized into groups of various sorts ranging from legislatures to solidarity groups. Authorities and partisans also see conflict differently. Authorities are concerned with the impact of any particular conflict on the political system. Partisans tend to focus more on "who gets what." Authorities, however, are always potential partisans and vice versa.

We have seen, then, that there are many varieties of political involvement that are connected in complex ways to various personality and situational factors. Central to much of what has been said here is the notion that the decision to participate or not participate seems basically to hinge on the importance of politics to the individual. Is politics important enough to justify the time and energy it takes to participate?

To a great extent, our attitudes about politics and the importance of political involvement are conditioned by the way we are raised. They are also conditioned by the relevant experiences we have in childhood, adolescence, and our adult years. Thus, it is appropriate to turn to a consideration of political socialization—of *homo politicus* in the lifetime process of becoming.

4

POLITICAL SOCIALIZATION:
Homo Politicus in the Process
of Becoming

While we have discussed some of the characteristics and attitudes that are conducive to political involvement, we have ignored questions relating to the origins of these characteristics and attitudes. How did politically active people get to be the way they are? Why did they choose to spend a major part of their lives pursuing political goals as opposed to other sorts of goals, such as economic or spiritual goals? In chapter 3 we stressed the importance of an individual's perception that politics is important to his or her life and that efforts in the political arena have some potential for making a difference. Note that we use the term *perception*. Whether such assessments are accurate in any objective sense is not our concern here. It is sufficient if the perception leads to some useful level of political involvement.

As is the case with many other forms of social behavior, an assumption is made by both students of political behavior and interested laypersons that the origins of the impetus to political involvement lie in the formative years of childhood. Having said this, however, we hasten to add that the scholarly community offers few definitive answers about why most people develop the relationships to the political system that they do. There has been a lot of research, though, so there are some theories we can and will examine.

Students of political socialization bring two basic perspectives to their definitions of the topic. From an individual-level perspective the term, political socialization, can be defined as "the processes through which an individual acquires his particular political orientations—his knowledge, feelings, and evaluations regarding [the] political world" (Dawson, Prewitt, & Dawson 1977, p. 33). Much of what is to follow in this chapter will be focused on these processes. There is, however, a system-level perspective. From this point of view, political socialization can be defined as "the process through which citizens acquire political views *that become aggregated* in ways that have consequences for the political life of the nation" (Dawson, Prewitt, & Dawson 1977, p. 14,* italics in original).

Although this difference in perspective may not, at first, seem to be significant, one's point of view does color the approach one takes to any topic. In political socialization it has greatly influenced the kinds of questions researchers ask about their topic. Table 4-1 illustrates the extent to which one's perspective influences the questions one asks. The concepts used in the illustration—loyalty, tolerance, and democracy—are commonly used and important concepts in political analysis. The translation of those concepts into research questions, however, is idiosyncratic because of their high level of generality or abstractness. Give them to a person with one perspective and you get one set of questions; a person with the other point of view may come up with very different questions. Yet both persons will perceive themselves as concerned with political socialization.

These analytical perspectives have parallels in the day-to-day functioning of actual political systems. On an individual level parents may be concerned about the political beliefs and values acquired by their children. Children or adults may have experiences that influence their attitudes and beliefs regarding politics. These are both on the individual level of experience, and the focus is on what happens to the individual human being as he or she experiences life. On the other hand, a particular political regime may be very much concerned about the political beliefs and values held by the people—if only to be able to assess and, ultimately, insure their loyalties. In such a case socialization can be conceived of as something that is done to specific groups of people in a rather planned and systematic fashion, not something that just happens to people or is directed at individuals. These are more practical perspectives that parallel the analytic perspectives discussed previously. In both cases there is a distinction between a focus on the individual and a focus on groups of people.

Obviously, the individual level and system level are not discrete. They interact and influence each other in ways that can make it difficult to separate them analytically and often impossible to separate them in practical situations. Although in this chapter we will have a tendency to be

---

*Another way of conceptualizing this distinction is as a teaching perspective versus a learning perspective (Beck 1977, pp. 115–41).

TABLE 4-1   An Illustration of the Way in which One's Perspective Influences One's Use
of a Political Concept

Political Concept	Individual-Level Analysis of Political Socialization	System-Level Analysis of Political Socialization
Loyalty	How does a child learn to trust and have confidence in political leaders?	In trying to get citizens to obey the law does the government depend on the loyalty and patriotism of citizens, or must it use force and coercion?
Tolerance	As citizens grow up, do they accept or reject members of different races, ethnic backgrounds, regions, religions, and so on?	Are national politics characterized by cooperation or by conflict among the social groups that make up the society?
Democracy	What meaning does a citizen attach to the act of voting?	Is there widespread intelligent political participation in choosing the authorities and shaping the policies that govern the nation?

Adapted from R. E. Dawson, K. Prewitt, and K. S. Dawson, *Political Socialization,* 2nd ed.
p. 15. Copyright © 1977 by Little, Brown & Co. (Inc). Reprinted by permission.

more preoccupied with the individual, reference to system-level concerns
will be frequent. Individual-level and system-level attitudes and behaviors
interweave and interact, and a treatment of political socialization such as
this one cannot ignore that fact—in form as well as in substance.

THE POLITICAL-SOCIALIZATION PROCESS: ANALYTICAL PERSPECTIVES

Political socialization is, first and foremost, a process. It is a highly complex, interactional process, which—at least in theory—continues throughout a person's lifetime. There is a tendency among political scientists to
think of political socialization as something that is "done to" the individual
by such agents as the family, the school, the peer group, and the media.
To some extent, this is a valid conceptualization. Potentially socializing
messages do tend to flow to the individual from these sources. To consider only this aspect of the process, however, would be to oversimplify.
As we pointed out in our discussion of the interaction model in chapter 1,
the individual is not a passive recipient of messages from the outside

world. To the contrary, *Homo sapiens* is a complex creature with a lively and powerful inner life. Messages from the outside world have to contend with everything that is already inside our heads and even with the state of our glands and bodily functions.

As a result, people tend to mold—perhaps reject—any information that has the potential to influence the way they think and act. Therefore, in the study of a process such as political socialization it is important to take note both of the sources of potential influence on the persons being socialized and the characteristics of those individuals, which may temper the ability of any outside influence to bring about change. In short, socialization is a highly complex and variable process, which is perhaps best thought of in terms of the final interaction model presented in chapter 1.

One of the most important ways in which the interaction between individual, microenvironment, and macroenvironment come into play in the socialization process is in the form of certain types of situational effects that can influence whole categories of people (rather than more or less random individuals). Three of the more politically important are: 1) life cycle effects; 2) generational effects; and 3) period effects (Beck, Bruner and Dobson, 1975, pp. 16–19).

In the case of life cycle effects, we find a difference between two generations which stems from their different ages or the different stages they are at in the human life cycle. For example, it is difficult, if not impossible, for a teenager to imagine what life as a retired person might be like. One's own retirement seems remote enough to be irrelevant. Thus, a teenager who is vitally interested in policy regarding Social Security is, indeed, a rare commodity. Many persons in mid-life, however, see more clearly the relevance of Social Security to their own lives and are thus much more apt to take either an active or a passive interest in policy proposals affecting Social Security benefit distribution. And it is probably safe to predict that our hypothetical teenagers will—on the average— develop more interest as they grow older.

Generational effects can be seen in the fact that certain attitudes seem to be characteristic of certain generations or age cohorts and that these attitudes seem to persist throughout the life cycle. Thus, persons who went through their formative years during World War II may continue to see United States participation in the battles of U.S. allies in a much more patriotic and less cynical light than those who went through their formative years during the final phases of the Vietnam War. For the latter, war is much less a patriotic crusade to save those who both want and deserve to be saved from oppression. It was this generational difference during the 1960s that made it so difficult for many parents to understand or sympathize with their children's anti-Vietnam War protest activities.

Finally, period effects are reflections of events that have an impact on people of all ages. Some political events are of such magnitude that very few persons who are both alive and able to comprehend them are left untouched. The assassination of John F. Kennedy was such an event.

Ask virtually anyone who was around then and was old enough to have had some instant understanding of the magnitude of the event, and they will probably be able to tell you exactly where they were and what they were doing when they heard about the assassination. This is not just true of persons in the United States, but can be found even in persons as seemingly remote from the event as Soviet citizens—many of whom retain a distinct fondness for John F. Kennedy as both a seeker of peace and a brave, handsome, intelligent young man struck down before his time. Such nostalgia for a slain president can make a person like Teddy Kennedy a much more viable Presidential candidate than he ever would have been had he been virtually anyone else's brother.

Such effects exist within the context of individual socialization processes. And it is to the issue of the essential nature of such processes we now turn our attention. Scholars have tried to make sense of socialization processes in many ways. Generally, their analytical constructs fall into three groupings: (1) the social-learning perspective, (2) the psychodynamic perspective, and (3) the cognitive-developmental perspective. These are not mutually exclusive. In fact, they overlap and interact in some very complex and interesting ways. In framing our discussion under these three headings, we run the risk of provoking the ire of persons who may think that we have misclassified their favorite theory or who resent the fact that we have tried to "pigeonhole" these theories at all. It does seem helpful, however, to try to organize the discussion in some reasonable way, so we will proceed, with the caveat that the walls between these perspectives are to be regarded as highly permeable.

The social-learning perspective. In social-learning theories, the emphasis is on the messages the individual receives from the outside world. A person with a social-learning perspective might, for example, be interested in analyzing the political content of school children's textbooks (e.g., Cary 1976; Women on Words and Images 1972). Pursuit of this type of research would be based on the theory that "detailing the changing conditions of environmental stimulation in family, school, and peer group settings" has value in the identification and analysis of "the variables in the environment, both in the present and of the past, that control behavior" (Gewirtz 1969, p. 60).

The most obvious—though not necessarily most effective—form of social learning is direct instrumental training or tuition. To put it more simply, it is the situation where there is a conscious attempt by persons with a stake in a particular type of political socialization to make explicit attempts to socialize others. This might involve the decision of a political regime to set up civics classes in the educational system and to prescribe, generally or specifically, what the curriculum should be. It can also be seen in cases where parents might take their children along to, say, an antinuclear demonstration—not only to solve a babysitting problem but also to sensitize their children at a young age to the values that led the parents to want to participate in the demonstration. The vehicle for explicit socialization might be a discussion between parents and children before or after the demonstration about what the parents are doing and why.

The latter example, in a sense, is a bridge to the second form of social learning—observational learning and imitation. Not only do the children hear their parents telling them why it is important to oppose any increase in the number of nuclear-power-generating plants, they also see what their parents are doing and perhaps even join them on the picket line. Such behavior is especially compelling in childhood because it gives the children an opportunity to "act grown up." Indeed, Albert Bandura, a leading scholar in this area (Crain 1980, pp. 222–39), makes the point that

> It would be difficult to imagine a socialization process in which the language, mores, vocational and avocational patterns, the familial customs of a culture, and its . . . political practices were shaped in each new member . . . without the response guidance of models who exhibit the accumulated cultural repertoires in their own behavior. [Bandura 1969, p. 213]

Thus while social-learning theory emerged from the more mechanistic learning theory best known to the general public in connection with the work of B. F. Skinner, it deemphasizes the role of external, contrived stimulus response and reinforcement and stresses the importance of the ability of a person to be his or her own stimulus and reward. As Rohter points out:

> Human beings continually engage in self-evaluation and self-reinforcing behaviors. In social-learning language, the individual's own reactions become stimuli in behavior chains or response hierarchies. People set themselves certain standards and self-administer rewarding or punishing consequences depending on whether their performance meets their self-prescribed demands. The reinforcers may be tangible or secondary, such as self-praise or depreciation. [Rohter 1975, p. 148]

There are many ways of modeling behavior, some of which may involve the intent to socialize and others of which may not. Apparently the best way to model a particular behavior is simply to do it repeatedly in the presence of the person being socialized. For example, a child who observes her parents voting regularly at each election is likely to define voting regularly as something done by responsible mature adults and to imitate that behavior first during play and later by actually voting regularly. To date, the relevant research literature seems to indicate that this is the most effective form of modeling (Crain 1980, p. 236). Verbal modeling has been found to be much less effective, especially in the long run. The term *verbal modeling* is sometimes used to designate the giving of instructions or the issuance of commands.

The first way of conceptualizing the political-socialization process, then, is as a learning process that has a substantial social component. In school pupils are expressly taught how a "good citizen" behaves. If they see their parents acting that way in the community, the lesson is reinforced. The mass media may add to that message both by explicit teaching, as in broadcasts that urge us to "get out and vote!" Also, politically relevant behavior may be modeled by television personalities and programs. A prime example is the attitude toward war that is modeled by Hawkeye Pierce in "M*A*S*H."

But, what makes one socialization agent more effective than another? All persons who watch "M*A*S*H" reruns regularly do not adopt the antiwar attitude of Hawkeye. Why do some children follow in the political footsteps of their parents while others depart from them radically in belief, affiliation, and behavior (e.g., Flacks 1967; Keniston 1973; Rothman 1981)? For example, one wonders whether Donna's parents approve or disapprove of her participation in politics and the form it has taken. A person with a psychodynamic perspective on the political socialization process would probably suggest that we take a closer look at the emotional or symbolic relationship between Donna and her parents, as well as between her and the rest of her family, her childhood peer group, and her former teachers.

The psychodynamic perspective.   In the Freudian tradition persons who see the political-socialization process from a psychodynamic perspective tend to place great emphasis on childhood experiences. "A fundamental assumption, implied more often than stated, is that learning is permanent" [Miller 1969, p. 489]. In addition, "Traces of the earliest events have a special impact . . . and serve as a foundation for . . . later stages" (ibid., p. 489). From this perspective, then, the family assumes a special prominence (Langton 1980, p. 37). Attitudes toward the appropriateness of certain behavioral responses to one's father can be seen as generalizing to authority figures in the political system, such as the president and the police officer (Hess & Torney, 1968, pp. 116–20). Correspondingly, emotional reactions to other authority figures in the immediate environment can also be generalized to authority figures in government and politics. A generally benevolent father or teacher can thus engender a perception in the child that the president is also generally benevolent.

Also, beginning with Lasswell (1948) there has been a tendency for psychodynamically oriented political analysts to see the individual as adopting "outlooks toward the political world as a means of satisfying his or her own personal needs and personality dynamics" (Dawson, Prewitt, & Dawson 1977, p. 69). For example, a person can go into politics to gain power and, in this way, to satisfy a driving need for control that can be traced to childhood experiences of helplessness. Also, one can support and admire strong political leaders—perhaps even demagogues—because the perceived strength and wisdom of the leader gives the individual a buttress against his or her own feelings of anxiety and vulnerability.

Therefore, a socializing message that states that all good citizens should be politically active might be particularly persuasive to a person with strong control needs; the political system could be seen as a vehicle for satisfying those needs. Correspondingly, a person with a psycho-dynamically based urge to be given a feeling of security would be more susceptible to the socializing messages of a political demagogue who promises to solve their problems and keep them safe.

An important concept, which comes down to us from Freud, is that of identification,* the desire to be like another person. In Freudian theory a boy resolves his oedipal predicament by repressing his sexual feelings toward his mother and his rivalry with his father. In the process he identifies with, or becomes more like, his father, thus attaining a proper masculine identity. With this identity comes a bundle of traits. Among these can be politically relevant ones, like party preference (Connell 1971, pp. 77–78) or the tendency to be politically active. Perhaps Harry was more susceptible to the lures of political life than the rest of the "old boys" because one of his parents was politically active. Donna's father may have been a union organizer during the 1930s or the 1940s. Because of the underlying psychodynamic, the politically relevant traits acquired would be accompanied by an emotional intensity that would make them motivational forces of considerable strength. What we have, then, is not simple learning through reinforcement but learning or imitation buttressed or driven by something much more powerful.

Because of the emotional tone associated with the socializing agent or model the acquisition of the values, attitudes, beliefs, or behavior patterns of the model is more than mere imitation to the psychodynamically oriented interpreter:

> The typical psychoanalytic view appears to be that the relatively precise matching to the model's overt behavior in imitation is a transient, symptomatic, surface process, whereas the wider ranging, less precise behavioral matching in identification results from a more fundamental and dynamic underlying process. [Gewirtz 1969, p. 154]

Given Freudian theory, if the identification process is an important force in political socialization, one might expect to find the greatest similarity in political views between same-sex parents and children. To date, however, the research results on this issue are sparse and inconclusive (Connell 1971, pp. 79–82; Jennings & Niemi 1971). The fact that most recent political-socialization studies have been based on survey research, however, makes it inherently impossible to uncover the kinds of subtle influences involved in identification. Given the importance of this construct in con-

---

*This concept of identification is related to, but not identical with, the process of identification discussed in chapter 3, p. 62.

temporary psychology, it should be retained as a potentially important, but as yet unproven, dynamic in the process of political socialization.

The cognitive-developmental perspective. Scholars adopting this point of view put a great deal of emphasis on the changing ability of the individual to make sense of the political world. For example, at a fairly young age Donna may have seen or experienced things she thought were "unfair." At a later stage, she may have been able to relate them to certain social structures or political institutions. Finally, at an even more sophisticated developmental stage she was able to conceive of how political and social activism might bring about a more "just" distribution of societal resources. In other words, the cognitive-developmental perspective focuses on "the interaction between the environment and the developing capacity of the individual to deal with the environment" (Dawson, Prewitt, & Dawson 1977, p. 71).

> Cognitive development is a continuous cumulative process in which every step builds on what has come before. What the individual learns from a given experience is partly determined by how he represents and organizes that experience cognitively, but this depends on the schemas he has available to apply to the experience, which schemas are the products of prior experience. [Rosenau 1975, pp. 164–65]

An emphasis on development is not unique to this perspective. Proponents of all three perspectives discussed in this section see them as essentially developmental. All three are perspectives on a process that can be subsumed under the category social development. Social development in turn can be defined as "the restructuring of the (1) concept of self, (2) in its relationship to the concepts of other people, (3) conceived as being in a common social world with social standards" (Kohlberg 1969, p. 349). So what we have is a difference in emphasis.

The "father" of cognitive-development theory was Jean Piaget. In the course of a long and productive life he forged a theory of the growth of the intellect. Two of the most basic ideas are of particular relevance to political socialization. The first is that "children are not just taught by adults; they learn on their own." The second is that "children think differently from adults. They do not merely know less; they think in an entirely different way" (Piaget 1974; Piaget & Inhelder 1969). What this means, in brief, is that attempts to socialize and socializing influences will have varying impacts depending on the stage of development of the person who is the object of the socializing effort.

Piaget traced the process of intellectual development through a series of stages, which he asserted are invariant. Although any given individual may proceed through the stages at a rate different from the rate of another individual, everyone will proceed through the stages in the same order. A corollary is that some persons achieve higher stages than others.

All cognitive-development theories are interactionist in the sense that "they assume that basic mental structure is the product of the patterning of the interaction between the organism and the environment rather than directly reflecting either innate patterns in the organism or patterns of events . . . in the environment" (Kohlberg 1969, p. 350).

Like the psychodynamic perspective, the cognitive-developmental perspective is probably most useful in explaining more general, politically relevant concepts, such as attitudes and behavior with regard to authority or conflict. The emphasis is on the individual's growth in understanding political phenomena. This process is thought to "follow a natural progression" with sequence and content that is dictated by the experiences a person has and his evolving intellectual capacity to deal with them (Rosenau 1975, p. 174). Thus while a young child is able to think of the president in terms of an individual (probably the current incumbent or George Washington or Abraham Lincoln), an adolescent will usually have reached a level of cognitive development that will allow her to go beyond this very concrete conceptualization and to think about the presidency as an institution separate from any person who holds the office.

POLITICAL SOCIALIZATION AGENTS

There are basically two types of socialization agents. First, there are those over which a political regime can, if desired, exercise a great deal of control. The most important of these are the schools or educational system, the media, and specialized political-socialization bodies. Examples of the last type are organizations such as the American Legion and the League of Women Voters in the United States and AGITPROP in the Soviet Union. Second, there are those over which a political regime has, at best, much more tenuous control. The most important of these are the family, the peer group, and social groups or collectivities, such as religious and ethnic groups.

Given this diversity of important agents (not to mention a host of less obvious ones), the amount of information to which an individual can be exposed in the daily course of events is potentially enormous. To further complicate the matter there is also the fact that all of this information is usually not completely consistent. In fact, even in countries like the People's Republic of China or Chile, where there is an overt, concerted attempt to bring some consistency into the process, accomplishment invariably falls somewhat short of the goal. This is due, in part, to the complexity of the messages being conveyed. The opportunities for confusion and distortion are many. Also, given the number of people involved in both the sending and the receiving of socialization messages, some lack of coordination is inevitable. If you add to this phenomena such as selective perception and plain old-fashioned human obstinacy, the result is a situation where any given individual is inevitably going to have to deal with a more or less unique set of competing and often conflicting attempts to influence his or her beliefs, attitudes, and behavior.

Many people solve the problem by tacitly tolerating many inconsistencies in their own structures of attitudes and beliefs. More difficult, but not impossible, to ignore are inconsistencies between what one has chosen to believe and what one experiences in daily life. As a banker, for example, Harry inevitably was affected by various government laws and financial policies. These may have clashed with his notions about the role the government should (or should not) play in the banking industry. In turn, all of this might have been inconsistent with his patriotic beliefs about the goodness of American government. Becoming a member of Congress in order to effect needed reform was one way of dealing with this inconsistency. Personal experience, in fact, can be one standard for deciding which of the mass of competing messages to accept as valid and which to reject. Inconsistency, however, becomes most troublesome when a person is impelled, for one reason or another, to act in a way that is inconsistent with certain of his or her beliefs or attitudes. This situation is not only difficult to ignore but also, according to Leon Festinger's theory of cognitive dissonance (Festinger 1957), it can cause considerable psychological discomfort. A variation on this theme is the situation where a person realizes that he or she holds two beliefs or attitudes that have contradictory implications for behavior. Festinger would argue that in either of these cases the individual would seek to reduce the psychological discomfort by modifying the conflicting attitudes or beliefs in order to bring them into a relation of acceptable consistency with each other.

What one finds in research literature on the influence of one or another agent of political socialization is a wide variety of seemingly contradictory findings (Beck 1977, pp. 118–21). It seems virtually impossible to come to any definitive conclusions regarding the exact role or importance in the political-socialization process of agents such as the family, the school, or the media. Yet intuitively people seem to agree that they are vital. This can be seen in Richard Niemi's analysis of research on the politically socializing impact of the school:

> With all of these conflicting reports and conclusions, what are we to conclude about the school? One conclusion seems inescapable. The effects of the school are highly variable. . . . My own feeling is that the school has an enormous impact, but precisely what affects each student is so variable that it is difficult to measure the overall impact of any one component part. [1973, p. 131]

The same might be said for the other principal agents of political socialization mentioned above. The variability in their impact seems to be so great that definitive research results are at best elusive, and at worst unobtainable.

This should not, however, come as a surprise. If you have an extremely complex situation, it stands to reason that the analysis and understanding of that situation will not be an easy task. With this in mind, then, we will turn to a brief consideration of the most important agents of political socialization—understanding that a great deal of uncertainty must necessarily characterize any generalizations made.

The schools.   Every political regime engages in some sort of civic education. Frequently, especially in the media, the difference between education for good citizenship and propaganda and indoctrination turns out to be a function of whether the writer or speaker agrees with the message being transmitted. One person's terrorist can be another person's freedom fighter. For purposes of this discussion, we will avoid the issue of whether the message being transmitted should be applauded or condemned. Our concern is with the fact that some message is invariably transmitted and with the main channels of the transmission.

The classic, and perhaps the most ancient, means of structured and highly regime-accessible political socialization is probably the educational system, formal or informal. Today most developed countries have large, well-organized school systems, and most developing countries, if they do not already have modern educational systems, aspire to them. Obviously, it is desirable for children to learn certain skills and ideas that will help them function more effectively in the adult world. Basic literacy training is one of the most essential functions of any school system. In countries where there is an organized educational system of some sort, the political regime has at its disposal a vehicle for getting its message to most or all citizens at a formative stage in their development. Most regimes take advantage of this opportunity.

There are basically two approaches. Civics lessons can be used to teach what children will need to know in order to take their place as informed adult citizens. Usually included is information about the governmental structure and the belief system that informs that structure. Such civic education is found almost anywhere there is a formal civics curriculum. The second type is also present almost everywhere, but there is a great deal of variation in the emphasis placed upon it. This would be education that has as its aim the development of patriotic feelings and loyalty to the current regime. In countries such as Syria a great deal of overt emphasis is placed on such instruction. In the United States the approach is relatively more subtle.

Finally, it should be noted that the schools do a certain amount of politically relevant teaching even when they do not intend to do so (Hawley 1976). A school is a complex and sometimes very large organization. As such, it must be governed. If it is governed autocratically, the pupils will learn much about living under an autocratic regime. If it is democratic, the students will develop skills that will prepare them to function within a democratic political system. Most schools function somewhere between these two extremes, but the added subtlety should not lead us to discount the potential importance of this learning mechanism.

How does the school match up as an agent of political socialization when it is compared to other agents, such as the parents and the peer group? After a careful review of the literature, Beck concludes that:

> Research has failed to show that the school, either as an institution or in terms of the individual teachers within it, has much influence on the political learning of students. At most, it seems to be a source of complementary socialization for most Americans. [1977, p. 139]

While this may seem a gloomy conclusion to those who see the educational system as a convenient method for "mainstreaming" children into the dominant political culture, it should give comfort to those who fear the potential totalitarian reach of the government into the home via the school. Beck concludes that agents over which the regime has less capacity to exercise control, such as the family and the peer group, have a more potent influence on the shaping of an individual's political persona.

There is one aspect of the educational system that does seem to have a significant socializing influence: involvement in extracurricular activities (Beck & Jennings 1982, pp. 101–6). The influence seems to be related less to the content of the activities than to the experience gained and the activist style that a young person can develop and carry with her into the adult world. This would seem to confirm the assertion that extracurricular activities prepare children to assume adult participative roles. Although all of the adult participative roles at issue here are not necessarily in the political system, many are and this may be the most significant socializing impact of the educational system.

The media. The modern world is dominated by the pervasive presence of the second agent of political socialization to be considered here—the mass media. There is, however, a great deal of variation in media availability from country to country. Because most of the research on the relationship between media usage and political socialization has been done in the United States and similar countries, our comments will have to be limited to highly developed, industrialized nations where media access is not a major problem and where media use is high among all segments of society.

The media have not, until recently, received much attention in the research literature. There is evidence, however, that "mass communication plays an important, in some ways primary, role in the process of political socialization" (Chaffee 1977, p. 258). This is particularly true with regard to children whose reading levels limit their access to more sophisticated printed sources of political information and whose preconceptions are few. One researcher, in fact, has gone so far as to assert that the mass media are now replacing the family as the primary source of political information for youth ("News Roundup" 1979, p. 8). Adolescents and adults, also, tend to rely heavily on the mass media—especially television—for their political information. Connell's research in Australia indicates that "at all ages, the news is commonly seen as part of a normal evening's [television] viewing" (1971, p. 118). It is unlikely that the norm in the United States is much different.

The socializing effect of both the print and the electronic media is not necessarily a direct function of the content and frequency of politically relevant media usage. As was mentioned earlier, the orientation the consumer brings to the experience is crucial in determining the impact of the mass media. Persons tend to expose themselves to the media because they expect to derive some enjoyment from that exposure (Conway et al. 1979). Also for some persons the mass media constitute a prime (if not exclusive) source of political information, while for others the media are secondary. Finally, one must also take into consideration the phenomenon of selective perception. Not only can one choose whether to read or watch a particular source of political information, but one can also "tune it out" while ostensibly watching or reading it.

Although the research literature is still rather sparse, one thing that is relatively easy to measure is the relationship between media use and information. Preliminary results indicate that among young children broadcast-media usage seems to increase knowledge proportionally with the amount of usage. Among older people, however, the print media take on more importance, and persons who are frequent readers are more politically knowledgeable and active than those who are not (Chaffee 1977, pp. 231–40; *Behavior Today* 1979, p. 3). Obviously, the information broadcast or published is a function of editorial decisions. In the United States, uniformity can be attributed largely to similarity in the characteristics and values of the persons who control the various branches of the media. In authoritarian settings control is more centralized and institutionalized. Differences of orientation still exist, however, owing to the diversity of the persons who are charged with making day-to-day decisions. These differences are normally subtle and must fall within a certain allowable range, or the responsible decision makers will be replaced.

The specialized socializing organization.   This brings us to the third type of socialization agent, the specialized socializing organization. This is an organization with goals that entirely or largely involve political socialization and with a program of activities intended to carry out these goals. Organizations with the exclusive function of political socialization are most common in countries with strong ideologies and authoritarian regimes. In other countries such organizations usually have major functions other than the socialization function, although the latter may permeate most of their overt activities.

Examples of U.S. organizations that are largely, but not wholly, devoted to activities with a political-socializing intent are the American Legion, the Girl Scouts, the Boy Scouts, and the League of Women Voters. Although attempts to influence people, especially young people, to develop more patriotic values (as the organizations define them) is a primary goal, it is not the only goal of the organizations. One prime example of an organization devoted entirely to the political socialization of a largely adult population is the Department of Agitation and Propaganda of the Central Committee of the Communist party of the Soviet Union (AGITPROP). Although AGITPROP may sponsor ostensibly social activities, such as dances or concerts, the underlying goal is to gather together a large number of people in order to make them sit through a political lecture as a quid pro quo for allowing them to attend the social event. Every Soviet institution or organization of any consequence has its center for agitation and propaganda. In addition, agitators and propagandists are sent out to do their work less formally in field, park, or neighborhood gathering places. Although there is little rigorous research (for public consumption, at least) on the effectiveness of AGITPROP, it is probably safe to assume that it has some effect—if only by sheer force of persistence.

Of the three types of socializing agents discussed in this subsection, the specialized socializing organization is probably the most accessible to regime influence. The accessibility of the school system varies with the amount of decentralization, although under local control schools often make substantial efforts to socialize young people to the political values predominating in the locality. Thus while school systems are utilized by local political authorities as political-socializing agencies, the degree to which the message is congruent with the values of the central political regime of the country can vary greatly. Finally, central regime control over the media can also vary greatly—from minimal in countries like the United States and England to massive in countries like the People's Republic of China and Libya. Even assuming, though, that central control is all-pervasive and reasonably effective, there may be countervailing influences from socializing agencies over which the regime can exercise less control. The most important ones are the family, the peer group, and the collectivity.

The family. Herbert Hyman in his landmark book, *Political Socialization,* waxed eloquent over the importance of the family in the political-socialization process, calling it "foremost among [the] agencies of socialization into politics" (1959, p. 69). Although there is some question as to whether the empirical research upon which he drew really supported such an extreme position (Beck 1977, pp. 122–23), it is not an unreasonable position given the natural advantage the family has over all other agents of political socialization. First, from a social-learning perspective, it is important to note that a person spends an enormous amount of time with other members of his or her family, especially parents. Although this effect has probably been diluted to some degree in the contemporary world (at least in the more developed nations) by television, the opportunities for persons, especially children, to learn from and imitate other family members are legion. From a psychodynamic perspective, the emotional ties in most families are strong and complex. Even when there are strong negative overtones, their influence cannot be denied, and there is considerable opportunity for children to identify with family members in either case. Finally, from a cognitive developmental perspective, the intimate knowledge possessed by family members makes it possible for them to gear socializing efforts to the developmental level and abilities of other family members.

The major empirical studies of the 1960s and early 1970s lent only partial support to this view of the importance of the family. Most important was the work of Jennings & Niemi (1968, 1974), who found family influences on political socialization to be relatively weak, except in the case of party preference and candidate preference. The Jennings and Niemi research was particularly well suited to an exploration of this issue because they studied both children and their parents. While previous studies had gathered data on children in the aggregate and parents in the aggregate, the Jennings and Niemi study made it possible to study parent/child pairs. Whereas the earlier studies had found high agreement between the parent groups and child groups (Renshon 1975, p. 32), the Jennings and Niemi study found that the agreement within parent/child pairs was not nearly as impressive. This caused scholars to reconsider the importance of other agents of political socialization, since it appeared that the importance of the family might be more related to the context in which they placed their children (Connell 1971 and Renshon 1975, pp. 47–49). In other words, the agreement between certain types of parents and certain types of children might be more related to common experiences and influences and less related to more direct forms of parent/child interaction, such as imitation or identification.

Thus there appeared to be a discrepancy between theoretical expectations and empirical results. When such a discrepancy occurs in any field of research, there are two basic ways of resolving the problem. First, one might reconsider the theory. Perhaps the results could be better explained by some other notion of the way the political-socialization process works—some notion that would trace important socializing influences to sources outside the family or perhaps within the person himself. Second, one could look more carefully at the methodology that yielded the incongruous results and try to develop a research technique that might better identify family influences that exist but have been poorly measured or analyzed by existing techniques. Efforts along one or the other of these lines have generated a substantial body of literature, which cannot be exhaustively discussed here. Several examples, however, might be illustrative of some of the ways in which current scholarly opinion is moving.

One of the most interesting trends to come out of this controversy is a series of findings that seem to indicate that the family may regain some of its former importance in scholarly thinking on the subject. First of all, parents seem to have more influence on their children when mothers and fathers share common views of politics and when they make an affirmative effort to communicate these views to their children (Beck 1977, pp. 126–27). As a corollary, the importance of politics to the parents seems to be salient. If politics are important to the parents, and if the children have an accurate perception of their parents' political views, the correspondence between parent and child political positions seems to be much greater on the average (Tedin 1974). Finally, using the Jennings and Niemi data but using a different method of statistical analysis, Dalton found much more correspondence between parent/child pairs than had been found previously. He concluded: "To the extent that high correlations are accepted as evidence of causality, parents exert a much larger impact in these areas than recent research has generally concluded" (1980, p. 429).

What are the areas that have been studied? Dalton looked at partisanship, racial values, political knowledge, political efficacy, civil tolerance, and political trust. Other studies have explored such matters as attitudes toward the president (or other heads of state) and toward less exalted political figures, such as the policeman. What all of these (and many others too numerous to mention here) have in common is a focus on the adult political system. Several scholars have suggested, however, that real parent/child political socialization takes place on a completely different level. Stanley Renshon, for example, suggests that at least three psychological levels must be considered: (1) opinions, (2) attitudes, and (3) beliefs (1973, 1974). He thinks that in order to study the most important parent/child influences, one must go below more superficial opinions and attitudes to look more closely at the formation of basic beliefs or personality orientations. This type of study, he avers, would not only show much greater parental influence but would also tap a much more potent force in political behavior (Renshon 1974, 1975).

Another scholar, James C. Davies, takes a similar but distinct point of view, asserting that "some of the tendencies of people to act that are politically most crucial are firmly established well before a child ever leaves home, and a few of them before it even leaves the womb" (Davies 1977, p. 142). For example, Davies proposes that children who have experienced severe physical or emotional deprivation early in life are highly unlikely to become politically active as adults. To put it in Davies's own words:

> Most infants do not rise in their cribs and pledge allegiance to the flag, the party, or the leader. But most children before they ever go to school have developed a particular and a lasting sense of being secure or insecure about getting food, affection, and recognition. Most children, long before school starts for them, have learned to return in kind the last two of these (plus trust or mistrust) to those who have schooled them as to what they can expect from individuals and society. And these childhood established expectations about food, affection, and recognition profoundly influence political behavior in adulthood. [1977, p. 162]

All of these factors are clearly related to child-rearing practices, not only on an individual family level but also on a cultural level. These influences on subsequent political behavior are, however, potentially quite subtle and not easily studied using prevailing research techniques, such as survey research.

Finally, Beck and Jennings (1982, pp. 96–97) present evidence that the socioeconomic status of the parents exerts a powerful influence on the propensity of young adults to be politically active. They see parent socioeconomic status contributing to offspring political activism in several ways. First parent socioeconomic status is a significant determinant of child socioeconomic status. Second, in the United States, at least, there are substantial differences among socioeconomic strata in child-rearing practices. Third, socioeconomic status influences the milieu in which a child grows up. The higher the socioeconomic status, the more likely the social environment will contain substantial influences encouraging civic attitudes and political involvement (Jennings & Niemi 1974).

These are only a few of the avenues that are currently being explored by researchers on childhood political socialization. Although the exact nature of the role played by the family is far from clear, there seems to be an emerging consensus that the subject cannot be adequately studied without additional methodological and theoretical refinement. With the current growth in interdisciplinary research in political socialization as well as political psychology, it is probably safe to predict that the findings of the last two decades will be considerably modified during the decades ahead.

The peer group.   Most children spend enormous amounts of time with peers. In spite of this, relatively little work has been done on the influence of the peer group in the political-socialization process. Many of the factors that give the family its salience (in theory at least) also apply to the peer group. This is particularly true as the child grows up and out of the tight circle of the family. Thus while the importance of peer influence in early childhood should not be underrated (Barner-Barry 1977), the possibilities grow as the individual moves into adolescence and adulthood.

In countries like the United States the peer group is relatively autonomous and highly influential during the period of a person's life when she is establishing her individuality by asserting beliefs and engaging in behaviors that may be contrary to those inculcated by family, school, or social group. During some periods of U.S. history the peer group has socialized individuals in a way that had a direct and obvious impact on their political behavior. An example would be the participation by adolescents and young adults during the 1960s in the civil-rights movement and the anti-Vietnam War movement. At other times in U.S. history peer-group norms have encouraged political apathy and quiescence. The 1950s are often cited as such a period. In the Soviet Union, where there is an active adult attempt to harness the peer group to the purposes of the political system, fragmentary evidence indicates that political apathy may be the prevailing peer-group norm among Soviet adolescents.

From the point of view of social learning, the potential is enormous. A minimal amount of time spent observing any children's play group will demonstrate the extent to which young children imitate the interesting or amusing behaviors of other young children. Adolescents, of course, are notorious for this proclivity to imitate peers. As people grow into adulthood the effect becomes more subtle, but it is there. The "dress for success" phenomenon in the business world and the political bandwagon effect are illustrations of the tendency of adults to imitate each other as well as learn from each other's social behavior.

From the psychodynamic point of view, there is a tendency among people, especially grade-school children and adolescents, to look toward role models and to identify with them. In peer groups there is a definite tendency toward contagion in this process. As adults, we may observe the behavior of the boss for clues to the proper image one should project in order to become a boss some day. This may even mean becoming active in the Republican party. In the process, for rather complex reasons, a person can become convinced of the rightness of the Republican cause and of the wisdom of the boss (Bem 1970, pp. 54–69). It is not without reason that Kurt Vonnegut implicitly cautions his readers to be careful that they not become what they pretend to be (Vonnegut 1966).

Finally, in the course of cognitive development people become more capable of abstract thinking and more aware, at the same time, of the adult political system and the possibility that they may play a role in it. This can be particularly important to adolescents who are trying to establish their personal independence. Developing one's own political philosophy and political preferences, as well as being able to discuss them knowledgeably, can be equated with grown-up behavior. Becoming politically independent of one's parents, while being capable for the first time of arguing the issues on their level, can be a heady experience for an adolescent. If one is going to have a political opinion independent of one's family, the easiest place to pick up the necessary knowledge is from peers, and correspondingly one's peers are the easiest people on whom to try out one's newly found opinions. Thus whether one plays the role of an opinion leader or a follower can be determined by one's stage of cognitive development and can, at the same time, be closely intertwined with one's position as a member of a peer group.

The influence of peer groups starts as soon as a child is able to toddle out and engage in something more than parallel play. It extends through the play groups of childhood to the gangs of adolescence. There is a tendency to think that it stops there. Adults, however, have their friendship groups, which are often outgrowths of such groups as unions, professional groups, and work groups, as well as religious, fraternal, sports, and civic organizations. It is at this point that any consideration of the influence of peer groups shades into a consideration of the influence of collectivities.

The social group.   Even in early childhood, the members of peer groups tend to have certain characteristics in common. These might include age, sex, socioeconomic status, race, religion, and ethnic background. At this point in the life cycle such clustering often has more to do with propinquity than with choice (at least on the part of the children). With growth, however, and the added mobility and opportunities that increased age brings, the driving force seems to be a strong tendency for like to seek out like. A casual glance at the lunch room of most racially integrated schools will lend support to this proposition. Also, in recent years there has been an increased emphasis on such factors as racial and ethnic pride. Added to previously existing pressures for people of similar religion and socioeconomic status to "stick with their own kind" this has produced a tendency for collectivities to play a potentially important role in the political process. For example, given the polyglot population of New York, political parties in that state have usually tried to field "balanced" tickets during election campaigns. Efforts to appeal to the black vote or to the Catholic vote or to the labor vote are often driving forces behind the behavior of both candidates and incumbents.

The tendency for children to begin to identify with ethnic, racial, or other collectivities can come quite early in life—especially if the group with which the child identifies is perceived as a minority group (Edwards 1972, pp. 17–19). This process tends to be influenced by cognitive-developmental factors; younger children place emphasis on concrete factors such as skin color and neighborhood church attendance while older children are capable of using more abstract definitions of group membership, such as black or Catholic. Piaget and Weil (1951) studied the relationship of cognitive development to group identification in terms of national identity. Their research suggests that a child's notions about collectivities develop in three stages. During the first stage the child has difficulty even grasping the notion of a country or group. Subsequently, the child becomes able to identify with a nation but is not too clear on how that relates to familiar entities, such as neighborhood and town. This also applies to other collectivities. The social environment has a determining impact on the child's emotional reaction to other nations and other groups. Finally, the child develops the ability to have a fairly abstract concept of the relationship between groups or entities that include the self and those that do not. It is at this point that the child develops emotional reactions toward these differences that Piaget and Weil aver will be relatively basic and enduring. Thus the process of socialization for a significant number of people involves a growing awareness of shared ideas and interests. This group awareness in turn results in a group consciousness, which involves cognitive, affective, and behavioral orientations tied to the awareness of similarity.

The importance of the social group may rest on whether it encourages or discourages political activity. If it does encourage political involvement, the question becomes: What kind of political behavior is promoted as appropriate or advantageous? Conversely, what sorts of political participation are considered anathema? Obviously, the answers to these questions change from collectivity to collectivity and within collectivities over time.

Thus membership in a social group—be it formal or informal—has the potential for generating powerful socializing influences. Unlike the family, whose direct influence wanes as the individual grows up, the social group remains a potentially powerful political rallying force over the entire life cycle. Therefore, any consideration of collectivities as socializing agents must range from gangs of ghetto youth to groups of Gray Panthers.

SOCIALIZATION NEVER ENDS

From one point of view, one can assert that there is never an outcome to the political-socialization process, since it continues throughout the entire life cycle (Kellerman 1979). On the other hand, since political socialization derives its chief significance from its impact on political behavior, it might better be conceptualized as having a series of continuing outcomes. In other words, the effect a socialization process has had on an individual at any particular moment is only the current outcome of the process for that individual.

Though the person's orientation and resultant behavior may change, that future part of the socialization process can have no impact on the current state of the political system. Thus, the socialization process always has an impact equivalent to what it would be if it were complete; the difference is in the potentiality for change that is implicit in the fact that socialization continues throughout the life cycle. Nothing is writ in stone—though it may seem to be at times. Change is always possible.

The picture that seems to emerge is one in which the socialization process generates ever-changing political players each of whom reflects the outcome of a blend of forces, some common to the individual's social and cultural milieu and some unique. Each politically socialized person behaves (or refrains from behaving) in ways that are a special blend of societal and cultural influences in disparate proportions. The blend is ever changing but relatively stable at any given moment and thus capable of driving political behavior at any particular time. This fragile stasis is capable of being modified in both the short and long terms by influences that emanate from the environment and from within the individual. Thus while each of us is a product of the political-socialization process, the behavior of any individual *homo politicus* cannot be rendered easily predictable by the study of aggregate processes.

SUMMARY

The study of political socialization is the study of how people come to choose political activity as a significant form of personal activity. By implication, it also deals with why some people do not. That, however, is not a major focus in the research literature and, correspondingly, it has not been a major focus in this chapter. Students of political socialization tend to focus on the process from either of two basic perspectives: 1) an individual-level perspective that emphasizes the experiences an individual has which influence the nature of her particular political orientations; and 2) a system-level perspective that emphasizes the ways in which citizens are inculcated with political beliefs that have consequences for the particular political system within which they live. These perspectives influence the way researchers think about political socialization and condition the approaches of those who become active in the political socialization process.

Human beings are not just passive recipients of socializing messages. They screen and mold the influences to which they are subjected and can even be socialized by messages or events that were never intended to have a socializing effect. The important point is that people are not passive recipients of socializing experiences, they are active participants in the process—whether consciously or unconsciously. Also, political socialization never really ends. It is always happening and continues up to the point of death for most, if not all, people.

Scholars have tried to make sense of the socialization process in at least three basic ways. First, some have taken a social-learning perspective which emphasizes the messages which the individual receives from the outside world. Second, the psychodynamic approach leads people into the Freudian tradition which places great emphasis on a child's reactions to early childhood experiences. It also stresses the importance of unconscious forces. Finally, the cognitive-developmental perspective focuses on the maturation process and the effect it has on the ability of the individual to make sense of and act appropriately in the political system.

Much of the research on political socialization centers around the role of socializing agents. These come in two basic varieties that, in turn, can be related to the two basic perspectives on socialization discussed at the beginning of this chapter. First, there are those agents over which a political regime can potentially exercise a great deal of control. These include the educational system, the media, and specialized socializing organizations. Second, there are agents over which a regime has, at most, limited control. These include the family, the peer group, and the social group. The combined effect of all of these agents is the exposure of the citizen to an enormous amount of information—not all of which is entirely consistent even in cases where the government makes an attempt to exercise maximum control over the process.

Literature on the influence of socializing agents is large and diverse. It contains a variety of seemingly contradictory findings, making it difficult to come to any definitive conclusions as to the relative influence of these agents. The only possible conclusion is that, intuitively speaking, they seem quite important in ways it has been difficult to study or to specify with any degree of confidence.

With the next chapter we begin a series of four chapters in which we will explore four of the most basic types of politically relevant behavior: leadership, persuasion, bargaining, and the use or threat of force. Because of the magnitude of each of these four topics, a single chapter barely allows us to introduce them in a superficial way. What we hope to accomplish is to suggest at least some of the ways in which these behavior types can be analyzed from the perspectives of psychology. We turn first to that most glamorous of political behaviors—leadership.

5

LEADING AND FOLLOWING:
Who Is "In Charge"?

Trotsky's appearance and speech still thrilled the crowd. But he no longer seemed to find the intimate contact with his audiences which he found unerringly during the civil war, the contact which Lenin invariably established by his unobtrusive appearance and simple expression. Trotsky on the platform appeared more than life-size; and his speech resounded with all its old heroic tones. Yet the country was tired of heroism, of great vistas, high hopes and sweeping gestures; and Trotsky still suffered from the slump in his popularity caused by his recent attempts to militarize labor. But the spell was already shot through with doubt and even suspicion. His greatness and revolutionary merits were not doubted; but was he not too spectacular, too flamboyant, and perhaps too ambitious?

His theatrical manner and heroic style had not struck people as odd in earlier years when they accorded with the drama of the times. Now they carried with them a suggestion of histrionics. Yet he had behaved as he did because he could not behave otherwise. He did not posture to appear more than life-size—he could not help appearing it. He spoke in an intense and dramatic language not from affectation or craving for stage effect, but because this was his natural language, best suited to express his dramatic thought and intense emotion. . . . [Deutscher 1959, pp. 26–27]*

Thus writes Isaac Deutscher in his biography of Leon Trotsky. He describes the waning influence of this man who, along with Lenin and others, "made the revolution" in Russia, who led the Red army in its

*I. Deutscher, *The Prophet Unarmed: Trotsky: 1921–1929* (Oxford: Oxford University Press, 1954).

successful battles against forces antagonistic to the revolution and who, after the death of Lenin, found himself displaced and outmaneuvered by Josef Stalin; indeed, it was Stalin who had him exiled and eventually murdered.

Of all the political processes, leadership seems to many the most intriguing, the most important, and yet the most satisfying. Take Deutscher's description of Trotsky's waning influence. Consider first the man himself. He was a person whose style as "heroic man in historic action" was not a pose; it was deeply rooted in his character, so much so that he spoke with the same fervor, intensity, and theatrical manner whether at a political meeting, during a public speech, or alone with family and friends!

But this rigidity in Trotsky's style clearly foreshadowed his impending downfall. Trotsky did not change, but the *perceptions* and *expectations* of the Russian people did. What in an earlier period had been perceived as heroism, what had evoked the sense of historic mission, was subsequently perceived as "histrionics," and provoked uneasiness and suspicion of Trotsky's motives. The answer must be sought in both macroenvironmental and microenvironmental factors as they interacted with Trotsky's style as a leader. In the civil war period Russia was threatened by forces determined to destroy the Revolution. Hence, someone who could increase people's morale and solidarity through evocation of great principles was of value. At the end of the civil war, with millions dead on the battlefield, starvation and disease rampant, and a society in chaos, the Russian people looked for ways in which to knit together the torn social fabric. In this Trotsky suffered by comparison to Lenin and other more seemingly pragmatic leaders. Moreover, much of the good will felt toward Trotsky had been diminished by Trotsky's attempt to militarize labor. Trotsky's relationship to his "followers" was changing and his microenvironment (his relationship to Lenin, Stalin, and other figures jockeying for power) was changing as well.

DIRECTIONS AND DEFINITIONS

This brief discussion illuminates two major directions in the modern study of political leadership and followership. These are: describing the behavior of leaders and followers as an interaction of person and situation, *and* focusing on the mutual and reciprocal relationship between leaders and followers.

In the first direction, behaviors of leaders and followers are thought to emerge from the interaction of person and situation. Thus, the study of leadership is *not*, as many people commonly suppose, about the traits or qualities of persons we call "leaders" or "followers," although it would be hard to understand something about, for example, Trotsky's fate without understanding something about his personal characteristics. Nor is the study of leadership or followership about the nature of environments, although, again, it would be impossible to explain what happened to Trotsky without understanding quite a lot of things about his micro- and macroenvironments.* Rather, the task is to understand how person and situation interact in influencing the phenomena we label leadership or followership.

In the second direction, the *relationship* between leaders and followers is taken as the unit of analysis. A number of related questions suggest themselves: What brings leaders and followers together; why do they remain in the relationship; why does the relationship maintain itself, change, or terminate? Thus the task is to account for the *mutual* and *reciprocal* effects leaders and followers have on each other (where mutual means that leaders affect followers and vice-versa, and reciprocal means some sort of balance in the importance of the effects). Obviously, these two directions in the study of political leadership are not completely independent. One might want to understand the leader-follower relationship as influenced by person-situation interactions. But as should become clear, the theoretical and empirical work of the last few decades divides roughly into these two directions.

Let us make our task clearer by describing some typical "dilemmas" of political leadership.

1. Consider the dilemma of the "frailty" of leadership. The noted anthropologist Samuel Gluckman (1956), in his study of tribal leadership in Africa, has made the important point that all authority is "frail" in the sense that there is always some gap between the expectations one has for a leader and the reality of the leader's performance. Since no human is perfect, any leader will ultimately exhibit weaknesses that will disappoint her followers, lead them to turn against her and, perhaps, look for another leader. Gluckman made the point that while this disappointment may be disruptive in the short run, in the long run it may contribute to social cohesion and stability. That is, if new persons periodically get a chance at leadership (whether this is through the ballot or through rebellion), it reinforces the ideals of leadership, since each new aspirant to office must justify herself in terms of societal ideals. A possible exception to this is what we call "revolutionary" change, in which the societal ideals of leadership may be called into question (see Chapter 8).

For example, to get elected, a candidate must sell herself by emphasizing her most positive virtues. The candidate who advertises herself "warts and all"—emphasizing her weaknesses as well as strengths—is taking a real risk (although the virtues of honesty as a persuasive technique should

---

*Most people have implicit, commonsense theories of leadership which *do* focus only on characteristics of the person as explaining leadership, or only on characteristics of the situation as explaining leadership, but rarely on their interaction. Appendix A contains an extended discussion of points of view in the history of scholarship on political leadership which have emphasized either person or situation.

not be overlooked). Nonetheless, there is almost always some discrepancy between what a candidate promises and what it is possible for her to deliver. If popular disappointment is keen enough, other candidates may aspire to the office. They must, however, "sell" themselves in terms that conform to the same ideals of leadership. Thus it seems as if there is something built into the leader-follower relationship which creates forces for change in that relationship although, paradoxically, those forces for change may ultimately lead to great social stability. Further, the effect of the talents, faculties and personal characteristics of a leader on her behavior will interact with the microenvironment of expectations in which the leader must operate.

2. *Consider the dilemma of "multiple pressures."* If we think about the "leader" as embedded in a complex framework of relationships where different individuals and groups are making contradictory demands, we can understand "frailty in authority" in a somewhat broader perspective. In a complex society like the United States, where many different partisan groups make demands and everyone cannot be satisfied, the best strategy for a leader is often to "manage discontent" (Gamson 1968). Therefore, it is not surprising that the popularity of recent presidents starts off high and gradually slides downhill over time—with exceptions based on events.

Another extension of this theme is more Marxist in flavor. In the Marxist perspective, the political leader is a representative of centers of economic power in the society. In this formulation, the leader is an extension of those interests; he is "captured" by them and, therefore, is limited by the need to respond to them. As our discussion in Chapter 1 indicates, the matter is obviously more complex than this. Nonetheless, it does suggest that not all "competing interests" are necessarily equal and that the "management of discontent" requires attention to who is wielding the greatest influence.* Thus the leader's potential range of behavior will be conditioned on the need to respond to pressures from various groups, some of whose capacity to exert pressure is greater than others.

3. *Consider the dilemma of "omniscience."* The leader is often charged with both innovating and conserving what is best. This requires that he strive for omniscience regarding what is going on, both in the group and outside the group. The dilemma is that:

> [O]n the one hand, he needs to know what the group is and what it can become, while on the other, because of both the volume of information and the built-in resistances to self-awareness, he cannot know all that persons are, all that is happening. In short, the demands of his role are impossible to fulfill (Mills 1967, p. 97).

4. *Consider the dilemma of "omnipotence."* "[E]ven though [the latter's] assessment might indicate what in the group should be changed . . . cer-

---

*In this connection see Seymour Hersh's (1983) fine account of the 1973 overthrow of the democratically elected government in Chile.

tain basic properties of persons, groups, and the context—as he may have
discovered through assessing the situation—are impervious to the will of
him who wishes to change them" (Neustadt 1980, p. 98). This echoes a
familiar complaint of modern presidents, perhaps best exemplified by
John Kennedy, who remarked that he entered his office on the first day,
wanted something done, pressed a button—and nothing happened!
That's a nice way of saying that there are personal, situational, and relational resistances to a leader finding out what he needs and doing what he
thinks needs to be done (Neustadt 1980).

   5. *Finally, consider the dilemma of "unintended consequences."* If we look at
leadership as a process that unfolds over time, we can see that history itself
creates a dilemma for political leadership. This issue is highlighted when
we try to define what is meant by leadership "effectiveness." "Effectiveness" or "success" are value judgments which may change over time. Thus:

> [C]onsider the reaction when John F. Kennedy 'stared the Russians in the
> eye and the Russians blinked' during the Cuban missile crisis of October
> 1962. Kennedy received plaudits from a relieved and grateful citizenry for
> his tough and apparently successful dealings with the enemy. After all, the
> Soviet Union removed its missiles from Cuba, didn't it? But the more de-
> tached analysis (for example, Wills 1982) leads to the following observations:
> Kennedy did not initiate any attempts to negotiate, at first; rather he
> pursued a more extreme course, thereby escalating the conflict into a crisis.
> Instead of arranging a diplomatic trade by offering to dismantle our obso-
> lete and unreliable missiles in Turkey, Kennedy demands submissiveness
> from the Soviet Union. "If Kennedy's first and only concern was the mis-
> siles' removal from Cuba—as he and his defenders proclaimed—then a
> trade was the safest, surest way to achieve that goal" (Wills 1982, p. 269).
> But instead he forced upon Krushchev a humiliating posture. It was the
> Soviet leader, not Kennedy, who was the one who showed restraint, and who
> "had to back down, admit his maneuver had failed, [and] take the heat from
> internal critics of his policy" (Wills 1982, p. 269). Well, all the better, the
> U.S. citizenry might have said at the time—President Kennedy was all the
> more effective because he (a) got the Soviets to withdraw their missiles while
> (b) holding on to ours in Turkey and (c) thus humiliating his adversary.
>   But Krushchev's retraction probably contributed to his later downfall,
> "depriving us of a leader who was easier to deal with than his successors"
> (Wills 1982, p. 271) . . . as Garry Wills concludes, "We purchased submission
> at the price of later intransigence, which is often the case after gratuitous
> humiliation" (p. 271). (Wrightsman 1982, pp. 9–10)*

The point of this example is that what might seem at a particular
time to be an effective exercise of leadership may have unpleasant consequences later. While Wrightsman implies that this outcome might have
been foreseen, it is often the case that the long-term consequences of
"exercising leadership" may not be possible to anticipate. Hence, the resolution of an issue in the present may give rise to consequences leading to
further problems subsequently.

*L. Wrightsman, The social psychology of U.S. presidential effectiveness. Unpub-
lished paper, 1982. Used with permission.

As the reader can see, all these "dilemmas" illustrate the obvious fact that leadership and followership do not occur in a vacuum. They refer to behaviors that result from persons and situations as they interact, and one never occurs without the other. The truism that "there is no leadership without followership; there is no followership without leadership" denotes the critical idea that leadership or followership *always* implies a relationship. Understanding the dynamics of that relationship, then, is one of the "proper studies" of leadership.

The reader may now be impatient for us to get on with the discussion of explanatory perspective brought to bear on followership and leadership. Before we can satisfy that impatience, however, we need to clear away some of the confusion surrounding the terms "leadership" and "followership." In the first part of the present chapter, we discuss the definition of political leadership and followership, using descriptions of political behavior. We ask: How can we productively describe what is going on when "leadership" or "followership" is occurring? The outcome of this discussion is a vocabulary of leader and follower behavior which we employ later in the chapter; in that part, we turn our attention to selected psychological perspectives, looking at them in terms of the answers they provide to questions posed by the two directions in studying political leadership discussed earlier. Finally, we evaluate the perspectives, weighing both their weaknesses and strengths and considering some general insights which emerge from our review.

Definitional problems.   What problems are involved in defining the term "leadership"? Our review of a wide range of definitions of leadership (Bass, 1981) indicates three overlapping themes that these definitions share. First, people seem to want to use the word leadership in a political context when one individual (or a group of individuals) affects the behavior of others by moving them in some direction. "Direction" might have to do with shared goals of leaders and followers (Burns 1978; Edinger 1964; Gibb 1958; Hollander and Julian 1969; Stodgill 1950). It might have to do with "giving structure," which means specifically organizing a group, soliciting and integrating follower contributions, and proposing policies or courses of action (Kirscht, Lodahl, and Haire 1959). Thus in the example given earlier, Trotsky appeared to people to enunciate clear directions for the Revolution in its early stage, but later seemed less persuasive in this regard.

Second, political leadership is associated with positions within some set of political structures. It is characteristic of individuals in such positions to have the *right* to exercise control over resources. Hence, political leadership is about positions in which decisions are made about public resource allocation and control. Katz (1973) puts it nicely:

The chairman of a meeting, in following parliamentary procedures can assume the role of expert or the role of political leader. If the chairman is there because he is a knowledgeable parliamentarian and because he plays his role impartially, political leadership is not involved. If, however, he uses his chairmanship to recognize his friends and to gavel down his opponents—in other words, if he becomes a partisan—he is exerting political influence. (p. 132)

Having invoked, with this second point, the concept of positions within organizational structures (see Chapter 1), we are forced to clarify the ambiguity which exists in separating the concepts of leadership from those of *power, authority,* and *legitimacy.* Let us spend a few moments clarifying the difference.

A pervasive theme in political sociology is that political leadership is about *power;* a political leader is one who represents a particular group or class of individuals interested in maintaining their control over resources. C. Wright Mills, for example, studied American society from the perspective of the relationship between centers of power in politics, economics, and the military, trying to show how these "power elites" overlap and interact with one another (1959). Thus the study of leadership can center on the way the leadership process operates to protect the interests of the "power group."

Tucker (1981) has made the point that this kind of analysis is not an analysis of leadership as a process, but rather an analysis of the goals of leadership. The primary question is not so much "How does it work?" but rather "To what ends?" It is not that the latter question is unimportant. Surely the content of the activity we call leadership must have some effect on its process. It would be a strange analysis of, say, political leadership in South Africa which did not take into account the role of political leadership in maintaining the system of apartheid, a system for perpetuating the dominance of the white minority over the majority of blacks and other people of color. But equally a power analysis is not a process analysis, and leadership may be exercised for ends other than power.

Authority and legitimacy are often defined in intertwined ways. *Authority* has been defined as "the right to command and to induce compliance" (Bass, 1981). Usually regarded as the foundation of authority, *legitimacy* is a perception that a person occupying a particular formal or informal position has the right to exercise influence over others, i.e., to make demands, give orders, and give directions.

Legitimacy is often perceived as having two bases. First, it can be associated with a position in some social structure. The person in that position has her legitimacy, and consequently her authority, merely by virtue of occupying it. The teacher in the classroom has the right to give assignments and tests and to make rules for classroom procedures because she occupies the position "teacher." Second, legitimacy can arise from the behavior of the individual as it is perceived by his followers. Here, legitimacy comes from operating within the "rules" for the position and exhibiting behavior perceived as competent by the followers.

This distinction may be made clearer by an example. One of the authors and a friend once went to the Hollywood Bowl, a famous open-air concert theater. Before the concert Richard Nixon, then the vice-president of the United States, was introduced to the crowd amidst the strains of "Hail to the Chief." The friend was not a great admirer of Nixon, and as the rest of the crowd rose to its feet, he paused for a moment. Then he slowly rose, saying, "I'll rise to the occasion, not the man." In this case, he was recognizing the legitimacy that came with the office of vice-president—regardless of the incumbent. He was, however, making it clear that he did not regard Nixon as a worthy occupant of that position because Nixon had exhibited behavior that the friend did not regard as competent or within the "rules." In the earlier example, it is clear that Trotsky was suffering from a crisis of legitimacy in that people perceived him not to be as competent in his role, a little too "spectacular, flamboyant, and ambitious." In sum, political leadership has to do with the control and management of resources, but as a descriptive concept, it needs to be clearly distinguished from power, authority, and legitimacy.

This brings us to the third theme. Leadership is often associated with the concept of influence. This theme is perhaps broadest of the three. Some social psychologists, among them Elliot Aronson, want to define the whole field of social psychology as the study of social influence (Aronson 1980). To the extent that you adjust, modify, change your behavior in response to what I do, you could say I have influenced you. But if the concept is so broad, how can it be useful in defining or understanding leadership? The answer is that nobody will call something leadership if it does not in some way change or affect the behavior of the person toward whom the leadership activity is directed. Influence, therefore, becomes important as part of the definition of leadership because it *defines the essence of follower behavior*. That is, we want to define leadership in a way that takes into account the phenomenon pointed to in the Trotsky example: a person is a leader to the extent that others will accept her or his influence.

Describing leadership behavior.   What are the behaviors we would like to consider leadership as a set of activities. In describing political leadership, we have suggested that the definitions are pointing to the giving of direction, resource control, and influence. But clearly we want to be more specific than this. Certain kinds of behaviors get labelled as "leader" behaviors while others do not. Can we define some set of behaviors that will be useful to us in thinking about leadership and about which we can agree? Although some lists of behavior can be quite specific (see Bass, 1981) or very general (see Paige, 1977), and still other lists can be generated in terms of quite specific political situations (e.g., the American presidency—see Wrightsman, 1982), we prefer defining leader behavior so that it more closely conforms to our conception of the political process.

A useful approach is suggested by Robert Tucker (1981; see also Mills, 1967 and Parson, Bales and Shils, 1955). Let us assume that a political system is "in the business" of dealing with problems concerning the allocation and distribution of valued public resources (Easton, 1965). Let us imagine that when these problems arise, individuals within the system may respond in four general ways.

First, and most obviously, they observe what is happening in the system, keeping an eye open for what problems are arising and defining these problems for others (recognizing and defining function). Second, they may formulate plans of action (formulation function). Third, they may find ways of carrying out these action plans (implementation-mobilization function). Fourth, they may monitor the consequences of carrying out these plans (evaluation-monitoring function). Each of these functions defines a set of activities that can be labelled as "political leadership"—activities occurring in the context of problems or demands being made on or within the political system. For example, when the Environmental Protection Agency or the National Academy of Science warns against the effects of acid rain, it is *recognizing* and *defining* a problem. If the president or Congress develops a plan of action (say, to cut the amount of sulfur dioxide emissions into the atmosphere by a certain proportion), they are exercising the *formulation* function. The president may try to persuade Congress to support his or her particular plan of action with legislation and both Congress and the president may, in turn, try to get industry to comply with the action plans, that is, attempt to *implement* them. Finally, the Environmental Protection Agency or its inspectors in the field will attempt to *monitor* compliance with the plan.

One thing that may be puzzling to the reader in this approach is that the definition of *leadership as a set of activities* does not require leadership to be centralized in one individual or a small group of individuals. This idea runs counter to the common-sense notion that leadership is a specific role or position within a group. Indeed, it is characteristic of human groups to establish a structure in which a single individual is elected, appointed, or emerges to take responsibility for these activities (Ridgeway, 1983). But one must be careful not to confuse leadership activities with the leadership role. As is pointed out in Chapter 1, a role is a set of expectations for behavior associated with a position.

Tucker (1981) provides a telling example. In February 1946, George F. Kennan, chargé d'affaires of the U.S. Embassy in Moscow, wrote an eight-thousand-word message to the State Department in which he sought to define the problem he saw arising between the Soviet Union and its former Western Allies as caused by the uncooperative and possibly dangerous conduct of the Soviet Union. Kennan not only diagnosed the emerging situation, but suggested several lines of policy on the basis of the situation as he defined it. As Tucker notes, it "produced an electrifying effect in and upon official Washington. It was read by the President, by members of his cabinet, and by very many U.S. Government officials down the line" (p. 37). It may be, of course, that Kennan's message served as a catalyst for an already emerging set of foreign policy objectives on the part of political authorities in the U.S. (e.g., D. F. Fleming 1961). Nonetheless, this little-known officer in the Foreign Service had performed an act of political leadership that influenced America's posture in the subsequent years of the Cold War. Later, Kennan also became an effective part of the implementation of his policy recommendations by mobilizing support through a long article in the influential periodical *Foreign Affairs*.

There is another important implication of the point that leadership activities may be distributed through the system, rather than centralized. When we think about political leadership, we tend to think about *constituted*—that is, formally recognized—leadership. But sometimes constituted leadership may not be willing to recognize problems, or, if it recognize them, to formulate appropriate policies and implement them. In these situations, *nonconstituted* leadership may carry out these activities (Tucker 1981). That is, individuals within the body politic may engage in unofficial leadership activities in response to problems or issues they see as critical. Thus, social movements (arising out of perceptions of injustice) and the leadership that develops within these movements are as much a part of the analysis of political phenomena as leadership in constituted positions. To put this in a way discussed in Chapter 3, leadership may be exercised by authorities or it may be exercised by partisans. This is one reason why we consider leadership to be a process for regulating conflict (see also Chapter 10).

Describing followership behavior.   What are the behaviors we would describe as followership? As with leadership, we would like to describe followership as a set of activities. We began this chapter by indicating that one key issue for understanding political leadership lies in an analysis of the relationship between leader and follower. We have suggested that "leadership" refers to a set of activities that may or may not be carried out by a single individual. Can we make a similar statement about followers? Is there a corresponding set of follower activities?

A commonsense approach sees no real problem in defining sets of follower activities. It can be identified by acts that signal *acceptance of influence and direction.* To the extent that a person accepts a definition of the situation, agrees with a formulated policy, goes along with the way in which the policy is implemented, or accepts the evaluations based on feedback about those policies, we can say that "followership" has occurred. But notice a problem in the very language we have used— "accepts," "agrees with," "goes along with." Obviously, there are *degrees* of acceptance of influence and direction. Other ways of describing acceptance come to mind: "accepts influence up to a point," "accepts influence but only under certain conditions," "enthusiastically supports." Clearly, follower activities are no more descriptive of a simple response than leader activities.

Common sense also tells us that follower activities are not a constant.

They vary over time and can be affected by a wide range of factors including the number of followers. Moreover, a near–far distinction becomes important here. On the one hand, we have a person in a leadership position relating to his subordinates in face-to-face situations. On the other hand, there is Fidel Castro standing in the square in downtown Havana exhorting a crowd of 20,000. And there is the candidate trying to attract voters through the use of TV commercials. Thus, followers may accept influence from many different degrees of remoteness within the political system, and the amount of remoteness may affect the kind, quality or degree of acceptance of influence.

Common sense, however, takes a blow when we consider the following: Imagine a voter considering candidates whom he mostly "interacts with" via watching commercials, press conferences, and news reports. Imagine that the voter's first response to candidate A is negative; he wouldn't vote for that "bum" if you gave him a million bucks. As the campaign wears on, however, and as all the candidates come more clearly into view, candidate A starts to look better. In fact, as time passes, he begins to look good (at least relative to the others). On election day, we find our voter going to the polls and pulling the lever for candidate A. Clearly, this voter wasn't a follower at the beginning. By the end, however, he seemed more willing to accept the candidate's attempts to influence and direct his behavior. But if follower activities mean only accepting influence and direction, then we should not be interested in looking at the follower in the earlier stages when he was resistant to, and, in fact, rejected influence. This posture is patently absurd and for an obvious reason. Just as with leaders, we are not only interested in people who follow, but also in how they came to be followers. In other words, we need to look at individuals in terms of *potential* for being influenced.

We would like to suggest that a fruitful way to define follower activities is to begin with the dimension of *supportiveness vs. resistance*. Degrees of supportiveness or resistance can be colored by how *positive or negative* the person feels in giving support or resistance and also by the *degree of activity or intensity* of involvement a person expresses. Let's take one example. Imagine a follower who is supportive—but whose support is expressed negatively—and who exhibits a low level of political involvement. This set might very well describe begrudging support for a candidate, perhaps the kind of support one gives when one feels a duty to vote but dislikes the candidates. The example should make clear how it is possible to generate a wide range of different follower activities (see Bales 1950; 1970, and particularly 1979, on whose work this formulation is based).

In sum, these three dimensions can offer us a vocabulary for describing follower behavior that can be coordinated with leader activities as described earlier. Thus we are now in a position to explore answers to the questions posed by the two directions in the study of political leadership. That is, how do person and situation interact to produce the phenomena called leadership and followership? Second, how do we account for the

characteristics of the leader-follower *relationship* and the mutual and reciprocal effects leaders and followers have on each other?

SELECTED PSYCHOLOGICAL PERSPECTIVES

Richard Nixon's frantic efforts to extricate himself from the Watergate
scandal; Woodrow Wilson's fight with the U.S. Senate to secure American participation in the League of Nations; the enthusiastic support of
the German people for Adolf Hitler; the mayor of Allentown, Pennsyl-
vania trying to defend the idea of historical districts; a precinct captain
working to get out the vote; Trotsky's decreasing popularity with the
Russian people—all these examples constitute what most people would
call leadership and followership. Is it possible for such a seemingly disparate set of things to be understood within a single framework? While
there is little agreement at this time that any *one* psychological perspective is powerful enough to explain everything about leadership, there
are a number of perspectives that contribute to our understanding. At
present, we see the following perspectives providing useful concepts,
theories and methods: the group dynamics perspective, the conflict perspective, the learned needs perspective, the actualization perspective, the
exchange perspective, and the cognitive perspective. Within each perspective, we will focus on certain approaches that provide some special
insight or empirical findings.

The group dynamics perspective.   Group dynamic approaches to
leadership generally start with the assumption that a group can be considered as a single entity with certain properties and special characteristics
over and beyond the properties and characteristics of the individuals in
the group. One approach which has been of special importance is the
structural-functional approach. Imagine that a group is something like an
organism (there is some debate over what kind—see Mills 1967). An organism exists in an environment and has, as its first priority, survival.
How does an organism survive? By solving those problems of living with
which every organism has to deal (food, water, elimination, etc.). Now
consider the group as an organism. What problems does it need to solve,
or to say it somewhat differently, what *functions* must it perform (or have
performed for it) to survive? One could generate lists with any number of
items. One list of special importance to studying leadership has four problems on it. Two of these problems concern the *internal* life of the group.
The group must solve problems related to keeping interpersonal tensions
at a level low enough for members to work together. It must also find
ways of getting members to coordinate their activity and stay together
long enough to work on the group's tasks. The other two problems concern the *external* life of the group. The group must generate the skills and
resources necessary to reach the group's goal, and the group members

must organize well enough to work on tasks necessary for reaching the goal (Parsons, Bales, & Shils 1955).

You may have already guessed at the answer this approach would give to the issues of leader-member relationships, since it follows in a straightforward manner from the argument. Leadership emerges in a group because it is a way of solving some or all of the problems confronting the group. As we have already pointed out, these activities or problem-solving behaviors either will be distributed throughout the group or, as is more likely in human groups, will be centered on some single individual or subgroup of individuals. But what does this approach tell us about who comes to be a leader, who becomes a follower, why this relationship is sustained, or why it weakens and changes?

Consider for a moment that a group has different problems at different points in its existence. For example, if a country is threatened with a powerful external enemy, it will mobilize its resources and organize to deal with the threat. In short, it will have primarily external problems. On the other hand, if a country is relatively affluent and has no particular external problems, questions about interpersonal tensions and commitment to group tasks may be of greater importance. It has been suggested (Bales 1953) that all groups have this equilibrium problem, that is, the group seems to swing back and forth between two kinds of problems— external and internal—and that the leader-follower relationship changes as the group shifts from one set of problems to another. Thus, a certain individual who is particularly adept (or perceived to be adept) at external problems may be very attractive to group members (followers) when external problems are most important. When internal problems become increasingly important, the external leader will become less influential and the group members may become more susceptible to influence from an internal leader.

Bales and Slater (1955) have distinguished between an "instrumental" leader and a "socioemotional" leader. The former is "in charge" of getting organized for the tasks of the group. The latter is mostly concerned with the general level of tension between members and the internal commitment of members to each other and the task. Notice that external and internal problems are related. That is, work on the external problems of the group tends to generate tension and threats to commitment, requiring increased attention to internal problems so that the group can get on with its work (Bales 1953). Thus we might anticipate a cyclical strengthening and weakening of the ties between certain leaders and followers as attention is paid to first one set of problems and then the other.

A popular example used to illustrate this point concerns the career of Winston Churchill. Churchill came to power as prime minister of England at one of the most critical points in its history. It was 1940, and England was at war with Germany. The preceding administration had been particularly weak and incompetent in dealing with the growing German threat, while Churchill had been speaking out vociferously about it.

Now Churchill took charge. He rallied the people of England (and the world, for that matter) with powerful and eloquent rhetoric and moved quickly to put the country on a war-footing. In short, *given the historical situation,* Churchill performed marvels of recognizing, formulating, implementing-mobilizing, and evaluating. For this, he was praised and loved by the English. Yet when the war was almost over, the English people voted him out of office and installed a Labor party government dedicated to building strong and comprehensive social programs for the middle-class and workers. What had happened? From a structural-functional point of view, Churchill was a brilliant external leader and, when those kinds of problems were most critical, people were willing to accept influence from someone they perceived as being able to deal with those problems. As the war ended, these external problems seemed to be approaching resolution. But the people of England had suffered considerably and sacrificed much during the war. Therefore, they became more concerned with internal problems, particularly those related to mending the social fabric. The leadership of the Labor party offered alternatives which spoke directly to these internal problems. On the other hand, internal problems were not of central concern to Churchill. Therefore, one finds a shift in attraction to internal leaders and a waning in attraction to the external leader.

In sum, a functional approach to leadership looks at the structure of the leader member-relationship in terms of its effectiveness for solving group problems. Group members are attracted to leaders whose skills and abilities address whatever problem is most pressing at the moment. When new problems arise, group members become attracted to individuals or groups of individuals perceived as able to handle those new problems. We have used Winston Churchill's political career as an example, but one can see that the example of Trotsky's career might also be understood in this framework (i.e., Trotsky was well-suited to the demands of "making the revolution" but less well suited to the problems of the post-civil war period).

Although this approach has its obvious merit, we will note two problems here. First, the concept of a functional basis for group behavior has not been without controversy (see Abrahamson 1978), even though *functionalism* as a school of thought in the social sciences has been predominant for several generations (see, e.g., Merton 1957). Second, the functional approach is not clear about the specific micro- and macroenvironmental characteristics in which the leader-follower relationship takes place. Thus it may be true that the kinds of functional problems with which the Russian people had to deal were changing and thus Trotsky's effectiveness and influence as a leader were waning; however, many other aspects of Trotsky's microenvironment, such as his relationship with other revolutionary leaders and the controversy over which direction the revolution would take, were also changing. As attractive as the structural-functional position is, it is not sufficient by itself to account for the dynamics of the leader-followership relationship.

Another group dynamics approach starts with the idea that the effectiveness of the leader in relation to followers is based on certain properties of the person and a set of important characteristics of the environment. This *contingency approach* (Fiedler 1978) begins by looking at the two types of leaders described in the structural-functional approach, that is, a task leader and a socioemotional leader. It then asks, however, what properties of a group allow one or the other type of leader to get her job done most effectively. Three properties of a group have been explored (Fiedler 1977). The first is the *power position* of the leader—that is, the tools available for influencing the behavior of others at the leader's disposal. The second property is the quality of relations in the group—that is, how warm, friendly, and close people feel toward one another. The third property is the degree of structure in the task—that is, how clear it is to members of the group what precisely has to be done or how it is to be done.

In sum, the contingency approach specifies certain important properties of the environment of the group and then asks how different types of leaders operate within them. This approach is therefore more precise about situational factors as they interact with properties of the person in determining the nature of the leader-member relationship than the previous approach. However, unlike the previous approach, the contingency approach is not as concerned with the development of the relationship *over time*, although it would not seem difficult to combine the two approaches to take time into account (indeed, this has been done—see Hersey and Blanchard 1972). Certainly it might be possible to analyze Trotsky's situation in contingency terms. Over time, he appears to vary in position power, quality of relations among the Russian people changes, and we might say that the tasks of 1922 were less clear and more complex than in 1917. But herein lies a problem: How do we define what "complex" or "unstructured" is in relation to a task? Presumably, the leadership of Russia during that period was dealing with a multitude of tasks, some of which were less structured and others more structured. To which tasks, then, are we referring? Moreover, how do we assess how "bad" the relationships among the Russian people were? Surely they were suffering from the effects of famine and civil war. Was morale low? If so, how low is "low"?

This brings us to some general problems with group dynamic approaches. The tradition from which they spring is one of laboratory research. Groups of strangers or acquaintances are brought together for short periods of time and asked to perform certain tasks. Their behavior is observed. Leadership is generally treated as it *emerges* from the group. In other words, people are usually not appointed or elected to be leaders. Thus, not only must we generalize from small groups in laboratories to the world of politics, but we also have to generalize from the kind of leadership which is most *uncharacteristic* of political leadership in the real world.*

---

*An exception to this research is that of Hollander 1961, who has experimentally compared elected, appointed, and emergent group leadership.

Notice also another assumption in these two group dynamics approaches. A leader is either oriented toward tasks or is concerned with the quality of member-member relationships. Although no one would argue that both qualities could be combined in a single person, these approaches do assume a lack of flexibility on the part of the person. Although Trotsky does seem somewhat rigid as a person, the history of politics seems replete with leaders who were able to "shift gears."

Let us consider this point a bit further. If political leaders differ in their capacity to change when the environment demands it, where does this difference come from? For many theorists in the field, the answer to this question lies in a greater understanding of the personalities of the leaders involved. The next series of perspectives we will review, then, considers the question of leader-member relationships from the vantage point of personality structure and dynamics.

The conflict perspective. The term conflict as used here refers to inner conflict. Approaches within this perspective share the following assumptions:

1. The individual acts to maximize impulse gratification and to minimize the pain of anxiety and guilt.
2. The world, both physical and social, is seen to oppose or resist the demands of "human nature."
3. Humans find ways to "make peace" with the world, but exist in a state of *ambivalence* in relation to it. That is, all objects in the world are potential sources of gratification but also of pain and frustration.
4. All behavior is motivated by a mix of reality-oriented considerations and "irrational" impulses or motives.

Inner conflict, therefore, refers to the tension or conflict that exists between what the individual would like to do and what she knows the world demands of her.

If you had fallen asleep in 1884 and awakened in 1984, you might not have heard of Sigmund Freud. It is likely that virtually everyone else has heard of that singular individual, since Freud has been a dominant force in Western culture, as well as in psychological thought in this century. Indeed, his theories strongly influenced what Stone (1981) calls the "first phase" of political psychology in America, notably through the work of Harold Lasswell (1930; 1948; 1954).*

Harold Lasswell is sometimes dubbed the "father" of political psychology because of his work in the late 1920s and early 30s applying psychoanalytic theory to the behavior of political actors. The style of his work is perhaps as important as his insights. Indeed, the depth analysis of case studies of famous leaders, now usually termed *psychobiography* (that is,

*The following discussion assumes some familiarity with psychoanalytic theory. For those to whom this theory is unfamiliar, a brief review of its basic assumptions and vocabulary is found in Appendix B.

biographies in which the personality structure and dynamics are closely analyzed for their relationship to the leader's behavior) continues to preoccupy numerous authors to this day. One of Lasswell's contributions to this literature is the concept of "externalized conflict." That is, a person deals with inner conflict either by acting out this conflict in the world around him or by creating behavior in others which reinforces or supports a particular defense mechanism. For example, Lasswell analyzes a type of political figure he calls the agitator. According to Lasswell, an agitator is one who is primarily interested in invoking the emotional response of the public in regard to a particular policy. This response is important to the person because it vindicates a resolution of his inner conflict represented by that policy.

A good example of this style of analysis is afforded by a carefully researched and thoughtful study of Woodrow Wilson (George and George 1956). Wilson formulated many "idealistic" policies, particularly the League of Nations and "the 14 points," which affirm the need for self-determination and the protection of those unable to protect themselves. The Georges suggest:

> Wilson was plagued by bottled-up aggressive impulses which he could not bear to recognize. Most men in public life are capable of perceiving and accepting the fact that an element of self-interest and personal motivation is present in much of their political activity. Woodrow Wilson had what can only be described as a horror of being "selfish" and of the possibility of behaving aggressively for personal reasons . . . The aggressive tinge of his leadership he could justify only if he dedicated this leadership to the highest moral ends (1956; p. 160).

Following Lasswell's lead, the Georges further suggest that Wilson was motivated to overcome the sense of inferiority engendered by his father's scornful belittling of him. Thus he attempted to compensate for his "low self-esteem" through the doing of "great deeds," externalizing the conflict with his father onto those individuals who opposed his "high and lofty" policies (but see the discussion of narcissism below). A variety of other well-known leaders have been analyzed in a similar way, with greater or lesser success (e.g., Richard Nixon by Malish 1973; Lyndon Johnson by Caro 1982) and with a greater or lesser degree of theoretical sophistication. Notice, however, that in all these useful efforts, the idea of the leader-follower *relationship* is taken as a given. The emphasis is primarily on the way in which the leader's behavior (whether it be recognizing, formulating, persuading-mobilizing, or evaluating) is explained by the working out of inner conflict and other representative dynamics.

The authoritarian personality and followership.   The idea that externalization of conflict occurs found its most important expression in 1950. In that year, a group of social scientists (T. Adorno *et al.*) working at the University of California at Berkeley published a two-volume, one thousand-page work called *The Authoritarian Personality*. On one level, this research was an attempt to find the roots of anti-Semitism and to discover the nature of "anti-democratic tendencies" as they relate to anti-Semitism. On another level, this research was a response to the terrifying acquiescence, if not enthusiastic support, of the German people for the fascist and genocidal policies of Adolf Hitler. Thus, the authors had in mind not only to understand the relationship of personality structure and dynamics to "anti-democratic" tendencies but also understand why followers with these tendencies would be so susceptible to the influence of (and willing to enter into a relationship with) a person like Hitler and the particular policies he espoused.

There have been numerous critiques of this research and reviews of its history (e.g., Christie 1954; Brown 1965; Stone 1974; Altmeyer 1981), and we will not recapitulate that material here; the reader is referred to those sources if interested in pursuing this concept further. The methods used here and their assumptions, however, are interesting because they initiated a way of looking at leader-follower relationships and of understanding leader and follower behavior that has been extraordinarily influential in generating lines of research. The researchers first defined a constellation of attitudes that they felt "held together" and that defined an "authoritarian" perception of the world. Then they created a measurement instrument called the Implicit Antidemocratic Trends or Potentiality for Fascism scale (the F-Scale). The items on this scale were grouped into nine general characteristics. Table 5-1 indicates these characteristics, as well as representative items on the scale. These characteristics were derived from the authors' studies of anti-Semitism and ethnocentrism and from their understanding of psychoanalytic theory.

The personality which presumably underlies this collection of attitudes has been studied primarily through the investigation of single case studies. Whether or not an authoritarian personality exists (i.e., one that displaces aggression on to weak "outgroups" and glorifies strong "ingroups") is still unclear (see Stone 1976 for a good summary). In terms of the questions we are asking here, however, the evidence that these attitudes reflect factors other than personality is very interesting. For example, there is a strong correlation between the F-scale and both education and socioeconomic status (Christie 1954; Brown 1965; Altmeyer 1981). People who are low in education and socioeconomic status tend to be significantly higher in F-scale scores.

How might one explain this kind of correlation? One possibility is that the subcultural norms of individuals who are less well-educated and who are poorer may be "authoritarian" in the sense defined by the F-scale. An even more interesting possibility in terms of the interaction approach taken in this book is that individuals shift toward "antidemocratic" tendencies, as expressed in their attitudes, as economic stress increases. There is impressive evidence that F-scale characteristics significantly increased during periods of economic stress in America (the 1930s

TABLE 5-1   F-Scale Items by Clusters

(a) *Conventionalism:* Rigid adherence to conventional, middle-class values.

   12. A person who has bad manners, habits, and breeding can hardly expect to go along with decent people.

   41. The businessman and the manufacturer are much more important to society than the artist and the professor.

(b) *Authoritarian Submission:* Submissive, uncritical attitude toward idealized moral authorities of the ingroup.

   1. Obedience and respect for authority are the most important virtues children should learn.

   23. What this country needs most, more than laws and political programs, is a few courageous, tireless, devoted leaders in whom the people can put their faith.

(c) *Authoritarian Aggression:* Tendency to be on the lookout for, and to condemn, reject, and punish people who violate conventional values.

   25. Sex crimes, such as rape and attacks on children, deserve more than mere imprisonment; such criminals ought to be publicly whipped, or worse.

   34. Most of our social problems would be solved if we could somehow get rid of the immoral, crooked, and feebleminded people.

(d) *Anti-intraception:* Opposition to the subjective, the imaginative, the tender-minded.

   9. When a person has a problem or worry, it is best for him not to think about it, but to keep busy with more cheerful things.

   31. Nowadays more and more people are prying into matters that should remain personal and private.

(e) *Superstition and Stereotype:* The belief in mystical determinants of the individual's fate; the disposition to think in rigid categories.

   4. Science has its place, but there are many important things that can never possibly be understood by the human mind.

   16. Some people are born with an urge to jump from high places.

(f) *Power and "Toughness":* Preoccupation with the dominance-submission, strong-weak, leader-follower dimension; identification with power figures; overemphasis upon the conventionalized attributes of the ego; exaggerated assertion of strength and toughness.

   2. No weakness or difficulty can hold us back if we have enough will power.

   26. People can be divided into two distinct classes: the weak and the strong.

(g) *Destructiveness and Cynicism:* Generalized hostility, vilification of the human.

   6. Human nature being what it is, there will always be war and conflict.

   43. Familiarity breeds contempt.

(h) *Projectivity:* The disposition to believe that wild and dangerous things go on in the world; the outward projection of unconscious emotional impulses.

18. Nowadays when so many different kinds of people move around and mix together so much, a person has to protect himself especially carefully against catching an infection or disease from them.

38. Most people don't realize how much our lives are controlled by plots hatched in secret places.

(i) *Sex:* Exaggerated concern with sexual "goings-on."

35. The wild sex life of the old Greeks and Romans was tame compared to some of the goings-on in this country, even where people might least expect it.
39. Homosexuals are hardly better than criminals and ought to be severely punished.

Table 7 F-Scale Clusters: Forms 45 & 40 (p. 255–57) from *The Authoritanian Personality* by T.W. Adorno et al. Copyright 1950 by the American Jewish Committee. Reprinted by permission of Harper & Row.

depression) and significantly decreased in more affluent times (Sales 1973; Padgett & Jorgenson 1982). These results have important implications for the person-situation interaction issue we are addressing in this chapter. When are people ready to accept influence and direction from a person espousing more authoritarian policies? The answer may be that in periods of economic stress, people begin to find themselves more sympathetic to F-scale type attitudes. This answer would explain why Hitler's messages did not attract much attention through the 1920s in Germany but were dramatically successful once the depression descended on Germany (see Toland 1976).

But why should economic stress have this effect? The answer may lie in the nature of the stress itself. First (as we will discuss in Chapter 9), stress, in the form of anxiety, tends to make people think in narrow, less complex, and more rigid ways, particularly if the stress is great. Moreover, times of economic stress typically tend to create needs for both problem definition or recognition and new policy formulations. These terms should sound familiar, since they are categories of leader behavior. Note that these categories derive from a functional conception of the political system. Thus, if people fear that the system may not survive (certainly a strong feeling during the depression of the 1930s), they may very much become receptive to people who seem to have a sense of the problem and some simple solutions. Simple solutions are appealing because, under stress, people tend to think in less complex ways. This again sounds very much like the situation in the early years of the depression in which Hitler's popularity vastly increased.

What all these results seem to tell us is that followers (or potential followers) will indeed be susceptible to influence by individuals who express "authoritarian" attitudes (or policies based on those attitudes) but that this susceptibility only occurs in specific situations (e.g., economic stress). Is it possible that economic stress stirs up certain characteristic inner conflicts in followers that are then externalized in the form of these attitudes? Perhaps. But it seems more likely that stress induces a certain rigidity of thought and a desire for simple answers. Thus, leader-follower relationships of this kind flow from an interaction of persons and situations.

Data of the sort just discussed have led researchers to wonder if authoritarian attitudes might be better explained in some other way. For example, it has been suggested that one alternative way to interpret responses to the F-scale is that what is being measured is the degree of cognitive flexibility, or the degree of "openness" or "closedness" of the mind (Rokeach 1960). Rokeach calls this dogmatism, which, as Stone (1974) points out, is authoritarianism with the specific political content removed.*

Alternative explanations for authoritarian attitudes.   Another fashionable explanation suggests that every individual has a *latitude of acceptance* and a *latitude of rejection* in terms of their attitude system. For example, on the question "Should we negotiate with the Russians about nuclear arms?", attitudes may range from "No under any circumstances," to "Yes, no matter what the circumstances" with different variations on these attitudes arrayed between them. Let's suppose there are 12 different attitudes from one extreme to the other. One person may endorse (or be ready to endorse) attitudes 1 through 4 but rejects 8 through 12. Another person accepts 5 through 8, but rejects 1 and 2 as well as 11 and 12. It has been shown (Sherif 1976) that the more extreme one's attitudes, the fewer attitudes are in the latitude of acceptance and the more in the latitude of rejection. Moreover, endorsing an extreme attitude is usually associated with a very high involvement in the issue and subsequent rejection of other alternatives. Indeed, high involvement in an issue, whether extreme or not, results in rejection of most other attitudes. Therefore, what we see as authoritarianism (i.e., endorsement of extreme attitudes) may be, at least for some people, an expression of involvement in specific issues, perhaps as reflected in one's social relationships, rather than as an expression of some specific underlying personality configuration.

There has been recent interest in reinterpreting authoritarianism in terms of some other personality configuration, particularly one seen as having greater relevance to understanding the dynamics of leader-follower relationships. One such concept is *narcissism*. Since the late 1950s, the concept of narcissism or the narcissistic personality has become increasingly interesting to psychologists (Kohut 1966; Kernberg 1975), political psychologists (Tucker 1977; Etheredge 1979) and com-

---

*However, the evidence for left-wing authoritarianism (as opposed to the right-wing authoritarianism presumably tapped by the F-scale) remains controversial (Stone 1980). Readers interested in this question of authoritarianism on the left may want to consult Stone (1980) or Rothman (1981) for a review of the literature.

mentators on the cultural scene (Lasch 1978). Narcissism refers to interest or investment in the self, to self-regard. While a reasonable degree of self-regard is considered by theorists to be "normal" (if only in the statistical sense), conflicts around narcissism may arise in development. In particular, as the result of real or fantasied wounds to one's self-regard, individuals may develop a split in the way they perceive themselves and their relation to others (although this split may be unconscious). On the one hand, the person may feel bad about the self—more specifically, weak, needy, depleted, full of self-doubt, inadequate, insecure, ashamed, and the like. On the other hand, the person may develop a grandiose image of the self. This image may include drives for greater accomplishment, and a need for the admiration and adulation of others.

Tucker (1977) has reinterpreted the Georges' view of Wilson's behavior as president from this perspective. He argues that Wilson was filled with self-doubt in compensation for which he had an enormous thirst for great accomplishment. He explores the way in which Wilson had a never-ending need for adulation and admiration from others and how violently angry and rigidly obstinate he became when he felt others (particularly those who opposed America's entry into the League of Nations) resisted his "magnificent" ideas. The anger is explained, therefore, not as projection of displaced hostilities from his repressed feelings toward his father, but rather as reaction to the thwarting of his desires for glory. Tucker observes that Wilson's drive for grandiose accomplishment inevitably provoked some resistance. How could it not, given the scope of his plans? Wilson thereby provoked the very opposition he found so infuriating.

This perspective seems to address some of the contradictions in Wilson's behavior, giving a reasonable explanation for the nature of his policies as well as for the style with which he tried to persuade others (implementation function). But how does this approach help with the leader-follower relationship? Obviously, it specifies a certain kind of relationship between the leader and the follower, one in which the follower is required to act in an adoring, uncritical way. Presumably, this is one of the attractions of politics; it allows individuals to achieve narcissistic gratifications through the "cheers of the crowd."

Another interesting possibility is provided by considering the posture of the narcissistic leader in relation to the follower. Part of the grandiose self is to present an image of complete self-confidence and lack of conflict about one's actions. This posture may be particularly attractive to individuals who are themselves in a state of conflict, ambivalence, anxiety, and/or doubt. The narcissistic leader may represent a kind of ego-ideal (see Appendix B) of unconflicted self-assuredness which the conflicted follower finds reassuring (see also the "Learned Needs" perspective). This point may also help us to understand why relationships of this sort can be unstable. Any questioning of the leader's policies is likely to be seen by the leader as betrayal and resistance, and the leader is therefore likely to turn against his followers. Thus, Wilson took any questioning of his policies by even his most loyal followers as signs of betrayal.

Fantasy and the leader-follower relationship.   So far we have struggled with conflict approaches that focus on the personality of followers or leaders and attempt to show how a particular personality configuration may lead, for example, to acceptance of certain kinds of influence. But there are conflict approaches that speak directly to the nature of the leader-follower relationship itself.

Wilifred Bion (1959) suggests that under conditions of stress, particularly when they are feeling helpless and unable to cope with the world or internal conflicts, people have access to three fantasies which help them to cope with the facts of group life. In the *dependency* fantasy, the group (let's call them followers) wants security, reassurance, and protection. In this model, individuals experience themselves as weak, depleted, bad, and they look for a leader who will be strong, nurturant, all-knowing, protective. In the *fight-flight* fantasy, followers mobilize to defend, or flee from some feared external object. In this mood, the followers look for a leader who can mobilize them. Finally, in the *pairing* fantasy, followers look to certain individuals to create or nourish new growth in the group. The leader is expected to nurture and encourage this growth.

Hartman and Gibbard (1974) add a fourth fantasy called "utopian." In this fantasy, followers come to desire a conflict-free set of relationships with others. They wish to emphasize similarities, not differences, positive feelings, not negative (i.e., competitive, jealous) ones, so they look for a leader who will help them attain this desired state. Such individuals are trying to identify with what they perceive as good feelings and are trying to repress, deny, or otherwise distort the presence and operation of bad feelings. Two recent analyses using these concepts have been applied to political life (Little 1980; Hartman 1977). We will briefly illustrate this approach with Hartman's analysis.

Hartman asks this question: How was it that the Democratic party, historically riddled with factionalism and having a long history of extremely contentious conventions, was able to achieve an unprecedented degree of unity and lack of conflict in the 1976 Convention? It could not have been that the Democrats needed unity to win; that has always been the case. It could not have been because of the organizational skills of the convention organizers of delegates; those were also available previously. Moreover, even though Jimmy Carter came into the convention with a "lock" on the nomination, there were ample opportunities for contention over the platform, the rules, and the vice-presidency. Instead, as Hartman clearly documents, there were virtually no conflicts, even when the occasion arose.

Where did this surprising and unprecedented unity come from? Hartman suggests that it was a manifestation of a shared utopian fantasy, one that derived its strength from the period of chaos, disillusionment, disunity, and conflict which had characterized not only the two previous Democratic conventions but the nation as a whole: the Vietnam War, the Watergate scandals, and the resignation of Richard Nixon. What was this fantasy? At a deep psychological level (according to Hartman), it represented the hope of gaining contact with the good, nurturant, and protective aspects of group life and the suppression or denial of the bad, abandoning, and destructive aspects. On the surface, it represents an attempt to create an atmosphere of warmth, mutual understanding, and harmonious living—an idealized group in which spontaneity, sharing and cooperation exist and competition, jealousy, envy, and greed do not. In terms of leadership, group members (followers) who share this fantasy will look for someone who seems to embody the philosophy, personality, and ideals that can best fulfill these "utopian" wishes. Hartman makes the case that Jimmy Carter was that person, a born-again Christian, whose projected image was of a man guided by love and goodness. Moreover, Hartman suggests, the Carter campaign cleverly played upon the notion of Carter as a "savior," as the new creative force who could bring about this hoped-for utopian community.

It is clear that Carter came across (at that time) as a complex but integrated (hence unified in the utopian sense) individual, able to appeal to all segments of the electorate as both liberal and conservative, scientist and humanist, outstanding yet ordinary, sophisticated in an urban sense and yet rural in his origins, a white man who had the respect of blacks, unthreatened by women and yet possessed of certain "feminine" traits of nurturing, healing and gentleness. For an electorate caught up in the wish for utopian community, Carter clearly "fits" the fantasy.

Several interesting points about the leader-follower relationship flow from this analysis. First, *followers find leaders* (cf. Little 1980). That is, people tend to evaluate potential leaders in terms of their ability to achieve the fantasied goals. Second, these are fantasies. People are different from each other, conflict exists, anger and negative feelings exist, competition exists. Thus, the fantasy is unrealistic. Therefore, the utopian leader will always fail, since it is not possible in reality to bring off the utopian vision. Moreover, if a leader is selected to satisfy a fantasy (dependency, fight-flight, pairing), her behavior will be severely restricted. For instance, if the most appropriate leader for people caught up in the fight-flight fantasy is a "paranoid" leader, that is, one who is good at targeting an external enemy whether it exists or not, then the leader must maintain a "hard line" toward the enemy. To soften or try to convey the idea that the enemy is not quite as bad as originally thought, or that confronting the external enemy is not the main problem, risks losing the capacity to influence followers. Furthermore, as the shared fantasy changes the followers will start to seek out different leaders who embody a different kind of fantasy. One might think about the change from policies of détente and reconciliation with the Russians (Carter) to policies that emphasize confrontation and hostility (Reagan). Note that we are not saying that a change in group fantasy was the major or only reason the American electorate preferred Reagan to Carter in 1980, only that this is an illustration of the kind of analysis which this theoretical position yields.

Let us summarize what we have learned so far. Within the conflict perspective two general approaches to leadership and followership are taken. First, authors analyze the ways in which attitudes, policies, and other political behavior represent defensive solutions to inner conflict. The work on authoritarianism is particularly interesting because it directly addresses the question of susceptibility to influence. To put this another way, the authors of the original study tried to explain why people would choose to enter into a relationship with Hitler (by voting his party into office) and why, once he was in office, continued to support him enthusiastically. Dogmatism, latitudes of acceptance, and narcissism are alternative ways of dealing with the same issue. Second, certain conflict approaches directly address the question of relational dynamics between leaders and followers. Bion's fantasy analysis is used as one illustration of this approach (for other alternatives, see Redl 1942; Freud 1922).

In the foregoing discussion, the reader will have noticed that we have generally moved away from considering leadership within an environmental context. Conflict approaches often lend themselves to a lack of concern with micro- and macroenvironmental factors, since one becomes preoccupied with the intricacies of internal dynamics. Yet some authors seem more sensitive to this matter. The Georges' biography of Wilson (1956), for example, is notable for its fine analysis of the political realities with which Wilson had to deal.

Two authors working from conflict approaches have been especially sensitive to environmental factors and their work bears mention here. The first author, Erich Fromm, returns us to authoritarianism as a concept. In a well-known work which had considerable influence on the authors of *The Authoritarian Personality,* Fromm (1941) advanced the thesis that the rise of capitalism severed human beings from primary group ties. In a capitalist society, with its emphasis on individual striving, people characteristically experience anxiety over being alone. These feelings are extremely painful and, allied with a sense of powerlessness, lead individuals to try to escape from the freedom which accompanies individual effort within the capitalist framework.

Our second author, Erik Erikson, returns us to the problem with which the authors of *The Authoritarian Personality* were most concerned, the rise of Adolf Hitler and the German people's receptivity to his message. Erikson (1950) has done an extensive analysis of the relationship between the German people and Adolf Hitler. In it, he attempts to relate historical and social factors as mediated through the family to the creation of the kind of personality susceptible to fascist ideology. The analysis is complex, but some aspects can be presented here. Erikson saw in Hitler and generally, in the German character, a "peculiar combination of idealistic rebellion and obedient submission" which were linked to a conscience which was:

self-denying and cruel . . . its ideals are shifting and, as it were, homeless. The German is harsh with himself and with others; but extreme harshness without inner authority breeds bitterness, fear, and vindictiveness. Lacking coordinated ideal, [one approaches] with blind conviction, cruel self-denial and supreme perfectionism many contradictory and outright destructive aims (p. 293).

But where does this harshness and lack of "coordinated ideals" come from? Erikson thinks it derives from a common family scenario in which a submissive, restricted mother is dominated by an outwardly domineering, but inherently weak and frequently distant father who enacts harsh retributions against the son.

But where did *this* pattern come from? Here Erikson looks at a number of historical and cultural factors which made it impossible for the German father to feel that he was "participating in an integrating cause." He thus lacked the capacity to be dominating and harsh, as well as to be an apt model for the child. In this connection, Erikson points to the curious historical position of Germany in the center of Europe. Historically it continually changed its boundaries as the result of wars of conquest. Therefore, Germans were constantly reminded of their vulnerable position. Further, Germany was thereby exposed to a multitude of foreign influences and values, making it difficult to crystallize a single integrated set of values. Exacerbating this in the 1920s was Germany's defeat in World War I and the harsh treatment it received in the Treaty of Versailles which again partially dismembered the country and forced large reparations upon it. Also, there was a breakdown in the cultural traditions which dealt with adolescent conflict, such that there were more "alienated adolescents" available for recruitment by the Nazis during the 1920s. This brief description leaves out much of Erikson's analysis (particularly his discussion of the role of the mother and of women). It does, however, give a picture of the way in which historical and political factors translate into patterns of socialization which produce individuals with authoritarian tendencies.

What seems so very neat about Erikson's analysis is that it combines a concern for person-situation interaction with an equal concern for understanding the relational dynamics of Hitler and the German people. In doing so, then, it combines the two directions of modern study of political leadership in ways that show them to be complementary. (See also Erikson's extended discussions of the life of Gandhi, 1971; 1969.)

In sum, conflict approaches sort themselves into two categories. First, there are the approaches that focus on ways in which the individual leader or follower externalizes conflict. Here it is assumed that the leader-follower relationship is based on the capacity of leaders and followers to provide support for their defensive strategies. Second, there are approaches that focus on the fit between inner fantasy on the part of followers and the way in which leaders are perceived to gratify those fantasies. In these perspectives, followers find new leaders to supplant the old as fantasies change or as reality makes clear that the leader cannot be gratifying. Generally speaking, conflict approaches are vague or ignore micro- and macroenvironmental factors. However, Fromm and particularly Erikson provide a much broader context of historic events and social organization in which to consider leader-follower behavior.

Learned needs perspective.   Conflict approaches often seem complicated and difficult to people encountering them for the first time, since they often require special vocabularies and also suggest complicated inner dynamics. The next perspective that has been applied to the study of political leadership, the *learned needs* perspective, often seems more commonsense. We often speak of specific kinds of needs being related to specific kinds of situations. For example, we may talk about a politician's "need for recognition" or his "need to be liked." In short, we often try to explain political behavior as if it gratified or satisfied a need to get something from other people.

The major assumptions of learned needs approaches are:

1. Human beings are motivated to seek rewards and avoid costs.
2. "Motivation" refers to needs whose origins arise out of early family experiences through which individuals learn both that 1) certain kinds of behaviors will characteristically lead to certain rewards, and 2) that there is a connection between certain kinds of situations and those rewards (hence, *learned* needs as opposed to physiologically based needs, which presumably are innate).
3. Needs are conceptualized as potentials for action "within" the individual.
4. Needs may be expressed in action when the individual perceives that the situation is one which would gratify a particular need.
5. Individuals are not passive in relation to the need-gratification potential of situations. They therefore may seek out those situations in which needs may be gratified.

The propensity of people to seek rewards and avoid costs seems very much like the proposition in conflict approaches that people act to maximize gratification and minimize punishment (including feeling anxious, guilty, or depressed). This is because both approaches flow from a venerable philosophical position called "hedonism," that human beings seek pleasure and avoid pain. However, in the present approach, no inherent conflict is seen between the individual's need for satisfaction and environmental demands.

Henry Murray's theory of learned needs (1938) has strongly affected much of the theory and research. As elaborated in the works of Atkinson (1958), McClelland (1961), Veroff (1950), Winter (1973), and others, Murray's theory directed researchers toward a simultaneous focus on the situation and the person. For Murray, a situation is understood in terms of its effect upon the individual: "Does the (situation) physically harm the subject, nourish him, excite him, quiet him, exalt him, depreciate, restrain, guide, aid, or inform him" (1938, p. 117–18)? Murray used the term "situational press" for that property of a situation which directs or elicits behaviors relevant to certain needs. Thus, a learned needs perspective is always interactional and concerned with the person-situation issue since, by definition, one looks for those characteristics of an environment that allow one to satisfy one's need. By the same token, one can see that the learned needs concept would appeal to those interested in the dynamics of leader-follower relationships, since leaders and followers can fulfill each other's needs.

One can, of course, generate different lists of learned needs. Murray, for example, discusses over 25 different kinds of needs related to other people and the gratifications one derives from the behavior of others. Political psychologists, however, have tended to concentrate on three kinds of needs, sometimes breaking these needs into finer categories of analysis. The three needs are affiliation, achievement, and power (see also Chapter 3). Affiliation refers to gratification associated with friendly interaction with others, to liking and wanting to be liked by others, and sociable activities. Achievement refers to striving to achieve some standard of excellence or some unique accomplishment. Power refers to concerns with the potential for controlling the means of influencing others or with having impact (Winter 1973).

One might immediately think that the major need gratified by the political process is power. After all, in our view, politics is about controlling decisions concerning the allocation of valued public resources. Interestingly enough, however, there is data that clearly indicates that politics provides a wider range of gratification than is generally thought to be the case. James David Barber (1965) studied 27 legislators serving their first term in the Connecticut state legislature, and his findings serve as an example of the way the need for power relates to political behavior. Based on the legislators' level of activity in their jobs and on their willingness to return for a second term, Barber defined four groups: (1) *Lawmakers*, who are characterized by high needs for achievement, unusual empathic abilities, and willingness to profit from experience; (2) *Advertisers*, who are like the lawmakers except that they are also high in fear of failure and hence are less likely to see politics as a career; (3) *Spectators*, who are low in legislative activity but who want to make politics a career primarily because they find pleasure in being appreciated, approved, loved, and respected by others; and (4) *Reluctants*, who are neither active as legislators nor much interested in continuing to serve, that is, people who serve out of some sense of duty and tradition.

Notice that in these types there is not a single mention by Barber of anything that resembles a "need for power." Indeed, the gratifications of the role of Connecticut state legislator appear to be achievement, affiliation, and duty. Where are the power-oriented types? The answer may lie in the interaction of persons with levels of the political and other structures (see Chapter 1). Meaning no offense to the Connecticut legislature, there are lots of opportunities to exercise influence and control that seem much more significant than being a member of that august body. If we want to find people high in the need for power, we should probably look to political offices with more "clout" or to other more "powerful" positions, for instance, in business (Elms 1976). Thus, in an interaction perspective, we would expect to find that individuals who have a need for power are more likely to gravitate to the highest possible position from which to exercise control over others, assuming other factors are not operating.

But what other factors might deter individuals who need power a great deal from seeking the highest possible position of influence and control? Two interesting possibilities have been suggested by David McClelland (1975). For Americans, he suggests, there is an extreme sensitivity to the potential for abuse of positions from which control can be exercised. In fact, there are strong norms against the appearance of enjoyment in exercising control over others. Americans tend to be suspicious of those who gravitate to powerful roles. Characteristically, we require that people justify their desire to occupy these positions by appealing to higher values or by indicating how they can serve others. In other words, the *style* by which one exercises control must be carefully crafted so that it does not violate norms about power assertion. Thus, there is an interaction between the need for power and the norms which regulate the assertion of control and influence through political positions.

A second interaction issue that may limit the fit between those needing power a great deal and their seeking positions from which control can be exercised is the *form* which a person's need for power might take. There are four such forms (McClelland 1975). First, a person may feel strengthened (or threatened) by a powerful force outside the self. This often happens in relationships with religious mystics or with powerful political figures through whom one can experience power. The relationship of authoritarian individuals to powerful leaders may be of this kind. Second, a person may be oriented toward the things that make her feel powerful. Such individuals are probably more attracted by policies which allow the possibility of their strengthening themselves than they are to gaining strength through "identification" with a powerful leader. Third, a person might be centrally concerned with having an impact on others. In this case, the need for power is expressed through competition and strategic manipulation of others; it is what most people mean when they talk about "power oriented" individuals. Finally, people may express their need to control or have impact on others by viewing themselves as instruments of some higher good. While this kind of expression may seem like a hypocritical justification for the gratification of personal needs, it should be remembered that great religious and political leaders from Jesus Christ to Mahatma Gandhi to Martin Luther King have felt that they were instruments of a power higher and greater than themselves. Indeed, we delegate responsibility to individuals in the political system to act on behalf of the collectivity. Their actions are usually based on some higher level of principled assertion—such as a constitution or laws—that they can use to appeal to their followers.

As is true for so many other concepts used to explain leader and follower behavior, we need to be aware of the micro- and macroenvironments in which people are operating. To reiterate one theme in this book: The relationship between internal factors is never simple, whether we are talking about attitudes, needs, or any other factor inside the person.

We have briefly discussed an example of how one need might be related to leader or follower behavior, and some personal and situational factors which affect the relationship between needs and political behavior. What does a learned needs perspective offer for understanding the dynamics of leader-follower relationships? Consider the following example (Winter 1973). Male students were asked to view a film of President Kennedy giving his inaugural address. Measures of the need for power were taken before and after the students had viewed the movie. It was found that measures of themes related to power needs were much higher after viewing the film. How can we account for this finding? One suggestion is that the students perceived Kennedy as a person who could gratify their power needs. What does this mean? One possible explanation is that these students saw Kennedy's behavior a way of completing themselves. That is, these men may have felt that they lacked certain qualities or characteristics necessary for them to gratify their power needs and that by entering into a relationship with Kennedy (if only in fantasy), they could feel completed in their capacity to satisfy their need for power. This *need-completion principle* is similar to Freud's notion of the ego-ideal (see Appendix B).

A similar idea is the *need-complementarity principle* (see Knapp 1981). Here, the basis for the relationship is seen as something like a lock and key. For example, my need to be friendly to others may be complemented by your need to be liked by others. In this instance, a person's need for power (that is, to control the means of influencing others) might be complemented by another person's need to be controlled or influenced by others (Schutz 1958). One would guess that the latter need might be related to issues of self-esteem and locus of control (see Chapter 3). Indeed, a recent analysis of Jim Jones's cult which, after locating in the country of Guyana, came to a brutal and murderous end (Osherow 1981) provides an explanation based partly on the needs the cult members had to be controlled by a powerful other and Jim Jones's powerful need to control others, on low self-esteem on the members' part, and on their feelings of having little control over the environment.

A third principle used to account for the ways in which needs may provide the basis for leader-follower relationship is the *need similarity* principle. This principle suggests that leaders and followers are attracted to each other because they have needs that are similar or at similar levels of intensity. For example, followers may be attracted to leaders because they perceive them to have similar needs for achievement, since achievement-related behavior expresses a commitment to the *value* of achievement (see following discussion of belief and value similarity in the "cognitive perspective"). However, one might guess that people with same needs for power would *not* be attracted to each other since the competitive behavior that might follow would cause tension between them.

In considering leader-follower relationships from a learned needs perspective, then, one finds many subtle variations, both stable and changing. If one considers that people have many learned needs, then leaders and followers can be bound together by different principles of need complementarity, competition, and similarity, depending on the particular need. The relationship may change or weaken as followers feel that their needs are not being gratified or sense that someone else can more adequately meet their needs.

The Machiavellian.   A final point needs discussion in light of this perspective. In 1513, Niccolò Machiavelli wrote a treatise called *The Prince,* advocating what we would call an extreme prescription for success. He suggested that the ruler practice extreme cynicism, and promoted the "virtues" of deceit and exploitation in the ruler's behavior. Moreover, he recommended that the "prince" see others around him in a similar light—untrustworthy, deceitful, and cruel. Over 450 years later, Richard Christie and Florence Geis suggested that there may indeed be such a "power-oriented" individual—one characterized by a relative lack of emotion in interpersonal relationships, a lack of concern with conventional morality, low ideological commitment, and pleasure in manipulating others (1968). Does this person sound familiar? In some ways, it is almost a stereotype people have of politicians. But are politicians like this? Studies like those on the Connecticut legislature show a much more varied and complex picture. Nonetheless, it is important to understand something about Machiavellian types, if only because of the possibility that such characters may find their way into political life. We are all the more concerned because studies have shown that "high Machs" (that is, people who score high on a scale of Machiavellianism developed by Christie, Geis, and their co-workers) lie more plausibly, can more creatively devise ways of manipulating or persuading others, and are particularly adept at bargaining, apparently because they can keep their emotions out of the decision-making process.

Do such individuals find their way into political life? Etheredge (1979) believes that not only they do, but that once there they practice a kind of politics which he terms "hard-ball"—in which the major goal is to win by any means necessary. (Etheredge prefers to subsume the concept of Machiavellianism under the rubric of narcissism.) A more productive question to ask from an interactional point of view is: What *kind* of political roles, or situations, would most likely be attractive to this kind of individual? Machiavellian types are attracted to situations where they can be face-to-face with those they wish to manipulate, where there is considerable latitude for improvisation, and where they can exercise their "cool" in the face of the opponent's emotional responses (Cooper & Peterson 1980). Machiavellian types can be particularly effective when "they are sent on what amounts to detached service in which there is freedom to wheel and deal to both their own and [their] organization's benefits" (Christie & Geis 1970, p. 234). Elms (1976) has given a brilliant portrait of Henry Kissinger, advisor to presidents from Nixon to Reagan, as a Machiavellian whose role—particularly in the Nixon administration—was made to order. He had extraordinary freedom to wheel and deal on his own and to be in "detached service" on behalf of his government. Elms chronicles the nonideological enjoyment Kissinger derived from his role, an enjoyment consistent with the pleasure such a type of person would take in manipulating and controlling the behavior of others.*

In sum, learned needs approaches provide some interesting additions to our understanding of leader and follower behavior and the leader-follower relationship. By definition, learned needs approaches require close attention to the nature of the environments that stimulate any given need or set of needs. From this kind of analysis, it is only a short step to thinking about those factors present in persons or situations that increase or decrease the correlation between the stimulation of a need and behavior related to gratifying that need. In our earlier discussion, we briefly illustrated this point using the need for power.

The principles of need-completion, complementarity, and similarity also provide an important avenue to an analysis of dynamics of the leader-follower relationship. Different patterns of these principles may help to explain why leaders and followers are attracted to each other and why the relationship may be sustained or change. Finally, we briefly considered the Machiavellian individual, a "power-oriented" type who is likely to be found in certain kinds of political roles.

The actualization perspective.   In Chapter 1, we said that one of the complexities of dealing with the concept of attitude was that attitudes are organized, for instance, in clusters and networks. It seems a commonsense observation that needs might also be organized. Indeed, some concepts of personality are based on the notion of interlocking and systematically organized needs (Maddi 1968).

One such approach that has been influential in political psychology was developed by Abraham Maslow (1954). He proposed that there are at least four groups of needs for which human beings seek gratification:

---

*Space does not permit a more extended discussion of Machiavellianism. It may be useful to point out that like the authoritarianism concept, Machiavellianism was originally approached by creating a scale of Machiavellian beliefs (Christie & Geis, 1968) based upon Machiavelli's principles and concept of a Machiavellian personality. Whether or not one needs the personality formulation in order to understand responses to the Mach. scale is not clear (see Hunter, Gerbing, & Boster 1982). Nonetheless, much research has been generated by the concept (cf. Harrell & Hartnagel 1976; Cooper & Peterson 1980).

physiological, safety, affection, or inclusion (similar to the need for affiliation described above), and "growth" needs. The latter refer to needs for
expanding one's inner potentialities ("actualization"). Individuals seek to
gratify these needs sequentially, starting with physiological needs and as-
cending the hierarchy to growth needs. Of particular interest is Maslow's
claim that a "lower" level need must be satisfied before an individual can
seek to gratify a "higher" need.

Jeanne Knutson (1972) uses this idea to explain both attraction to
leadership roles and kinds of follower behavior. For example, she points
out that individuals with greater physiological needs tend to exhibit more
intense anxiety, close-mindedness, and a greater sense of being threatened (her sample consisted of several hundred teachers, hospital employees, and wood and paper processers in Oregon). Not only did these individuals exhibit a low level of participation in political activities, they also
actively avoided positions of political leadership. Knutson also makes the
point that if a person of this sort were to become a political leader, even
with all the comforts this might offer, she or he would be likely to continue to act like those who experience "the hunger and the cold." Another
interesting finding was that individuals whose priority needs concern
safety and security are likely to regard political activity as futile, but feel a
duty to participate. Again, people at this level tend to avoid leadership
roles: "To be inconspicuous is a necessary concomitant to safety" (1972, p.
191).

James McGregor Burns (1978) has made remarkably creative use of
this general Maslowian formulation to understand the nature of leader-
follower relationships. We will focus here on what he calls "transformational" leadership (a second type, "transactional leadership," will be discussed later). First, he points out that leaders make followers accept their
influence by sensing where the followers are in the hierarchy of needs
and responding to this. Moreover, leaders and followers engage in a
process by which they move toward higher levels and in which the purposes of leaders and followers are fused in pursuit of "higher-order"
goals.

Burns thinks the best example of this transforming leadership in
recent times is Gandhi, "who aroused and elevated the hopes and demands of millions of Indians and whose life and personality were enhanced in the process" (1978, p. 20). Thus, there is reciprocity between
leaders and followers. As Burns puts it, "transcending leadership is dynamic leadership in the sense that the leaders throw themselves into a
relationship with followers who will feel 'elevated' by it and often become
more active themselves, thereby creating new cadres of leaders" (p. 20).

Exactly how does a transforming leader elevate followers through
the hierarchy to higher-order ends? Here Burns is less clear. Part of the
problem is that transforming others in the service of some higher-order
good is an end of leadership. In other words, it describes an outcome of
the leadership process. There are different types of transforming leader-

ship: intellectual leadership, reform leadership, and revolutionary leadership. Burns briefly discusses the roots of each; for example, he suggests that intellectual leadership arises out of inner conflict expressed during periods of social and moral conflict. But the precise mechanisms through which leaders and followers become involved in a transformative relationship are not spelled out. Still, the concept is important. In some little-understood way, certain leaders and followers contrive to move beyond lower needs toward growth and change.

A sophisticated version of this approach puts the issue of leader-follower relationships in a broad interactional and situational framework. This version ranks governmental goals in terms of a "national needs" hierarchy and then relates needs of individual leaders and followers to this governmental goal hierarchy (Sloan & Whicker 1983). The authors identify five levels of governmental goals: developing an economic infrastructure, having internal security, creating political and social cohesion, establishing mobility and status, and enhancing the quality of life. Leaders are successful in moving followers through this goal hierarchy to the extent that they are sensitive to the needs of the average citizen. But this sensitivity is dependent on the degree of centralization or decentralization of governmental structure. The more highly centralized the government, the less likely it is that leaders will be sensitive to the average individual's location in the need hierarchy. Moreover, success in moving up through the hierarchy of government goals will also depend on larger macroenvironmental interactions with other nations in the international arena. These interactions may include, for example, economic competition and technological innovation (losers in this competition are likely to slip down along the hierarchy of governmental goals, no matter how sensitive the leaders are to followers) or Great Power manipulation of countries at lower levels in the goals hierarchy. Thus the capacity of leaders to transform followers is seen to be dependent on complex interactions in the internal and external environments of a country.

In sum, the actualization approach, particularly Maslow's version, has been of considerable interest to political psychologists. A virtue of this approach is that it not only focuses us on the way leaders must identify the specific needs of their followers, but also suggests that part of the dynamic relationship between leaders and followers has to do with movement either up or down an organized hierarchy of needs. Finally, the concept of "transforming" leader comes closer to capturing the quality of many leaders who have been called "great," although the precise mechanisms by which this transformation occurs is not yet clear.

The exchange perspective.   In the conflict, learned needs, and actualization perspectives it was implicitly assumed that the relationship between leaders and followers yielded certain rewards for both participants, whether these rewards were reduction of anxiety, gratification of a particular need, or movement towards greater actualization. Indeed, we com monly understand that leader-follower relationships exist because each party to the exchange "gets something out of it." Imagine a constituent who goes to his representative in Congress and asks for help on a matter of personal importance. Immediately, the member of Congress makes a few phone calls or dispatches a few notes and, within a few hours, the problem is solved. Relieved, the constituent departs. What has each one gotten from this exchange? The constituent has obviously been rewarded with a solution to his problem. The member of Congress, in return, has received good feeling, support, and the likelihood that she will be able to influence that constituent in the future (i.e., if the member of Congress wants something, like a vote, the constituent will provide it).

Thus, an *exchange* has occurred. As in a marketplace, one person has given another something that has been matched by something of presumably equal value. Particularly at lower levels of the political structure (see Chapter 1), most leader-follower relationships involve exchanges of this sort. Burns (1978) has called this kind of leadership "transactional." Such leadership occurs when "one person takes the initiative in making contact with others for the purpose of exchange of valued things" (1978, p. 19). Transactional leadership is relatively fragile: "the bargainers have no enduring purpose that holds them together; hence they may go their separate ways" (1978, p. 20). For Burns, there is a "what have you done for me lately?" quality to leadership based simply on exchange:

> The marketplace is just that—a mart. It is a place of quick connections and quick fixes. It is a place of multiple leaders and followers, a place where leaders can move from follower to follower in search of gratification and followers can respond in the same way to leaders. . . . Relationships are dominated by quick calculations of cost-benefits. (p. 258)

Burns has an ideological concern about defining leadership in this way. He quotes the oft-told story of the Frenchman sitting in a café who, hearing a disturbance outside, jumps to his feet, crying, "There goes the mob. I am their leader. I must follow them!" (1978, p. 265). The leader who seeks to lead by mirroring attitudes and immediately expressed concerns (as through opinion polls) is at the lowest level of what Burns calls "transactional opinion leadership" (p. 265). But Burns also recognizes another problem about the stability of transactional leadership. How does a leader operating transactionally "store up" enough support so that it will be available for periods in which the leader cannot successfully reward followers?

Here Burns takes a broader and politically useful view. A transactionally oriented leader may try to organize a large personal following, individuals whose commitment to the leader may override later breakdowns in the exchange process. She may try to mobilize support by appealing to overriding class interests. She may use the political party as a source of legitimacy for the presentation of ideas that otherwise may strike followers as "costly" or unrewarding. In all of these cases, the process is fundamentally transactional; what Burns describes are essentially "banking" strategies allowing flexibility and adaptability, the keys to transactional leadership.*

The idea of transactional leadership as an exchange process is, of course, not dependent simply on the use of material rewards. The leader can give psychological support. The point is that these immediate needs are not bound up in some shared purpose or direction to which the immediate needs are either subordinated or transformed into "higher-order" needs.† Thus, Burns is sensitive to the ways in which transactional leadership can be stabilized and how micro- and macroenvironmental factors play a role.

In sum, an exchange perspective describes leader-follower relationships as we most immediately experience them. A central issue to be explained, however, is how such relationships can be stabilized. An exchange of resources results in an evaluation of relative fairness of transactions, and the continual calculus can lead to potential disruptions as one or another parties feels unfairly treated (see discussion of justice in Chapter 10). Burns' analysis of "banking" strategies is helpful. However, a transactional or exchange analysis does not specify the exact nature of the rewards. Indeed, most exchange analyses see the leader's primary reward as "support." However, both our discussion of follower behaviors and material discussed in previous perspectives would lead us to believe that the nature and type of rewards to be exchanged (and their associated costs) must be part of an interaction framework.

The cognitive perspective.   It has been said that the growing area in psychological research on political leadership and followership is the area of political cognition (Hopple 1982). In this regard, political psychology follows trends that are more generally characteristic of psychology. There are a number of reasons for this intense interest, not the least of which is that a variety of interesting methods have been developed to study political cognition. Where methods evolve, interest often follows, and this is certainly the case with the study of cognition.

*The capacity of some leaders to survive catastrophic errors of judgment in which the outcome would appear to be not only lack of reward for followers, but something akin to punishment, has long been a problem for political psychologists. In some cases, failure seems to lead to *increased* support for the leader (e.g., Kennedy's rise in the public opinion polls after he admitted his mistake in the (1961) attempted invasion of the Bay of Pigs). Hollander (1961) suggests that failure of a popular leader (one who has built up psychological "credits") is perceived by followers as a "crisis." Important, then, is how the crisis is subsequently handled. Kennedy's apology for his mistake was apparently seen as a gracious gesture indicating his capacity to be flexible and undefensive. However, it is generally considered by historians that the (1962) Cuban missile crisis, which was perceived as a success by the American people, was important in shoring up Kennedy's support.

†One additional benefit of "banking" credits for a leader is that it may allow her latitude for trying new policies or for failure. This may be especially true if the leader earns credits not only for demonstrating competence in helping followers achieve their goals but particularly for adhering to group norms of expected behavior. For a further discussion of the concept of "idiosyncrasy" credits, see Hollander 1960, 1961.

What assumptions underlie approaches in a cognitive perspective? As you will remember from Chapter 1, cognition is about information and how it is processed by individuals. How do individuals select, organize, generate, and combine information in order to understand the world? It is assumed that political behavior can be understood as a reflection of these organized ways of dealing with information—that cognitive organizations, however conceptualized (as implicit theories, categories, schemas, etc.), predict future political behavior.

Thus students of political cognition have been busy trying to understand the thinking of leaders (not usually followers) and then attempting to relate what they find to political behavior.* Yet we must confess to some disappointment with this cognitive literature. Throughout this chapter, we have tried to focus on both interactional approaches to leader and follower behavior and on the dynamics of the leader-follower relationship. Still, the vast bulk of the cognitive literature to date, has not been sensitive to the interactional nature of political leadership and followership and has been almost deadeningly silent on the issue of leader-follower relationships. The reader should, however, be familiar with the style of analysis that is characteristic of cognitive approaches. We will therefore proceed as follows: From the numerous approaches characteristic of the cognitive perspective we will, for purposes of illustration, select one widely used method of understanding cognitive structure, the operational code (Leites 1951; George 1969). We will then discuss two approaches that *have* made attempts to put cognitive concepts within a broader interactional framework. We should note that work of the latter sort is just beginning; in this book's epilogue we discuss how this research will probably look in the future.

The operational code approach is based on the concept of a belief system, a set of value and attitudinal elements, organized in a hierarchy from most general to most discrete. "Belief system" as used here is similar to the concept of ideology described in Chapter 1. The development of a person's operational code involves sampling from a belief system, especially central beliefs about the nature of politics and political conflict. Also important are views about the extent to which the individual can control the environment (see Chapter 3) and ideas about preferred or correct political strategies and tactics (George 1969). There are two categories of belief in an operational code. Philosophical beliefs refer to "fundamental assumptions" about the nature of politics, while instrumental beliefs reflect convictions about the styles and strategies that are appropriate to acting in the world. The integrated set of elements described here represent the way the person, in some fundamental way, "codes" the world around him, using this code to operate on the environment.

The method for defining the operational code can involve (George

---

*Some of this literature is reviewed in connection with the process of decision making we discuss in Chapter 9. Indeed, a considerable portion of the cognitive literature on leadership is about leaders as they engage in the process of decision making, whether it be in more "normal" situations (Jervis 1976) or in "crisis" situations (Snyder & Diesing 1977).

1969) posing ten questions and deriving a set of categories from the answers. These categories then allow the researcher to analyze statements made by leaders. The questions are:

Philosophical Beliefs

1. What is the essential nature of political life—harmonious or conflict-ridden?
2. What are the prospects for the eventual realization of basic goals and aspirations? Is pessimism or optimism warranted in assessing the prospects?
3. Is the political future predictable? In what sense? To what extent?
4. How much "control" or "mastery" can be asserted over historical development?
5. What is the role of "chance" in human development?

Instrumental Beliefs

6. What is the best approach for selecting goals?
7. How are the goals pursued most effectively?
8. How does one calculate, control, and accept the risks of political action?
9. What is the best "timing" of action?
10. What is the utility and role of differing means for advancing one's interest? (Hopple 1982, pp. 93–94)

You can see how these questions address leader activities as we described them in the first part of this chapter. Here the concern is to ask about the cognitive framework that underlies signalizing, policy formulation, persuasion and implementation, and monitoring. Figure 5-1 indicates how different leaders can be arrayed along dimensions of both philosophical and instrumental beliefs. We can see that former Senator Frank Church (C) of Idaho stands almost alone in comparison to the others in his belief in autonomy for our allies, is near the extreme in pushing for noninterventionist policies, and shares with the others a very high energy output. Similarly, John Foster Dulles (D)—President Eisenhower's Secretary of State—is at an extreme in believing in the conflictual nature of politics, and differs with the others in believing that history is predictable.

To what extent do these operational codes predict actual political behavior? Johnson (1977) was able to show that Frank Church's operational code was able to predict, for example, his antipathy toward U.S. foreign aid and intervention. Similarly, Walker (1977) was able to show that the patterns and sequences of U.S. and North Vietnamese behavior were congruent with instrumental beliefs expressed by Henry Kissinger. He notes, however, that certain discrepancies could be accounted for by bureaucratic constraints and the requirements of alliance diplomacy, underlining the environmental constraints on individual behavior.

Hopple (1982) is a good example of someone who takes seriously the idea that cognitive factors such as values (actually a hybrid concept—see Chapter 1) exert an impact on behavior—depending on environmental factors such as the organizational context, the level in the political system,

FIGURE 5-1 A Comparison of Church and Other Leaders Along Operational Code Dimensions

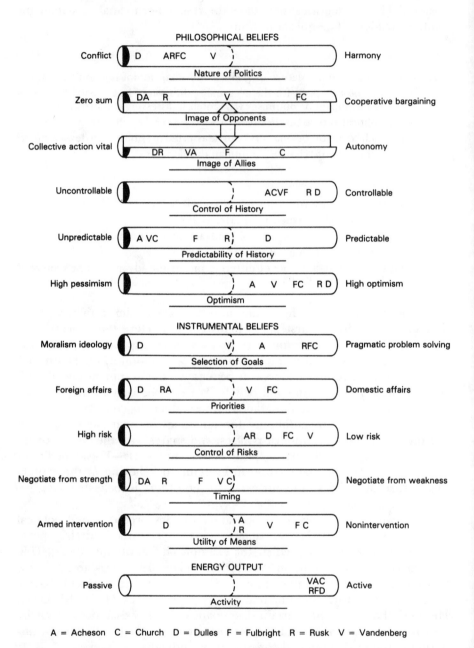

A = Acheson   C = Church   D = Dulles   F = Fulbright   R = Rusk   V = Vandenberg

Source: L. Johnson, "Operational Code and the Prediction of Leadership Behavior: Senator Frank Church at Mid-career." In M. Hermann (ed.), *A Psychological Examination of Political Leaders*, p. 102, New York: Free Press, 1977.

and the nature and type of government. For example, he found that the values placed on public security predicted constructive diplomatic behavior only in closed or nondemocratic societies. There was no relationship between constructive behavior and this value in democratic societies *or* in relatively unstable societies. In other words, whether a cognitive concept helps explain leader behavior depends on macroenvironmental factors. Hopple suggests that the reason for this finding is that in nondemocratic states there is a high concentration of power, and therefore the values of the leadership group will have a greater impact on behavior than in a democratic state, where—in contrast—power is more diffused and leaders are more constrained by the actions of others.

Although the leader-follower relationship has not been adequately addressed by cognitive political psychologists, cognitive social psychology offers a few intriguing suggestions. There is a wide range of evidence supporting the idea that people are attracted to those they perceive as similar to themselves in terms of attitudes, beliefs, and values. Rokeach (1979) has found that similarity of values outweighs substantial differences in race, socioeconomic class, and ethnic background. It would be fascinating to know the extent to which followers are attracted to leaders who are perceived to have similar cognitive characteristics. We can predict that the relationship between leaders and followers will change after changes occur in their perceived similarity of beliefs, attitudes, and values. Indeed, our Trotsky example might be analyzed in this manner. The Russian people's attitudes toward the revolution and those who led it were changing and Trotsky did not seem to be undergoing a similar change.

In sum, cognitive approaches assume a relationship between cognitive processes, however defined, and political behavior. Only recently, however, have researchers begun to question the assumption of a simple relationship between the two. Thus we are just beginning to get analyses that take into account the interactions of cognitions and other personal and environmental factors. An area of research that should be of increasing interest in the future is the relationship between cognitive processes in leaders and followers, whether this relationship is couched in terms of cognitive similarity–dissimilarity or in other terms.

SUMMARY

At the start of this chapter, we suggested that there were two directions in the modern study of political leadership and followership. The first direction tries to understand the behavior of leaders and followers as an interaction of person and situation. The second direction takes the leader-follower relationship as the unit of analysis, focusing on the mutual and reciprocal effects leaders and followers have on each other. We reviewed six different perspectives characteristic of leadership and followership as it is studied today. We are now in a position to ask how well these perspectives do in resolving the two problems of concern.

Group dynamic approaches have the virtue of locating the leader-follower relationship within the context of groups as they develop over time. Thus they allow us to see how changes in leader-follower relationships may depend on the kinds of problems or issues the group as a whole must face in order to survive. Further, they tend to be sensitive to the ways in which effective leader behavior is contingent on certain properties in the environment. On the other hand, they have been less forthcoming in providing appropriately complex portraits of real persons.

Conflict approaches are rich in detail of the internal dynamics of individuals, but are often vague or fuzzy about the interaction of these dynamics with the complexities of environments. One problem with this vagueness is that individuals with presumably different dynamics may behave similarly because of social pressures in the situation. An exception is the work of Erik Erikson: Erikson attempts to situate persons within a broad historic context, seeing leadership and followership as flowing from a complex interaction between history, patterns of socialization, and forms of social organization.

Learned needs approaches are based on the understanding that environments are analyzed for their capacity to arouse particular kinds of needs. This forces an investigator to look closely at the multiple forces operating that either constrain or encourage the individual expression of a need. Needs, through the principles of need completion, complementarity, and similarity, might very well form the basis for the dynamics of leader-follower relationships.

Actualization approaches take the learned needs idea a step further by suggesting that needs are organized into hierarchies. Leader behavior interacts with the need hierarchy of followers, and leaders are successful to the degree that they are sensitive to their followers' location in the hierarchy. However, leaders either may satisfy followers at that level, or they may seek to move them up the hierarchy toward presumably more growth-oriented needs. There is an interesting insight about the leader-follower relationship as it evolves through time that is implied in these approaches. Burns describes transformational leadership as a dynamic process in which leaders engage the growth needs of followers and, in so doing, excite them and involve them in ways that may create new leaders. Aronson's analysis of leadership in Israel (1982) makes this point in an ironic and pointed way. He notes that David Ben-Gurion, Israel's first president, was a powerful individual who organized and transformed people around him. Yet, it was this very capacity that led Ben-Gurion's disciples to break away and oppose him on important policy matters. In some sense, then, the transforming leader creates the kind of followers who will ultimately seek to displace him or her.

Exchange approaches describe what most of us consider to be the basic stuff of politics—namely, that there is a transaction between leader and follower from which both parties derive certain rewards. The focus of these approaches is primarily on leader–follower relationships; less concern is given to the person–situation interaction, except that environments need to be assessed for their potential rewards as these are available to either leader or follower.

Finally, cognitive approaches—perhaps the "hottest" area of interest in the field of political psychology today—are just beginning to focus on the environmental factors that enhance or reduce the connection between cognitive structures and behavior. Little attention has been given to the way in which cognitive processes provide a basis for leader-follower dynamics.

Let us conclude by recalling the "dilemmas" of leadership mentioned at the beginning of the chapter: the dilemmas of "frailty" in leadership, competing interests, leader omnipotence and omniscience, and the unanticipated or unintended consequences of leader behavior. Rereading these dilemmas, we are struck by how much we tend to demand of leaders. How could a sensible person believe that a leader would or could be omnipotent or omniscient? Aren't all consequences of actions, in some fundamental sense, ultimately unknowable? Doesn't the very definition of politics imply that there will be competing interests, even though some may be able to compete better than others? The fact is that while at one level we really do want political leaders to surmount these obstacles, at another level we are perfectly aware that to do so is impossible. Hence followers always exist in some state of ambivalence in relation to leaders. We know that there are no superhumans; yet at the same time, we may desire it in some deep way. Most people rightly feel that there are dangers in leaders who are too powerful. Still, there are times when humans have quite willingly given themselves into the hands of the most powerful of leaders. And so it goes.

What we are getting at is that leader-follower relationships are based on some kind of mutual understanding. Leader-follower relationships get into trouble when such understanding breaks down. Thus, Trotsky's fate was determined by the increasing lack of understanding the Russian people had for his behavior. What previously was heroic now seemed somehow out of touch, histrionic, and somehow suspicious. This theme runs throughout our perspectives. The need for flexibility in leader behavior as underlined in the group dynamic perspective, for instance, is another way of saying that the leader needs to know "where the followers are at." As another example: the transforming leader can hardly transform if he or she does not understand the needs of the followers, nor can the followers be transformed unless they feel there is a bond of mutual understanding between themselves and the leader.

This discussion brings us to our last point. In some important way, leadership and followership are about the *relationship of the individual to the group*. In a political sense, leadership is about agreements concerning the control of valued public resources. In essence, by becoming followers, we make a statement that others will have some measure of control over our lives. Thus, in relation to the needs and exigencies of group life, we take a certain stance about our position in regard to resource allocation and control. For example, when leadership behaviors are more clearly dispersed throughout a group, we are making a statement about how we want control over the allocation of valued public resources. Conversely, where leader-follower relationships are extremely hierarchical or where leadership behavior is concentrated in a few hands, we are making a statement (or having it made for us) about the way resource allocations decisions are made. Thus, in the most basic way, leadership and followership are central to an understanding of the process of politics (see Chapter 10).

Policies concerning the allocation of valued public resources are not worth much if they cannot be implemented. Nor can conflict be resolved if people cannot be persuaded to accept the outcome of a decision about resource allocation. It is to psychological perspectives on political persuasion that we now turn.

6

PERSUASION:
The Lubricant of the Political Process

I sit here all day trying to persuade people to do the things they ought to have sense enough to do without my persuading them. . . . That's all the powers of the president amount to.—President Harry Truman [as quoted in Neustadt 1980, p. 9]

At the heart of all political persuasion is communication. It makes sense, therefore, to begin with a brief (and admittedly oversimplified) consideration of the basic act of communication that is inherent in any persuasion. As Dan Nimmo aptly puts it (1978 p. 4), "definitions of communication are . . . a dime a dozen." Since the point of this chapter is to consider persuasion, and we will not focus on communication except as a vehicle for persuasion, a reasonably simple and straightforward definition will do. Thus we will introduce our consideration of communication and persuasion by defining communication as the transmission of information to elicit a response (Aranguren 1967, p. 11). In this case the response of interest is some indication of having been persuaded.*

---

*This response is often referred to as "public opinion." There is, however, some question as to the extent to which public opinion really exists independent of the results of political surveys (Converse 1964). We have decided to steer clear of this potential quagmire and concentrate on more basic underlying processes.

One of the problems with this definition of communication, however, is that it conveys the impression that communication is an intermittent, one-way, and intentional phenomenon. When one is thinking of communication in terms of persuasion, this is not necessarily a fatal flaw. It should be noted, though, that communication is constant and not necessarily intentional. If one considers the fact that communication may be both verbal and nonverbal, it becomes obvious that the only requirement for communication to take place is that one person be perceived by another person. Thus unless we are totally alone (and in the absence of such devices as TV cameras) we are continually and involuntarily communicating all of the time. In fact, anyone who has seen a professional dancer work alone before a mirror knows that it is possible to communicate in an intense and profound way with oneself.

There is a strong tendency in political science to think of political communication in terms of verbal communication. It is thus possible to consider politics as "the ongoing discussion of means and ends" (Mueller 1973, p. 4). Words and the way they are used certainly are important in political life, and the choice of words to express an idea and the impact of those words on their audience is a matter of some considerable interest to politicians, political journalists, and those who study political behavior (Graber 1976; Edelman 1977). In fact, one can assert that "it is language that evokes most of the political 'realities' people experience" (Edelman 1977, p. 3; Graber 1976, pp. 135–41). All sorts of nonverbal factors, however, contribute to this experience of political reality. Do the words come directly, over the telephone, through a TV set, or via the radio? What words are chosen? How are they joined together as sentences, and how are the sentences related to one another? What are the voice quality and speech mannerisms of the speaker? How is all of this modified by visual clues (if there are any)? In political discourse the way a thing is said can often overshadow in importance the substance of what is said:

> Roosevelt's flexible style centered in a way of relating to persons. He was not much of a speechmaker, but he slowly found out how to project to audiences his manner in conversation. As Assistant Secretary he got through best to the reporters, who saw his charm, simplicity, and enthusiasm at first hand. Similarly in campaigning FDR was most effective in his informal words with "My Friends" the voters, even when he had little of substance to say to them. In this as in most else he had great advantages in that the reporters and the public were curious to see what another Roosevelt would say and do. FDR exploited this attention unabashedly, as he did the social connections his family passed on to him. [Barber 1977, p. 231]*

This brings us to the second facet of political communication: nonverbal communication. The study of body language, kinesics, is a rela-

*From *The Presidential Character*, 2nd ed., by James David Barber, p. 231. © 1977, 1972 by James David Barber. Published by Prentice-Hall, Inc., Englewood Cliffs, New Jersey.

tively recent scholarly preoccupation. The potential of nonverbal behavior to express such politically relevant relationships as dominance and power has only begun to be explored by scholars (Henley 1977; Scheflen 1972). Appreciation of its importance to expressly political behavior has more often been acknowledged in the abstract than systematically explored. The potential of this line of research for generating suggestive insights is great, as illustrated by Roger Masters's empirical research on nonverbal communication by presidential candidates. In the following passage he discusses the television debate between Reagan and Carter:

> Reagan exhibited a high frequency of relaxed appeasement or submissive gestures during the debate: he looked down frequently, smiled frequently, and—in speech patterns—hesitated. It was Reagan who crossed the space between the candidates to initiate hand-shaking. In contrast, Carter stared directly at the camera, smiled rarely, and generally appeared tense and threatening. On the non-verbal level, therefore, Carter's *gestures* indicated that *he* was the threatening or aggressive candidate, not Reagan. For the cross-pressured voter, this non-verbal message contradicted Carter's verbal insistence that it was Reagan who was a "dangerous" man, hence negating the principal argument against the Republican challenger. [Masters 1982, p. 12]*

The "presentation of the self" (Goffman 1959) in political life is obviously important and deserving of more systematic research than it has been afforded to date.

THE NATURE OF THE PERSUASION PROCESS

The whole point of the Reagan-Carter debate was to persuade—to persuade voters to vote. The only rationale for participation was that each candidate hoped he could use the forum the debate provided to persuade more voters to vote for him. In fact, there is very little in the realm of political behavior that does not involve the attempt to persuade others to share the persuader's notion of the proper or just allocation of scarce societal resources.

One of the most important functions of political persuasion may be its use in influencing the choice of issues to be dealt with by political means (Schattschneider 1960, p. 68). As we indicated at the beginning of this book, there are many latent or potential public resource allocation problems. The political process, however, is not activated by any of them until someone—authority or partisan—perceives that there is a problem to be solved and decides to do something about it. At this point, the concerned individual must persuade others of the importance of the issue

*Roger D. Masters, "Nice Guys Don't Finish Last: Aggressive and Appeasement Gestures in Media Images of Politicians," paper delivered at 1982 Annual Meeting of the American Association for the Advancement of Science, Washington, D.C.

and the necessity to find some political solution. This process has been called political agenda-setting (Kingdon 1984; Shaw & McCombs 1977). Thus it is that public attention is drawn to some questions and—if only tacitly—away from others. Since persuasion is a major weapon in the arsenal of all combatants in political conflict, we turn to a closer consideration of the nature and characteristics of the process of persuasion.

As Reardon (1981, p. 24) points out, the major distinction between communication and persuasion is that, unlike communication, "persuasion is always a conscious activity." Not only is persuasion a conscious activity on the part of the persuader, but there is also a conscious element of participation on the part of the persuadee (Roloff 1980, p. 30). Thus persuasion can be conceptualized as a creative transaction in which the persuadee takes an active part by responding to the cues furnished by the persuader as well as to the environment or situation. From this point of view persuasion becomes a "process in which both persuader and persuadee are responsive, not reactive to each other; their behavior is constructive, interpretative, and minded rather than passive and mindless" (Nimmo 1978, p. 119). This point of view runs counter to much writing on political persuasion that focuses on the intent of the persuader and the persuasive strategy and (usually implicitly rather than explicitly) treats the persuadee as a mere reacting mechanism.

It is also important to note that persuasion must take place on the basis of shared meanings, symbols, or myths (Nimmo & Combs 1980). People carry around in their heads a personalized set of images concerning the political system. These images influence what they see and how they interpret it. In turn, new images are formed. When we perceive something, these images give our perceptions symbolic value (Edelman 1971; Nimmo 1974). Thus the White House is not just another building. Depending on the imagery of the viewer, it can symbolize the essential goodness (whiteness) of the United States, a place of power and authority, or a historical landmark of more than ordinary importance. One of the purposes of the political-socialization process is to create a certain amount of shared imagery among the citizens of a particular nation. Thus, at the very least, the White House should represent something positive to the average American citizen and not something negative (such as the center of power of an imperialist nation). As former Vice-President Spiro Agnew noted when he resigned from office, in the political realm imagery can be powerful—no matter how much it approaches or deviates from anything that could reasonably be regarded as "objective reality":

> In this technological age, image becomes dominant; appearance supersedes reality. An appearance of wrongdoing, whether true or false in fact, is damaging to any man, but—more important—it is fatal to a man who must be ready at any moment to step into the presidency. [As quoted in Nimmo & Savage 1976, p. 1]

As Spiro Agnew pointed out, much of what we have to deal with in the political realm is out of the scope of our direct experience. Therefore, there is a certain point—difficult to locate generally or specifically—at which imagery and symbolism shade over into mythology. There are many definitions and concepts of what a myth is (Nimmo & Combs 1980, pp. 7–24), however most of the important characteristics of political myths are captured in Murry Edelman's definition: A myth is "a belief held in common by a large group of people that gives events and actions a particular meaning; it is typically socially cued rather than empirically based" (1971, p. 14).

The first important point is that a myth is a belief; it is something that we assume to be true—usually without any desire to closely examine it or have our assumptions challenged. Second, it is a belief held by a substantial number of people. This is what gives it its importance in much of the political-persuasion process. Although there are times, as in the cloakrooms of Congress, when one individual focuses in on another to make an attempt at persuasion, more commonly political leaders are engaged in trying to persuade groups, or even masses, of people. It is the fact that myths give meaning to events and actions shared by significant numbers of persons that allows myths to form the basis (as a shared meaning) of a persuasive message. It is very difficult, if not impossible, to successfully persuade a group of people unless they share some common notions about the world with each other and with the persuader. Finally, Edelman makes the important point that myths are based more on social cues than on empirical evidence. This is what renders the truth or falsity of a particular myth irrelevant in many instances of persuasion. There is a sense in which there is no such thing as absolute truth. What we judge to be true, even in scientific inquiry (Babbie 1973, p. 19), tends to be what works for us in the sense that it is useful in understanding and coping with the world around us. As the history of science amply demonstrates, it can be exceedingly difficult to disprove an idea that has been reasonably serviceable to date.

Thus, in order to persuade, one must share with the persuadee at least a minimum of images, symbols, and perhaps even myths. The outcome of the persuasion process, if successful, should be a change in behavior. At this point it is necessary to pause and to consider the assertion that the desired outcome of an attempt to persuade is a change in *behavior*, not merely a change in attitude. As was discussed earlier (in Chapter 2), the relationship between attitudes and overt behavior is extremely complex. One thing, however, is clear. It is unwise to make the assumption that because a person expresses a particular attitude she will necessarily act in a way consistent with that expressed attitude at any point in the future. Furthermore, since in political life some premium is placed on "getting things done," overt behavior is of more interest as an indicator of persuasion than as an expressed attitude. In more practical, concrete terms, it is usually more important to find out how an individual voted on a particular issue than how the same individual said he or she felt about that issue. The bottom line is usually some form of overt action, not the mere expression of an attitude (Oskamp 1977, p. 226; Zimbardo et al. 1977, p. 50).

It is at this point that Ajzen and Fishbein's theory of reasoned action (in Chapter 2) becomes useful again. If, as they assert, beliefs are at the basis of any behavior, the way to change behavior is to change beliefs.

> By influencing beliefs about the consequences of performing the behavior we can produce change in the attitude toward the behavior, and by influencing beliefs about the expectations of specific referents we can affect the subjective norm. A change in the attitudinal or normative component is likely to be reflected in the person's intention and behavior, provided that the component affected carries a significant weight in the prediction of the intention. [Ajzen & Fishbein 1980, pp. 223–24]

Thus if we were trying to persuade a legislator to vote for a certain bill that would require a new type of safety device in all automobiles, we might try to convince him that a vote for this legislation would save lives (a change in the attitude toward the behavior). Also we might try to argue that his constituents expect him to vote for legislation that protects their safety (affecting the subjective norm). Thus if one wants to change behavior, the persuasive effort should be directed at either behavior beliefs or normative beliefs or both. This means that the persuasive message should carry information connecting the desired behavior to various outcomes, or it should contain information about the normative expectations of persons who are important to the persuadee. Finally, a persuasive message that affects only one or two beliefs is seldom sufficient. The message must bring about a shift in the total set of underlying beliefs before it can be expected to cause a change in behavior.

THEORIES OF ATTITUDE CHANGE

Ajzen and Fishbein to the contrary notwithstanding, psychologists have tended to see persuasion in terms of attitude change (Berkowitz 1975). In their efforts to understand attitude formation and attitude change, they have developed a wealth of theories about how people's minds can be changed. Assuming for the moment that changing people's minds is a desirable, if not necessary, prerequisite to changing their behavior, let us take a look at these theories with an eye to what they offer in the way of strategies for the political persuader.

The theories that have stimulated the greatest amount of research activity can be grouped together loosely under the term *consistency theories*. In these theories the individual becomes aware of a discrepancy in her life that she finds psychologically troubling, and she is impelled to do something to remove or reduce the discrepancy. First, we will consider an approach that focuses on a situation in which an individual's attitudes or behavior is at odds with the norms of a group with which that individual identifies. This approach is not usually classified with the other consistency theories, but there is an underlying similarity that makes it logical to deal with it here. Subsequently, we will deal with an example of the more well-known, "mainstream" consistency theories. These focus on the attempts people make to try to maintain consistency among their beliefs, attitudes, and behaviors. Thus in the first case the individual is dealing with an inconsistency that she finds in the relationship between herself and her microenvironment. In the second she is trying to reconcile discrepancies within the self.

The notion that people try to maintain a reasonable level of consistency between their own beliefs and attitudes and those of the groups with which they associate was an outgrowth of the research of Kurt Lewin (1947) and his associates. Often referred to as the group dynamics approach, it stresses the pressures toward uniformity that groups exert on their members. The power of the group has two general bases. First, the groups with which we associate normally fill certain of our needs. For example, Leon Festinger has theorized (1954) that we need to be able to compare ourselves to others in order to evaluate our own abilities and ideas. In this process, however, we do not compare ourselves to just anyone; we compare ourselves primarily to others who are similar to us. The members of the groups with which we associate, therefore, are a valuable resource in this comparison process.

The tendency to compare oneself to others is particularly significant in the formation of policy opinions because there is usually no objective standard against which the individual can measure her ideas. For example, if an individual were in favor of maintaining the status quo in spending for social programs, she might regard herself as a liberal in comparison to a reference group of conservative Republicans. Among social workers she would be likely to regard herself as a conservative. If she were to become active in a professional organization of social workers, it is likely that she might eventually find herself lobbying for at least some increases in spending for social programs.

A second source of pressure toward uniformity stems from the fact that a person who is perceived as being too different from the other members of a group will tend to be ostracized or rejected. Since our group memberships fill our needs, we value them and generally strive to maintain them. For example, if an individual was a member of a professional organization of social workers who specialized in working with senior citizens, he might find it difficult to advocate a policy change that would eliminate Medicaid or Medicare. If he persisted in doing so, he might find that his relationships with his fellow workers were becoming distinctly cooler, if not hostile.

From the point of view of persuasion, this approach deemphasizes the importance of the persuasive message. The social influence here stems not from an overt attempt to persuade but from more subtle social pressures that are operating in the microenvironment in which the individual finds himself. Depending on his personality characteristics and the effects of the macroenvironment, these pressures can be more or less powerful. In the case of persuasion, however, they can be quite effective due to their very subtlety. By being placed in the right microenvironment, we can change our political attitudes or behavior without realizing that we have been persuaded because we tend to think of political persuasion in its more blatant forms, such as propaganda or political advertising.

Mainstream consistency theories picture human beings as basically rational, although not necessarily strictly logical. Fritz Heider is generally credited with being the "father" of consistency theory (Oskamp 1977, p. 193). His original idea, balance theory, has given rise to a host of variations, not all of which can be dealt with here. What they have in common is the idea that people attempt to maintain some degree of consistency among their beliefs, attitudes, and behaviors. If one becomes aware of an inconsistency, one becomes uncomfortable and tries to remedy the situation. Thus if you wish to change someone's attitude, you can expose him to information that is inconsistent with his beliefs or attitudes, or you can call his attention to another of his attitudes that is inconsistent with the one you are trying to persuade him to change.

Leon Festinger's cognitive dissonance theory is, perhaps, the best known of the consistency theories (1957; Brehm & Cohen 1962). Festinger posits *cognitive elements*, which can be attitudes, beliefs, or pieces of information. Any two of these elements can be consonant (compatible or consistent) with one another or they can be dissonant (incompatible or inconsistent). They may also be irrelevant to each other.

What if you are a Republican, but have a basically liberal set of political beliefs? The father of one of the authors dealt with this situation by claiming for years that he was a "Rockefeller Republican" (Nelson Rockefeller at that time represented the far left wing of the Republican Party). During the 1960 Presidential campaign, he found it impossible to vote for Richard Nixon, so he voted for John F. Kennedy and wore his arm in a sling for the rest of the day. When the 1964 election presented him with the arch-conservative Barry Goldwater as the Republican candidate, and when Nelson Rockefeller was shouted down as he tried to address the Republican National Convention of that year, the discrepancy became more than he could bear, and he changed his registration from Republican to Democrat. Since he was highly interested in politics the issue assumed great importance for him. Had he been a basically apolitical or apathetic Republican, he would not have been as bothered by this movement toward extreme conservatism in the Republican Party. With his long history of political involvement, though, he experienced such severe psychological discomfort that he felt impelled to resolve it by finally making the drastic (for him) move of changing his party registration.

One implication of the theory of cognitive dissonance is of particular interest with reference to the process of political persuasion. First of all, the theory suggests that people will tend to seek out information that reduces dissonance and avoid information that increases it. The extent to which this applies in political life is in dispute. In their study of the 1972 election Patterson and McClure (1976) found that the people most likely to watch political telecasts that run longer than an advertising spot were already highly partisan in favor of the candidate. In fact, such broadcasts are "a gathering point for the faithful few, and a means for raising funds . . . *not* the means to communicate with a cross section of the American electorate" (p. 121). Short political advertising spots, on the other hand, tended to overcome this tendency, and frequency of television viewing seems to be a better predictor for exposure to these than partisan identification or candidate support. On the other hand, there is evidence (Kaid 1981, pp. 257–58) that partisan selectivity and the tendency to watch persuasive political programming are unrelated.

Selective perception, not selective consumption, seems to be the most powerful force here (ibid.). This is in line with Festinger's suggestion that when exposure to dissonant information is unavoidable, people will defensively misperceive or misunderstand the message. Other ways of dealing with such dissonance are discrediting the source or balancing the dissonant information by exposing oneself to consonant information from another source. Thus a political candidate may be able to get a large number of voters to expose themselves to his messages, but this does not mean that they will be "converted." This tendency toward selective perception and misunderstanding is also a problem for politicians in office who must sell an unpleasant (e.g., belt-tightening) message to the public. While much of the public might watch or read what she has to say about the implications of the policy, there is a good chance she will later be blamed for not informing them about the very things her message was intended to convey.

Another influential interpretation of the phenomenon of attitude change is the *functional approach*. Although this approach informs the work of two groups of researchers (Sarnoff & Katz 1954; Smith, Bruner, & White 1956), for the sake of clarity of presentation this discussion will rely heavily on the writings of Daniel Katz (1970, 1972). The central focus for both groups of researchers is the functions that attitudes perform for the persons holding them. Katz states the basic assumption of the functional approach as follows:

> . . . both attitude formation and attitude change must be understood in terms of the needs they serve and that, as these motivational processes differ, so too will the conditions and techniques of attitude change. [1970, p. 293]

Attitudes are seen as being organized hierarchically into value systems. If an attitude is associated with a value system closely related to a person's self-concept, then it is more difficult to change. If it is more complex in cognitive structure, it is more difficult to change. Finally, some attitudes are more closely related to behavior than others. Thus there is a distinction between those attitudes that tie the emotional reaction to verbal expression and those that tie the affect to behavior.

Attitudes perform four major functions for the personality. First, there is the *adjustment function*. Attitudes associated with this function are the means for getting something desirable or avoiding something undesirable. They can also be emotional reactions based upon past experiences in attaining important satisfactions. An example would be the attitude of a businessman opposing legislation that would increase taxes on his profits. The second function is the *ego-defensive function*. Ego defenses include the psychological devices used by an individual to avoid facing either the inner reality of the kind of person she is or the outer reality of the dangers of the world. Thus when a person cannot admit to herself that she has profound feelings of inferiority, she may project these feelings onto a minority group. Regarding them as inferior allows her to feel superior. She may further bolster this fragile sense of superiority by actively supporting political policies that will create or perpetuate an inferior status for that minority group. In this case, though, it is important to recognize that the attitude is not created by the minority group but by her own inner emotional conflicts. She will not recognize this, though, because people are ordinarily unaware of their defense mechanisms and will resist efforts by others to make them aware.

The *value-expressive function* gives positive expression to an individual's central values and the kind of person he conceives himself to be. This is based on the notion that people gain satisfaction from expressing attitudes and values that reflect their cherished beliefs and self-images. The rewards include confirmation of a positive self-identity and the satisfaction generally associated with the exercise of our talents and abilities. Thus an individual may oppose additional spending for defense weapons as an expression of deeply felt humanitarian impulses. Similarly, an individual may become a Marxist after being dramatically exposed to the sad lot of the economically underprivileged. Finally, there is the *knowledge function*. Human beings tend to seek knowledge to give meaning to the confusion they experience in the world around them. Knowledge can impart standards or frames of reference that allow the individual to better understand his world. Such attitudes give us a way to interpret things we perceive to be important for us.

Attitudes based on the adjustment function can be changed by the creation of new needs or levels of aspiration. Also the rewards and punishments associated with the object of the attitude can be modified. For example, in order to convince the businessman to favor legislation that would increase taxes on his profits, you might have to convince him that the tax revenues would be spent in ways that would benefit him as much as, or more than, the additional profits. Alternatively, you might try to point out to him that shifting an unavoidable tax burden to other segments of society might cause increased worker demands or decreased spending power among his customers. Attitudes based on the ego-defensive function can be changed by the creation of conditions that make the outer world seem less threatening, thus increasing the individual's subjective feeling of security. Alternatively, some form of psychological therapy might be used to help the individual construct a more attractive inner self. When a person lessens her feelings of inferiority, she also lessens her need to find others in the outside world whom she can perceive as inferior to herself. Thus an improvement in the status of minorities may no longer be seen as threatening.

Attitudes based on the value-expressive function can be changed by inducing some degree of dissatisfaction with the self. Once this has been done, it becomes easier to demonstrate to the individual how a new attitude might be a more appropriate expression of a new, improved self-identity. Also the environment might be changed to make old values less attractive and new ones more attractive. Thus the person who became a Marxist might be persuaded to abandon his Marxism after living in a country where Marxist ideals are professed by the political leadership but the lot of the economically underprivileged is not appreciably improved. Finally, attitudes based on the knowledge function might be changed by introducing new information that would either be more meaningful or would create ambiguity for the individual in her interpretation of the world. Many persons who thought that nuclear power was a safe and economical way to generate energy have had to adjust their frames of reference as a result of the crisis generated by the accident at Three Mile Island and the information on the safety of nuclear-power generating plants that has become available to the public following that incident.

Another set of research approaches to attitude formation and change are based on learning theory or *social learning theory*. Basically, this theory holds that learning processes are responsible for attitude formation and change. A great deal of emphasis is put on the characteristics of the persuasive stimulus, which in this case would be the source of the persuasion and the content of the persuasive message. Also stressed is the process of reinforcement in attitude change. In other words, if you want a person to adopt a new attitude, make sure that the adoption of that new attitude leads to pleasant or rewarding experiences.

The leading researchers in this tradition were Carl Hovland and his associates at Yale University (Hovland et al. 1953). In considering the source of the persuasion, Hovland and his associates did a great deal of work on the effect of the credibility of the communicator. Generally, they found that a message from a highly credible source will be a more effective persuader than a message from a low-credibility source. Of the various bases for credibility, expertness was found to be the most effective. In considering the persuasive message, these researchers spent a great deal of time studying the effect of fear appeals. Most recent evidence indicates that strong fear appeals produce more attitude change than weak ones

(Leventhal 1970; McGuire 1969b). This generalization seems to hold up rather well except in the case of very high fear levels. Then the persuasive message seems to trigger a reaction of defensive avoidance and discounting mechanisms decreasing attitude change (McGuire 1968; Janis & Mann 1977, pp. 96–98).

Finally, there has been a great deal of recent interest in the study of perception—the way in which people see and make sense of other people and things in their environment. From this point of view the problem of persuading a person to change his attitudes resolves itself into the problem of creating a change in that individual's perception of the object of the attitude. The variation on this theme, which will be the focus of the following discussion, is *attribution theory.*

As we noted in chapter 1, an attribution is the act of inferring that oneself and other people have certain qualities or characteristics. These in turn become the vehicles for us to reach conclusions about the causes of other people's behavior. Whether or not these attributions of causality are as a matter of fact accurate, they will affect our behaviors, beliefs, and attitudes if we regard them as accurate. In the immediate context we are interested in the fact that the goal of the persuader is to change or control attribution (Jones 1982).

Attribution theorists usually make a distinction between internal attribution and external attribution. Internal attribution is the idea that the reason for an individual's behavior is a personal characteristic. For example, we might make the assumption that people enter political life because they have a need for power. In fact, just such an attribution was at the core of Harold Lasswell's early analyses of the political personality (e.g., 1948). External attribution is the perception that the reason for a person's behavior is outside that person; it stems from something in the situation in which that person finds himself and to which he reacts with the behavior in question. For example, James David Barber concluded, on the basis of his study of the history of the presidency in the twentieth century, that the American people tend to elect presidents "on the basis of widely shared common experience" (1980, p. 6). Thus, "candidates who suit their times are more likely to win than those who contradict them" (p. 5).

If a person's attributions are stable and he is confident about their accuracy, they will be more difficult to change. If, however, his attributions are tentative or unstable, he will be much more open to persuasion. Some of the reasons for attribution instability are "little social support, poor or ambiguous prior information, problems which are too difficult for the person's abilities, beliefs which have been disconfirmed, and other experiences which lower the person's self-confidence" (Oskamp 1977, p. 216).

Based on his research on the Arab-Israeli conflict, Daniel Heradstveit has come to the conclusion that national decision makers find it very easy to avoid cognitive change in their beliefs about international relations (1979, 1982). He bases this conclusion on the dynamics of favorable and unfavorable attributions. More specifically, he found that when decision makers perceive that the enemy is doing something good, they tend to attribute it to situational factors (external attribution), but bad actions are attributed to personal factors (internal attribution). For example, if you think that Arabs are irrational (internal attribution), this severely limits the policy alternatives you are likely to consider trying. But if you think they are reacting to the situation in which they find themselves (external attribution), there are many more options (Jervis 1982, p. 19). On the other hand, when the decision makers' own country does something bad they are likely to explain it in situational terms, but if the action is good the explanation is likely to be dispositional. If you think that the "good guys" are always us and the "bad guys" are always them, it will be very difficult to change your mind about any detail of this formulation. This is especially true if any information that contradicts this generalization can be dismissed as something bad "we were *forced* to do because of the situation in which we found ourselves" or something good "they were *forced* to do because of the situation in which they found themselves."

THE ELEMENTS OF PERSUASIVE COMMUNICATION

Any persuasive communication must have a *source*—the persuader or persuaders. Although there is substantial evidence of the superior persuasive impact of face-to-face communication (Oskamp 1977, pp. 153–54), relatively few attempts at political persuasion take place on a face-to-face basis. In fact, in a study of political conversations, Bernard Berelson and his associates found that only 6 percent involved any argument or attempt to persuade (Berelson et al. 1954). Most of our exposure to sources of political persuasion is second hand, usually via the media (Oskamp 1977, pp. 159–60).

Thus the actual sources, or originators, of political persuasion are usually far away from us, intent on persuading large numbers of us as efficiently as possible. This precludes much in the way of face-to-face communication despite its apparent superiority. Although it can be said that anyone in a political situation is a potential political persuader, as a matter of fact only a few categories of persons engage in political persuasion on a sustained basis. These are the politicians, the professional political communicators and the political activists (Nimmo 1978, pp. 24–32).

Politicians are people who aspire to or hold public office. In the process of trying to get elected or to achieve certain goals once they have been elected, they find it necessary to do a great deal of persuading. In fact, as the Truman quote at the beginning of this chapter illustrates, some politicians have moments when they see persuasion as virtually 100 percent of the job.

Political activists like Donna Franklin may be engaged in politics full time, but commonly their commitment to political life is different from that of the professional politician. The chief indicator of that difference is that they are not ordinarily interested in holding political office. One type of activist, the spokesperson for an organized interest, has a role very similar to that of the officeholder. Her constituency, however, is composed not of voters but of persons interested in the goals of the organization she represents. Less formal is the role of the opinion leader, the person others seek out for advice and information about politics. Opinion leaders used to be seen as the key people in the political-communication process: They got their information from the media and passed on to less interested citizens. Subsequent research (Oskamp 1977, pp. 155–56) suggests that there are many types of opinion leaders, some more inclined than others to try to persuade their acquaintances to their point of view. Thus opinion leaders may be important, but it is as part of a multistep, circular process, in which some are generally more active than others and the activity level of any opinion leader can vary greatly from issue to issue.

Professional political communicators are relatively new on the political scene. In a sense they can be regarded as a by-product of the rise of the media in modern life. A professional communicator becomes a kind of "communications go-between," who links politicians or activists with the general public or certain target audiences. In this role he or she becomes an integral part of the persuasion process. Generally, there are two types of professional political communicators—journalists and promoters. These two types differ in the extent to which they work independently of the persons paying their salaries. Promoters are in the pay of politicians or organizations. Journalists may—but do not always—have more freedom to be impartial.

As was mentioned earlier, the major factor that seems to condition the persuasive power of any source is credibility (Nimmo 1978, p. 106; Cohen 1964, pp. 23–29). In the short run, at least, the best basis for credibility is expertness. All three of the types of political persuader mentioned above can fairly be said to be experts in politics and, especially, the political issues about which they try to persuade others. Potential persuadees, however, also take other things into consideration. For example, it can lessen a source's persuasive power if his audience perceives him as biased, having ulterior motives, or having the intention to influence. An image of disinterestedness is definitely a help, but aside from some journalists and opinion leaders, this impression is difficult to convey for most political persuaders.

The next element of a persuasive communication is the persuasive *message* itself. In most cases political persuasion is aimed at accomplishing a change in behavior or instituting a new type of behavior. Occasionally it might have other functions, such as reinforcing an existing tendency or simply making the audience aware of new possibilities or potentialities as prelude to trying to induce the desired behavior (Wiebe 1969–70). If one accepts the relationship between belief, attitude, and behavior posited by the theory of reasoned action (see chapter 2), then the most obvious aim of the message should be to try to change the primary beliefs that underlie the behavior or behaviors of interest (Ajzen & Fishbein 1980, pp. 225). If one accepts one of the other theories outlined above, the aim might be to change situational factors, personality characteristics, or attitudes. In either case the ultimate goal is to change behavioral intention and, subsequently, behavior. A persuasive message, then, tries to get at what is going on in people's heads.

As a general rule, there are at least three parts to any persuasive message. First, there is a set of arguments designed to persuade the listener or reader of the merits of the proposed course of action. Second, there is the factual evidence, which is selected and presented in such a way as to support the arguments. Finally, if the goal is behavior change and not just a change in attitudes or beliefs, there must be some recommendations regarding desirable forms of action.

In constructing a message the persuader must be aware of, and responsive to, several characteristics of his audience (Graber 1976, pp. 28–30). First, he must be aware that for any audience certain types of words are likely to elicit reasonably predictable responses. Thus the persuader must consider past responses of the audience in trying to estimate the most probable responses to a variety of options in message content (Barber 1977, p. 229). Second, the persuader must have some knowledge about the needs, conflicts, and psychic structures of the members of his intended audience. For example, Lyndon Johnson was one of the most successful persuaders ever to serve in the United States Congress. In reminiscing about their days together in Congress, Hubert Humphrey made the following observation:

> Early on in our Senate days, Lyndon started inviting me up to his office, and we'd talk. From the very beginning, it seemed to me, he understood the most intricate workings of the Senate. It seemed that he got there aware of the backgrounds of most of the members, and he took the trouble to find out about the ones he didn't know about. He was like a novelist, a psychiatrist. He didn't stop until he knew how to appeal to every single senator and how to win him over. [As quoted in Miller 1980, p. 181]*

Also different situations place different demands on the credibility of a persuasion attempt. What you can say credibly will depend greatly on what has already happened and how it has been perceived by the audience. Here attributions can play a crucial role. To a member of the Palestine Liberation Organization who sees the United States as an ally of Israel, any protestations of good faith on the part of U.S. officials are likely to be viewed with considerable suspicion, if not outright disbelief. Finally, it is necessary to consider the condition under which the message is received. If there is an international crisis, persuasive messages might more easily be seen as covertly threatening than would be the case in a period of international tranquility.

*This and following passages reprinted by permission of the Berkley Corp. from, *Lyndon: An Oral Biography.* Copyright © 1980 Merle Miller.

Some of the more common forms for messages involving political persuasion are the face-to-face discussion, speeches, advertising, and propaganda. Face-to-face political persuasion is powerful because it has an immediacy that allows the persuader to choose the time and method of proceeding based on a direct reading of the persuadee's motives, attitudes, and moods.

There is a feedback mechanism built into face-to-face encounters that allows the persuader to modify his approach, to meet any objections, and to emphasize the arguments that seem to be more effective at the time. Also there is that subtle social pressure on the persuadee that encourages him to yield in the interest of maintaining a harmonious social relationship with the persuader. Even physical contact can affect the outcome of a face-to-face encounter:

> When he talked to somebody, [Lyndon] Johnson used to get right up close and poke him in the chest; at the same time he would drop his head and cock it to one side and really come in to talk to you with his head coming in under your face. And he would poke you in the chest with his finger and cock his head under and look up at you and talk, all at the same time. [William Jorden, as quoted in Miller 1980, p. 213]

A popular, relatively new form of face-to-face discussion is the televised political debate (Kraus & Davis 1981). Debates are not new to the campaign process and can be traced rather far back in political history. Their current popularity can be traced to the televised Kennedy-Nixon debates during the presidential campaign of 1960. Unlike most other forms of face-to-face political persuasion, televised debates are not intended to persuade either of the participants. They constitute a persuasive appeal aimed exclusively at the audience, and in this way they are more similar to the second form of message, the political speech.

Political speech making is an old and honored form of political persuasion. In fact, it can be argued the "politicians rise to power because they can talk persuasively to voters and political elites" (Graber 1981, p. 195). Of course not all of this persuasive talk is in the form of speeches, but much of it is. Moreover, the political speech affords a politician the opportunity to get his message across not only by verbal communication but also by nonverbal communication. In fact, in any form of political communication in which the communicator can be seen by the audience persuasive appeal may rest as much on what is indicated nonverbally as on what is said verbally.

In political advertising the nonverbal message may be considered as important as the verbal message, and in some cases it may be the most important part of the commercial. Up until the 1920s political advertising played a relatively minor role in political campaigning. The emphasis was on mobilizing the faithful and getting out the vote. About 1916, though, the emphasis started to shift to a mode of political persuasion closely resembling marketing. Appeals began to be directed at the undecided and wavering voters as well as at the party faithful. Elections came to look more and more like sales campaigns (Nimmo & Savage 1976, pp. 7, 110–12). It is, however, not clear what all of this has accomplished, since it is difficult to separate the effects of commercials from the effects of other campaign efforts (Graber 1980, p. 156; Kaid 1981).

Much advertising is intended to project a certain image for the candidate. The public is to be persuaded that here is a person who looks suitable to be an incumbent of the contested office. It is aimed more at emotional reactions than it is at the audiences' rational processes or intellect (Nimmo & Savage 1976; Nimmo 1978). In contrast, issue advertising tries to appeal to cognitive functions in its persuasive messages. Its aim is to inform the potential voters about the candidate's position on issues and to persuade them to vote for the candidate on the basis of shared issue judgments. In their study of the 1972 presidential campaign Patterson and McClure (1976, p. 108) found that the political spot advertising was "a blend of soft imagery and hard issue material."

Finally, there is propaganda, a form of political persuasion specifically designed to appeal to large groups of people rather than individuals (Ellul 1973, p. 6; Nimmo 1978, pp. 102–3). The message in propaganda is perhaps the most simplified because if you have to appeal to a large undifferentiated audience, you must gear your message to the lowest common denominator. Thus Hitler observed:

> ... All effective propaganda must be confined to a very few points which must be brought out in the form of slogans until the very last man is enabled to comprehend what is meant by any slogan. If this principle is sacrificed to the desire to be many-sided, it will dissipate the effectual working of the propaganda, for the people will be unable to digest or retain the material that is offered them. [As quoted in Zimbardo et al. 1977, p. 32]

As a concomitant to this, propaganda is not designed to appeal to people's intellectual or rational faculties. Ellul, in fact, asserts that one of the effects of propaganda must be to short-circuit cognitive processes (1965, p. 27). The appeal to emotional processes is primary. Again, Hitler understood this well, affirming that the essence of propaganda is "a positive and a negative; love or hate, right or wrong, truth or lie, never half one thing and half the other" (as quoted in Maser 1971, p. 260). It is on this basis that many people draw a distinction between propaganda and education.

The presentation and content of propaganda also emphasize its emotion-based nature. Hitler was unrivaled in presenting his message in such a way as to appeal to the strongest emotions in his audience:

> Four nights later he addressed a large, excited throng at the Zirkus Krone. At 8:30 P.M. there was a shout from outside of "Heil Hitler!" and the band struck up a rousing march. Hitler entered, wrapped in trench coat, followed

by his entourage. He quickly strode down the aisle as the audience cheered, feet stamped. Once Hitler reached the platform there was abrupt silence. Then 200 Brownshirts marched in preceded by two drummers and the flag. The audience broke into thundering Heils and held out arms in Fascist salute. On the stage, Hitler stood stern-faced, his right arm out. The music mounted, flags passed by the stage, glittering standards with swastikas in wreaths and eagles, patterned after the banners of the Roman legions. The S.A. men took position below the stage except for flag- and standard-bearers riveted at attention behind the speakers.

At first Hitler spoke slowly, deliberately, then the words began tumbling out in a torrent. According to one police reporter, his gesticulations as he jumped excitedly back and forth fascinated "the spell-bound thousand-headed audience. When he is interrupted by applause, he extends his hands theatrically.". . . It was an inspirational exhibition, notable not for what he said but how he said it. [Toland 1976, pp. 302–3]*

This passage emphasizes the way in which Hitler was able to take advantage of the tendency of an emotion to diffuse through a crowd. Ellul points out that such an effect is not limited to people in face-to-face crowds, but can also happen when the group members are physically scattered (1973, p. 8); an example would be television viewers. The important thing is that each person feels some direct relationship with the propagandist and the experience activates his or her need for self-affirmation. Another factor operating here is group pressure (Asch 1973). Finally, there is preliminary evidence (Newton & Mann 1980) that the sheer size of a crowd matters—the larger the crowd, the more easily persuaded are its members.

Propaganda reaches people in terms of the collectivities in which they are socially embedded (Ellul 1973, pp. 6, 34, 50). These social groups can be of diverse types, including racial groups, religious groups, nationalities, and socioeconomic groups. The vital factor is that the members of the group share known or knowable beliefs, symbols, and myths and care what each other thinks. If they do and if the propagandist can gear his or her persuasive message to appeal to the emotions generated by these shared ideas, then the effectiveness of the resulting propaganda is likely to be enhanced.

In the modern world a political-persuasion message is most likely to be disseminated through the mass media. The relationship between the use of the mass media and the ability to persuade is a perennially controversial one (e.g., Lemert 1981). It should be kept in mind, however, that it is quite easy to overestimate the power of the media in the persuasion process (Graber 1976, p. 139; Patterson & McClure, 1976, pp. 21–24). There are two general types of media, the print media and the broadcast media. The print media are more suitable for persuasive messages that are inherently complex. They also produce a product that is somewhat less ephemeral than that of the broadcast media. A persuasive message or

*Excerpt from *Adolf Hitler* by John Toland. Copyright © 1976 by John Toland. Reprinted by permission of Doubleday & Company, Inc.

a piece of information in the print media can be more easily retrieved to be pondered over than it would be from the broadcast media. The broadcast media, however, reach the largest audience (Patterson & McClure 1976, p. 48). Broadcasting has an immediacy that newspapers and magazines lack. This means it is well suited for simple but emotionally evocative messages. There is evidence that television is the most important medium for political information and persuasion attempts (1973; Siune & Kline 1975, p. 72).

There is, unfortunately for the persuaders, a catch. Most persons expose themselves to the mass media primarily in the hope of being entertained. Their desire for information or enlightenment, when it exists, tends to be a secondary motivation. In fact, one of the reasons why presidential election campaigns tend to be relatively popular mass-media events is that they make rather good entertainment (Chaffee 1975; Stephenson 1967); they are contests and can on occasion have the entertainment value of a horse race or a game show. The general run of political-persuasion attempts, however, are much less popular. Even during election campaigns, how many voters use the time durng a television political spot in order to do a chore or go to the kitchen for a snack? On the other hand, though, the value of the media for persuasive appeals should not be underestimated, since there is evidence that appeals to specially targeted audiences can sometimes have considerable effect (Mendelsohn 1973).

Exposing an audience to a persuasive message is only part of the job. The persuader must also be concerned about how much people get out of what they see, hear, or read, not to mention how accurate their impressions are. This topic is not very well explored (Oskamp 1977, p. 147), so most estimates are more or less educated guesses. One thing is fairly well supported though; print-media consumers tend to comprehend more than consumers of the broadcast media (Wade & Schram 1969; Patterson & McClure 1976, p. 51). There is, however, a self-selection process operating here, which makes it difficult to distinguish media effects from audience characteristics. That is, print-media consumers may simply be different from broadcast-media consumers in ways that predispose them to get more out of whatever sources they attend to. Also there are very few people who expose themselves exclusively to only one type of media, and this adds a further confounding element.

Being exposed to a persuasive message and understanding that message are not sufficient for persuasion. It is still necessary for the persuadee to accept the message and for this acceptance to last long enough to be translated into some sort of behavior. Unfortunately, the most common finding in research on this topic is that there is no clear relationship between getting the persuasive message and some sort of behavior or attitude change (Fishbein & Ajzen 1975). In fact, the theory has been advanced that those persons most likely to comprehend the persuasive message are the least likely to be persuaded by it (McGuire 1968, p. 182). This is related to personality characteristics. For example, a person who has high self-esteem is likely to be quite able and willing to listen to and understand a political argument. The person who has low self-esteem, however, is more likely to be converted by the persuasion attempt.

There are various types of persuasion. A person may indicate that he has been persuaded in terms of expressed attitude or overt behavior, but not really change much internally. For example, a Soviet citizen may say and do all of the right things in order to get himself a membership in the Communist party—not through sincere conviction but to garner the rewards that come with party membership (Barry & Barner-Barry 1982, p. 112–13). This type of acceptance of a persuasive message is known as *compliance.* A person might, however, yield to a persuasive message in order to be like some admired individual or group in the hope that by so doing she will be liked and accepted by them. This is known as *identification.* For example, a Soviet citizen might become a dedicated member of the Communist party because of the political activism of a respected and loved teacher or relative. Finally, a person might *internalize* a message under conditions where that message is intrinsically rewarding or fits in well with one's other values. If a Soviet citizen has been properly socialized during childhood and early adulthood, aspiring to membership in the Communist party should come as an outgrowth of the human desire to express his value system through his behavior.

In general, the consensus of research to date seems to be that persuasive political messages tend to reinforce or marginally alter already held attitudes and behaviors rather than make any great change in them (Chaffee 1975, pp. 106–7). This is, however, a generalization to which one may find exceptions.

The *audience* for a persuasive message should never be regarded as a "terminal receiver of messages nor a passive object to be manipulated, but as an active participating agent in deliberations" (Bitzer 1981, p. 244). As was pointed out earlier, the persuasion process is one that is creative and transactional. The persuadee is an active participant, constructing meaningful responses to the persuasive message. This being so, it is fitting to conclude our discussion of the persuasive process with some consideration of the audience or, more correctly, the audiences at which political persuasion is commonly directed.

In considering the persuasion potential of any particular audience, one of the primary things to be considered is the involvement of those people in the political system or in some aspect of the political system. Most of the research on political involvement has been done in the context of political campaigns (Kaid 1981, pp. 259–61). These studies seem to indicate that a low level of involvement in politics makes an individual more susceptible to persuasion. Thus it makes sense to look at the people comprising the audience for political persuasion in terms of their involvement in politics.

Steven Chaffee, a communications specialist, has developed a typology of levels of orientation to a political system that is based on the level and type of involvement of citizens (Chaffee 1975, pp. 103–4). The least involved level are those he labels apathetics. Although they are supportive of the system in a diffuse way and they have minimal information, they can be characterized as passive. They have little interest in either the demands currently being made on the system or the decisions officials are making in response to those demands.

Next come the conservatives. They are also basically supportive, but they express their support in a somewhat more active manner, engaging in boosterism or Fourth of July patriotism. They are usually resistant to people who would make stressful new demands on the system. In short, they like things the way they are and try to discourage any political activity that holds the potential for substantial change. On the third level are persons who are highly concerned with the decisions being made by political officials—the outputs of the system. Those who follow politics quite closely without being directly involved are the inside-dopesters. Those who are directly involved in either carrying out or reacting to public policies are the Establishment. Finally, those who are involved not just with the outputs of the system but also with the inputs in terms of making demands on the system are referred to as the liberals or the radicals. They are liberals if they are basically reformist in orientation, accompanying their demands by strong basic support for the system. If their support is withheld, or at least suspended, pending satisfaction of their demands, they are the radicals.

Thus the typology moves from the apathetics who are least involved and who can probably be equated with the mass public mentioned in many studies to the highly involved liberals and radicals for whom politics approaches or is a way of life. If studies of noninvolvement hold true, the persons most easily persuaded should be the apathetics. There is, as a matter of fact, research evidence for this (Hoffstetter, Zukin, & Buss 1978; Patterson & McClure 1974, p. 128; Hoffstetter & Buss 1980; Rothschild & Ray 1974). Those least amenable to political persuasion would probably be the liberals and radicals, if only because they are likely to be engaging in political-persuasion efforts themselves. Thus as one moves up in levels of involvement, one meets an increasing vested interest in not being persuaded. The more involved you are, the more likely you are to have firmly held, well-examined beliefs and attitudes as well as definite habits of behavior. While becoming increasingly apt to be a political persuader yourself, you are less apt to be open to the blandishments of others.

What other characteristics increase or decrease one's persuadability? Given the demonstrated importance of party affiliation in the United States, it is probable that psychological tendencies such as selective perception would make the members of one party resistant to the persuasive efforts of the other party (Nimmo 1978, pp. 112–13). Also, Americans tend to have a positive bias. This is a tendency to give preferential attention to positive messages over negative messages (Sears and Whitney

1973, p. 272). This means that positive persuasive messages will be more likely to be effective than negative ones. Self-esteem has been mentioned at many points in this book and apparently is also significant here. The lower one's self-esteem, the more easy it appears to change one's mind and, perhaps, behavior (Nimmo 1978, p. 113). The less anxious one is, the easier it is to consider alternative views and try new behaviors. Bettinghaus (1973) found that people low in dogmatism or authoritarianism are more open to persuasion. Finally, those who tend to see the similarities, as opposed to the differences, in thinking about the world are more likely to be amenable to persuasive appeals.

SUMMARY

Communication is the means by which persuasion is both attempted and accomplished. Political communication is usually thought of in terms of verbal communication, but recently there has been an increased appreciation of the importance of nonverbal communication in influencing behavior in the political arena.

The process of persuasion is an extremely complex intentional activity that can be conceptualized as a creative transaction between two or more people based on shared meanings, symbols, or myths. The creation of these shared meanings, symbols, and myths is one of the outcomes of the political socialization process. The result of persuasion should be an effective change in behavior—not just a change in attitude. The Theory of Reasoned Action suggests that the way to accomplish this is to bring about a shift in the total set of underlying beliefs that are relevant to the behavior at issue.

Most psychological theories, however, have focused on attitude change. To date, consistency theories have sparked the most interest and research. They view the problem as one of inducing in the persuadee an awareness that there is some psychologically troubling discrepancy in his or her life. This will impel the persuadee to do something to remove or reduce the discrepancy. Consistency theories tend to deemphasize the importance of the persuasive communication and to emphasize more subtle social and psychological pressures operating on individuals. Another set of theories focuses on the functions which attitudes perform for the persons holding them. These functions include: 1) serving as a means for getting the desirable and avoiding the undesirable; 2) avoiding of realities which are threatening or unpleasant; 3) expressing one's central values and self-image and 4) giving us information we need to interpret things which we perceive as important. Thus, attempts to change attitudes must be sensitive to their functional significance for the person holding them.

Another set of theories on attitude change takes a social learning approach which holds that learning processes are responsible for both attitude formation and change. Thus, much emphasis is placed on the nature of the persuasive communication and the assertion that attempts to change attitudes must be associated with pleasant or rewarding consequences. Finally, there are attribution theories that see attitude change as a problem of creating a change in the persuadee's perception of the object of the attitude. The attributions at issue might or might not be accurate; it is sufficient that they will affect our attitudes, beliefs, and behavior if we regard them as accurate.

Persuasive communications normally have a set of elements which includes a source, the persuasive message itself, a medium through which the persuasive message is conveyed and an audience. In the case of political persuasion, the source tends to be the professional politician, the professional political communicator or the political activist. The political message generally contains a set of arguments, supporting evidence and recommendations regarding desirable forms of action. In the modern world, the medium is most likely to be the mass media which tends to bias the form the message takes in the direction of entertainment, rather than education. Exposure is not the end of the process; the message must be accepted and acted upon. The dynamics of this process are currently poorly understood, but it seems that persuasive political messages tend to reinforce or slightly alter already-held attitudes, rather than change them in a more dramatic way. Finally, the audience must be regarded as an active participant in the persuasion process—not a passive message recipient. Here the salience of and involvement in politics of the members of the audience seems to condition their responses to the message.

A DEMURRER

When all is said and done, however, there are some aspects of the persuasive process which are difficult, if not impossible, to capture by hard, cold analysis or theorizing. They are the unique things that people do. Take again the master persuader, Lyndon Johnson. Many of the strategies and techniques he used can be analyzed in terms of the variables discussed in this chapter. But some aspects were uniquely Johnsonian:

> When Johnson wanted to persuade you of something, when you got the "Johnson treatment," you really felt as if a St. Bernard had licked your face for an hour, had pawed you all over.
> When he was in the Senate, especially as majority leader, it was like going to the zoo. He never just shook hands with you. One hand was shaking your hand; the other hand was always some place else, exploring you, examining you.
> And, of course, he was a great actor, bar . . . none the greatest. He'd be feeling up Katharine Graham and bumping Meg Greensfield on the boobs. And at the same time he'd be trying to persuade you of something, some

times something that he knew and I knew was not so, and there was just the trace of a little smile on his face. It was just a miraculous performance. (Benjamin C. Bradlee, as quoted in Miller, 1980, pp. 212–13.)

The "Johnson treatment" was not the only factor that made Lyndon Johnson the most successful Senate majority leader of all time. He was also very gifted at that art that can be seen as the essence of the legislative process—the art of bargaining. This is obvious from the following tribute paid him by a fellow Senator, John Stennis—a colleague who disagreed with him on many an occasion:

> He was very skillful in taking an issue and getting a group, like a conservative group, to have a prominent conclusion about certain phases of the bill, and then he could influence the liberals with some other parts of it or some other emphasis. In that way he could gradually narrow the gap as far as getting the vote. . . . I think that was one of the great secrets of his success. [as quoted in Miller 1980, p. 218]

Given this, it seems appropriate at this point to turn our attention to a consideration of bargaining and negotiation.

7

BARGAINING AND NEGOTIATION:
Semiritualized Combat

The greater the scarcity of resources and the more complex the exchange arrangement, the more applicable is [the] concept of give-and-take bargaining. A marketplace must be created in which this intricate and continuous bargaining can take place. One important function of government is to establish such a marketplace where the many exchanges can transpire efficiently. In addition, the government lays down the ground rules for bargaining, so that all participants can communicate meaningfully. [Reilly & Sigall 1976, p. 8]*

What Reilly and Sigall fail to note in this comment is that governments can themselves be parties to a political bargaining process, as in the case of international treaty negotiations. In fact, bargaining is one of the most continuous and characteristic modes of behavior in political life. Political bargaining can involve something as simple as the attempt to resolve a dispute regarding stolen cattle in Tanzania (Gulliver 1979, pp. 194–96) or something as complicated as the attempt to get all the nations of the world to agree on a way of regulating the exploitation and conservation of resources in the world's oceans (Wertenbaker 1983, pp. 60–61).

These and all other cases of political bargaining have certain core

---

*Reilly & Sigall, *Political Bargaining*. ©1976, W. H. Freeman and Co.

characteristics in common. First, in all cases individuals are engaged in joint decision making over issues that are in conflict. Second, they are trying to resolve the conflict through a process of exchanging offers and counteroffers during which they attempt to narrow their differences and arrive at some mutually acceptable solution. Finally, this process is affected by the interactions between the characteristics of the individuals involved and the situations in which they find themselves.

In this chapter we will take a look at what contemporary researchers have found out about how bargaining and negotiation processes work using as examples instances of political conflict. Although some investigators (Druckman 1977; Rubin & Brown 1975) make no distinction between bargaining and negotiation, we will follow Gulliver (1979) in defining *bargaining* as the actual process of presenting proposals, counterproposals and concessions in the attempt to reach agreement on particular issues. *Negotiations* will be defined more broadly as the whole range of interactions between the parties to a conflict in which the central conflict-resolution mechanism is bargaining.

The following discussion of bargaining and negotiation essentially takes an information-processing approach. You will remember from Chapter 1 that this approach focuses on how people select information from the world around them, how this information is organized, how it is combined, and how new information is generated. The work of Glenn Snyder and Paul Diesing (1977) and particularly that of P.H. Gulliver (1979) have been especially influential in this regard, and the discussion below relies heavily on ideas developed by these social scientists.

At the outset it should be noted that both bargaining and negotiation involve *cyclical and developmental processes.* That is, they both unfold over time and involve learning, motivational, and cognitive processes. These intrapersonal processes interact with social and environmental factors. Thus in an international negotiation the parties are representatives of their respective governments, societies, and cultures. What they do is conditioned by their sense of how their important reference groups will respond. For example, Israeli negotiators continuously consider the reactions not only of the Israeli government but also of the Israeli people, Zionist groups in the United States, and the United States government itself (since it is Israel's chief weapons supplier). Less tangible factors such as cultural norms come into play as well. For example, during the Law of the Sea Conference representatives from African countries were influenced by the Organization of African Unity, but they were also influenced by widely shared normative standards regarding what constitutes a breach of faith. Personalities, relationships, cultures, and social and economic imperatives all form the interlocking framework in which political bargaining and negotiation take place.

One of the most trite observations about bargaining and negotiation is that they take place over time. Yet this turns out to be an important consideration. The heart of the bargaining process is a *sequential exchange* of proposal, counterproposal, concession, retraction, and compromise leading ultimately to some outcome—including the breaking off of negotiation. But what is this exchange really about? In effect, it is an exchange of *information.** No participant in a negotiation has perfect knowledge of the other. Rather, to get a better understanding of the intentions, preferences, strategies, and expectations of an opponent a negotiator has to give information to the opponent. This in turn creates opportunities for him to get feedback from the opponent, as the opponent reacts to the information. These reactions, then, create opportunities for the negotiator to adjust his own expectations, demands, and strategies. Each succeeding round requires both revealing information and processing new information from the opponent. Thus negotiations can be seen as a cyclical process (Gulliver 1979). At every turn of the cycle information is collected from the opponent, assessments are made of the current situation, and a reassessment is made of one's preferred alternatives and tactics as well as one's expectations regarding the opponent's future moves. All of this culminates in another tactical decision representing yet another offer, counterproposal, concession, retraction, or compromise.

An information-processing approach to bargaining and negotiation necessarily reminds us of our discussion of cognition in Chapter 1. As Snyder and Diesing point out (1976), any act of interpretation by a negotiator will involve some selectivity and organization based on the negotiator's implicit theories about negotiation and bargaining and about the political process in general. Interpretation will also depend on the attributions about the nature and causes of behavior of the other party (they call this latter the "image" of the other). Moreover, they note that interpretation will be further influenced by one's expectations concerning the behavior of the other. Thus, strategies and tactics (see following discussion) will be based on our predictions about how the other will respond to our behavior. Snyder and Diesing give some interesting examples of these concepts. For example, John F. Kennedy held the implicit theory that "most wars result from miscalculation." Dean Acheson (Secretary of State under president Truman) held that "concessions to an aggressive opponent will always be interpreted as weakness." Neville Chamberlain (Prime Minister of Great Britain during the late 1930s) believed that most, if not all, international conflicts could be "settled by calm, reasonable discussion" (p. 286). Implicit theories in conjunction with images lead to expectations for the behavior of the other. For example:

> In 1950, the German foreign office held the theories, based partly on some successful tactics by Bismarck, that opposing alliances can be broken by pressure and that other states can be attracted to an alliance with one's own

---

*The reader may wonder why negotiations are not "about" resources. Of course, the *outcomes* of political negotiations are indeed about resource allocation. The point we are making, however, is that the actual *process* of negotiation by which resources are ultimately allocated is about information as it is exchanged by specific parties and as these groups or individuals process that information (that is, select, organize, combine, and generate information).

state by demonstrations of power. The image of Britain was that of an untrustworthy ally who would renege on alliance obligations rather than incur
sacrifices. The first theory therefore applied to Britain and the Foreign Office "deduced" the expectation that Britain would back out of its . . . obligations to France under German pressure. (Snyder & Diesing 1976, p. 287)

This discussion leads us to the premise that participants in a negotiation are informationally dependent on each other (Kelley 1966). If we
think of negotiations in this way, we can see that there are always two
dilemmas for the parties. First, is the other's information a true reflection
of her underlying objectives? If not, how can one translate her pattern of
offers, proposals, and counterproposals into an accurate picture of where
she stands? This is Kelley's "dilemma of trust." Second, how much of
one's own intentions and objectives should be revealed? How much deceit
should be used? This is Kelley's "dilemma of honesty and openness." In
part, a successful negotiation outcome depends upon the resolution of
these dilemmas.

It follows that if participants are informationally dependent on each
other in negotiation and bargaining, they will have somewhat different
perceptions of the situation at different points in the process or sequence.
Thus what any given move means will depend on where it appears in the
negotiation and bargaining sequence (Gulliver 1979). For example, in his
study of the U.S.-USSR nuclear test ban negotiations of 1958–63, Jönsson
(1979) found that Soviet perceptions of tractability of the United States
government changed over time. Early in the negotiations the Soviets
viewed the U.S. as recognizing the two countries' common stake in a
cessation of nuclear testing. During the course of the negotiations they
seemed to see American test ban opponents as gaining the upper hand,
and their suspicions increased. The 1960 shooting down of the American
U-2 spy plane over the Soviet Union was a key catalyst in solidifying a
Soviet image of the U.S. as controlled by aggressive forces that were
actively trying to prevent a test ban agreement. Subsequently, at the time
of the Cuban missile crisis the Soviets seemed to take certain events, such
as the peaceful resolution of the crisis and a conciliatory speech by President Kennedy, as signs that more peaceful elements had again gained the
ascendancy and that cooperation was again possible.

Gulliver (1979) uses the term "phase" to denote different points in
the sequence of cycles. He argues that the developmental aspect of bargaining and negotiation refers to the changes in understanding during
each phase that are brought about by the processing or interpretation of
information from either inside or outside the negotiations. In our analysis
of political negotiation, we take Gulliver's sequence of phases as our
framework. As Gulliver points out, the phases are not empirically veri-
fied. Rather, they are derived from a descriptive and logical analysis of
the phases through which many negotiations pass. There is, therefore,
some degree of artificiality to this approach, since any particular negotiation might not proceed in such an ideal and complete fashion. This ap-

proach, however, does allow us to do two things. First, we can emphasize the sequential and time-bound nature of bargaining and negotiation processes. Second, we can highlight specific factors affecting these processes at a time in the sequence when they are most likely to be important. This latter point, though, comes with a caveat attached. While a given factor may be of particular importance in a given phase, most of the factors we will consider have some degree of importance in almost all phases. For example, the effect of constituency pressure may be of special importance during the initial presentation of demands (phase 4), but it is clearly relevant at every step in the process.

One final point needs to be made before we begin our phase-by-phase analysis. Conclusions about the nature of political bargaining and negotiation come from a variety of different sources. There is a lengthy and detailed body of data derived from laboratory experiments (e.g., Rubin and Brown 1975; Druckman 1977). There is also a somewhat smaller body of experimental data generated by simulations (e.g., Druckman 1968). Finally, there are numerous anecdotal and descriptive accounts of specific real-world negotiations at many levels of the political process, from labor negotiations to international negotiations (e.g., Newhouse 1972; Strobe 1979; Jönsson 1979; Allison 1971).

Are all of these accounts comparable? How generalizable to the real world are laboratory studies? Indeed, can we compare senators negotiating over how much money to allocate to one senator's pet project with strategic-arms-limitation talks where the fate of the world may hang in the balance? Given the state of research at this time, it is not possible to answer these questions. What we can do is to draw on all of these sources and to provide what seems like a coherent and reasonable account of the factors affecting the genesis, development, and outcome of bargaining and negotiation.

PHASE 1: BEFORE THE CURTAIN RISES

Why should people—or nations—enter into a bargaining relationship? If a conflict exists between or among parties, why should they choose to negotiate? Consider the lengthy negotiations that culminated in the Law of the Sea Treaty signed by a large proportion of the members of the United Nations in 1983. Early in the 1970s, many nations began to realize that (1) there were tremendous resources to be found on the bed of the ocean (other than the fish in the ocean itself), and (2) some countries were already beginning to exploit these resources. The latter was of particular concern for smaller, poorer nations, since it was the more advanced and affluent countries that were getting a head start. But even the larger countries were finding that they had similar designs on undersea resources and that those resources were limited. What alternatives were there to resolve these conflicts? One was to ignore the problem and to continue activities as before. But the diplomatic pressures were enormous. Also the countries that continued undersea exploitation of resources risked losing credibility within the world community and outright confrontation with other countries. Another alternative would have been to turn to some central decision-making body and to abide by its decisions. But so far the countries of the world have not been able to create such a central governmental body with the strength to back up its decisions. Finally, one nation might have tried to persuade all the others of the "rightness" of some particular allocation of resources. It is unlikely that such efforts would have succeeded, for each country was likely to come up with a plan biased by its own self-interest. Hence, the stage was set for some form of negotiation.

This example illustrates two points. First, negotiations typically occur when there is some degree of common, as well as conflicting, interest. The countries of the world have differing notions of what should be their piece of the pie. On the other hand, they have a common interest in avoiding war and the breakdown of international order. To put it another way, the parties to the conflict can be said to be *interdependent*. That is, neither side can receive its own desired outcomes without the cooperation or consent of the other. In his discussion of the Cuban missile crisis of 1962 Graham Allison emphasizes, quite eloquently, this aspect of the relationship between President Kennedy and the head of the Soviet government, Nikita Khrushchev:

> This nuclear crisis seems to have magnified both rulers' conceptions of the consequences of nuclear war, and each man's awareness of his responsibility for these consequences. This consciousness not only set each man apart from his associates; it set them apart in a way that left the two alone— together. For they were equally yoked with responsibility for irreparable consequences: either man could cause both to fail; each would have to cooperate if they were to succeed. Indeed, it is a central feature of the crisis that these two men were partners in a game against nuclear disaster. [Allison 1971, p. 212]

This is, perhaps, an extreme example of the degree of interdependence that may exist between and among the parties to a negotiation. Such interdependence may vary from extreme to moderate to almost nonexistent. For example, in the latter case one country may enter into negotiations with another country not because that other country has something of vital importance to offer but because the first country wants a platform for airing its position or interpretation of the situation. More typically, however, each party has some significant stake in what the other will do, be it relatively large or small. In other words, each party holds the key to achieving the goals of the other.

Obviously, this interdependence is not a sufficient condition for negotiation to occur. Frequently nations or people who would seem to have a common interest in avoiding violence begin fighting instead of negotiating. This leads to the second point. Parties to a relationship, such as negotiation, make a decision to enter that relationship based on their *preferred alternatives*, the set of possible ways in which they might obtain their desired ends—one of which is entering into the negotiating relationship. Thibaut and Kelley (1959) suggest that parties who enter into a relationship first compare where they are currently with where they want to be. Thus a nation that would like to avail itself of the resources contained in the seabed would compare each acceptable alternative with all the others in order to decide which are the most likely to lead to the achievement of a desirable level and type of access to seabed resources.

In the real world parties to a potential negotiation may not be entirely clear about their preferences. That is, they might not have a good idea of exactly what the payoffs might be or even how strongly they feel about each alternative. The evolution of the Strategic Arms Limitation Talks (SALT) between the United States and the Soviet Union offers an example of this point (Newhouse 1972). By the middle of the 1960s it had become apparent to Secretary of Defense Robert MacNamara that the two superpowers were poised for another major jump in arms spending. He was well aware of all the drain on national resources this would entail and also of the danger of a destabilization of the world order. It was also clear that the Soviet Union was struggling with the same issue. On the other hand, there was intense debate and political in-fighting between factions, both in the federal bureaucracy (including the military) and within Congress, on the wisdom of undertaking SALT. To simplify, the debate raged not only around whether negotiations should be the preferred way of dealing with the USSR but also around what the specific goals of such negotiations should be. For this reason Dean Rusk, the secretary of state, predicted that SALT would be "the world's longest permanent floating crap game." Apparently a similar debate took place within the Soviet Union.

Moreover, not only are the relative evaluations of preferences not necessarily clear or precise, but the preferences themselves may not be consistent with each other. To make things even more complicated, the preferred alternatives may change during the course of negotiations (Gulliver 1979, pp. 88–89). Interestingly, the process of negotiation itself may be seen as the continual refinement of preferences through a gradual clarification of one party's goals in relation to its perceptions of the behavior of the other party. This idea follows from the notion that negotiation essentially involves a process of information exchange.

Another important factor in the decision to enter negotiations is the *power differential* between the parties to a conflict. For example, during the nineteenth century labor unions in the United States were few and relatively weak. Employers could refuse to negotiate with them and, if the workers refused to work, could hold out (or bring in other workers) until economic privation forced the workers to return to their jobs—often under worse conditions than before. During the 1880s, however, the formation of the American Federation of Labor (AFL) marked a turning point (Truman 1971. p. 69). By 1902 the membership of the AFL exceeded one million. It became obvious to employers that the power of the unions was growing, and they gradually became more willing to negotiate. The first year of the Roosevelt administration also illustrates how extreme differences in power between parties to a conflict can affect the choice to negotiate. Roosevelt came into office in 1933 with an overwhelming Democratic majority in both the House and the Senate. The large amount of legislation passed during the first 100 days was made possible by the lack of any need to bargain, since the Republicans could be easily outvoted, both in committee and on the floor of Congress.*

Other factors may enter into a decision to negotiate. For example, the degree to which you know, or think you know, the other parties involved will affect the calculation. How strong are they? How needy are they? How trustworthy are they? Similarly, the effect that the pursuit of one's objectives will have on the continuing relationship with the other party will be a factor. Certainly, one strong country can "hog" the resources of the sea, but what effect will this have on its relationship with other interested countries in the future? What sort of risks are run by opting to refuse to negotiate? Further, a history of successful negotiation may play a role. If negotiation has yielded positive gains in the past, it is likely to be one of the parties' more preferred alternatives for resolving the conflict. In the same way, prior experience with conflict-resolution methods other than negotiation may play a part. Thus negotiations between countries or between parties within a country may seem preferable after the terrible results of violence have impressed themselves on the participants.

Finally, it should be noted that in the real world of politics bargaining may occur *along with* other modes of conflict resolution. Thus in the passage of a budget through Congress, it is almost always the case that bargaining occurs simultaneously with the use of a number of other strategies and tactics (Wildavsky 1984, pp. 63–126). It also takes place within microenvironmental and macroenvironmental conditions that make certain budgetary objectives easier to obtain than others. For example, in 1981 the Reagan administration came into office supported by a strong conservative coalition in Congress and spurred by a mandate to "put America's economic house in order" (Budgeting for America 1982, p. 1). A major element in Reagan's approach to economic recovery was the reduction of federal spending for social problems. In 1981, using the parliamentary device of reconciliation as a tool, the Reagan administration managed to cut billions of dollars from hundreds of federal programs, shift much of this money to the defense program, and use the budget process to make fundamental changes in the federal government's

---

*It should be noted that the sense of crisis and the need to "get things done" also contributed to this burst of legislative activity.

role. This was accomplished through a process that included not only bargaining but persuasion, parliamentary and legal manipulations, intrigue, fear tactics, media appeals, and many other methods.

Thus the decision to bargain or negotiate is usually a complex one in which the parties take into account many diverse and often conflicting factors. Also a decision to bargain or negotiate does not necessarily preclude the use of other conflict-resolution tactics and strategies to buttress the process and increase the chances that the parties will gain the maximum possible from the process.

PHASE 2: CHOOSING A SITE

Once the parties to a dispute have agreed to negotiate, it would seem that the choice of a place to negotiate would be easy. Yet location often turns out to be of critical importance, and negotiations have, on occasion, floundered over a failure to agree on where to hold them. There are a number of reasons for this. First, there may be actual physical dangers for some participants at a given site. In 1983 the various parties to the conflict that was then raging in Lebanon agreed to negotiate. They chose Geneva, Switzerland, because negotiations in Lebanon were impossible; there was literally no place that was sufficiently "neutral." Everywhere there were groups and factions with strong hatreds and a willingness to use violence against one or another of the negotiators.

Choice of site is also important because of the significance of the effects of *territoriality* on the negotiation process. Territoriality refers to that physical space a person or group regards as "theirs," which they would defend if it were to be intruded upon by others (Scheflen & Ashcraft 1976). Research has shown that individuals feel more confident and relaxed, and most importantly, more in control when on their own territory. Similarly, people on the territory of others are likely to feel less in control, less relaxed, and less comfortable (Conroy & Sundstrom 1977; Dyson-Hudson & Smith 1978; Edney 1975; Fried & DeFazio 1974, and Vanden Berghe 1977). In a laboratory study of negotiations, Martindate (1971) found that bargainers were more assertive on their "home turf" and less on their opponent's territory.

In short, place may affect the psychological climate of the negotiations to the advantage of one party or another. George Ball has provided an interesting analysis of Richard Nixon's problems in traveling to China for the first time in 1972. It illustrates the implications of territorial relationships:

> Because it was considered an act of grace for the Emperors of China to grant any foreign visitors passage to Peking, it was understood that they come as supplicants bearing tribute. This traditional Chinese arrogance toward foreigners points up at least a theoretical risk in the President's trip: that the Chinese leadership might, either during the visit or beforehand

deliberately take some action to embarrass the United States. . . . it is this possibility which points up one of the costs of summitry, for during the period that a summit meeting is pending . . . the President becomes, in effect, a hostage to the situation. . . . [As quoted in Ruben & Brown 1975, pp. 82–83]

The psychological climate of negotiations may also be affected by the symbolism inherent in the physical arrangements of the actual bargaining. For example, the participants in the Vietnamese peace talks, held in Paris in 1969, took several months to resolve the issue of just where individuals representing different groups would sit during the sessions. Of particular concern was the fact that the North Vietnamese did not recognize the South Vietnamese government as legitimate. They therefore balked at having the South Vietnamese sit side by side with the American negotiators, asserting that this would imply the same degree of legitimacy. Similarly, the South Vietnamese did not recognize the National Liberation Front as an equal partner in the negotiations. In time a complex arrangement was worked out; South and North Vietnamese sat at certain angles to each other (Zartman 1974). Although there is no direct research on the effects of proximity on negotiations, there is much evidence, both observational and laboratory, that indicates that people with different kinds of interaction goals (e.g., competitive versus cooperative) will want to sit at different distances from one another or at different angles in relation to each other (Sommer 1965).

Agreement over the site, since it involves informational exchange, is in effect the beginning of negotiation. The willingness or intransigence of one or another party during the process of choosing a site may reveal some thing about that party's expectations and preferences. It also may be a first tactical move, which it is hoped will reveal something about how the other party is likely to respond later in the bargaining. Indeed, it may provide information about the probable nature of the other party's opening position (e.g., extreme or moderate).

PHASE 3: DEFINING THE AGENDA

It may seem odd that the agenda should be a problem; don't the parties know what the conflict is about and what issues need to be resolved? In fact, however, the question of the content of the agenda not only is a problem at the outset but may continue to be a problem throughout the negotiations. A not unfamiliar scenario in political negotiations (and one that can lead to a breakdown) may go like this: The initial issue at stake is fairly clear—say, proposed legislation funding the acquisition of additions to a wildlife sanctuary. Subsequently, however, this may be augmented by dormant issues (such as concerns about particular endangered species), new details (such as disagreement about how certain sections of the provision should be worded), or ideological concerns (such as conservation versus development). When this happens, other people may insist on becoming part of the bargaining, either in conjunction with the original parties or as parties in their own right. These new parties, then, may want to introduce other issues, particularly ones that reflect the special interests about which they or their groups are concerned.

Agendas for political negotiations are often complicated in this way because even very closely defined issues may have the potential for "spread." In short, the *manifest* conflict to which the negotiations are originally directed may mask one or more *latent* or hidden conflicts. For example, in the early 1980s the problem of huge federal deficits was of considerable concern to both the executive and the legislative branches of the U.S. government. Under these conditions spending money for any project, however worthy, immediately became entangled in larger philosophical and practical issues related to the size of the budget deficit and in turn the effect of the deficit on the nation's economic health. Thus it can be said that the issue of agenda formation is never completely finished. As problems, particularly complex ones, become more clearly defined during the bargaining process, one or another party may want to add new items to the agenda. Indeed, including new items in the agenda may be a tactic to influence the process itself.

Since the way an agenda is defined will, of course, affect the way negotiations are carried out and the outcomes of those negotiations, we might ask what it is about the issues on an agenda that might be important factors in affecting the course of negotiations. First, there is the problem already alluded to, namely, *single versus multiple issues.* Although we have introduced the problem above, we need to point out that the more issues there are on an agenda, the greater the time that it will probably take to conclude negotiations successfully. When there is a time limit this becomes a problem in and of itself. Time limits or time pressures have a marked effect on the likelihood of agreement as well as on bargaining aspirations, demands, and bluffing. The relationship, however, between the number of issues and time is not an absolute. Other factors may affect the time needed to reach agreement. For example, when issues are perceived as exceptionally important in terms of their payoffs (arms negotiations and national survival, for instance), the parties may be prepared to take an exceptionally long time to reach agreement. The U.S. and the USSR have been engaged in arms negotiations more or less continually for over twenty years.

As the number of issues in a dispute grows, there is the impetus to differentiate between the issues on some basis (Rubin & Brown 1975, p. 147). How might issues be differentiated? Frequently this is done by creating subsets of related issues and treating them as one (e.g., all matters having to do with fringe benefits in a labor contract). The subsetting of issues would seem to be increasingly effective as the number of issues increases. Because there has been little research on this it is not clear when pressures for differentiation begin to operate (at five, ten, fifteen, or twenty issues?). Also, differentiating may be dependent, as well, on both the personal characteristics of the negotiators and situational factors—not to mention their interaction. For example, cognitive factors related to organization of information may affect the number of issues negotiators can comfortably deal with. Moreover, the sets of issues that are grouped together may reflect the ease with which these issues can be perceived as similar.

The differentiation of issues may also occur as a function of the scale of value appended to each issue. That is, one might put together issues that seem of minor importance and thus differentiate those few issues that are perceived to be of substantially greater importance. Obviously, the magnitude of the issue at stake is a function of the importance either or both parties to the conflict give it. One factor may alter this ranking. Fisher (1964) notes that overtly tangible issues may implicitly be symbolic of intangible issues such as pride, honor, group status, or individual respect. This may alter the magnitude of an issue all out of proportion to its tangible value. For example, the history of conflict over national boundaries in the Middle East has been a long and often bloody one. Much of the time the parcels of land in dispute have had little or no intrinsic value but were of high symbolic importance to the opponents.

The question of *tangible versus intangible issues* turns out to be of particular importance in political negotiations. Characteristically, agendas are about specific tangible issues, such as how certain resources could be allocated and which solution would satisfy interest-group demands. Intangible issues, however, involve such factors as interest-group honor, self-esteem, respect, face, status, or "appearances," which are often implied by the tangible issues or become imposed on them. What affects the emergence of intangible issues? At the stage of agenda formulation, each party often has stereotyped expectations and perceptions of the other. Harsanyi (1962) calls these "stereotyped utility functions." These are the expectations parties to a conflict have regarding what they may be able to get from each other. Of particular importance is the perceived status or power position of the other. Where status distinctions are unclear, contested, or viewed as illegitimate, intangible issues are likely to be imposed on the tangible ones (ibid.).

The importance of intangible issues is brought out by events that took place during the last stages of the Cuban missile crisis (Allison 1971, pp. 220–27). After sending President Kennedy a conciliatory private letter that suggested that the Soviet Union would remove the missiles if the U.S. would end the blockade and promise not to invade Cuba, Khrushchev issued a public letter that contained the following proposal:

> We agree to remove those weapons from Cuba which you regard as offensive weapons. We agree to do this and to state this commitment in the United Nations. Your representatives will make a statement to the effect that the United States, on its part, bearing in mind the anxiety and concern

of the Soviet state, will evacuate its analogous weapons from Turkey. [U.S. Department of State 1962, p. 743]

Since the missiles in Turkey had been determined to be obsolete, and since President Kennedy had twice ordered their removal, acquiescing to this demand would not have meant any significant loss in military strength to the U.S. or to NATO. However, this option was rejected because it was felt by several influential members of the decision-making group that the Soviets would see the removal of the weapons as proof of American weakness. In addition, it was felt that such a concession would cause the United States' European allies to suspect that America would sacrifice their security to protect its own interests and safety.

In this example Kennedy also showed his sensitivity to the issues of status and face, repeatedly avoiding moves that would damage Khrushchev's pride or face (Allison 1971, p. 214). Subsequently, he stated in his celebrated American University speech: "Above all, avert those confrontations which bring an adversary to the choice of either a humiliating defeat or a nuclear war" (as quoted in Allison 1971, p. 214). The perception of justice is critical. If the other side is perceived to be unjustly demanding, if the other side is seen as asking for more than what they deserve, intangible issues related to honor, self-esteem, and respect are likely to emerge (Rubin & Brown 1975, p. 132). Notice that while this is clearly a factor in actual negotiation, it is also a factor in agenda preparation. That is, if one or the other party anticipates unfairness, intangible issues may affect the setting of the agenda.

In addition, if either party anticipates that the other will attack its status, esteem, or public image, it may adhere to the agenda more rigidly in order to preserve the appearance of strength. This can be less than productive, since "looking strong" can lead to competitive, threat-oriented, exploitative behavior during the bargaining process (Deutsch & Kraus 1962). Moreover, such perceptions are conditioned on the image each party wants to project during the negotiation—which in turn is dependent upon the role of their political constituency or audience. To put this another way, the negotiators may want to initially appear as tough as possible to satisfy the demands of those they represent and to assure them that their interests will be adequately represented at the bargaining table.

In the negotiations between the Lebanese government and the Israeli government in April 1983 the tangible issue was withdrawal of Israeli troops from Lebanon. In this situation there was a clear and significant power differential between the parties. The Lebanese government was weak and admittedly represented only a small fraction of the Lebanese people. The Israelis had recently fought their way to the Beirut area and had decimated the Palestine Liberation Organization. At that point they controlled a large portion of the country. Within this context the Lebanese government sought to limit the discussions strictly to the question of Israeli withdrawal. It did not want to deal with the related question of recognition of Israel. That was too dangerous, since Syria (which occupied another large portion of Lebanon) and the other Arab countries were adamant that Lebanon not give formal recognition to Israel. Israel, on the other hand, was eager to have the Lebanese government go on record as formally recognizing Israel as a sovereign state. To this end the Israelis insisted that the agenda also contain such issues as trade and the exchange of ambassadors.

Although these issues were tangible and seemingly straightforward, intangible issues transformed them. Lebanon, in the low status, low power position (and threatened by its Arab neighbors), had to maintain its opposition to broadening the agenda, for the sake of both its honor and its fragile existence. The Israelis, in the more powerful, dominant position, also had much invested in recognition as a sovereign state by Lebanon. Thus much of the initial bargaining was about the agenda. It is reflective of the relative power positions of the two parties that the Israelis were able to force some concessions about issues such as trade. Interestingly, Israel did not insist on formal recognition; the Israelis apparently decided that formal recognition would result in the collapse of the nascent Lebanese government—a collapse that would not be in Israel's best interests.

It appears, then, that much bargaining goes on before the participants actually sit down to the formal or informal exchange of proposals, compromises, reformulations, and concessions. In fact, bargaining about the agenda may continue throughout the course of the negotiations. Moreover, stereotyped perceptions and indirect communication lead to what we will call internal negotiation, that is, attempts at formulating proposals by each party based on sources of information other than direct, face-to-face bargaining. At some point, however, phase 3 yields to phase 4. Each side must formally present its ideas for solutions to the conflict. In order to understand what happens in phase 4, it is important to recall that negotiations are, in essence, the exchange of information and the processing of information. Opening moves, then, are important because they convey a multitude of signals.

PHASE 4: THE OPENING GUNS

What kind of information is conveyed by opening proposals or offers? To answer this question, we first must understand the *role* of the negotiator more clearly. When negotiators begin "actual negotiations"—or even before this phase—the role of negotiator becomes extremely important to the process. This role is inherently conflictual. It is a "boundary role" in the sense that the negotiator must respond to demands from the group she represents and, at the same time, be responsive to the demands of the other negotiators. There is a wide range in the extent to which this "boundary conflict" restricts the behavior of the negotiator. On the one hand, negotiators may come to the bargaining table ready to exercise a great deal of discretion in order to get their constituency the most advantageous agreement possible. On the other hand, negotiators may come with fairly rigid instructions that allow little latitude for the individual to bargain more creatively. For example, Fred Ikle and Edward Rowney, negotiators for the United States in the abortive arms control discussions with the Soviet Union in 1983, found themselves in trouble with the Reagan administration for advancing proposals made in one-on-one negotiations with their Soviet counterparts.

Between these two extremes is an area in which the skilled use of *impression management* can be crucial. Ideally, the negotiator wants to convey an impression that her moves coincide with her constituency's expectations, while at the same time conveying an impression to her opposite number that she is willing to yield up to a certain point. In short, she must be firm without appearing to be too rigid, and willing to yield without appearing too conciliatory. This is the "paradox of negotiation." In order to appear competent, tough, and representative of constituent interests, negotiators may resort to various face-saving techniques. To pick one example, Ikle (1964) describes "hedging against failure," commonly used by international negotiators. This may involve not discussing specific issues, withholding information, and emphasizing one's magnanimity, morality, or willingness to sacrifice when making concessions. It may also take the form of bluffing or deception in order to ward off possible damage to one's personal or national image or reputation (Brown 1977, p. 279). Attempts to forestall negotiations by procrastinating, holding unduly long caucuses, perseverating on irrelevancies, creating distractions, and bringing in side issues—all of these may represent attempts to keep an impression of "weakness" from leaking out.

Fear of losing face, then, may lead to a rigid, unyielding stance. What can be done about this problem? Both parties must be sensitive to this possibility and find ways of creating face-maintaining or face-restoring situations (Brown 1977). In some sense, what the other party does in response to a bargainer's moves may have an influence. For example, concessions that are responsive to the intent of the other are likely to lead to her feeling more capable and effective. This, in turn, may lead her toward more cooperative behavior. Rubin and Brown (1975) suggest that bargainers are most likely to behave cooperatively when they think they are able to exert systematic influence on the other party. "By making positive concessions, bargainers may communicate their perception of the other as a strong, worthy, and tough opponent and in so doing increase the likelihood of inducing positive concessions in return" (Rubin & Brown 1975, p. 278).

The answer to our initial question—what kind of information is conveyed by opening proposals or offers?—is that first and foremost, an opening move conveys an image of the kind of negotiator a participant will be. Will he try to drive a hard bargain? Will he work toward a more cooperative outcome? Will he be competitive and dogmatic? Does he convey a suspicious or trusting image of the other party? Does he pay due respect to the other's "pride"?

We have said that concessions which are responsive to the intent of the other are likely to lead to the other side's feeling more competent and effective. But this gets us ahead of the game. What about opening moves?

One of the major findings in the experimental study of negotiations is that early cooperative moves tend to elicit greater trust, which encourages cooperative bargaining. Early competitive moves, on the other hand, tend to induce mutual suspicion leading to a less cooperative relationship (e.g., Deutsch 1967). This finding presents a curious problem. In the real world negotiations tend to open with assertive, dogmatic, and highly polarized offers—often accompanied by the immediate rejection of the other's offer as absurd and impossible to meet.

Moreover, along with the establishment and embellishment of maximum positions, there are often "shows of strength and suggestions or forthright assertions of resoluteness and threat" (Gulliver 1979, p. 137):

> Comments are made on the alleged moral and practical weakness of the opponent and the errors or mendacity in his statements. Personal and group animosities are often brought into the open: animaversions to social, moral and personal faults in *ad hominum* attacks on members of the other party, in contrast to the high motives and meritorious qualities of one's own party. Ideological banners are waved (e.g., workers' rights, the moral unity of one's own group, ideal norms of neighborliness) and supporting references are made to cultural rules, ethical standards, and evocative symbols. . . . There is a wide and free-ranging reference to, and partisan exposition of, everything on the agenda and, in effect, of more or less everything touching the parties' statuses, relationships, past histories, and future prospects. [ibid.]*

One sees this in disputes over dowries in certain African societies as well as in American labor negotiations. Yet if the data suggest that the way toward cooperative problem solving is to begin with more reasonable demands, why is that suggestion seldom followed?

This question penetrates the core of the negotiation process. First, it is at this phase that both sides are least sure of where the other side is in terms of what they might be willing to accept. Both sides are likely to find it to their advantage not to set limits that might later seem too narrow. Since neither side has complete knowledge of what the other might be willing to concede, it makes subjective sense to start at the extremes and to work toward some middle ground. Thus there is a tendency to bring in everything possible rather than forfeit advantage at a later time.

All these reasons, therefore, may account for the disparity between the experimental literature and studies of "real world" negotiations. Rubin and Brown (1975) offer an interesting explanation for finding that, in real world contexts, extreme opening offers lead to more satisfactory outcomes. Their explanation centers on the informational value of such

---

*Reprinted with permission.

moves in a context where there is partial and vague information about the other. The opening offer is designed primarily to explore the dimensions of the ground upon which negotiation can occur. Thus, by making an extreme offer a bargainer does three things (see also Ramberg 1977, p. 687). First, more time is gained to assemble information about the other's perceptions and expectations. Second, he provides the other with valuable information about the range of possible expectations for payoffs. Finally, an extreme move presents an image of the negotiation process that indicates that no exploitation will be tolerated.

The final point has particular relevance not only to the question of the presentation of the self but also to the question of the appearance of the negotiators to their constituencies. Even during the budget-cutting fervor in Congress in 1981 most members were careful not to bargain away important pork-barrel projects (*Washington Post,* January 9, 1983, p. A1). Even the most avid conservative Reagan allies "dipped into the 'pork barrel' and pulled out a variety of parochial projects, making sure that new courthouses, dams, highways, inland waterways, and nuclear plants continue[d] to find their way into their home states" (Howie Durtz, as quoted in Ripley 1983, p. 313).

Although there is much anecdotal evidence concerning the importance of a negotiator's constituents, there are few empirical studies. Negotiators, however, do seem to need to get a positive evaluation by their constituents (Brown 1968). In American society this is associated with appearing to be competent, strong, effective, and resistant to exploitation by others (Deutsch & Kraus, 1962). This leads to "the paradox of negotiation" (Rubin & Brown 1975). One must retain the appearance of being unyielding while making concessions in order to reach agreement. In part, then, the posturing of the fourth phase may be accounted for by the need of the negotiator to conform to the image of the "good" representative of her constituency. In other words, the accountability of the negotiator to a constituency generates strong pressures toward loyalty, advocacy, and commitment to that constituency's preferred position (Druckman 1967).

Therefore, the opening of formal bargaining and the unveiling of first moves has a ritual character to it. This may be why so much apparent antagonism, flag-waving, and so on, may go on without an immediate rupture in the negotiations. Both sides recognize that it is necessary to establish the credibility of the negotiator "back home" and that extreme moves reflect an attempt to define the range for the coming bargaining. This is perhaps the reason why separation, difference, and antagonism— social distance—is emphasized during this phase. Ultimately, it clarifies the movement of the parties toward each other as well as more clearly defining the field within which bargaining will take place.

Finally, the extremity of initial offers affects an individual's latitude of acceptance or rejection (see Chapter 5). If the negotiator feels constrained to begin by making an extreme offer, one it is clear the other side cannot accept, it may also be the case that, at this stage in the process, the kinds of proposals the negotiator is willing to accept are in fact fewer than will be the case as the negotiator later moderates his position. As pointed out earlier, the degree to which the person is willing to moderate his position may depend on his degree of involvement in the issue. But to understand how positions are moderated, we must turn our attention to the next phase.

PHASE 5: NARROWING THE DIFFERENCES

At some point the negotiators finally get down to the serious business of bargaining, moving from the expression of antagonism and posturing to the coordination of activities so that differences can be narrowed and some agreement reached. At its core the bargaining process consists of the "trading" of a sequence of offers and counteroffers. Each side works toward a better understanding of the real intentions, expectations, limitations, and levels of aspiration of the other side. These are revealed by the "moves" (offers and counteroffers) and by the behavior accompanying these moves (e.g., threats and promises). In turn, each side makes continual adjustments in its own expectations and levels of aspiration.

How do bargainers narrow their differences? What factors affect this process? We might first distinguish between the view that parties to the conflict have of each other in general (that is, based on long-term experiences) and those views parties have of each other in the immediate situation. Snyder & Diesing (1976) call these the "background image" and the "immediate image" of the other. The relationship between them is probably always important, but particularly so in international conflict where both parties perceive that a crisis is occurring. In circumstances of this sort, there is likely to be little relationship between the negotiator's image of the opponent and the opponent's image of herself. Thus both parties are likely to perceive their actions in the crisis as legitimate expressions of their interest while seeing the other side as pursuing illegitimate aims. In such circumstances, interpretations of the other side's behavior are likely to lead to increased mistrust and polarization.

This discussion suggests that how differences are narrowed depends on the climate of trust or mistrust generated by implicit theories, images, and expectations. But precisely what do negotiators do that generates information for the other party, and how do participants respond to this information? Let us distinguish first between a tactic and a strategy. A *tactic* refers to a specific position to be taken or a specific maneuver to be made at some point in the sequence. A *strategy* consists of, or describes, a series of organized bargaining tactics to be used throughout the process.

One tactic is the tough initial offer in which much is asked and little given. A second tactic has to do with the size of concessions. Generally, bargainers are likely to make small concessions if possible—particularly if the goal is to obtain outcomes equal to or better than one's opponent. In other words, as with hard-line opening proposals, the bargainer tries not to "give too much away." Making large concessions leads to several risks, including having too little to bargain with later and giving the appearance of being exploited. A third tactic has to do with the finality with which offers and concessions are made. This is related to the degree of cooperativeness with which the bargaining process has been approached. Making and withdrawing offers can be used as a test of the other's intentions and limits.

Finally, promises and threats may be seen as tactics, usually employed along with offers and concessions. Promises and threats are common in negotiations (Pruitt 1981; Rubin & Brown 1975; Deutsch 1973). The reason is obvious. The parties to a conflict have the power to inflict both harmful and beneficial outcomes on each other. Thus the threat to leave or the promise to remain in the negotiation can become a major tactic. In 1983 during arms-control negotiations between the U.S. and the USSR, the U.S. deployed medium-range Pershing II and Cruise missiles at certain NATO bases in Europe. The Soviet negotiators threatened to walk out of the negotiations if the missiles were deployed, and when the missiles actually arrived at the bases, they walked out of the negotiations on medium-range missiles. Subsequently, they also "suspended" talks on limiting intercontinental nuclear weapons (*Washington Post*, December 9, 1983, p. A1). American negotiators responded by calling the Soviet move a bargaining tactic and by expressing confidence that the Soviets would soon return.

Threats and promises, therefore, convey information about a party's preferences and intentions. For example, the willingness to back up an offer with a threat may convey information about seriousness of intention. Further, succeeding moves (after a threat is made) may give some information about the readiness of the other to bluff, which in turn may say something about their intentions, tactics, and strategy.

A good example of the complex pattern of threats and promise, as they may be employed sequentially, and their effects is the pattern of negotiations over the threat by the Chinese government in 1958 to take over the islands of Quemoy and Matsu off the coast of China. These islands had been occupied and fortified by the government of Taiwan (then Formosa). The mainland Chinese began to bomb these islands on August 4, 1958, and intensified the bombing in late August. As the bombings intensified, the U.S. government made more threatening comments, coupled with assertions that defense of the island was part of our defensive commitment to the government of Formosa. In early September, Secretary of State John Foster Dulles made explicit that the United States would defend the islands, and hinted that this defense might involve bombing the mainland. At the same time, Dulles made clear that the United States wanted to resume talks at Warsaw with the Chinese government. Thus, increasingly escalated threats were coupled with a promise of accommodation. The Chinese temporarily halted the bombardment and agreed to resume talks. However, the crisis did not pass until the United States helped break a blockade of the islands, while at the same time disavowing any commitment to help the Formosan government return to the mainland and further hinting that cessation of the bombardment might lead to the withdrawal of Formosan forces from the islands (Snyder & Diesing 1977, pp. 258–60).

Notice the probable information conveyed by actions of both parties, and the probable interpretations made by each. The United States responded to the Chinese as if the resolve of the United States was being tested. They presented a "tough" face but coupled this toughness with a conciliatory offer. After the initial threat, succeeding moves were designed to communicate to the Chinese that the United States was not "bluffing" but was in earnest about the commitment to Formosa (and the islands). On the other hand, in order to give the Chinese a way to back out, the United States made a clear commitment not to support an invasion of the mainland, and offered the "carrot" of a possible withdrawal of Formosan forces from the island.

The terms of a promise may also communicate how important the particular offer is to the other party. For example, during the Cuban missile crisis President Kennedy refused publicly a Soviet proposal that the U.S. remove its missiles in Turkey if the Soviets removed their offensive weapons from Cuba. Using his brother Robert Kennedy as intermediary, however, he indicated to Khrushchev that within a short time after the resolution of the crisis the Soviet leader could be sure that the missiles would be quietly removed from Turkey. Thus by making a private promise along with his public offer of a solution, President Kennedy signaled to the Soviets his high level of concern that the crisis be resolved peacefully.

In short, the timing, nature, and frequency of threats and promises may provide an important avenue for gauging the real intentions of the other party. In addition, because threats and promises tend to personalize a bargaining relationship, they may also convey information about how one side perceives the other (e.g., that the other side is exploitable).

Threats and promises tend to come into play when bargainers perceive that they cannot exert influence in other ways. Thus the use of threats or promises may signal an impending breakdown or impasse. The research literature indicates that promises elicit more positive responses than threats and increase the likelihood of reaching a mutually favorable agreement (Rubin & Brown 1975). The research also indicates, however, that threats are often effective in eliciting further concessions and counteroffers. This curious contradiction can be explained by the vulnerability of both parties. They are in the negotiation because they see this as the best of their alternatives. Therefore, any threat jeopardizes the negotiation process itself and may elicit responses designed to save the negotiations.

Agenda manipulation strategies. Bargainers need to concern themselves with two sorts of strategic problems. First is the problem of handling multiple issues on the agenda. Differentiating the agenda in various ways affords both sides an opportunity to begin bargaining. During the process of narrowing differences, differentiating issues may seem an attractive way of proceeding. The bargainers can decide which issues are the one or two most important and deal with them first. The expectation is that if these can be resolved, the other issues will quickly fall into place. Of course, a major problem here is agreeing on what are the more important issues. In turn, this may be affected by the extent to which intangible issues come into play. Alternatively, the parties can agree to deal with the simpler issues first. This strategy often recommends itself because less important issues are less likely to be weighted with intangibles and therefore are usually less complex. Moreover, one or another party may simply withdraw an issue or quickly accede to demands. This may provide a climate of cooperation easing the problems of getting agreement on the more difficult issues.

Bargainers can also opt for a simple agenda strategy. Here the issues are taken one at a time with no concern for degree of importance or difficulty. This is the least desirable kind of strategy since there is both the problem of order and the threat that the bargaining can reach an impasse on a given item. Indeed, such a strategy often affords any party that wishes to slow down the negotiations process an opportunity to make an issue of any agenda item. A simple agenda strategy is sometimes used when other ways of approaching the agenda cannot be worked out. At least it offers the opportunity to begin the process, although it is likely that eventually the sides will want to manipulate the order of priority.

Another strategic approach is to try to reduce all items on an agenda to a single common objective, such as monetary profit or honor. During the Cuban missile crisis the overriding objective of both sides became avoiding nuclear war. Such a strategy requires that the bargainers downplay certain attributes of issues. Also, a single common objective is extremely likely to take on intangible values. Although this strategy is infrequently used, it may be particularly effective where a dangerous or costly impasse is threatened because it can help to clear away much of the complexity of the typical-bargaining situation (Gulliver 1979).

Finally, bargainers may engage in the trading of issues, i.e., "I will agree to your position on issue A if you will agree to my position on issue B." This process, known in Congress as logrolling, is illustrated in the following comment by former Senator Sam Ervin: "I got to know [Senator] Milt Young very well. And I told Milt, 'Milt, I would just like you to tell me how to vote about wheat and sugar beets and things like that, if you just help me out on tobacco and things like that' " (quoted in Ripley 1983, p. 129). Such packaging of issues is attractive because it can signal significant concessions. At the same time it can be a way of probing the other party for areas of potential concession and flexibility.

Offer and concession strategies.   But agenda-manipulating strategies are not the only ones bargainers must consider. A second class of strategies deals with the pattern of offers and concessions. Hamner & Yukl (1977) have described four types of "offer" strategies: the tough strategy, the soft strategy, the moderately tough strategy, and the fair strategy.

The *tough strategy* suggests that one will obtain higher pay-offs by opening with a tough offer, making very small concessions (always smaller than the opponent's), being unyielding for as long as possible, and having a high level of aspiration. Use of such a strategy requires that one make a concession only if the other makes no concession. If success follows (i.e., the opponent makes a concession), then no further concessions should be made. If failure follows (i.e., the opponent makes no concessions), then the negotiator should make further small concessions to the level of aspiration and stop. If the opponent makes concessions, then one should raise one's level of aspiration. This strategy is likely to project an image of toughness and enable the bargainer to make concessions without going below her aspiration level. Also, as in all bargaining, the strategy may yield information encouraging the formation of more realistic levels of aspiration.

The *soft strategy*, on the other hand, suggests that one side should unilaterally initiate small concessions and continue to do so even if the other side does not immediately respond with concessions. Thus while this strategy is similar to the tough strategy in suggesting that a small concession be made if the other side does not make one, it is "softer" on how long and when such a process should be undertaken. Osgood (1962), in suggesting a model for mutual arms reduction between the super-powers, described it as GRIT (graduated reciprocation in tension reduction). John F. Kennedy actually tried a form of this strategy in his policy toward the Soviet Union (Etzioni 1967). In 1963 he made a conciliatory speech and announced the cessation of all U.S. atmospheric nuclear testing, stating that the U.S. would resume testing only if another country began testing. In doing so he was making only a small concession, since there was no immediate need to do more testing. Khrushchev responded by making a similar set of small concessions. In this way there was initiated a process that culminated in the signing of a nuclear test ban treaty and other major tension-reducing agreements (Freedman & Freedman 1975, pp. 208–9).

The third strategy, the *moderately tough strategy*, lies somewhere in between the tough and soft strategies. Unlike the tough strategy, however, concessions may be more generous than those of the other bargainer. This generates an image of the bargainer as a little less tough and more conciliatory. Unlike the soft strategy, the moderately tough strategy does not depend on conciliatory moves in the absence of concessions from the other bargainer. In effect, this might be viewed as a matching strategy in that one side's offers and counteroffers match the degrees of conciliation of the other side.

Finally, the *fair strategy* suggests that the bargainers find the solution that is fair to both sides and, once that solution is identified, make the agreement. In following such a strategy, the idea is not to exploit or bluff but, instead, to indicate where the point of equality lies and to stay there until agreement is reached. While on the surface this would seem ideal, there are many different notions of what is a fair solution (Pruitt 1972). If there is considerable disagreement about what constitutes fairness, there is the temptation for bargainers to resort to pressure tactics to impose their own solutions. This in turn strains the entire negotiating process.

Interestingly, of these strategies, the one least likely to be used is a soft strategy such as GRIT. Yet the few times this strategy has been used, particularly at the international level, it has usually been successful. The reasons for the reluctance to use this strategy seem obvious if we consider the "paradox of negotiation." A unilateral move to give something up, even if it is quite unimportant or harmless to the side making the move, runs the risk of making the negotiator look "weak" to her constituency. In other words, it is read by the constituency as a sign that the negotiator's resolve is weakening, or is least not as tough as they thought. Moreover, it is often believed that such a move communicates to the opponent that one is indeed vulnerable, and the fear is then that the opponent will take advantage of the move, even though the evidence does not suggest calamitous outcomes (Druckman 1977).

Factors in the choice of strategy and tactic. What factors account for the choice of strategy and tactics? What are the circumstances under which a given strategy or tactic yields a satisfactory outcome? Four factors seem to be of particular importance: the type of outcome desired, individual differences between the parties, the relationship between the parties, and the rules and norms governing the negotiation process.

The type of outcome desired. Parties to a conflict may enter a negotiation with one of two orientations. First, they may want to win. That is, they may want to try to extract from the other the largest possible number of concessions without allowing the relationship to break down. This kind of orientation often leads to "compromise" bargaining (Pruitt & Lewis 1977). The bargainers make concessions along some dimension to a point part way between their initial preferences. This approach is very characteristic of bargaining in Congress, where it is often easiest to "split the difference." It is also frequent in treaty negotiations. For example, in the U.S.-USSR test ban negotiations, the United States wanted an annual quota of from twelve to twenty inspections. The Soviets held that inspections were unnecessary. After some maneuvering, both sides agreed to the establishment of unoccupied monitoring stations and two to three annual inspections. The Soviets still expressed the opinion that no inspections were necessary but insisted they had agreed to some in the interests of compromise (Jönsson 1979, p. 64).

Alternatively, the negotiators may try to find those options that give maximum benefits to both sides. This "integrative" approach (Walton & McKersie 1965, pp. 144–83) requires that the parties adopt a more cooperative, mutual problem-solving attitude. This can lead to a search for solutions not immediately apparent to the participants. The orientation here is that both sides can win, given concern for finding a mutually beneficial solution.

In political negotiations the bargainers often have mixed motives. On the one hand, they may want to win. On the other hand, they may perceive that in the long run finding a mutually satisfactory solution may be best for all concerned—even at the cost of short-term dissatisfaction among constituents. For example, in the 1983–84 Congress it was generally perceived that some combination of tax increases and cuts in spending were necessary to deal with the enormous projected budget deficit. Such "integrative" solutions are inherently unpopular with a broad range of constituents. Hence, it becomes difficult for members of Congress to agree to such a package without getting something for their constituents to offset the inevitable dissatisfaction that will be generated by a combination of tax increases and spending cuts.

The type of strategy pursued by a negotiator will reflect whether that negotiator's desired outcome is winning or integrative. Tough or moderately tough strategies are more likely to be employed when the desired outcome is winning, while fair or soft strategies may be followed when the desired outcome is integrative. Of course, it might be argued that it is in the interests of both parties to seek integrative outcomes, and in our discussion of the next phase we will present some proposals for how this might be done.

Individual differences.   Earlier we discussed the "boundary role" of the negotiator and the peculiar "paradox of negotiation" generated by these boundary characteristics. But since *individuals* must cope with these problems, it is therefore useful to know something about the individuals' characteristics which interact with properties of the environment to produce negotiation behavior. Of course, in the situation where the negotiator has rigid instructions from which she cannot deviate, the effects of personal characteristics will be significantly reduced. In the case where there is discretion on the part of the negotiator, personal factors will, to some greater or lesser extent, come into play. What factors seem of special relevance to the negotiation process? We will discuss two important factors, the first of which is the *motivational orientation* (MO) of the parties involved.

Deutsch (1973) has suggested that there are three kinds of motivational orientation toward negotiations. A *cooperative* orientation is one in which the negotiator is interested in the best integrative solution (i.e., both sides win). A *competitive* orientation is one in which one negotiator attempts to beat the other by winning more. An *individualistic* orientation is one in which the negotiator plays to win as much as possible without regard to the implications of the other's outcome.

Rubin and Brown (1975) have suggested a second characteristic or dimension of *interpersonal orientation* (IO). At the high end are those who are, by and large, responsive to the interpersonal aspects of relationships. They are interested in, and reactive to, variations in the behavior of others. At the low end are people who are nonresponsive to interpersonal relations. They see behavioral variations in others as deriving from the situation, not from idiosyncracies in personal style. The low IO does not respond to his opponent with comparable moves; he simply acts for his own gain. The high IO, on the other hand, will be more likely to empathize and act accordingly. To put this difference in terms from Chapter 1, low IOs tend to attribute differences in people's behavior to factors in the situation, rather than the person. The reverse is true for the high IO person, who is more likely to attribute differences in behavior to factors in the person and act accordingly.

This notion can be used to summarize results from a very large research literature on individual differences such as age, sex, nationality, intelligence, social status, need for achievement, and authoritarianism. For example, persons high in Machiavellianism tend to behave like high IOs. That is, they enter the bargaining relationship with an eye to taking advantage of the other, tending to be suspicious of the other party's behavior (expecting her to respond with competition rather than cooperation) and to perceive her as untrustworthy (expecting her to respond to cooperation with exploitation rather than reciprocation). Cooperative behavior will be seen as weakness to be exploited, while competitive behavior will reinforce suspiciousness and competitiveness.Thus the high Mach person is sensitive to the others but in a manipulative way. Correspondingly, individuals low in authoritarianism tend to behave like cooperatively oriented high IO's, while those high in authoritarianism behave like low IO's. That is, the latter exhibit a pattern of rigidity and general insensitively to others.

Snyder and Diesing (1976) have described two kinds of information-processing styles of bargainers. The first, or "rational," style is one in which the bargainer is aware that he does not know "at the start . . . what the situation is . . . but is one whose initial judgment may be mistaken and who knows it, and who is able to correct initial misjudgments and perceive the outlines of the developing bargaining situation in time to deal with it effectively" (p. 333). The rational bargainer is someone who has "low confidence" (p. 334) in his diagnosis of the situation and is generally aware that his implicit theories about the other party may be faulty and in need of modification to a greater or lesser degree. In short, a negotiator with this style is relatively open to new information and is continually engaged in appraising that information as a way of changing or modifying his expectations for the other, and therefore his bargaining tactics.

The "irrational" style, however, is characterized by a rigid belief system (categories, implicit theories, attributions, or whatever version one wishes to use) that dominates his behavior. The first few behaviors or bargaining moves by the other party are interpreted entirely as confirming the beliefs about the other. Thus, as Snyder and Diesing note (with tongues planted firmly in cheeks), "he knows from the onset . . . what the opponent is up to because he has studied the opponent thoroughly and understands his ultimate aims, bargaining style, preferences and internal political problems. He is also a keen judge of men on his side, knowing whose opinions to value and whose opinions to ignore or bypass . . . knowing the opponent as he does, he is not going to be duped by the opponent's tricks . . . nor is he going to lose heart at temporary setbacks, alarms and rumors, but continues firmly on his chosen strategy through all diversions and difficulties" (p. 337). In short, this kind of negotiator makes up his mind early and sticks to his original plan, not allowing new information in or taking new information and reinterpreting it in terms of the original beliefs.

How important are individual differences? This will depend on the level at which the negotiations are carried on and the role of the negotiator. For example, Woodrow Wilson simply could not bargain successfully with Henry Cabot Lodge over United States membership in the League of Nations, a failure that was primarily a result of the personality of Woodrow Wilson. His personality "was such that *any* compromise was anathema. . . ." (Stoessinger 1979, p. 23). A more pragmatic leader could have accepted most of the changes Lodge and the other senators demanded, but "to Woodrow Wilson, it was all or nothing" (ibid.).

Where bargaining goes on in a highly visible context, situational factors may loom larger. It would be hard to imagine, however, that the personalities of Anwar Sadat, Menachem Begin, and Jimmy Carter did not play some important role in the 1978 Camp David agreements between Israel and Egypt.

Finally, in considering Snyder and Diesing's two "styles" of bargaining, we can see that "rational" and "irrational" are two sides of a single dimension of general rigidity of thought. Although we could categorize negotiators as proponents of one style or the other, it is likely that most negotiators fall somewhere in the middle of this spectrum—perhaps more to one side than the other, depending on factors both in the person and the situation. Thus, as we noted in Chapter 5, situations experienced as stressful may lead people to be more rigid in their thinking than otherwise would be the case. This point is similar to our criticism of conflict approaches in Chapter 5 and indicates one of the general weaknesses of any "personality" explanation of any political phenomena, including bargaining and negotiation.

Relationship factors. In discussing impression management and face, we stressed the importance of considering the mutual and reciprocal influences of the parties to a relationship. The nature of relationships has a considerable impact on the course and outcome of negotiations. In discussing Israeli-Lebanese negotiations, we emphasized the relative power inequality between the participants and the effect this may have had on the outcomes. The degree of power equality or inequality is an important factor in the negotiation process. Research tends to show that bargaining is more satisfactory to both sides when the participants are of approximately equal power.

Why? First, each side can provide commensurate threats and promises. *Credibility* is important here. Bargainers who are of approximately equal power can more clearly assess whether the other is bluffing when threats or promises are made. Moreover, neither side has to proceed from a position of defensiveness. Thus it it possible for the process to be more straightforward, since face, vulnerability, and weakness are less likely to be issues. This straightforwardness can, however, be mostly a matter of *perception*, as who is or is not more powerful can often be a real question—as in the case of the U.S. and the USSR (G. Smith 1974).

What happens under conditions of power inequality? Many laboratory studies indicate that bargainers with more power are likely to behave in a manipulative or exploitative manner, while those with less power are likely to behave submissively (Rubin & Brown 1975). Thus the more powerful are inclined to adopt tough strategies and to stick to them, as well as to employ threats. Correspondingly, they are less likely to pursue "package-deal" strategies or other stances of accommodation.

We should emphasize that power is not a simple matter. Thibaut (1968) has suggested that we look at the *kinds of power* available to bargainers. Power may be exerted by control over the division of resources and by withdrawal from the negotiations. When both forms of power are available to both parties, the course of the process may be smoother, since either side can be threatened by the other. This situation tends to lead to the evolution of a contract or set of norms that explicitly forbids such threatening behavior.

Bargaining effectiveness may also be influenced by the *amount of power* possessed by the parties. The more coercive power potential there is in the relationship, the more the bargainers tend to expect that the other side will use it. This, in turn, can lead to the preemptive use of power. Also, an increase in overall power may heighten concern with intangible issues, thereby making agreement more difficult (Thibaut 1968). Arms limitation negotiations between the US and the Soviet Union have been largely concerned with assessing the relative power positions of the two nations with an eye to reducing and equalizing the amount of military force they command (Strobe 1979).

To further complicate the matter, there are interactions between and among motivational orientation (MO), interpersonal orientation (IO), and power status. For example, if bargainers share a cooperative MO and are of equal power, each is in a position to facilitate the other's outcomes, since both the desire and the resources to do so are present. Moreover, the relationship is less likely to be clouded with intangible issues, since both sides are more likely to trust each other. A cooperative MO on the part of the bargainers should also mitigate the problems attendant on power inequality, since the orientation is toward integrative solutions. In contrast, parties who share a competitive MO are out to beat each other and are thus inclined to exploit and manipulate each other. Therefore, the general finding that the more powerful are more likely to exploit is exacerbated by a competitive MO. High IO bargainers will be more effective when power is equal (Rubin and Brown 1975). In a situation of power equality, high IO individuals tend to perceive the situation as democratic—the rights of others should be respected. When power is unequal, the relationship tends to be perceived as undemocratic, lending itself to exploitation.

There is an additional aspect of power in a relationship that affects bargaining. In legislative bargaining, for example, it is often the case that many individuals are involved. That is, legislators representing different constituencies see a common interest in passing or blocking a particular piece of legislation. This opens the way to the formation of *coalitions*. In general, coalitions tend to form when parties think they are seen by others as weak, vulnerable, or lacking in resources. They then join forces to increase their individual strength. But if the initial distribution of power is seen as too overwhelming, it may seem futile for the weaker parties to combine. Coalitions also tend not to form when the stronger party actively interferes with their formation. Thus management may refuse to bargain with a coalition of unions because the strike potential is greater. It can retain its bargaining power by dealing only with individual unions. Much of the history of the labor movement in the U.S. has been the struggle to form increasingly more powerful coalitions of workers, countered by the efforts of management to prevent this.

Finally, coalitions may not form (or may fall apart) because of differences between the partners. Coalitions are often marriages of convenience between partners who come together because they perceive a common interest in one issue. Beneath the surface of unity may lie very strong differences about other matters. Part of the difficulty of grassroots organizing is the problem of bringing together groups whose philosophical or strategic differences prevent them from maintaining sufficient unity to undertake effective bargaining with those in power.

Rules and norms.   We have noted that Thibaut (1968) sees equality in power between negotiators as generating a pressure toward the formation of a "contract" that specifically prohibits the use of threats or coercive power. Because the preservation of face may be critical, there tend to

197 Bargaining and Negotiation 197

arise rules or norms of bargaining conduct. If a rule or norm is present, a negotiator can point to it as a constraint on his behavior and thus is "taken off the hook" with his constituents. In general, rules and norms function to reduce the pressure of intangible issues. This is particularly the case when questions of justice and fairness become central.

One of the strategies discussed earlier was the fair strategy, in which one side puts forward some concept of what a just agreement would be and works toward that. The problem with this strategy is divergent opinions among the negotiators about what constitutes justice or fairness. (See Chapter 10 for a more extended discussion of the psychology of justice.) As the bargaining process continues, however, the parties may begin to move toward agreement on what principle of justice will govern the final agreement. As differences narrow, one norm that seems to operate is the norm of *reciprocity*. That is, as issues become clarified, reduced, or dropped from the agenda, the question of whether one side is better off than the other becomes increasingly salient.

Norms and rules are important in a tactical sense also. One can gain negotiating strength by evoking claims to conformity with the norms and rules that govern "civilized" behavior. Such evocation of norms is often a tactic to increase outsider support as well as a means of shoring up constituency approval for one's behavior. For example, it is common for one party to claim that an offer by the other not only is insulting but also, by implication, violates the rules of fair play, equality, and justice. The fact that the evocation of norms is used as a tactic, however, means that it is seldom convincing in its own right. Both sides may have their own ideas of what is right and fair, so both sides can play the game of trying to appear in better conformity to shared rules of human behavior.

The strategies and tactics employed by bargainers to narrow the differences are many and varied. Their choice is affected by both situational and individual factors. But it should be remembered that negotiations are a relationship. All negotiators are simultaneously both senders and receivers of information, and both sides are dependent on each other for information to use in making decisions about what can realistically be hoped for from the relationship. Thus individual and situational factors not only affect bargainer behavior but also affect the relationship itself. It is a tribute to the complexity of such relationships that, after several decades of experimental research, Pruitt (1981) can say that we are just beginning the study of bargaining and negotiation.

PHASE 6: PRELIMINARIES TO FINAL BARGAINING

Sooner or later, the parties come to a point at which the real differences are clear and the issues are reduced to a small number. The stage is set for some final agreement—or failure to agree, as the case may be. What does it take for negotiators to realize that they have reached the point where the other side cannot give more, where it is no longer possible to move in one's desired direction, and where one can accept the current state of affairs?

The major issue here is determining the *viable range for bargaining* (Gulliver 1979, p. 153). All along, of course, both sides have been sending signals about the minimum they will accept. At this point the dilemmas of trust and of honesty and openness become critical. The parties have a clearer picture of what their differences are, and the issues have been narrowed down. Can the other side be trusted in its claims regarding what it can or cannot accept? Do we dare reveal something about our true intent?

Much depends on the amount and quality of information available to the negotiators. Both sides may now search for additional information from outside sources or, perhaps, through the use of a mediator. Moreover, both sides may feel some impatience to conclude an agreement. This sets up a "positive goal gradient" in that the appeal of an agreement and an end to conflict begins to exert its power on both sides. This may precipitate a surge of bluffing, threats, walkouts, and so on (Bross 1969). On the other hand, one may find, given the gradual increase in trust that characterizes successful negotiations, that both parties may act as if willing to settle for what they can realistically get—as opposed to what would be ideal.

Nicely calculated ranges of acceptable outcomes are not always possible; in fact they may seldom be possible (Gulliver 1979). Gulliver calls this the "cheese, chalk, and honor" problem. Suppose we have disagreement about how much cheese each side should have, how much chalk should be mined, and what will satisfy the honor of both sides. How do we weigh the importance of cheese and chalk against the claims of honor? Does honor plus cheese balance chalk mining? Will chalk mining and an agreement on cheese balance honor? Moreover, the relative importance of each may change during the course of negotiations. In short, multiple and changing criteria influence negotiators' judgments about the solutions that will be acceptable. Nonetheless, there is usually a rough, general range within which potentially agreeable solutions can be found.

It is during this phase that certain strategies become more attractive. These include side agreements, package deals, and, generally, the reduction of factors considered to be important. Further, it is in this phase that more attention is given to converting winning into integrative options (Pruitt & Lewis 1977). Pruitt and Lewis suggest three forms such solutions might take. First, if the conflict results from resource shortage, attempts might be made to increase the size of the pie by finding new resources. Thus a conflict over the funding of domestic versus foreign government programs might be resolved by levying a new tax. Second, the parties may take turns in choosing the preferred alternative, as when a couple takes turns in planning vacations from year to year. Third, and most important, the bargainers can begin to develop trade-offs, exchanges of concessions on issues of differing importance to the parties. This is always an option for bargainers, but it becomes particularly attractive at this point. Obviously, such logrolling will be more difficult if the parties insist on a sequential agenda (taking one issue at a time and resolving it before going on to the next). Something that is tantamount to logrolling occurs in a sequential agenda, however, when the party with a stronger investment in a given issue prevails over a party with a weaker commitment and then, at a later point, the situation is reversed (Pruitt 1972).

Trust is important in logrolling. When one party perceives the other as having done her a favor, she may feel compelled to make a concession on an issue to return the favor. In conditions where trust is weak, substitutes may be found, including the reversible concession (one that can be withdrawn if the other fails to reciprocate) (Deutsch 1958). One final characteristic of this phase is an extension of this point. The parties, in defining the viable range, may attempt to develop a formula according to which final bargaining can occur.

Generating a formula requires the bargainers to assess the history of the negotiations in order to find some set of principles to govern the final outcome. In fact, Zartman (1975) believes that this is the primary operation in this phase and questions the notion that bargaining is always an incremental, concession-making process by which the parties gradually approach each other and come to an agreement. He avers that negotiators are always reevaluating, reassessing, and reconstructing their positions in order to come up with formulas. He gives the following example from the Vietnam negotiations in the early 1970s:

> The negotiations passed through two distinct phases, reflected in the two types of final documents that resulted. The first, from October 1970 to October 1972, concerned the American attempt to find a formula acceptable to both sides—freezing of the stalemate in place without removing either the North Vietnamese or the Saigon regime from South Vietnam—and selling it to Hanoi. The second, in the following three months, concerned a suspicious search for the details that followed from the agreed image. [p. 73]

PHASE 7: FINAL OR END-STATE BARGAINING

At what point do negotiators realize that they have the makings of a satisfactory agreement? What precipitates a final agreement? Four situations can lead negotiators to realize they are within reach of an agreement. First, the viable range of options may have been narrowed to such a degree that the advantages of further bargaining seem marginal. One might expect this to be the case where integrative solutions have been proposed or where bargaining has occurred within a cooperative, trusting atmosphere (Rubin & Brown 1975). Second, considerable agreement may have been established, but the details need to be worked out. End-state bargaining on these "little" matters may often be very hard, particularly if the participants have a history of suspicion or antagonism.

A third situation is one in which the viable range is pretty well-known, but the perception is that considerable gain may still occur in any final settlement. Often this gain may superficially appear to be about a very narrow point but, on closer examination, it turns out to have significant consequences for both sides. One popular song makes this point nicely:

> 7½ cents doesn't mean a helluva lot,
> 7½ cents doesn't mean a thing,
> But give it to me every hour,
> Forty hours every week,
> That's the way you'll have me
> Living like a king.*

Note that the gain is not only financial, but a symbolic gain in status.

Finally, there is the situation in which both parties feel the pressure to come to final agreement but have not been able to define a viable range. There may remain a great deal of ignorance on both sides as to the real intentions and expectations of the other. In such situations there is the risk that both sides will perceive the outcome to be more or less arbitrary; they may see no obvious way to resolve the impasse. This can lead to participants' becoming locked into more aggressive, competitive bargaining (Kerr 1954).

What affects the occurrence and form of a final agreement? Obviously, much less is needed to reach final agreement in the first situation than in the fourth situation. But there are other important factors. First, time limits can affect the generation of final agreements. The "eleventh-hour" effect is widely recognized although little studied. It is the tendency to reach agreement just before a deadline. The problem with a deadline is that each side may delay making its viable range known until the last possible moment. On the other hand, time limits appear to squeeze elements of bluff out of the bargaining. They bring pressures on the parties to settle for less favorable terms and thus may pave the way for a final settlement (Stevens 1963). Thus bargaining aspirations, demands, and the amount of bluffing are all reduced under time pressure.

Yet many negotiations taking place under time limits break down. Why? In part it has to do with countervailing pressures that lead bargainers to resist any significant lowering of their aspirations. Here again the constituency makes itself felt. It is especially important for the bargainer to maintain credibility and to elicit a positive evaluation when the outcome of the negotiation needs to be ratified. This is the case, for

*From "7½ Cents," *The Pajama Game.* Reprinted with permission of The Songwriters Guild.

example, with labor negotiators whose final contract proposals must be approved by the rank and file and with United States diplomats whose treaties must be ratified by the Senate.

A further impediment to settlement, even under time pressure, is the re-arousal of intangible issues. As the probable outcome emerges, so do ideological commitments, notions of what constitutes justice, and evaluations of the image one is projecting (e.g., weak versus strong, vulnerable versus assertive). Also, the threat of breaking off negotiations becomes more salient as final agreement approaches. Hence there is often an upsurge in the use of all types of threats as a bargaining tactic. One party may try, for example, to convince the other that the threat of deadlock is higher than it really is. At this point all sides must assess the risk of such threats. Is the risk of a breakdown in negotiations worth it? How likely is it that the probable outcome can be altered in one's favor? These issues will be clearer in situations 1 and 2 than in situations 3 and 4.

The use of promises raises similar issues. Each side must weigh the advantages of making large concessions at this point. This is a particular problem in situations 3 and 4. Cross (1969) argues that a large concession in end-state bargaining may project an image of exploitability, which will cause the other party to harden its bargaining position. On the other hand, making no concessions can lead to deadlock or force the bargainer to make a larger concession at a later time. In short, concessions at this stage convey more information than is the case in earlier phases.

Finally, for reasons not completely understood, one party may suddenly jump to an outcome for which there has been little preparation. Also, parties that have long resisted any significant concessions may suddenly come to an agreement. Schelling (1960) has suggested that there are so many factors weighing on bargainers at this juncture that nonrational factors can play a large part. Perhaps agreement becomes more important than any *particular* outcome. Mediators sometimes take advantage of this mentality by focusing on a solution halfway between the positions of the two parties.

What all of this seems to suggest is that there is a flaw in the assumptions underlying much of the research literature. These assumptions include the propositions that people know their subjective utilities, that these remain relatively fixed, and that bargainers make rational calculations concerning the risks and advantages of certain moves. On the contrary, observations of actual negotiations present a picture of much less rationality and calculation (Luce & Raffia 1957; Rapoport 1968).

PHASE 8: RITUAL AFFIRMATION

Political negotiations often end with some ritual affirmation of the agreement. This is particularly likely to happen when the negotiations have been protracted or when the agreement reached is unusual. For example, important bills passed in Congress after extensive negotiations are often celebrated by a ceremonial signing at the White House. Typically, the president sits at a desk with all of the participants in the negotiation arrayed behind him. During the ceremony, the president may hand out mementos—usually the pen or pens with which the bill was signed. As part of the ceremony during which he signed the Civil Rights Act of 1968, Lyndon Johnson dedicated the legislation to Martin Luther King, Jr., who had been assassinated seven days earlier (M. Miller 1980, p. 627). One feature of such ceremonies is that all the participants who may have been bitter antagonists now appear to smile and shake hands. It affirms that the political process does work, that important relationships have not been irreparably harmed, and that future conflicts may also be resolved through negotiation.

Also, affirmation rituals give the parties an opportunity to defend their actions before their constituents. As noted above, this may be of crucial importance if ratification is needed. During such occasions the parties usually take pains to present each other in the best light possible. This not only reflects an awareness of the need of each party for constituency support but also may help repair any residual damage to the "face" of other participants. After all, these negotiators may very well find themselves face to face in another bargaining situation in the future.

THIRD-PARTY MEDIATION: CAMP DAVID

In November 1977, four years after the Arab-Israeli war of October 1973, Anwar Sadat, president of Egypt, flew to Israel and became the first Arab leader to set foot on Israeli soil since Israel was founded in 1948. This was one of the most dramatic and, to many people, hopeful moments of that decade. Here was an Arab leader, presumably a sworn enemy of Israel, coming to Tel Aviv, addressing the Israeli Parliament, and proclaiming a desire for peace. In effect Sadat was saying, "War is no longer an acceptable alternative. We must use peaceful means to resolve our differences."

But during the months that followed the Sadat visit his courageous act seemed doomed to lead nowhere. Sadat was under enormous pressure from his constituents to get back the Sinai territories lost in the war. Equally powerful were pressures from other Arab nations to find a settlement for the Palestinians on the West Bank of the Jordan River and the Gaza Strip. Menachem Begin, prime minister of Israel, insisted, from both personal belief and pressure within his political coalition, that no Palestinian state should be allowed to rise on the West Bank. The West Bank was seen as an integral part of Israel. Direct contacts and preliminary negotiations between the two leaders appeared to be going nowhere (Bradley 1981). Early in 1978, however, Jimmy Carter, then president of the United States, decided that the differences between Sadat and Begin might be resolved through third-party mediation.* Accordingly, he convinced both leaders to come (with their advisers) to Camp David, the presidential vacation retreat in the Maryland mountains.

Up to this point we have discussed negotiations that are primarily face-to-face confrontations between the parties to the conflict or their representatives. There are many situations, however, in which suspicion and antagonism are so deep, or the issues so divisive, or the grounds for agreement so lacking that a neutral, third party is needed to assist in the negotiations. The conflict between Egypt and Israel met virtually all these criteria. We will use the Camp David negotiations to illustrate the workings and problems of third-party mediation. We will also see how some of the principles discussed above are exemplified by the Camp David negotiations.†

Let us begin by considering some general characteristics of the role of the third-party mediator (TPM). This role varies in (1) the structural properties of the role; (2) how the TPM fits into the ongoing negotiation process; and (3) what the TPM actually does.

Jimmy Carter was president of the United States. He had put himself and the credibility of his administration on the line in this bold attempt at conflict resolution through negotiation. He therefore had a personal investment in achieving a favorable outcome. As the leader of the United States he had available enormous power and resources which could serve as tools in the negotiations.‡ Moreover, Carter specifically stated that he would not impose an agreement on the two parties but would work with them to find solutions to their problems.

Carter's stance illustrates the dimensions along which the structural properties of the TPM's role may vary. First, a TPM may or may not tie his credibility to the outcome. Second, he may or may not make it clear that he is neutral in the sense of having no personal stake in any particular outcome. Third, a TPM may have little to contribute to the negotiations except for skill in helping both parties reach mutually satisfactory solutions. Fourth, a TPM may insist that the solutions worked out by him will be accepted by the parties to the conflict—in other words, binding arbitration. Finally, a TPM may, unlike Carter, keep a relatively low profile, acting as a kind of communications specialist by limiting himself to conveying information and helping to clarify issues.

Moving to the second characteristic of the role of a TPM, the way in which he fits into the ongoing negotiation process is complex. Remember

*It should be noted that Sadat's initiative came as a surprise to the Carter administration, which had embarked on an ambitious multilateral negotiation plan. Carter's decision to become personally active in the Arab-Israeli conflict resolution effort meant abandoning this more comprehensive approach (Bradley 1981).

†Carter's account of the Camp David negotiations is not necessarily the most accurate or unbiased account of the proceedings. Our intent here is to use his account only to provide examples of the issues involved in third-party mediation. There is no attempt here to evaluate Carter's role in these negotiations nor the outcome. Bradley's account (1981) of the period from 1978 to 1981 contains a good description of the events that followed the Camp David accords.

‡Within, of course, the constraints placed upon him by Congress and political reality.

that the heart of negotiation is the exchange and interpretation of information. The crux of the whole business is the reciprocal evaluation of moves by the parties. Like each of the parties, the TPM is also a trader in information and its interpretation. The TPM's job is to acquire the most valid information possible about the intentions and goals of each participant. But unlike the principals to the negotiation, the TPM must be an advocate for both parties and at the same time must be an interpreter of each side to the other. Thus the TPM faces the dilemmas of trust and of honesty and openness as well as the paradox of negotiation, with reference to *both* sides.

There are numerous examples of this point in Carter's account of the Camp David negotiations. For example, Sadat complained to Carter that Begin appeared to be a man obsessed with the past and insensitive to Egypt's problems, saying, "Begin is not ready for peace" (Carter 1981, p. 360). Carter responded:

> Mr. President, Begin is a tough and honest man. In the past he has been quite hawkish. He sees his proposals as a starting point, and he has been quite forthcoming compared to other leaders of Israel who preceded him. His present control over the Sinai was derived from a war which Israel did not start. That is Begin's perspective. Thus he feels he has been very cooperative with his proposals. . . . [pp. 360–61]*

Here Carter is redefining Begin for Sadat in terms of Begin's "real" intentions, self-image, and problems with his constituency. Similarly, Carter repeatedly stressed to Begin that Sadat had acted with great courage and personal sacrifice in making the peace initiative.

A TPM is, in one sense, another party to the negotiations and yet not a party to them. This is particularly true when the TPM conceives his role in a highly personal and active way—as did President Carter. On the one hand, the TPM has the responsibility for successfully shepherding the parties through the phases of negotiation. On the other hand, the TPM is identified with each of the sides and bargains for it with the other. As a "shepherd," the TPM has to deal with his own dilemma of trust. Are the participants willing to reveal their "true" intentions? Of course, this is complicated by the fact that the participants may change their ideas about this during the course of the negotiations. Also, as a participant, the TPM has his own dilemma of honesty and openness. What kind of strategy and tactics should be used to move the parties closer? How much bluff, deceit, and "gambits" (not to mention threats and promises) should be employed? Moreover, the TPM has to confront the problem of manipulation. Each party is likely to try to use the TPM as a tool in attempting to influence the direction and outcome of the negotiations. Clearly, the TPM cannot allow himself to be perceived as the ally of one participant. On the

*This and following examples from Jimmy Carter, *Keeping Faith*. New York: Knopf, 1981. Used with permission.

other hand, though, these attempts to put the TPM in a compromising position are useful to the TPM as information.

This delicate balance is reflected nicely in an incident that occurred during the third day of the Camp David negotiations. Carter was speaking separately with Begin and his advisers about the key problem of West Bank control. At one point, Carter became irritated and said:

> What do you actually want for Israel if a peace is signed? How many refugees and what kind can come back? . . . What else do you want? If I know the facts, I can take them to Sadat and try to satisfy both you and him. . . . I must have your frank assessment. My greatest strength here is your confidence—but I don't feel that I have your trust. . . . I believe I can get from Sadat what you *really* need, but I just do not have your confidence . . . You are as evasive with me as with the Arabs. The time has come to throw away reticence . . . My belief is that Sadat is strong enough to make an agreement here—and impose it on other nations. I believe I can get Sadat to agree to your home-rule proposal if you convince him and me that you are not planning to keep large parts of the West Bank under your permanent control. [ibid., pp. 348–49]

This excerpt reflects much of the TPM's job and many of his problems. Like any participant in a negotiation he must try to discern the real interests of the parties—remembering, of course, that they may change. He cannot, however, perform the task of presenting the best case for a side if that party does not trust him enough to reveal its "true" position.

Further, we can see Carter defining Sadat to Begin, i.e., how Sadat will respond if the Israelis are "sincere" about not keeping control of the West Bank. This action by Carter reflects the delicate balance between the TPM's "shepherd" role and his bargainer role. He holds out a reward for agreement on the home-rule proposal, if the Israelis make certain concessions. Notice also that he "allies" himself with Sadat (" . . . if you convince him and me . . . . ") in what is clearly a tactical maneuver to engage the Israelis in what Carter conceives of as productive discussion.

These considerations lead to the final characteristic, what a third-party mediator actually does. For Carter being a TPM meant attempting to guide the negotiations through every stage. This included not only setting the agenda but also providing what Kelman (1972) considers one of the more important elements of negotiation—a place that is insulated from outside communication. The latter helps mitigate constituent pressures and the paradox-of-negotiation problem. It also provides opportunities for the parties to be separate from each other as well as together. In addition, Camp David offered opportunities for relaxation and recreation, a not insignificant factor in a very tense situation.

Fisher (1983) has pointed out that the function of a TPM is to induce positive motivation, improve communication, diagnose the problems, and regulate the interaction. Carter (presumably without having consulted Fisher) attempted to do these very things. He continually reminded both parties of the historic importance of their task, the esteem in which history would hold them, and the dire consequences of failure. He adroitly played on the different bargaining styles of Begin and Sadat to regulate the interaction between them.

Sadat tended to move away from details and words into the realm of general principles and broad strategic concepts; Begin was continually preoccupied with minutiae or semantics. Sadat, on arriving at Camp David, had immediately outlined two or three points on which he would not yield and then gave Carter a virtual free hand to negotiate with flexibility on all other issues. By contrast (according to Carter), the Israeli delegation was extremely reluctant to trust Carter with a revelation of its "real" positions or areas of possible compromise. Thus Carter developed the following technique:

> I would draft a proposal I considered reasonable, take it to Sadat for quick approval or slight modification, and then spend hours or days working on the same point with the Israeli delegation. . . . On any controversial issue, I never consulted Sadat's aides, but always went directly to their leader. It soon became obvious to all of us, however, that [Begin's aides] could be convinced on an issue more quickly than the Prime Minister, and they were certainly more effective in changing Begin's mind than I ever was. . . . Had both men been preoccupied with semantics or details, my job would have been much more difficult. [ibid., pp. 355–56]

Indeed, much of Carter's time was spent in drafting and redrafting proposals and then discussing them with the two sides separately. We have already noted how Carter attempted to allay suspicion on both sides by continually defining the "real" intents of each to the other. In this sense, he was trying to improve communication. On the other hand, he was not averse to forming a temporary coalition with one party to push for concessions from the other (ibid., p. 366). We might interpret Carter's actions here somewhat differently. We might say that Carter was attempting to shift the range of the participant's latitude of agreement and rejection. By continually reformulating the proposals in ways that made them increasingly less extreme, he was in effect trying to get their areas of agreement to overlap to an increasingly greater extent.

Bargaining and negotiation are about relationships and the mutual and reciprocal dependencies the parties have upon each other. The dynamics lead to escalating or deescalating spirals of conflict between the sides. Hence, the function of the TPM that may be most valuable is getting the participants to reflect on the *process* by which conflict is or is not resolved or managed. It is very interesting that Kelman (1979) and his colleagues, who have run workshops for participants in intersocietal disputes (e.g., Greeks and Turks, Arabs and Israelis), have found process observations by the TPM to be extremely critical.

Just as Jimmy Carter discovered, they also found that a key element in the learning that takes place is a new awareness of the significance of symbols and the importance of national identity. We might also include, as Carter did in explaining the behavior of Begin to Sadat, the perception by the participants of their own history. It is this capacity to bring out intangible issues and show how they affect the process that is probably critical in successful third party mediation. But of course this is just another way of saying that bargaining and negotiation, like all of the phenomena considered in this book, are most accurately conceived as involving complex interactions between multiple elements.*

SUMMARY

Bargaining is one of the most continuous and characteristic modes of behavior in political life. At its core, political bargaining is characterized by 1) joint decision making; 2) the exchange of offer and counteroffer; and 3) the effects of the interactions among the characteristics of the people involved. Bargaining and negotiation are cyclical and developmental processes involving the sequential exchange of information in pursuit of some mutually acceptable solution to the problem at issue. They are conditioned by intrapersonal processes, social and environmental factors, and the bargainers' sense of how their important reference groups will react. The key to the process is the fact that bargainers are constantly exchanging information and that they are informationally dependent upon one another.

A bargaining or negotiating process can be conceptualized as a series of phases during which changes of understanding are brought about by the processing of the information that becomes available during each phase (Gulliver 1979). The first phase is the process of deciding to enter into a bargaining relationship in order to deal with a conflict. Such a decision usually depends on some degree of interdependency between or among the parties, as well as a decision that bargaining is the best alternative, an approximate power equality, each party's knowledge of the other party or parties, and opportunities for the concurrent use of other modes of conflict resolution.

The second phase is the deceptively simple-seeming task of choosing a site. The factors that can complicate this phase include fears of physical danger, feelings associated with "territoriality," and other considerations

---

*Space does not permit us to explore the issue of third party intervention more fully. However, as Rubin (1981) has pointed out, a TPM may be effective by modifying the communication structure between the participants or the structure of the site or location. He may manipulate certain resources, such as his own services (i.e., by threatening to withdraw), access to the media, or by "sweetening the pie" (as Jimmy Carter did by agreeing to build the Israelis a new airfield in exchange for evacuation of the Sinai). We earlier discussed the question of shifting and changing the agenda and of the changing way in which issues on the agenda were "packaged." Obviously, a TPM will be centrally involved in these kinds of issues. For a further discussion of the role of the TPM at the level of international negotiation, see Rubin's (1981) volume on the role of Secretary of State Henry Kissinger at the conclusion of the October 1973 war between Israel and Egypt. The resolution of this conflict was one of the factors ultimately leading to Camp David.

that may affect the psychological climate of the negotiations. Once a site has been chosen, an agenda must be defined. Negotiating agendas are often complicated and have a tendency to expand in unanticipated ways. Thus, the issue of agenda formation can keep cropping up throughout the course of a negotiating process and can even be used as a tactic by the parties. This is important because the way an agenda is defined will affect the course of the negotiations, as well as their ultimate outcome. In short, it is necessary to bargain over the definition of the bargaining issues.

During the fourth phase, each side formally presents its proposals for solutions to the conflict. These opening moves give the parties valuable information about their adversaries and can also significantly affect the subsequent course of bargaining. Opening moves set the boundaries on the potential for flexibility of each of the parties, and convey a message to the constituencies of the bargainers—a message about how well they are being represented in the process. Once opening positions have been established, the bargainers begin the process of narrowing their differences. This involves the "trading" of a sequence of offers and counter offers, accompanied by such tactics as bluffing, threats, promises, and concessions. There are a number of ways in which these components can be assembled into strategies The strategy selected will, in turn, depend on the type of outcome desired, individual differences in negotiators' styles, factors in the relationships between and among the parties, and the rules or norms that govern the actions of the parties.

At some point, the parties come to the phase where final agreement seems near. Strategies not previously used may become attractive, and the attention of the bargainers may turn to integrative options. In the process of redefining the viable range of solutions, the bargainers may be able to develop a way of concluding the bargaining in a mutually acceptable way. This often takes the form of a set of principles that will govern the final outcome. Sooner or later the bargainers will probably find themselves considering a viable final agreement. How they handle this situation can be affected by time limits, intangible issues, and the advisability of further concessions. Once agreement is reached, there is usually a ritual that affirms the solution; typically it involves the exchange of copies of the final agreement and, perhaps, some signing ceremony.

Sometimes negotiations take place under the auspices of a third party mediator. Such was the case when President Carter brought Anwar Sadat and Menachem Begin together to try to reach some accord on their differences regarding the Middle East situation. Third party mediators can vary on at least three factors: 1) what they really do, 2) how they fit into the bargaining process, and 3) what form the role of mediator takes in a particular situation. How each of these is handled by the mediator can significantly affect the outcome, and this, in turn, reflects both the personality of the mediator and the situation in which the bargaining takes place, as well as the relationship between the two.

WHEN ALL ELSE FAILS . . .

Part of the urgency with which President Carter approached the Camp David talks stemmed from the fear that delay would permit the repetition of what had come to seem an endless series of outbreaks of violence in the Middle East. The historical importance attributed to the Camp David talks was proportional to the probability that without such an intervention Israel and Egypt would soon be involved in yet another inconclusive and devastating war. No consideration of the mechanisms by which politics is pursued would be complete without at least a brief consideration of the use or threat of force to achieve political ends. Thus we will now turn our attention to what happens when leadership, persuasion, and bargaining fail or perhaps are not even seriously tried.

8

CONFLICT AND THE USE OF FORCE:
The Ultimate Bargaining Chip

All political structures use force, but they differ in the manner in which and the extent to which they use or threaten to use it against other political organizations. These differences play a specific role in determining the form and destiny of political communities. [Max Weber, quoted in Gerth & Mills 1958, p.159]*

Max Weber, the great German social theorist, saw force so central to political processes that he defined the state in terms of force: ". . .a state is a human community that (successfully) claims the *monopoly of the legitimate use of physical force* within a given territory" (Gerth & Mills 1958, p. 78, italics in original). Thus no discussion of the major means by which political systems manage and regulate conflict would be complete without at least a brief consideration of the use of force or the threat of force to achieve political ends.

Before we consider coercion as a means of regulating and solving political conflict, it is necessary to take a closer look at the nature and characteristics of political conflict. So far we have been discussing conflict management by peaceful means. In this chapter, we will focus on situa-

*From H. Gerth & C.W. Mills (eds.), *Max Weber: Essays in Sociology* (New York: Oxford University Press, 1958). Used with permission.

tions in which either the previously discussed methods of regulating and resolving conflict have not worked or were not used. In either case, the obvious question is *why?* In order to deal with this question, we must have a more complete understanding of the nature of political conflict.

This chapter will begin, therefore, with a discussion of the nature and structure of political conflict. From there it will move to the question of the roots and causes of the human propensity to solve problems, political or otherwise, through the use of force or the threat of force. Finally there will be a consideration of the major ways in which coercion is used for the achievement of political ends.

THE NATURE AND STRUCTURE OF POLITICAL CONFLICT

Conflict pervades political life (Nimmo & Ungs 1979). Politics is, in essence, "a process in which regulated or unregulated conflict plays a central role" (Gamson 1968, p. 3). The underlying premise of the political process is that all parties to a particular political conflict cannot be completely and simultaneously satisfied. Some must lose so that others can win. This is a view of politics which stresses the fact that the parties to a political conflict have different ideas concerning how valued human and material resources should be distributed and utilized. They have, in short, incompatible political goals.

Political conflict is seen as arising out of the parties, pursuing of goals that the parties perceive to be incompatible (Mitchell 1981, p. 21). The term "perceive" here indicates the importance of psychological factors in the process. On one hand, the goals may as a matter of fact be incompatible. If the territory currently known as Israel is ruled exclusively or predominantly by Jews, it cannot be ruled exclusively or predominantly by Palestinians. On the other hand, the parties to a conflict "may perceive that their goals are incompatible at a given point in time when, in fact, their perceptions are incorrect" (ibid). Such misperceptions arise primarily from two sources. One is a fallacious assumption of logical mutual exclusivity between or among goals. The other is a faulty reading of the other party's goals. Such misperceptions are common "particularly given the propensity of goals to change over time, or the causes of a given situation to remain ambiguous or unknown (ibid.).

In politics the goals tend to be either material resources or positions (Easton 1971, p. 127; Hirsch 1977). For example, material goods may include things as diverse as a strip of land in the Sinai Desert or a contract to build a section of interstate highway. Political positions can range from the position of dog catcher to that of president of the United States or general secretary of the Communist Party of the Soviet Union. These two types of goals can be interrelated in many ways. For example, the Camp David negotiations involved a tangible issue that was material—the disposition of certain territories on the West Bank and Sinai—as well as an intangible issue that was positional—the future of Begin and Sadat as leaders in their respective countries.

The occupation of an important political position or the possession of valued political resources carries with it the opportunity to participate in decision making concerning the allocation of future valued positions or goods, as well as the potential for influencing the implementation of those decisions. Also, a history of success in winning political conflicts leads to an assumption on the part of both the self and others that this propensity to emerge a winner will persist. Thus political influence can be defined in terms of assumptions about the outcomes of future political conflicts, i.e., about who will decisively influence those outcomes.

The stakes are high, but the process is not neutral. Certain "rules of the game" tend to give an advantage to persons with certain resources and skills. For example, in American politics those with lots of money and outgoing personalities tend to be more successful than the poor and the introverted. In a political system such as the Soviet Union's, skill in political infighting is probably more important than either money or gregariousness. This is because the two countries have different rules for the game of political conflict. In trying to understand political conflict in any particular instance or in an entire political system, it becomes important to take a look at the rules that govern the conflict and the way in which they structure (or fail to structure) the behavior of the political combatants.

In any reasonably orderly society, political conflicts must be bound by some generally agreed-upon rules. Political and legal institutions may be seen as ways of expressing this structure. Indeed, political and legal institutions can be said to represent a set of methods by which conflict is structured and thereby regulated. Some political scientists define politics within this framework. For example, Dan Nimmo notes that "politics is that activity whereby the members of a society endeavor to regulate their conflicts and maintain a sufficient level of consensus to make living together possible" (Nimmo 1974, p. 9). One of the contributions psychology can make to understanding political phenomena is to call attention to the nature of these structures.

In the following discussion, we have been somewhat selective in the material we have emphasized concerning political conflict. There are two reasons for this selectivity. First, we chose those ideas which seemed to be particularly relevant to the model of the political process briefly outlined in Chapter 1 and developed more fully in Chapter 10. Second, as noted in Chapter 1, we tried to keep the focus on *psychological* perspectives about the characteristics of political conflict. We realize that a fuller treatment of this issue would require an integration of traditional political and sociological explanations of political conflict with these psychological perspectives; however, space prevents us from pursuing that end here.

Philip Brickman, a social psychologist, devoted a good deal of thought to the issue of the structuring of conflict relationships. His structural analysis of conflict relationships (Brickman 1974) can be used as a vehicle for exploring the relationship between differing degrees of structure and political conflict. Brickman discusses three prototypes of conflict relationships: (1) fully structured, (2) partially structured, and (3) unstructured. He also adds a fourth, somewhat different from the preceding three, which is conflict over the rules of conflict. Not all political conflicts can be classified neatly into one of these categories. In reality, there is a continuum of structure in conflict relationships which ranges from highly structured to relatively unstructured. A given real-world case might (and probably will) fall somewhere between two of Brickman's ideal types, but closer to one than to the other in the sense that it would have more of the characterisitcs of one than of the other. Thus these categories or ideal types cannot be used to infer information about any particular conflict relationship. Rather, they can be used as benchmarks for the analysis and comparison of particular instances of conflict.

Fully structured conflict relationships.   In fully structured conflict relationships, the roles and behavior of the parties to the conflict are prescribed by social norms or laws. The options or moves open to the participants are clearly specified as rights or obligations. These situational factors may completely suppress or highly ritualize the dispute so that overt, unritualized conflict will break out only if somebody violates or challenges the rules. "The orientation of parties in fully structured conflict relationships is a moral orientation, involving a concern with the other primarily as a moral agent whose actions are either right or wrong" (ibid., 1974, p. 12).

In the political world the activities of courts of law furnish the closest approximations to fully structured conflict relationships. In American courts the behavior of the officials of the court, as well as of the parties to a case, is under the normative control of a highly specified set of laws, rules, and customs. The participants are strongly constrained to behave in certain ways toward each other. The emphasis is on procedure rather than substance; if the procedures have been faithfully followed, there is the assumption that the substantive outcome is "just" or "right." Even though the parties to the case may loathe each other, they are constrained to be polite and proper in their interchanges. The role of lawyers as representatives is crucial here. The extent of the conflict or animosity becomes apparent only if and when someone violates the rules —as when a defendant leaps up and accuses his opponent or the judge of being a "dirty Fascist pig." Order is quickly restored (reestablishing the structure) even at the expense of having one or more parties to the case physically restrained or removed from the room.

The placement of the various participants in physical space, the arrangement of the physical space itself, and the dress of the participants emphasize not only the orderliness of the proceedings but also the relationships of the various participants to each other. The judge sits above everyone else, dressed in black robes, and is the focal point of the process.

The parties are seated opposite (opposing) each other and face the judge upon whom their fates ultimately rest. The spectators are usually walled off from the scene of action by some sort of fence, which symbolizes their passive role in the process. The jury, if there is one, is often on some sort of raised platform, but off to one side. It does not occupy the commanding position of the judge, but its importance is designated by its physically intermediate position between the judge and the parties to the case. Finally, the language one hears in courtrooms is full of references to moral values—to notions of rights and obligations and to judgments of right and wrong.

Partially structured conflict relationships.

In partially structured relationships, there are some limits on behavior of the parties in the form of agreements or rules. They do not govern all important aspects of the conflict, however, and do not as completely mask or ritualize the conflictual nature of the proceedings, as is the case in a court of law. The crucial factor is that "each party sees the other primarily as a competitive actor rationally pursuing his own self-interest" (Brickman 1974, p. 11). Because the structure is only partial, the participants have considerable room for maneuver in the use of tactics such as threats, lies, deception, promises, rewards, and bribes. "Intentional or selfish aggression, activated by calculation that this aggression will be rewarded by more favorable outcomes, is an important part of partially structured conflict" (ibid., 1974, p. 11). So the behavior of each party tends to be selfishly calculated, and each assumes that the behavior of the other is equally selfishly calculated. Some moral considerations or normative constraints enter into the social exchange, but they play a much less important role than they do in fully structured conflict relationships.

Political campaigns provide an example of partially structured conflicts. As Murphy and Schneier (1974, p. 156) point out, "Whatever constraints there are on the behavior of American politicians, few of them are written into law. Even the laws of libel and slander tend to be enforced far less strictly with regard to candidates for public office than for others." The most obvious constraints on election campaigning are the laws that specifically govern elections and campaigns, such as campaign finance legislation (Alexander 1976). The other major regulator is the American notion of fair play. One person's fair play, however, may be another person's immorality.

One practice that crosses party lines is the use of public opinion polling techniques to garner support. Polls are used by candidates in two basic ways, neither of which has much to do with an honest attempt at information gathering. First, polling is often deliberately done in such a way as to enhance candidate visibility. The bias of the procedures—usually sending a questionnaire to everyone in a given voting district—makes these polls worthless as an accurate reading of public opinion. The aim of such a poll is to make the voter aware of the candidate and to get the voter to think that the candidate cares about his and her ideas. Second, a poll showing that the candidate's pet policies are popular or that the candidate is apparently winning or gaining strength is useful as a psychological tool. Even if it was poorly done and the results grossly invalid, few candidates can resist releasing such results to the media. Such use of polling offend some persons' sense of fair play, but most consider it an acceptable if somewhat cynical tactic.

Somewhat more marginal is the practice of infiltrating the campaign staff of an opponent. One of the best-documented cases of this practice surfaced in connection with the Watergate investigation. The following excerpts from three White House memos (Committee on the Judiciary, 1974)* will illustrate the nature of this tactic. At this point in the 1972 presidential primary campaign, the Democratic frontrunner was Senator Edmund Muskie of Maine. The memos from which the following excerpts were taken are from Gordon Strachan to H.R. Haldeman and are marked "Administratively Confidential":

Memo dated August 13, 1971:

A plant will be in Muskie headquarters beginning October 1. [p. 6]

Memo dated October 27, 1971:

Magruder is meeting with some success in implementing Buchanan's suggestions for causing Muskie difficulties during appearances. Recent reports he has submitted have copies of the media coverage given to white and black pickets with anti-Muskie signs. The Muskie office plant is also producing speeches prior to delivery, recipients of Muskie materials in certain states, and films of certain files. No other intelligence activities against any of the other Democratic contenders is being pursued by Magruder. [p. 28]

Memo dated January 18, 1972:

Opposition Material—Through various sources Ashbrook's first mailing, Muskie's plans for newspaper ads on youth on January 26th, Muskie's fund raising mailing, minutes of Muskie's Domestic Issues meeting, and YAF's confidential mailing have been received. These materials are attached at Tab D. [p. 79]

Such efforts are not limited to the Republican Party (*Washington Post*, July 10, 1983, A1). Also, this undoubtedly was not the first time such a "plant" was made successfully, nor will it be the last.

In 1983 it was reported that a "mole" in the Carter White House had passed information to Reagan's campaign workers during the 1980 election campaign (*Washington Post*, July 7, 1983, p. A1). A *Washington Post/ABC* News Poll demonstrated that while people tended not to approve of

*Committee on the Judiciary, Political Matters Memoranda: 8/13/71–9/18/72 (Washington D.C.: U.S. Government Printing Office, 1974).

such tactics, they thought that such behavior was common in political campaigns (*Washington Post*, July 6, 1983, p. A3). Because political campaigns are partially structured conflict relationships, a situation is created that makes such activities possible if either (or both) of the candidates judge them to be part of a potentially winning strategy.

Finally, the point should be made that some candidates or their supporters engage in practices that are clearly against the law. For example, in connection with the 1972 presidential election campaign, twenty-one companies were charged with illegally contributing almost $968,000 to the campaigns of both Democratic and Republican contenders. All pleaded guilty (Alexander 1976, pp. 113–16).

Unstructured conflict relationships.   In unstructured conflict relationships the social constraints on the parties are minimal or totally absent. As a practical matter, the tactics and strategies available to the parties are limited only by constraints which they either possess inherently or impose on themselves—that is, by their own capacities and dispositions. Each party "sees the other primarily as a source of threatening or painful stimulation that needs to be escaped, avoided, or destroyed" (Brickman 1974, p. 9). An important element is impulsive or emotional aggression, and "the reactions of the parties are often immediate responses to internal drives or external shocks rather than the results of rational calculations of the nature and purpose of the other party" (ibid., 1974, p. 9).

Politically, an example of an unstructured conflict relationship is one in which prominent government officials (or members of their families) are killed or wounded by political terrorists in a seemingly random, unpredictable way. This is unstructured in that there is no obvious pattern to the attacks, apart from the characteristics of the victims, who are chosen from a relatively large population of potential victims. There is no external structuring of the alternatives either for the terrorists or for the potential targets. The rules that structure this situation are minimal in that there are no substantial limits on what the terrorists can do to gain access to their victims—except perhaps the limits inherent in having killing or wounding as a goal and in the terrorists' capacity to devise new and ingenious ways to accomplish their goals, neither of which amounts to or implies much of a rule structure. As Walter Laqueur states, "Even in civil war there are certain rules, whereas the characteristic features of terrorism are anonymity and the violation of established norms" (Laqueur 1977, p. 3).

In addition, terrorists and their victims and potential victims tend to perceive each other as sources of "threatening or painful stimulation that needs to be escaped, avoided, or destroyed."* In the case of the victims, the emphasis is on escape or avoidance; in the case of the terrorists, it is

---

*Instances where the victim develops positive feelings for the victimizer might constitute an exception (the so-called Stockholm Syndrome). This phenomenon is still poorly understood and somewhat controversial, and it will not be dealt with here.

on destruction. The potential for impulsive or emotional aggression on the part of one or both parties is virtually always present, strategies for dealing with the situation frequently tend to be ad hoc, and the decision making process tends to have a heavily emotional rather than rational flavor.

Conflict over the rules of conflict. This is conflict over what the structure of the conflict should be. Brickman calls this "revolutionary conflict," a term that indicates the most obvious political example. In its basic form, revolutionary conflict implies that the parties "differ over whether particular options, moves, or means should be considered legitimate or not" (Brickman 1974, p. 13). Thus there is a necessary challenge to the rule structure currently in existence by persons or groups who will benefit from a change—or who perceive that they will benefit from a change. Usually their objection to the existing state of affairs possesses strongly moralistic overtones. The current arrangement is somehow unfair or immoral. "Revolutionary change is change in the rules of the relationship, and revolutionary conflict is disagreement over whether or not such change should take place" (ibid., 1974, p. 15).

Revolutionary change can take place without revolutionary conflict—if there is a consensus between or among the parties regarding the change in rules. Correspondingly, revolutionary conflict does not necessarily result in revolutionary change: The defenders of the status quo may prevail. In either case, there is no need for either revolutionary change or revolutionary conflict to be violent or dramatic, though they may be.

In the political system, however, significant revolutionary changes do tend to be dramatic. The classic political revolution, one that aims to overthrow a regime or to change a system of government, is invariably violent to some extent. Mostafa Rejai (1977, p. 7–8) has proposed a definition of political revolution that emphasizes its nature as a conflict to change the rules of conflict. All revolutions, he maintains, are forms of change which are relatively abrupt and affect the behavior patterns of a significant proportion of the people. In order to be a "political" revolution, an upheaval must also: (1) involve a mass movement; (2) be aimed, at least initially, at the political/governmental apparatus; (3) seek a power transfer that will result in broader social change; (4) be illegal or extralegal; and (5) take place through violence.

What is sought in political revolution is a change in the rules by which valued resources are distributed (i.e., broad social change), as well as in the structure that controls this allocation and administers the rules which structure conflict in other key segments of the society (i.e., the political/governmental apparatus). This goal is sought not through the established rules and structures of the society but extralegally—outside the rules and institutions of the society. In and of itself, a political revolution dramatizes the revolutionaries' disdain for the rules that ordinarily structure conflict and their wish to supplant those rules with rules of their own.

Societal conflict, then, is to a greater or lesser extent structured by the laws, customs, and institutions of society. Some of the most important of these are political and governmental. The extent to which a conflict is thus structured influences what we can reasonably expect concerning the way in which the conflict will be waged, the attitudes of the parties toward each other, and the impact of any given instance of conflict on the society as a whole. Different types and amounts of structure are deemed appropriate for a given type of conflict in different societies. While decisions regarding the type and amount of structure to impose are not totally arbitrary, there is room for discretion. The way in which the discretion is exercised by institution builders and government rule makers will have a tremendous impact on the political stability of the society and the predictability of the everyday lives of its people.

What has all this to do with coercion? Except in some relatively rare situations (e.g., capital punishment), the use of violence is not part of the rules of the political game. In fact, the presence of a reasonably well-defined set of rules tends to discourage the resort to force. But it is difficult to think of a highly unstructured political conflict that does not involve a high probability that violence will erupt. And of course, conflict to change the rules of conflict—revolution—connotes violence to many if not all people. The choice to use force as a tactic or strategy becomes more available as the conflict becomes less structured by any set of rules or norms. Even in relatively structured conflicts, however, some people have a greater tendency than do others to choose violence rather than peaceful means.

But the structure of conflict is also related to the dynamics of the political process. For example, in highly structured, rule-bound conflict situations, authorities have the opportunity to make it difficult for partisans to assert claims on public resources. On the other hand, the existence of procedures and rules may make it possible for those who feel they have been unfairly treated to gain access to public resources in ways that might not be possible in unstructured conflict situations. There is clearly a complex relationship among the structure of conflict, the relative advantages of winners and losers, the perception of justice, and the resolution of conflict. Chapter 10 discusses some of these issues in more detail.

THE CHOICE OF COERCION

In conventional political analysis, a common assumption is that political actors use force or the threat of force instrumentally. That is, they use it in a conscious and premeditated fashion because they think (perhaps misguidedly, perhaps not) that it will enhance their probability of achieving a certain political goal or set of goals. When a terrorist kidnaps a government official or when one nation threatens to attack another, political scientists are prone to ask: What do they expect to accomplish by this action? Such behavior is seen as "controlled by consequences" in the sense that force is used to master a problem (Berkowitz 1975, p. 232; Gamson 1975, pp. 81–82; Mitchell 1981).

Unlike political scientists, psychologists tend to see politics as an arena in which emotions originating elsewhere are stimulated and played out. This is an expressive view of political conflict (Mitchell 1981, pp. 26–27). So although the users of political violence may give reasons for their acts and may talk about them in terms of concrete goals, the psychologist is inclined to ask: What nonpolitical frustrations or drives are at the base of this behavior? Berkowitz (1975, p. 229) points out two basic variations on this theme. First is the situation in which an individual is suffering from the effects of very unpleasant present or past conditions (e.g. painful events or frustrations). This will give rise to a "fairly specific internal inclination to be aggressive" (ibid., 1975, p. 229), which can be triggered by some political situation or event.

For example, Jeanne Knutson's research (1981) convinced her that victimization is the motive force behind much political violence in the contemporary world. Victimization is a personally experienced injustice which the victim knows to be unnecessary and which creates a basic fear of annihilation. Discrete victimization events that have the strength to change the victim's perception of the world can cause the victim to act in defense of himself and his group in order to reduce the chances for further aggression against the self. One such case might have been the effect on Lenin of the execution of his older brother for political terrorist activities against the czarist regime. Even more on point, Hitler was a formerly abused child who discovered his oratorical power at a time when Germany was in desperate economic straits as a result of the agreements that ended World War I.

Berkowitz's second variation (1975) is that a person may merely be excited or aroused. This general, initially nonaggressive arousal can—under appropriate conditions—be channeled into political violence. The classic example is that of a large group of people that suddenly turns into an angry, violent mob. For example, at about 3:45 A.M. on July 23, 1967, a curious crowd had gathered to watch a police raid on an illegal after-hours drinking club in a predominantly black section of Detroit. Bystanders began to taunt the police and throw bottles at police vans. Soon this developed into a major race riot involving over 10,000 people and millions of dollars of damage, not to mention the death of forty-three persons (Eldridge 1979, pp. 60–67).

As political psychologists we are inclined to look at instances of the use of force or the threat of force in terms of both of these perspectives—instrumental and expressive. Each such act is usually based on some mixture of instrumental motivation and underlying psychological dynamics. Rather than ask *which* of these underlie a given act of political violence, it is more useful to try to ascertain the particular mix. As has been true so many other times in this book, we are faced with a dimension rather than a clear-cut dichotomy.

For example, let us take an instance of political assassination—that of Robert Kennedy during the 1968 presidential campaign. The goal of Sirhan Sirhan, the assassin, was to protect his fellow Palestinians from what he perceived as the danger implicit in Kennedy's support for the sale of arms to Israel. On this level, then, his act was instrumental and goal directed. On another level, however, it is appropriate to ask why he chose assassination as a means to achieve this goal when hundreds of equally concerned supporters of Palestine were trying to achieve the same goal by more peaceful means. In finding him guilty, rather than not guilty by reason of insanity, the jury indicated that it perceived him as acting primarily in an instrumental way to achieve his goal. Any pathological aggressiveness they might have seen in him apparently was judged of secondary importance.

The use of force or the threat to use force usually implies the use of some form of violence.* The question of the origins and triggers of human violence has intrigued students of human behavior at least since the earliest days of written history. During the twentieth century, scholars have advanced a wide variety of theories of human aggressiveness. These can be roughly divided into three categories. First, there are the biological theories, including the psychophysiological, the sociobiological, and the ethological. Second, there are the psychological and social-psychological theories, ranging from Freudian theories to theories of situational conformity. Third, the relatively young discipline of political psychology has generated several theories in its quest to better understand terrorism and international violence. Two of the more recent of these will be outlined below. Though space does not permit a detailed discussion, this brief sampling will convey the flavor of recent scholarly thinking on the topic.

Biological theories.   The central issue in most ethological or sociobiological theories of aggression is whether the human propensity to commit acts of individual or collective violence is primarily innate or primarily learned. Note that the previous statement assumes both an innate and a learned component. Although this has not always been the case, very few people any longer attempt to discuss the question in terms of nature *or* nurture. Rather there is general acknowledgment that human behavior stems from a complex interaction among the many components of our genetic inheritance and the multitude of learning experiences we have during our lifetimes.

While twentieth century psychology has by and large supported a view of aggressiveness as primarily learned behavior, many scholars

---

*Because of the general tenor of this chapter and the limits on its length, we will omit any discussion of structural violence. The interested reader is referred to Gurr and Bishop, 1976.

relying on empirical and theoretical ethology as well as sociobiology, have argued for a significant behavioral genetic contribution (Taylor 1984). A major impetus was the 1966 publication of Konrad Lorenz's book, *On Aggression*. In it (to oversimplify a complex argument) Lorenz argues that a propensity toward aggression is rooted in the genetic inheritance of homo sapiens. A Nobel-prize-winning ethologist, Lorenz wrote *On Aggression* to be understandable to the interested nonspecialist. It immediately sparked a wave of controversy and a series of rejoinders from scholars who took exception to Lorenz's assertions (Alland 1972; Binford 1972; Goldstein 1975; Montagu 1968; Schneirla 1968; Scott 1968; Tinbergen 1968). About the time the furor over Lorenz's book was subsiding, E.O. Wilson published *Sociobiology* (1975), and the arguments pro and con were rekindled within a broader context in which violence and aggression were seen as part of a more complex structure of animal and human behaviors.

All of the arguments that revolve around such theoretical formulations hinge on several questions—none of which can be answered definitively. First, do we have all the necessary evidence regarding the aggressive behavior of those animals most closely related to homo sapiens? Given the amount of ethological field research currently being conducted, as well as the recent findings of field researchers, it is difficult to assert that we do. Second, even if animal research were to demonstrate conclusively the presence of an innate aggressive drive, could this finding be generalized to homo sapiens? Generalization of the results of animal research to humans is a mainstay of much biological, biomedical, and learning-theory-oriented psychological research. But even in these relatively more well-developed fields, scientists make such generalizations not because they have absolute faith in them but because the nature of the research often means that similar experiments on human beings are not a feasible option. The animal research is considered "better than nothing" rather than "the best way to go." Such issues of generalization become even more serious when we turn to the analysis of social behavior. Finally, even if humans do behave in many ways like our animal relatives, what are the implications of our being much more complex creatures living in a much more complex world? Human beings have more intricate brains and nervous systems than our nearest mammal relatives. Also, the structures of our many behavioral systems, as well as the situations we must deal with on a daily basis, far exceed in variety and complexity those faced by any other species. Given these factors, how much of our behavioral repertoire could possibly be pre-programmed?

Though much of our aggressive or violent behavior is probably instinctual, the genetic contribution is likely to be quite small (Mark & Ervin, 1970; but see Taylor 1984). Given the enormous variety of behaviors demanded of human beings by the situations in which they continually find themselves, it is unlikely that large components lie completely outside our conscious control. More convincing is the notion that we inherit certain propensities which may or may not be activated and which (in psychologically normal people, at least) cannot result in significant violence without some conscious decision making. One example is the tendency to fight or flee in response to stressful stimuli. Many an ulcer has been generated as the result of conscious and successful efforts to resist both of these strong innate tendencies.

Rather than looking at human beings as a species and asking to what extent homo sapiens is aggressively inclined, the psychophysiologically oriented researcher looks for physiological characteristics that may contribute to making one member or one category of members of the human species more aggressive than others. Psychophysiological researchers have identified several physiological characteristics which they assert are associated with an increased probability of violent behavior. One that achieved a considerable amount of notoriety several years ago was the XYY chromosome. Most males have an XY chromosome that determines their sexual characteristics (women have a corresponding XX chromosome). About one male in 1,000, however, has an extra Y chromosome (Taylor, 1984, p. 75). In the 1960s and early 1970s several studies reported that the number of XYY males jailed for violent behavior exceeded their proportion in the general population (e.g. Hook, 1973; Jacobs et al 1965; Jarvik et al 1973). Other scholars (e.g., Montagu 1968) were quick to point out, though, that over 95 percent of those incarcerated for violent behavior were *not* XYYs. Therefore it is likely that the XYY chromosome's contribution to violent behavior, if any, is slight, and that it requires precipitating conditions before violent behavior will occur.

An increased probability of violent behavior has also been associated with other physiological factors, such as certain brain abnormalities, certain chemicals, and high levels of testosterone (Davies 1984; Goldstein 1975, p. 9; Hook 1984; Larsen 1976, p. 31; Levine & Conner 1969; Mark & Ervin 1970). Similarly, it has been demonstrated that it is possible to stimulate the brain in such a way as to control aggressive behavior in both animals and humans (Delgado 1969; Heath 1963).

It would seem that, to some extent, violent behavior can be related to physiological factors. This should not be taken to mean, however, that violence is *caused* by body chemistry, brain chemistry or genetic abnormality. Some stimulus has to activate the process, and there has to be an appropriate target for attack. Also, socialization plays a major role (Berkowitz 1969b; Montagu 1968). So while body physiology and chemistry have a place in the production of aggressive behavior, in most real world situations it is probable that the necessary neural changes are stimulated by any of a host of cognitive and environmental events (e.g., Berkowitz 1970; Kaufmann 1969a,pp. 29–30). While biology plays a role in violence, it is highly unlikely to be the sole cause of any particular violent event.

Psychological and social-psychological theories.   Psychologists have developed a variety of theories concerning aggression and violence. Since these are numerous and often complex, the discussion here can cover only the bare essentials of a selection of those that have been most influential. Like biologists, psychologists have been concerned about whether aggression is innate. Freud, the father of modern psychotherapy, thought human beings are instinctively aggressive (Freud 1959). He tied this aggressiveness to the death wish, which he saw as a desire to return to an inorganic state. Because human beings also possess life instincts that inhibit self-destruction, Freud theorized that aggressive acts result from the death instinct being directed outward, rather than toward the self.

More widely accepted in contemporary psychoanalysis is the idea that humans have an inherent aggressive tendency which can be displaced and used as a source of energy for socially useful behaviors (e.g., Storr 1968). An example would be a person who uses his aggressive drive to generate large amounts of energy which can be used to further his career. There is no good experimental evidence for such psychoanalytic theories, but many psychoanalysts find them intuitively appealing and claim that they are useful in treating patients.

During the 1930s Dollard and his associates (1939) wrote a book which advanced the thesis that frustration leads to aggression under proper conditions. The idea that frustration is a major motive force behind aggressive behavior has been enormously influential and is particularly evident—either tacitly or explicitly—in many analyses of social and political violence (e.g., Gurr 1970). In 1941, Miller, one of Dollard's associates, published a book which emphasized the point that frustration does not invariably lead to aggressive behavior. Rather, it can lead to other responses, such as apathy (Berkowitz 1969a; Maier 1949). Also, frustration is less likely to lead to aggression when it is perceived as reasonable than when it is perceived as arbitrary or unreasonable (Nye 1973, p. 68). For example, military basic training is characterized by many severe hardships and humiliations. A young person of college age is much more likely to accept the frustrations involved when such hardships and humiliations are inflicted in the context of actual basic training (especially during wartime) than when they are inflicted in the context of a college physical education course.

Social learning theory, which was discussed in Chapter 4, posits reinforcement and imitation as the main ways in which aggressive behavior is produced in human beings (Bandura & Walters 1963). According to the social learning theorist, someone who is exposed to the aggressive behavior of others and who is rewarded for her own aggressive acts will have a greater tendency to be aggressive in the future. This approach emphasizes the importance of the socialization process. Some societies and cultures inculcate the notion that aggressive behavior is appropriate in a wide variety of situations; others teach greater restraint and discrimination.

Sometimes people will act aggressively in response to a situation that seems to demand that type of behavior from them. In other words, they conform to a situation which encourages or dictates aggressive behavior.

The driving force behind such conformity seems to be a fear of social disapproval or social sanctions (Larsen 1976, p. 80). For example, early in this century in the southern United States, participation in a lynch mob carried a negligible (or nonexistent) social cost. On the other hand, a potentially high social cost accompanied refusal to participate. Here, as in so many other areas of social behavior, perceptions are the key. People differ in their calculations of social cost and in the extent to which they put a higher priority on positive social relations than on moral or value considerations.

A variation on this theme has been explored by Stanley Milgram (1974), whose research concerned the willingness of people to perform aggressive acts when told to do so by an authority figure (in this case, a person posing as a scientific researcher). Milgram's subjects demonstrated a much higher willingness to perform aggressive acts than had been anticipated. In interpreting his data, Milgram explicitly rejected the notion that the situation had merely given the subjects an excuse to act out innate aggressive impulses. Rather, he found that the persons who engaged in the aggressive behavior when told to do so "were performing a task that was distasteful and often disagreeable but which they felt obliged to carry out" (Milgram 1974, p. 167). The theme of social cost as a sanction is evident:

> The subject has found himself locked into a well-defined social order. To break out of the assigned role is to create, on a small scale, a form of anomie. The future of the subject's interaction with the experimenter is predictable as long as he maintains the relationship in which he has been defined, in contrast to the totally unknown character of the relationship attendant upon a break [i.e., a refusal to obey]. [Milgram 1974, p. 162].

Of particular interest in political analysis is ethnocentrism, which is a theory of aggressive behavior based on group dynamics (Sumner 1906). According to this perspective, groups tend to develop strong psychological bonds among members. Such group cohesiveness leads to a pattern of thinking in which the group to which we belong—the in-group—is seen in a positive light and everyone else—the out-group—is seen in a negative light. Ethnocentrism refers to a situation in which "one's own group is the center of everything, and all others are scaled and rated with reference to it; [where]. . .each group nourishes its own pride and vanity, boasts itself superior, exalts its own divinities, and looks with contempt on outsiders" (Sumner 1906, p. 13, as quoted in Eldridge 1979, p. 42). Such hostility toward out-groups can lead to aggression (LeVine & Campbell 1972). This can take the form of a syndrome in which intergroup conflict leads to greater internal group cohesiveness, which leads, in turn, to ethnocentric reactions causing greater intergroup hostility. The ultimate result of such a spiral can be violence (Deutsch 1973, pp. 76–77). This spiral is directly linked to a classic ploy of international relations in which a country instigates hostilities against another country in order to distract its citizens' attention from problems at home.*

Political psychological theories.   Two of the most eminent scholars in the emerging discipline of political psychology have been the late Jeanne Knutson and Lloyd S. Etheredge. Each has tried to shed new light on the conditions under which a decision is made to resort to the use of force or violence in order to deal with a political problem. Etheredge studied the effect of personality on decisions to use military force in international relations. Knutson studied the motive forces behind acts of political violence, particularly those commonly characterized as terrorist acts, by individuals. In both cases, their theoretical propositions are based on extensive empirical data.

As a result of his research, Etheredge (1978) concluded that the personality makeup of males who seek and gain high positions in the American foreign policy elite "contains those ingredients—and in significant measure—that make war more likely" (ibid., p. xiv). These personality characteristics can be grouped under the general heading, "male narcissism syndrome." Etheredge sees the root of the problem in the fact that decision makers in this area have to deal with ambiguous situations and to use crude, inadequately validated notions about human behavior. This causes them to resort to intuition and opens the door to the influence of their own "oppressive or domineering or menacing or intrusive predispositions" (ibid., p. 59). The result of such emotion-based, self-deceptive thinking is a decision "that *looks* like a rational decision, and *feels* like a rational decision, but which is in reality only a plausible, consistent decision" (ibid., p. 60, italics in original). In discussing the components of this personality type, Etheredge gives us the following description:

> . . .[M]achismo has many facets. To be strong, proud, powerful, hard, tough, particularly sensitive and alert to possible threats or domination by others, to be boldly assertive, are some of these. But male chauvinism also has connotations of paternalism, of providing security and valued gratifications, of being a protector, a leader, guardian, benefactor, a provider. . . .[S]ome of these men wish to be high status managers, leaders, and benefactors to the world—and they are willing to fight stubbornly rather than surrender America's chance to play this powerful role of active virility, guidance of others, self-worth, and generativity. (ibid., p. 61)

Etheredge sees John F. Kennedy as having such personality characteristics. All his life, Kennedy was attracted to tales of men who fought their way to the top and emerged heroically triumphant. He exhibited such a pattern in his behavior after his submarine was destroyed during World War II, in his comeback after a very serious back operation, in his

---

* But such hostilities may also have divisive effects under the right conditions. See Deutsch 1973, pp. 76–77.

competition with his older brother whom his father had wished to be president, and in his successful battle to win the presidency despite his youth and his religion. In this context, Etheredge thinks a case can be made that the disastrous Bay of Pigs decision was a product of Kennedy's male narcissism syndrome:

> President Kennedy's personality was the crucial ingredient in producing the Bay of Pigs decision. We would predict, on the basis of Kennedy's personality and pattern of behavior in other areas, that he would be more predisposed than men with different traits to perceive Fidel Castro and communism in Latin America as a challenge, that he would be more predisposed to favor heroic action to meet such a challenge, that he would be more predisposed to believe the Cuban challenge would be overcome successfully by brave and committed men in a guerilla invasion force. (ibid., p. 4)

Jeanne Knutson became passionately concerned with the riddle of the motive force behind political violence. What convinces dedicated people espousing just causes that violence is their only option? In the course of approximately a hundred personal interviews with perpetrators of political violence throughout the world, she slowly began to piece together an answer. Although the work remained unfinished at the time of her death, she did leave behind a partial manuscript that outlines her theory that the motive force is victimization.

A victim is one who has personally experienced injustice which he or she perceives as unnecessary and which creates in him or her a deep fear of annihilation. Discrete victimization events, or conversion experiences, "pressure the person threatened to increase his personal security by seeking to alter the world from the fearful visage that he now knows it to possess" (Knutson 1981, p. 37). Knutson tells the story of Francis Hughes, a young man of seventeen in Northern Ireland. Coming home from a dance he was stopped at a checkpoint by British soldiers. He and a friend were pulled from the car and beaten severely. Subsequently, he vowed that he would take care of himself and his friends, forming a unit that staged many ambushes of British soldiers and police patrols. The unit became part of the Irish Republican Army, and Hughes eventually reached the top of the British "most wanted" list.

Victimization tends to have an emotionally deadening effect for most people. Victims, like terrified animals, become emotionally immobilized. Powerful mechanisms of denial keep them from perceiving that the future may bring more experiences of similar brutality and, possibly, death. Any improvement in the situation can permit the surfacing of both rage and severe anxiety, as well as a conscious fear of future victimization. Accompanying these reactions is "the semiconscious inner knowledge that *passivity ensures victimization*" (ibid, p. 73, italics in original). "Only continued activity in defense of one's self (one's group) adequately serves to reduce the threat of further aggression against [the] self" (ibid, p. 74).

Assertive activities hold the promise of weakening the victimizing system's power. "Equally important, personal activity focused on eliminating the threat of further injustice dampens the victim's paralyzing *inner* anxiety over future loss" (ibid, p. 74, italics in original). Action is a tonic for fear. The first act of defiance causes the emergence of "a full, direct, emotional awareness of intense rage, as well as unbearable anxiety stemming from the possibility of the loss of even life itself for having dared to defy the aggressor" (ibid, p. 75). Thus, the perpetrator of political violence can reach the point of no return, and the fears aroused sustain further acts of violence. Also important is hope: it undergirds defensive aggression with the promise of success. The potential penalties for violence are perceived as less threatening than the certain results of passivity—severe chronic anxiety and the possibility of death.

Conclusion. That ends our sampling of the major biological, psychological, social-psychological, and political psychological theories that have tried to elucidate the topic of political force or violence. Some, like those of Knutson and Etheredge, have emerged in direct response to events in the political world. Others, like those of Dollard, have formed the basis for later, more politically oriented work. For example, Ted Robert Gurr (1970) has explicitly attempted to develop a theory of revolutionary behavior based on frustration-aggression theory.

With reference to the interaction model discussed in Chapter 1, it should be noted that each of these theories focuses on one segment of the model. For example, Freud, as well as Dollard and his associates and Etheredge, focuses on what is happening inside the individual. Situational conformity theory concentrates on what is happening in the microenvironment. Social learning theory, as well as Knutson's victimization theory, concentrates on the impact of both the microenvironment and the macroenvironment on individual behavior. Ethnocentrism focuses on the dynamics of the microenvironmental interactions within groups, as well as the macroenvironmental issues involved in the relationships between groups, which may consist of entire cultural or national collectivities.

Although the brief treatment we gave the theories in this chapter tends to emphasize these central foci, more detailed consideration brings out that all of them, to some extent, stress the importance of the personality-situation interaction. We would like to step back a little further and suggest that they (as well as others that we have not been able to mention) each highlight a particular aspect of an extremely complex process and that, within the context of an interaction approach, they can all be seen as making a potential contribution to any concrete instance of political force or violence. In other words, while we do not regard any one of them as being *the* one right explanation of human violence, we think that all of them should be taken into consideration in any attempt to analyze specific events involving the use or threat of force. Also, we see the whole issue of human aggressive behavior as involving a much more complex dynamic than any of these theories suggests—a dynamic involving elements within the individual, the microenvironment, and the macroenvironment, with the specific mix varying from concrete situation to concrete situation.

THE USES OF FORCE

In political life, force has two major aspects. Force or the threat of force can be used to reinforce and protect the status quo. It can also be used to change the status quo. Although scholars before and since Weber have understood the importance of the use of force to *maintain* the status quo, the use of force to *change* the status quo has commanded much more research attention. Events such as wars and revolutions seem to hold more intrinsic interest than, for example, police officers going about their daily business. In the following discussion, we will touch on some of the most obvious research findings that are relevant to our model of the political process. In particular, we will emphasize the different perspectives authorities and partisans have on the use of force to obtain public resources or to control decisions made about these resources. The structure of conflict may also be related to the use of force partly because of the capacity of authorities to control the rule-making process and thus give advantages to certain groups over others.

Status-quo-oriented force. Because rulers are invariably outnumbered by those over whom they wield power, they are perpetually in danger of being ousted, either by an overthrow of the existing constitutional order or by an overthrow of the current regime. "Whatever the psychological mechanisms involved, once individuals become part of a ruling political elite they strive to maintain and use their power for as long as possible" (Pirages 1976, p. 32). At least in part, they are aided by the prevailing apathy of most citizens toward their political system. They are also aided by the fact that good law enforcement both supports the existing regime and constitutional order *and* renders the lives of citizens more secure and predictable.

When the monopoly of legitimate force is not abused and is used with some degree of intelligence, with citizen welfare in mind, citizens tend to respond by abiding by the laws and giving the political system at least minimal support in the form of compliance. Also, as Pareto asserted, "no elite which [has] preserved its capacity for timely and effective violence, or for effective manipulation, [can] be successfully assailed, or perhaps assailed at all" (Eckstein 1972, p. 17). Legitimacy, of course, is the key. Any political status quo possesses a certain amount of legitimacy merely by virtue of its existence; and the use of force to maintain that status quo thus takes on a corresponding legitimacy. In fact, police and soldiers wielding force to preserve an existing political order may view themselves as highly moral and may be decorated or promoted as a result of having used violence (Ball-Rokeach 1972, p. 102).

The use of force is reasonably effective at eliciting compliance. It is far less capable of creating identification and may even be counterproductive with reference to internalization. Therefore, force is, perhaps, the least effective mechanism for conflict regulation and resolution. In addition, it is also an extremely expensive means of preserving law and order (Pirages 1976, p. 33). In economic terms, it takes a tremendous amount of money and resources to maintain large and effective police and military forces. In psychological terms, the use of force can affect regime legitimacy, because the use of violence raises issues of morality (Gamson 1975, p. 73), and the more often force is used, the more serious these questions become. Also, their possession of the skills and means of using violence tends to make both the police and the military potent political forces—at least potentially.

Let us take the police as an example. It is probably safe to say that, whether or not the police choose to exercise their political power, they are acutely aware that they possess it (Wilson 1968, p. 230). With reference to the United States, the task force report submitted to the National Commission on the Causes and Prevention of Violence asserts:

> In some senses the police are an even greater source of potential concern than the armed forces because of their closeness to the day-to-day workings of the political process and their frequent interaction with the population. These factors make police abuse of the political process a more immediate prospect. For example, bumper stickers on squad cars, political buttons on uniforms, selective ticketing, and similar contacts with citizens quickly impart a political message. (Skolnick 1969, pp. 286–87)

In cases where the police have rebelled against constituted political authority, they have proved formidable opponents (ibid., 1969, pp. 276–78).

With reference to a country like the Soviet Union, the potential for police interference with and control of political decision making is even more dramatic:

> A secret police develops its own laws of growth. The more discord it discovers or develops, the more indispensable it becomes. Its tendency is always to extend its own sovereignty, to seek to emancipate itself from all external controls, to become a state within a state, and to preserve the conditions of emergency and siege on which an expansion of its own power depends. Once terror becomes an end in itself, there is no easy and natural stopping place. From the viewpoint of the leadership, there is an even greater worry, the fear that as the secret police apparatus emancipates itself from external controls, it becomes a menace to the security of the highest Party leaders themselves. (Fainsod 1980, p. 143)

Using violence to maintain the status quo, then, can be a two-edged sword, because it requires the creation of a formidable force that may in the future be turned against its creators. Even where the police remain basically loyal, the result of achieving political ends by the use of force can be less than entirely satisfactory. To take an extreme example, Stalinist terror succeeded in maintaining Stalin in power until his death. In achieving the national objectives embraced by Stalin, however, it was largely disfunctional (Hendel 1980, p. 134).

As was suggested earlier, force can fill needs for a population as well as for its rulers. For example, a strong and efficient police and military can fill for the citizenry (in part, at least) Maslow's basic security need, and this is an important prerequisite for filling the other needs in his hierarchy (Knutson 1973, p. 7). Even where a police force is oppressive it can, in some curious and unexpected ways, fill citizen needs—perhaps even the needs of its victims. For example, during a television program on the fate of recent Russian immigrants in the United States, a former dissident Soviet writer noted that in his new country his work was not receiving the attention he felt it deserved. In this connection he made the following comment:

> I actually miss the KGB. They paid attention to me. They were the first ones to read my manuscripts thoroughly. It was wonderful to have real attention. (*Washington Post,*June 13, 1983, p. C1)

From a psychological point of view, the use of force or the threat of force to achieve political ends can be conceptualized in terms of aversive stimuli. Aversive stimuli, in lay terms, are forms of punishment. Behavioral psychologists have done a great deal of research on the effects of punishment on behavior, and several of the results of this research seem to have some applicability to our discussion of the use of force in political life. In terms of aversive conditioning citizens may be seen as obeying political authorities in order to avoid the pain that would be involved if the authorities were to use force. Force, or the threat of force, is used to exert political influence through fear: "He who controls pain also controls behavior. He who controls fear is the one who rules" (Freedman & Freedman 1975, p. 66).

Aside from tending to elicit compliance or at best, identification and, probably, to hinder internalization, force has other serious disadvantages as a means of governing. If fear is too strong, people may be unable to respond or, at least, to respond appropriately (Estes 1944). In his famous "secret speech" at the Twentieth Congress of the Communist Party of the Soviet Union in 1956, Khrushchev made the following observation about Stalin's use of force:

> We should also not forget that, due to the numerous arrests of party, Soviet and economic leaders, many workers began to work uncertainly, showed overcautiousness, feared all which was new, feared their own shadows and began to show less initiative in their work. . . . (Khrushchev 1980, p. 152)

Behavioral researchers have also found that punishment tends to suppress undesirable behavior only temporarily (Church 1963). This means that if punishment is being used to control behavior, it must be reapplied on a regular schedule (Freedman & Freedman 1975, p. 79). People must be watched carefully for undesirable behaviors; the threat must be kept fresh, and punishment must be administered when appropriate. This not only puts a tremendous strain on any political system but also harms a country's economy. Merle Fainsod has noted such effects with regard to the Soviet Union:

> A system which relies on a large secret police as a basic core of its power is highly wasteful of manpower. The main occupation of the secret police is that of spying, investigating, examining, guarding, and controlling others. Large numbers of talented people are removed from productive work . . . . The atmosphere of universal suspicion which terror breeds is not ordinarily conducive to creative thinking and displays of individual initiative. If the weight of terror becomes too great and the penalty of any administrative failure or mistake is MVD detention, it becomes difficult to persuade people to take responsibility . . . . Even those driven by fear of the secret police to work as they have never worked before, begin to crack under the strain. It is no easy task to apply terror and at the same time to hold it in leash. (Fainsod 1980, p. 143)

As a mechanism for those in power to use in managing and resolving political conflict, force tends to be used as a last resort, rather than a favored method. The threat of force can also be used to buttress other mechanisms of political conflict regulation and resolution, as when the use of violence is threatened if the other side will not make certain concessions during negotiations. In most cases, however, force is too uncertain and too fraught with peril to be used as a primary source of political influence. Since it tends to be of uncertain effectiveness and since there are other more attractive options in stable situations, force tends to be reserved for more extraordinary situations—as when there is an attempt to overthrow a regime or a constitutional order.

Change-oriented force. While the status-quo-oriented use of force tends to take the form of a tacit or explicit *threat* of force—most commonly the specification of sanctions for the commission or omission of certain behaviors—the *actual use* of force tends to be more common when the objective is change. Thus it is in the service of change that we see the more dramatic instances of the use of violent force: revolution, assassination, riots, terrorism, and coups, for example.

In addition, force in service of the status-quo tends to be used according to some generally agreed-upon "rules of the game." Most commonly in political systems these are embodied in a constitution, a body of laws, or a set of traditions. Modern political systems tend to have all three and to vary concerning the extent to which each is embodied in written form and the extent to which each constitutes an actual restraint on individual behavior. The difference in form is seen in the contrast between the United States, with its written constitution, and Great Britain, with its unwritten constitution. The difference in extent of restraint is seen in the contrast between the United States, where the constitution is taken very seriously as a guide to behavior, and the Soviet Union, where written constitutions have largely tended to be ignored. Although it has a written constitution like the United States, the Soviet Union tends in actual practice to resemble Great Britain, with its unwritten constitution. As Szamuely (1969, pp. 59–60) puts it, "the USSR *does* have a genuine constitution—unwritten, or rather, unpublicized, yet perfectly well understood and recognized by all concerned."

Force in the service of change tends to be used to change some or most of the "rules of the game," or at least, to modify the way they are translated into practice. Since we cannot do justice to even the major forms of this use of force in the space allotted here, we will single out one form, revolution. This is not a random selection, but a reflection of the particular place revolution occupies within the broader context of political behavior conceptualized as conflict over the allocation of societal or public resources.

All political conflict—whether or not it involves force—is limited to some degree by rules. The extent to which particular types of political conflict are rule bound varies greatly, ranging from the highly structured form courtroom conflicts take in the United States to the virtually unstructured or ruleless activities of political terrorists. Within this context revolution is particularly significant because it is, in essence, a political conflict over what rules should bound other forms of political conflict. As Brickman (1974, p. 13) puts it, "Revolutionary conflict necessarily involves some sort of challenge to an existing rule structure by a party who regards this structure as in some way unfair." It is "conflict oriented toward changing the fundamental rules of relationships" (ibid., p. 15).

The violence and general system breakdown usually associated with political revolutions are in part a function of the lack, in such situations, of a larger system or a superior authority to which a disagreement over the rules can be appealed. In this sense, revolutions are ruleless: They are open challenges to the very systems of rules that would otherwise bound and channel political conflicts. During the night of October 25, 1917, the Bolsheviks did not just overthrow a regime, they established a new legal order (Liebman 1970, p. 273) or set of rules governing political activities in Russia.

Also, revolutionary conflicts tend to be perceived differently. Most nonrevolutionary conflicts are over valued resources. Although the stakes may be high, the combatants are usually confident that—whatever the outcome—they will probably survive to battle again. In a revolutionary conflict there is much more uncertainty as to survival. First, physical survival may be an issue. One way of making sure that a given constitutional order does not return is to kill those who might be keys to its revival. Nicholas II of Russia and his immediate family were eliminated during the Russian Revolution—giving Russian monarchists no one around whom they could rally in an undivided way. Second, the issue may not be actual physical survival, but survival as viable contestants in the political arena. If a given state or constitutional order does not survive, certain individuals and groups may find themselves excluded from the political arena and from previously held advantages. Revolutionary conflicts may have a greater emotional intensity due to the perception (not necessarily accurate) of each side that its survival, physical or other, is at stake.

If we look at revolution as political conflict over what the structure of other political conflicts should be, we see that it is not an extraordinary occurrence at all, but one that would be expected to arise normally in the course of events. That is, if we assume that perfect fairness is not attained by real-world political systems and, further, that some of the participants in any political system will *perceive* it to be unfair, then challenges to the existing rules governing political conflict are natural. This can be thought of as the revolutionary potential within a political system. When the constituted authorities or the weakness of the institutional structure allow this perception of unfairness to become acute, the revolutionary potential can easily be translated into actual revolutionary activity (Aristotle 1951, p. 106; Johnson 1966, p. 4). In the case of the Russia of 1917, both the rigidity of the political institutions and the indecisiveness of the political leadership contributed to the movement toward the October Revolution (Liebman 1970, pp. 163–164).

Defining revolution as conflict over the rules of conflict has another important implication. Various authors have generated a number of different typologies defining the sorts of political conflicts that should or should not be considered "revolution" (Rejai 1977, pp. 15–25). If we define revolution as an attempt to change the "rules of the game," certain types of struggles are automatically excluded, most notably struggles that involve a change of regime but not a significant change in the constitutional order or the structure of laws, such as the conspiratorial coup d'état, which is merely a struggle over who should occupy certain positions within an existing structure.

Moving from the nature of revolution to the psychological dynamics of revolutionary activity, it should be noted from the outset that this is a topic about which theories abound and there is little contemporary agreement. We will limit our discussion to several related theories (Davies 1962; Davies 1969; Feierabend & Feierabend 1966; Geschwender 1964; Gurr 1970; Gurr 1972). Although these studies have been subject to criticism (e.g., Levy 1981), they are still the theories of revolutionary behavior that have been most influential to date.

While important differences exist among these theories, they all center on some concept of relative deprivation. The general idea behind relative deprivation is that people develop expectations about their future based on their past experience. The degree to which they feel satisfied with their present state is a function of the difference between what has been happening to them currently and their expectations. If there is a wide gap between what they are experiencing and what they expect, they are likely to experience feelings of dissatisfaction and frustration and to be prone to involvement in political unrest. Under the proper conditions this propensity to involvement in political unrest can lead to revolution.

While it is clear that this approach illuminates one possible factor underlying at least some revolutionary events, it is equally clear that the phenomenon of revolution is too complex to be satisfactorily and definitively explained by so limited a set of theories.* If you look at a list of preconditions for political revolution elaborated by one or more reputable scholars (e.g., Rejai 1977, pp. 27–28), you will see that they prove to be both numerous and diverse. For example, from the microenvironment we are told to look toward such factors as economic conditions (both good and bad), foreign rule, deficient political leadership, governmental inefficiency, and class antagonisms. Somewhat overlapping, but more geared toward the macroenvironment are such conditions as exposure to groups propagating alternative ways of government, and the perception of barriers to social or economic advancement. On an individual level there can be such psychological factors as relative deprivation, relative gratification, and alienation. The picture that emerges is one of an extremely complex phenomenon that is difficult to either analyze or explain with a small number of categories or factors. In short, although some good pioneering work has been done, there is much left to do before we will have a satisfactory picture of the dynamics of revolutionary behavior.

SUMMARY

Under the proper conditions political conflict can involve the threat or use of force. These conditions are related to the nature of political conflict and to the way in which it is structured in political systems. Political conflicts tend to arise over the distribution of public positions or public goods. In both cases, there is a perception on the part of one or more parties to the conflict that they are pursuing incompatible goals. This conflict process is not neutral. Some "rules of the game" always constrain the combatants. Some of the most important are the rules embodied in political institutions. They structure and constrain (or fail to constrain) the various encounters of the political combatants.

These structural constraints range from those which almost totally govern the conflict to those which govern it only minimally. The less structure, the more opportunities for the conflict to shade into violence. Both historically and theoretically, the greatest potential for violence resides in conflicts over the rules of conflict, because they are—by definition—essentially ruleless. When such conflicts arise on a large scale in a

*This does not detract from the pioneering efforts of these authors who, in all fairness, have never claimed to be definitive.

given political system, we tend to call them *revolutions* and to invest them with a moralistic flavor.

Political scientists tend to see the decision to resort to force as an instrumental one, while psychologists tend to look for underlying frustrations or drives for which violence can serve as an expressive outlet. Neither should be ignored in the analysis of instances of the use of force. Theories regarding the roots of human aggressiveness can be divided into three categories. First, there are those which emphasize biological factors; these include theories based on psychophysiology, sociobiology, and ethology. Second, there are the psychological and social psychological theories. Finally, there are those which have emerged from political psychology, especially those generated by concerned scholars in search of a better understanding of terrorism and international violence.

Force can be used to protect or to change the status quo. The latter use has, to date, commanded more research attention. The former use, however, is also important since it involves the complex relationship between the relatively small number of people who make authoritative decisions in a political system and the relatively large number of people who are affected by those decisions. The use of force is reasonably effective at eliciting simple compliance with such decisions. It is far less effective in eliciting loyalty—either to the rulers themselves or to the constitutional order of which they are a part. Force as a mechanism for conflict management and resolution, then, tends to be used as a last resort rather than the method of choice. It also tends to be used as a threat, rather than an actuality.

Change-oriented situations, on the other hand, are more likely to involve the actual use of force or violence. It is force in the service of change—assassinations, coups, wars, revolutions, and terrorism—that tends to be associated in people's minds with the notion of the use of force in political conflict. Also, force used to effect change tends to be less rule bound than force used in preserving the status quo. Revolution is a particularly significant form of force, because it threatens the rules that govern—to a greater or lesser extent—all other instances of political conflict.

TOWARD THE NEXT STEP IN THE PROCESS

Although the use of force is commonplace in many types of political conflict, the conditions surrounding its emergence and use are diverse, complex and, currently, poorly understood. What seems clear is that some situations, both microenvironmental and macroenvironmental, make the use of violence more probable. Also, certain biological and psychological characteristics in the individuals involved have a similar effect. Finally, in most cases, the outbreak of violence seems to be related to the failure to try to use or the failure to succeed in using other methods of conflict management and resolution.

Political conflicts, in essence, arise from political problems that need to be solved. The parties to such conflicts have differing views as to the means to be used in solving them or the nature of the ultimate solution. In either case, the methods discussed in this and the three previous chapters are designed to aid the parties in arriving at the point where they resolve their differences by making some sort of decision (including the decision not to decide) which will—at least for the moment—resolve or regulate their conflict. It is appropriate at this point to turn to a consideration of political decision making.

9

DECISION MAKING
The Quintessential Political Act

Governments must make decisions. In fact, it might be argued that the most important function of the government of any country is to make decisions—difficult decisions about "who gets what, when, how" (Lasswell 1958). Decisions, however, are not really made by some abstraction labeled *government*. Rather, they are made by people who are acting on behalf of that abstract entity. These people are for the most part quite ordinary individuals; some are brighter than others, some are wiser; but most can be characterized as normal human beings trying to do a reasonably good job. Why then are so many "mistakes" made? Why do so many decisions end up being widely viewed as "bad" decisions?

To some extent this is inescapable, because one person's bad decision can be another person's brilliant one. This is the stuff of which political conflict is made. There is more to it than this, however. Some decisions are virtually unanimously acknowledged to have been misguided or disastrous. Perhaps the prime example of this is the decision by John F. Kennedy and his close advisers to launch the Bay of Pigs attack on Cuba. Without question, this was one of the great fiascos in United States history (Stuart 1980, pp. 6–7). It is easy to identify many other equally ill-fated but less spectacular decisions ranging from those made by obscure civil servants working in obscure corners of local government right up to the president and his most influential advisers.

THE DECISION-MAKING PROCESS

Political and governmental decision making, in the ultimate sense, takes place within the human brain (Peterson 1981, 1983). Because decision making is a type of cognitive behavior, it is appropriate to begin with some consideration of cognitive theory on the functioning of the human brain (Steinbruner 1974, pp. 91–138). Human mental operations appear to be characterized by certain regularities in the way people structure their cognitive thinking (Rosenberg 1982, 1983). The actual content or ideas involved may vary greatly—perhaps virtually infinitely—but the way in which they are manipulated by the mind does seem to be reasonably comparable from person to person. Also, it seems that we use our entire mental apparatus even when we are engaged in simple mental operations, such as direct, immediate perception. Finally, much human mental functioning takes place at an unconscious level.

These principles of cognitive theory are important in any consideration of decision making, because they bear on the ability of human beings to deal with problem-solving situations involving high levels of both complexity and uncertainty (Jervis 1981). The most obvious source of complexity in any political decision-making situation is usually the complexity of the information the decision makers have to take into account (ibid., p. 3). A far more troublesome type of complexity, however, is value complexity. Any given issue in politics—unless it is quite trivial—is bound to involve many competing values and interests. It is difficult, if not impossible, for decision makers to generate guidelines that will encompass and aggregate all competing values and interests (George 1980, p. 26). To this must be added the problem of value extension. This is the "all too familiar tendency of policy issues to arouse a variety of motives and interests that are extraneous to values associated with even a very broad conception of the 'national interest' " (ibid., pp. 26–27). Thus, a decision maker might also be concerned with how his decision might affect his image in the eyes of his constituents. Public administrators are frequently concerned with how their decisions might affect their career prospects or the competitive standing of their agencies vis-a-vis other agencies.

Political decision making is also ordinarily characterized by high levels of uncertainty because decision makers in politics and government usually have insufficient information about the situations they face, as well as a limited capacity to effectively process the information they do have. Finally, more than one person is commonly involved directly or indirectly, and these people often are either connected with or representative of organizational units. The number of people involved in any decision can be thought of as a dimension, beginning with a single individual, as might be the case in autocratic or totalitarian settings.

The above factors lead to what Steinbruner calls the "complex decision problem," in which the following conditions hold:

1. (a) Two or more values are affected by the decision.
    (b) There is a trade-off relationship between the values such that a greater return to one can be obtained only at a loss to the other.

2. There is uncertainty.

3. The power to make the decision is dispersed over a number of individual actors and/or organizational units. (Steinbruner 1974, p. 16).

The value trade-off problem can be dealt with in a number of ways (George, 1980, pp. 30–34). First, the decision makers may try to resolve the value conflict. They may generate a policy that gives everyone something immediately, or they may give everyone something, but not at the same time. The first variation yields the old half-a-loaf problem and may create a situation in which everyone feels cheated and blames the decision makers. The second variation depends on the willingness of the representatives of some interests to wait while the representatives of other interests are satisfied. Such patience is a rare, but not absent, virtue in political life.

Another way of dealing with value trade-offs is by accepting the fact that they exist and that they must be resolved whether or not some interests are antagonized. In effect, the decision makers accept a role requirement to make decisions that favor some values over others and to live with the consequences—however unpleasant. President Truman defined this as his duty and placed on his desk a sign saying "The Buck Stops Here." Finally, decision makers can try to avoid the conflict of values by ignoring, discounting, denying, forgetting, or unintentionally misinterpreting information concerning the value trade-offs. They also may try to denigrate some of the values. Either way, this process interferes with the ability to process information and may therefore lead to serious miscalculations.

Only some of the many ways of dealing with uncertainty can be mentioned here. Decision makers can simply put off making the decision in the hope that the problem will go away or resolve itself. President Coolidge was a great advocate of "calculated inactivity." He defined very narrowly those matters a president *has* to decide and felt that almost everything could wait. "Coolidge himself could wait, with utter, unflappable calm, for longer than the last of his advisers" (Barber 1977, p. 149). Another way of dealing with uncertainty is by focusing on the good points of a preferred option and on the bad points of all other options.

Finally, there are numerous cognitive aids that decision makers can fall back upon. These aids are, in effect, ways of categorizing information that make complexity easier to handle. For example, they can resort to historical analogies, concentrating on what the historical event and the present situation have in common and ignoring the differences. Ideology is a powerful cognitive aid in that most ideologies contain guides for action based on the premises inherent in the ideology. If you make certain assumptions—which may or may not be valid—about the current problem, you can usually bring it within the ambit of the ideology; then the solution tends to more or less fall into place. Implicit theories (see Chapter 1) furnish similar guides to information processing in the face of uncertainty. In the political realm they provide what have been called *operational codes*. An operational code (as you may remember from

Chapter 5, p. 138–39) is "a set of general beliefs about fundamental issues of history and central questions of politics as these bear, in turn, on the problem of action" (George 1969, p. 191). This aspect of a decision maker's implicit theories can have a powerful influence on the decision-making process, because policy addresses itself not to the nature of the external world but to the image of that world in the minds of those who make policy. In this sense, ideologies and operational codes may be mutually reinforcing and even overlap to a great extent.

DECISION MAKING MODELS

People ought to be rather good at decision making; they certainly get enough practice. In fact, a large part of human life is spent in the process of iterative decision making. If practice makes perfect, then perfection should be all around us. Needless to say, it is not and this fact has caused many thoughtful people, both inside and outside of government, to do some hard analytical thinking about the nature of the decision making process and how it could possibly be improved.

The outgrowth of this process has been a set of models of how the decision making process should work. The two prototypical models are the rational-comprehensive model and the incremental model. A third, the mixed scanning model, is really a combination of or compromise between the other two. This section will consider these three models, as well as Janis and Mann's conflict model. Then, there will be a series of sections focusing on the nature of decision making by individuals, small groups and, finally, institutions or organizational units. The chapter will end with a case study of the decision making processes that took place in connection with the Kennedy administration's decision to support an invasion of Cuba at the Bay of Pigs. This case study illustrates many of the principles and problems discussed earlier in the chapter.

Rational-comprehensive.   In trying to give guidance to decision makers faced with complex decision problems, many students of decision making have tried to come up with some notion of how an ideal decision-making process should work. From this effort has emerged what is known as the rational-comprehensive model of decision making. The use of the term "rational" suggests "a decision process dominated by logical reasoning; conclusions are deduced from evidence and inferences made with a minimum of emotion" (Hartle & Halperin 1980, p. 126). This notion is intuitively appealing because it expresses a value system that is characteristically American and that we share with many other people, particularly in the developed nations of the world (Steinbruner 1974, p. 27). Whether ordinary mortals can achieve this level of dispassionate and orderly thought and behavior is quite another thing.

First, however, it is necessary to consider in more detail the elements of the rational-comprehensive decision-making model. Essentially this model posits a seven-step process:

1. The problem to be solved must be identified.
2. The goals or values to be realized in solving the problem must be specified and clarified.
3. Assuming that more than one goal or value is relevant, they must be ordered or ranked to show their relative priority.
4. All possible alternative means for solving the problem must be identified and specified (some would modify this to include only the most important, but in either case it is clear that the list of alternative solutions must be relatively comprehensive).
5. Each of the alternatives is studied to identify its costs and benefits in achieving the goals or values of the decision maker(s).
6. The results of this scrutiny are used to make a comparative analysis of the various ways of solving the problem.
7. The decision maker(s) then must select the alternative that is best in light of the goals or values which were earlier specified and ranked.

Many scholars have criticized this model of the decision-making process on the ground that the intellectual and emotional limitation of humans, as well as the constraints surrounding real-world decision making, are such that the rational-comprehensive model is unrealizable, and perhaps even impractical as a goal (Simon 1961, pp. 79–109). Let us return to the earlier point about the human mind. If people exhibit certain regularities in the way they deal with value trade-offs, complexity, uncertainty, and the necessity to accommodate to others, these will come into play despite the intention of decision makers to adhere as closely as possible to the rational-comprehensive model.

For example, the complexity and incompleteness of the information available regarding a policy problem may lead to methods of coping with uncertainty that will make it difficult for a group of decision makers even to agree on a clear definition of the problem to be solved or the values to be realized in solving it. That this method calls their attention to the inevitable value trade-offs involved in solving the problem may cause considerable psychological stress. The fact that values or goals must be ranked can only exacerbate the stress. This stress, to a certain point, can adversely affect the decision makers' ability to function (George 1980, p. 49; Ivancevich & Matteson 1980, pp. 192–200). For example, it can impair their ability to attend to the problem at hand and can even distort their perception of the problem. This means they may overlook important facets of the problem, conflicting values, possible alternative solutions, and new ways of gathering information. Stress causes "a tendency to fall back on familiar solutions that have worked in the past whether or not they are appropriate to the present situation" (ibid., p. 49). Stress can also increase stereotypic thinking and cognitive rigidity, which will impair the ability to improvise and be creative. Rigidity reduces people's openness to information not in keeping with their established beliefs. Decision makers under excessive stress will tend to devote less attention to the long-range consequences of decisions or to the side effects of alternatives and will press to make the decision prematurely in order to relieve the unpleasant tensions generated by the stress.

These are just a few of the ways in which the psychological characteristics of decision makers interact with the situation to make realization of the process of rational-comprehensive decisionmaking extremely difficult (Snyder & Diesing 1977, pp. 340–48). It is not surprising that recent government procedural reforms based on this model, such as planning, programming, and budgeting systems, have proved difficult to implement and are no longer mandated in the federal government or most other jurisdictions.

Incremental.   In a now-classic article called "The Science of Muddling Through," Charles Lindblom (1959) put forth an alternative decision-making policy model he claimed was more realistic in terms of the way decision making was really done. It highlights some of the methods decision makers use to cope with uncertainty and complexity (George 1980, pp. 40–41). This alternative model is generally referred to as the incremental model of decision making. Its main characteristics can be indicated in contrast to the framework established by the rational-comprehensive model:

1. As before, the problem to be solved must be identified, but rather than being relatively immutable, it is subject to considerable modification in the course of the decision-making process.
2. The specification and clarification of goals or values is a step that either receives much less attention or is permitted to be implicit rather than explicit.
3. Consideration of alternative solutions is limited to those that differ only incrementally from methods currently being used; there is no attempt to be comprehensive in listing alternatives.
4. The alternatives are evaluated, but not as final solutions; rather they are regarded as components in a perpetual series of attacks on the problem at hand.
5. There is no final or best solution to be chosen: Various promising alternatives are tried and then evaluated in a process that may not only result in the substitution of another alternative, but also may cause modification in the definition of the problem or the values to be realized in the decision-making process.

This is a view of decision making that emphasizes the recognition that very few problems are solved once and for all. Rather, it accepts the fact that solutions are rarely final and that solutions to existing problems tend to generate new problems. Also, problems have a nasty tendency to keep cropping up in new guises just when the decision makers think they are done with them and can turn their attention to other things.

The very tentativeness of the process makes it less stressful for the participants. Less stress makes it easier to achieve agreement on objectives in the face of value conflicts and uncertainty. If the policy does not work out, it is within the scope of the process to make needed adjustments. Indeed, the model assumes that such adjustments will be both necessary and forthcoming. The stakes in any particular choice, therefore, are not as large as they are in rational-comprehensive decision making, in which participants attempt to find the "best" solution the first time around and then to let it stand indefinitely.

The incremental model allows the decision makers to proceed under conditions that are less stressful, and so may help to avoid some of the problems outlined above. It does not guarantee that the process will yield ideal solutions, however. Trial-and-error approaches to problems can be quite costly and may not succeed in achieving a cumulative improvement in the situation. Also, incrementalism can encourage solutions that attack symptoms rather than basic causes. Thus, the decision makers may or may not muddle through successfully. Their gains will tend to be short-term rather than long-term, and the decision makers may overlook opportunities a more comprehensive approach would uncover.

Mixed scanning.   Following the elaboration of the rational-comprehensive and incremental models, Amitai Etzioni (1967a) suggested that there might be a middle-ground approach that would be more desirable than either extreme. This he called the *mixed scanning model*. In this model, Etzioni borrows from both the other models. A distinction is made between two types of decisions. First, there are the "contextuating decisions." These are decisions which are fundamental and tied closely to some conception of ultimate goals. Second, there are the "bit decisions." They are incremental in that they are made in pursuit of the objectives already set by prior contextuating decisions. The mixed scanning model of decision making emphasizes rational-comprehensive processes when fundamental or contextuating decisions are being made, and emphasizes incremental processes when relatively minor or bit decisions are being made. In other words, major decisions should be made in as rational a way as possible, and decision makers should strive to approximate as closely as possible the rational-comprehensive model when they are making such important decisions. On the other hand, when the decision to be made is of less significance, an incremental approach is probably the most practical and realistic given the normal limits on time, information, and human energy.

Conflict.   Recognizing that nobody is likely to use the same decision-making strategy for all decisions, Irving Janis and Leon Mann (1977) have tried to formulate a theory which would make predictions about the conditions under which people are likely to use various strategies of decision making. They call their theory a *conflict model* of decision making (see Figure 9-1). This model is specifically applicable to decision-making situations in which the decision will have reasonably substantial consequences for the decision maker. That is, an individual is placed in a situation where a decision must be made which will have the potential for generating unfavorable consequences for the decision maker or for other persons who are important to the decision maker. Such decisions cause psychological stress, which as we have seen, affects the way people go about the process of making the decision. The term *conflict* refers to decisional conflicts or "simultaneous opposing tendencies within the individual to accept and reject a given course of action" (Janis & Mann 1977, p. 46). Such conflicts lead to stress symptoms such as "hesitation, vacillation, feelings of uncertainty, and signs of acute emotional stress" (ibid.).

In line with their emphasis on the stressful nature of important decision-making situations, Janis and Mann outline the five basic coping strategies people are likely to adopt when faced with the necessity to make a consequential decision. The process begins when an individual is challenged by some troublesome information or event that calls her attention to a real loss that can be expected at some point in the future. She is constrained to appraise the risk she would be taking if she were to continue without modifying her current course of action. If she judges the risk to be inconsequential enough to be tolerated, she continues in her present course of action with relatively little emotional arousal or conflict. However, if she judges the risk to be certainly or probably serious, she proceeds to the next step. At this point, information about the potential risk of new courses of action is taken into consideration along with the previously considered risk of continuing her present course of action. If the risk of some new course of action seems less than the risk of continuing without change, she is likely to make a decision to change with little or no symptoms of psychological stress.

The effects of psychological stress come to the fore if the risks of changing and of staying the same both appear substantial. Then she must ask herself whether it is possible that with further effort she might be able to find a solution that is better than those she is presently considering. If the answer is no, she is likely to resort to defensive avoidance. The three basic types of defensive avoidance are procrastinating, shifting responsibility, and bolstering. If she can see no serious penalty for postponing the decision, the decision maker can stop thinking about the problem and avoid situations that might call it to her attention. If, however, she has a tight deadline with strong sanctions for postponement, the decision maker is more likely to resort to shifting responsibility or bolstering. If the former, she would try to get other persons involved in the decision-making process, rationalizing that they ought to make the decision—and also take the blame if it does not turn

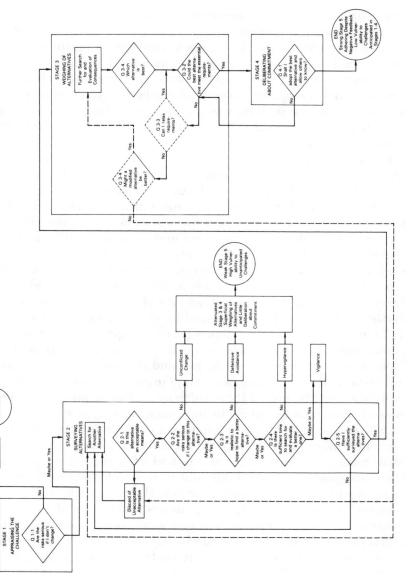

Reprinted with permission of The Free Press, a division of Macmillan, Inc. from *Decision Making: A Psychological Analysis of Conflict, Choice, and Commitment* by I. L. Janis & L. Mann. Copyright © 1977 by The Free Press.

FIGURE 9-1 The Conflict Model of Decision Making

out well. The latter is a way of minimizing stress by selective attention and distorted information processing.

There are various bolstering tactics.* A person might, for example, exaggerate the favorable consequences or minimize the unfavorable consequences of the most attractive of the available alternatives. He might also try to deny his negative attitudes about the bad consequences that would follow from the preferred policy alternative. For example, while accepting that armed conflict will be an outcome of his decision, he may take comfort in the fact that it will involve conventional, rather than nuclear, warfare. He might discount the negative consequences of a choice by assuming that he needs merely to announce his choice and then do nothing for such a long time that he can, as a practical matter, forget about it. For example, if forced to take a stand on a controversial issue, a candidate can come out in favor of a wildly unrealistic solution with the comforting thought that he will not have to do anything further about it until he is elected—if he is elected. Or he can make an excessive number of well-documented promises, as President Carter did—to his regret (Bell 1982, p. K1). A decision maker can assume that no one else will find out, or if they do find out, that they will not care about the consequences of the decision. The "dirty tricks" engaged in by Nixon supporters during the 1972 presidential election campaign were supposed to be secret. When they came to light, the defense was that they were the sort of thing that "everyone does during a campaign," and thus nothing to get upset about. Finally, a decision maker can attempt to minimize personal responsibility for the consequences of the decision by attributing his choice to the situational pressures under which he was acting. That is, he was forced to do what he did because of the circumstances in which he found himself.

If, on the other hand, the decision maker becomes aware of information that indicates it might be possible to find a better solution than the ones he is currently considering, he must then consider whether there is sufficient time to conduct the requisite search. If the answer is no, then he might go into a state of hypervigilance, which is a state of panic. Janis and Mann found hypervigilance a relatively rare state, even in cases of disaster and crisis. Therefore they did not deal with its consequences at any length, except to note that it effectively short-circuits the reasoning process.

If the decision maker comes to the conclusion that there is time to search for another, better solution to his problem, then the reaction is vigilance. Vigilance is a process of decision making that conforms as closely as possible to the criteria Janis and Mann claim characterize a thorough search, appraisal, and contingency planning process:

The decision maker, to the best of his ability and within his information-processing capabilities:

1. thoroughly canvasses a wide range of alternative courses of action;

---

*These are related to consistency theory, which was discussed in Chapter 6.

2. surveys the full range of objectives to be fulfilled and the values implicated by the choice;

3. carefully weighs whatever he knows about the costs and risks of both positive and negative consequences that could flow from each alternative;

4. intensively searches for new information relevant to further evaluation of the alternatives;

5. correctly assimilates and takes account of any new information or expert judgment to which he is exposed, even when the information or judgment does not support the course of action he initially prefers;

6. reexamines the positive and negative consequences of all known alternatives, including those originally regarded as unacceptable, before making a final choice;

7. makes detailed provisions for implementing or executing the chosen course of action, with special attention to contingency plans that might be required if various known risks were to materialize. [Janis and Mann 1977, p. 11]

A person who embarks on a decision-making process characterized by vigilance has a lower level of stress because she has confidence that an adequate solution will be found. A decision not to change or to change after consideration of only one other alternative, is not likely to generate much initial stress. It is more likely to lead to stress in the long run, however, because the decision maker is vulnerable to unanticipated challenges to her decision. Since her earlier confidence has left her unprepared to deal with any challenge, she is likely to become highly stressed and to overreact. Needless to say, strategies of defensive avoidance and hypervigilance are inherently stressful. No alternative except vigilance holds a reasonable promise that the decision made will be a good one.

What kinds of considerations make such decisional conflicts so psychologically stressful? Janis and Mann suggest four: (1) The expectation of utilitarian gains or losses for the self. What do I gain or lose as a result of having chosen this alternative? (2) The possibility of similar gains or losses for other persons who are important to the decision maker. Who else will it hurt and who else will it benefit? (3) The matter of whether the alternative chosen will generate a result in keeping with the decision maker's internalized moral standards and ideals. Is it the *right* thing to do? Does it reflect well on me? (4) The prospect of approval or disapproval by others whose opinion matters to the decision maker. What will *they* think of this decision? All four types of considerations are to some extent relevant to any decision, and the outcome of the decision-making process is determined by the relative strength of the incentives they represent.

Janis and Mann's conflict model of decision making encompasses the other models. Their criteria for good decision making closely resemble the rational-comprehensive decision-making model but are less stringent. Vigilance is the only strategy of coping that really can satisfy these criteria, and vigilance is the only strategy that can lead to decision making in which harmful effects of stress are minimized. This combination of factors suggests that incrementalism is likely to lead to unsatisfactory decisions if the decision is one of consequence, though not in relatively minor decisions. In this, the conflict model parallels closely Etzioni's mixed scanning model, but transforms it and enriches it by giving it a psychological dimension that was not originally there.

So far we have been concentrating on the processes by which decisions can be made. Now we shall turn to issues concerning the people making the decisions and the contexts within which decision making take place. Individuals making decisions bring characteristics and orientations to the decision making process that influence the way it develops, as well as the outcomes it yields. These interact with a context that is composed of elements from both the microenvironment and the macroenvironment. Thus, we have individual human beings—each one of whom is to some degree unique—functioning within an environment that is composed of many layers. The most important layers include culture, societal norms, specific orientation (in this case, governmental or political), and interpersonal involvement. Keeping this in mind, we will now consider the implications of the fact that governmental decision making is generally done 1) by an individual; 2) by a small group; or 3) by an organization or institution, such as Congress.

THE INDIVIDUAL AS DECISION MAKER

In 1954 a conference was held in Geneva, Switzerland. Among other things the agreement reached at Geneva provided for the withdrawal of France from Indochina and the partition of Vietnam into two sections that were to be unified by means of a general election two years later. Representing the United States was Secretary of State John Foster Dulles, and representing Communist China was Chou En-Lai, Foreign Minister. A brief personal encounter between these two men may have altered the course of history:

> Chou En-Lai, quite by accident, ran into John Foster Dulles in one of the corridors of Geneva's Palais des Nations. The Chinese statesman stretched out his hand to Dulles in a gesture of reconciliation, but the American put his hands behind his back and walked away. A good Puritan would have no commerce with the Devil. It is tempting to speculate about the repercussions of this episode. What if Dulles had responded? Might the Vietnam War have been avoided? We shall never know. But one is forced to wonder. [Stoessinger 1979, p. 102]*

While many important political decisions are made by individuals who have had time to study the situation, to consult with others, and to weigh the consequences of their alternatives, some are made as spur-of-the-moment reactions to unexpected events. Instances of individual decision

---

*This and following passages from J.G. Stoessinger, *Crusaders and Pragmatists: Movers of Modern American Foreign Policy*. New York: W.W. Norton, 1979. Used with permission.

making, then, fall along a dimension with one end representing a process approximating vigilance, or the rational-comprehensive decision-making model, and the other epitomized by Dulles's instantaneous decision to rebuff Chou En-Lai.

Although considerable work has been done on the influence of personality characteristics on individual behavior, almost none has focused specifically on political decision-making behavior until quite recently. One of the pioneering efforts in this area was the study of Woodrow Wilson by Alexander and Juliette George (1956). Subsequent studies have shown a strong tendency to follow in this tradition of using an individual in-depth case study (e.g., Mongar 1974) or a series of related case studies (e.g., Stoessinger 1979) to illustrate the relationship between personality and political decision making. More recently some scholars have tried to study this relationship quantitatively, but because of the difficulty of direct access to "real world" data, the researchers have had to rely on simulations of political decision making (e.g., Driver 1977; Crow & Noel 1977) or systematic analysis of the historical record (e.g., Hermann 1977). These approaches are less than entirely satisfactory from a methodological point of view. But because of the formidable obstacles to gathering large amounts of valid and reliable data on actual political decision making, they will have to suffice. While the discussion in this section should be regarded as suggestive rather than conclusive, the research done in this area to date has revealed information which is both intuitively appealing and potentially useful.

One way of approaching the issue of the relationship between personality and political decision making is by identifying broad personality configurations. This orientation is in the tradition of *The Authoritarian Personality* by Adorno and his associates (1950). It lends itself particularly well to the analysis of single or grouped case studies of important historical decision makers or decision-making situations. A relatively recent example of this type of analysis is *Crusaders and Pragmatists* by John G. Stoessinger (1979), in which he looks at a selected set of important U.S. foreign policy decision makers (mostly, but not exclusively, presidents). Taking into account both the background and personality characteristics of his subjects and the demands of the situations in which they found themselves, he analyzes their decision-making behavior in selected crises. For example, one of the events he studied is President Truman's decision to make a massive commitment of American troops to help defend South Korea in 1950.

The framework for Stoessinger's analysis is a typology of two basic personality types he claims "have characterized decision makers in twentieth century America" (Stoessinger 1979, p. xv). The first is the *crusader*. This type of individual is characterized by "a missionary zeal to make the world better."

The crusader tends to make decisions based on a preconceived idea rather than on the basis of experience. Even though there are alternatives, he usually does not see them. If the facts do not square with his philosophy, it is too bad for the facts. Thus, the crusader tends toward rigidity and finds it difficult, if not impossible, to extricate himself from a losing posture. He does not welcome dissent and advisers will tend to tell him what he wants to hear. He sets out to improve the world but all too often manages to leave it in worse shape than it was before. [ibid., p. xv]

The other basic personality type is the *pragmatist*. This type of individual "is guided by the facts and his experience in a given situation, not by wishes or unexamined preoccupations."

[The pragmatist] is generally aware of the alternatives to his chosen course of action and explores the pros and cons of each as objectively as possible. He encourages advisers to tell him what he ought to know, not what they think he wants to hear. Always flexible, he does not get locked into a losing policy. He can change direction and try again, without inflicting damage to his self-esteem. Neither hope nor fear but evidence alone governs his decisions. And when there is no evidence as yet, there is always common sense. [ibid., pp. xv–xvi]

After delineating these basic types, Stoessinger hastens to assure the reader that no real decision maker is ever a pure specimen of either type. Elements of both types are to be found in the personalities of all decision makers, but one tends to predominate. He finds that the crusading type predominated in Woodrow Wilson, John Foster Dulles, and Lyndon Johnson, while the pragmatic type predominated in Franklin Roosevelt, Harry Truman, and John Kennedy.

While Stoessinger finds it useful to analyze political decision making using broad personality configurations that are actually complexes of interrelated personality characteristics, other researchers prefer to narrow their scrutiny to more specific personality elements. One personality characteristic that has been found to be important in decision making is cognitive complexity. This refers to the number of dimensions an individual uses in characterizing his world and the number of rules he uses in integrating the information he takes in about that world (Schroder & Suedfeld 1971; Hermann 1977, p. 316). The higher the number of rules and dimensions, the more cognitively complex the individual.

Given what we have already ascertained about the complexity and uncertainty inherent in political decision-making processes, the value of the ability to use one's mental powers in a cognitively complex manner should be clear. Empirical research has shown that it tends to protect the decision maker against the tendency to be ethnocentric or think in terms of stereotypes (Adorno, et al, 1950). The ethnocentric person sees the world in terms of "us" versus "them." He is strongly attached to those whom he perceives as part of his in-group and highly rejecting of those who are not. In domestic politics this general orientation can lead to prejudices against persons of a different race, religion, or sex. In the international arena, it can lead to a fierce nationalism based on hostility and the willingness to be aggressive (Driver 1977, p. 347; Hermann 1977).

Thus, cognitive complexity can affect the perceptions decision makers have of significant people and events that are salient to the decision-making process. These perceptions, in turn, affect the attributions the participants make concerning the origins and nature of the problem that needs solving and the probable reactions of others to the various policy alternatives under consideration. Obviously, errors made in this attribution process can seriously misdirect the decision-making process.

Of particular importance in political life are those distortions related to self-presentation. Politicians are, by definition, public figures. Their success depends on presenting an attractive image to voters and to other influential people. Also, they can on occasion have a need or desire to protect themselves. For example, it is not unusual for political figures to manifest an exaggerated tendency to take credit for successes or a similarly exaggerated tendency to try to avoid blame. Thus, politicians can use an undue emphasis on the inevitable uncertainty and complexity of political decision-making to explain in advance possible failures in such a way that their positions or power will not be threatened. They can claim that unfortunate chance events produced the outcome—that it was beyond anyone's control. Made in advance of the actual failure, such an attribution could cause them to ignore potentially successful alternatives.

It is not just the ability to think in complex ways that affects the attributions made by political decision makers. Their belief systems or cognitive maps also condition their attributions by furnishing a filter for incoming information that is then used in the attributive process. In other words, cognitive maps are not direct guides to action in the decision-making situation. Rather, "they form one of several clusters of intervening variables that may shape and constrain decision-making behavior" (Holsti 1976, p. 34). First of all, they orient decision makers to the environment. They furnish a filter through which perceptions of the outside world are processed and given meaning. Cognitive maps help decision makers diagnose the situation with which they are presented. As mentioned earlier, they furnish a means for coping with uncertainty. And finally, they can function as a source of guidelines that may channel or constrain policy choices.

To say that such factors are operative when a politician participates in a decision-making process is one thing; to assert that she is aware of all of these factors is quite another. Human beings tend to assume that "we interpret events as we do because of the information in those events" (Jervis 1981, p. 1). When faced with something highly at odds with what we already believe, we tend to dismiss it more often than take it seriously (Etheredge 1978).

Lyndon Johnson could not accept the evidence that the wisest course could have been to pull the United States out of Vietnam as soon as possible after his victory in the 1964 election—as some people think Kennedy had intended to do (Paper 1979, p. 130; Miller 1980, pp. 463–64; also see Wills 1982, p. 281). The belief system underlying this perception of what was possible has been eloquently, if unsystematically, outlined by Tom Wicker:

> But how could Lyndon Johnson, in his moment of triumph, with his sense of the golden touch, doubt that his superbly equipped forces, representing all the technological and industrial genius of America, organized by the incomparable McNamara with his modern administrator's skills, trained and led by the impressive generals and admirals with whom Johnson had conspired politically in his congressional days, backed by the most powerful industrial capacity and the most impressive economy in history—how could he doubt that this juggernaut could deal with a few ill-clad guerrillas, if necessary with the old-fashioned Chinese-style infantry divisions of Vo Nguyen Giap, with an enemy who had to steal his weapons, bring in his supplies on bicycles and the backs of old women, and whose soldiers were regimented communist slaves without the incentives of freedom and democracy to make them fight well? [Wicker 1968, pp. 251–52]

As a result, Lyndon Johnson perceived the Vietnam War as being capable of being won, and in the process, lost a second presidential term, during which he might have been able to accomplish truly great things domestically.

Cognitive complexity and perceptual predispositions are not the only personality characteristics theorists or researchers have asserted are important in political decision making. Others include the tendency to be dogmatic, the level of self-esteem, the extent to which an individual is trustful or distrustful of others, and toleration of ambiguity. While this list does not exhaust the characteristics that have been considered important by one or another scholar, it is sufficient to indicate the type of personality characteristics that may come into play in individual political decision making.

Before we go on, however, we must pause to consider a final personality characteristic—narcissism—that has received increasing attention in recent years (see also Chapter 5). Of particular importance to the study of political decision making is the work of Lloyd Etheredge, who studied the factors that might predispose foreign policy decision makers to choose alternatives involving the use of force. He presents evidence that "the tendency to employ or oppose force within each situation reflects more general personality-based differences between individuals" (Etheredge 1978, p. 103). Central to his formulation is the "male narcissism syndrome" or "machismo syndrome." He found that persons who, to some extent, exhibit the ambitiousness and competitiveness characteristic of the syndrome play a key role in the initiation of war and the commission of errors in foreign policy making (but see Volkan 1980).

Thus there emerges a picture of the individual decision maker as highly fallible, and as subject—on an unconscious, as well as on a conscious level—to the imperatives of his own deep-seated personality characteristics. One approach to the solution of this problem is to limit the extent to which any individual is able to make important political decisions without the influence, advice, or participation of others.

Since most political decision making takes place within some sort of institutional or organizational structure, one of the most basic limitations on individual decision makers is the demands placed on the individual by the role she plays within the institution (Snyder & Diesing 1977, pp. 359–60). In other words, the way in which individuals adjust to institutional imperatives can have a substantial mediating influence on the decision-making process. Persons who occupy a given position or role within an organization are subject to the expectations both they and others have with regard to the way in which their decision-making task should properly be carried out. The individual develops a role orientation that is a set of expectations concerning the nature of proper decision-making behavior. In a study of the decision-making behavior of judges, James L. Gibson (1978) found evidence that judges do feel constrained by their notions concerning what factors can properly be brought to bear on a judicial decision. Judges differed in the extent to which they thought it was proper to take into account the personal characteristics of the defendant, the way the defendant had been treated in the criminal justice system, the conscious values or beliefs of the judge, and perceptions of the seriousness of the given crime in the judge's jurisdiction. He concluded that role orientations alone do not predict judicial decision-making behavior, rather, they "specify the criteria that judges rely on to reach decisions" (Gibson 1978, p. 22).

Another limitation on individual discretion in political and governmental decision making is the tendency or necessity for an individual to consult with advisers before arriving at a final decision. There are various ways by which such consultation may take place (Vroom 1980, p. 460). The individual decision maker can use advisers as sources of information but reserve the actual decision exclusively to himself. In such a case it is not even necessary for the decision maker to let his advisers know about the pending decision when he asks for their advice. Thus the adviser's role is limited to providing information and does not extend to generating alternative solutions. When the decision maker does share the problem with his advisers, he may or may not bring them together as a group. In either case, the decision maker can still reserve the final decision to himself, but he does have the advantage of other persons' ideas about potential solutions, as well as the relevant information they can furnish him. Finally, the decision maker can simply turn the decision-making task over to a group of which he is a member. The nature and impact of his participation will depend, in considerable measure, on his inclination to play a directive or facilitating role. He may even choose to adopt the stance of "just another member of the group," thus encouraging the emergence of a consensus decision of some sort. In order to do this, however, he must be willing in advance to accept and implement any decision that emerges from the group's deliberations.

THE GROUP AND DECISION MAKING

It is a truism that large groups of people, such as legislatures or political party conventions, are inferior forums for serious attempts at making important decisions. Out of sheer unwieldiness, the tendency is for large decision-making institutions to reflect—in part or completely—decisions that have previously been made by smaller groups. This may amount to simple rubber-stamping, as in the decision-making processes of the Supreme Soviet of the USSR. In American government and politics, this tendency is less extreme, with Congress really exercising its theoretical prerogative to modify or overturn the decisions proposed to it by its leaders or committees. The frequency with which this prerogative is actually exercised can vary from issue to issue, and over time with regard to the same issue. The centrality of the smaller group, however, cannot be denied, and this fact is amply demonstrated by the amount of attention students of American legislatures pay to committees. The other main type of large group or institutional decision-making forum that plays an important role in political systems is the bureaucratic organization or ministry. Here again, however, the small group is central. For the most part, "the bureaucratic organization is not an alternative to the face-to-face group, but rather a special kind of setting or added layer of context in which a network of smaller groups operates" (Hermann 1979, p. 3).

In short, it makes sense to regard the small group as a central decision-making structure in most political systems. This means that in our attempt to better understand governmental and political decision making, we can draw upon the vast literature on small groups that has been generated by social psychologists and allied researchers. This analysis will be broken into two segments. The rest of this section will be devoted to consideration of the advantages of group decision making. Then we will shift our attention to the structural variables relevant to small-group political decision making and the issue of group dynamics.

As we have seen previously, essentially uncontrollable factors may influence the quality of the decisions made by individuals acting alone. One remedy for the undesirable aspects of individual decision making is to bring more people into the process, the theory being that this will dilute the effects of arbitrary factors on the final decision. Opinions vary greatly as to whether group decision making is superior, inferior, or equal to individual decision making. It is possible, however, to outline the assets and liabilities of group decision making, as well as to delineate leadership effects on this process (Maier 1980).

As a decision-making body, the small group has much to commend it. Each member of the group brings to its deliberations a unique contribution of knowledge and experience. Thus the informational resources available to the decision-making process are greater than in the case of an individual decision maker, no matter how thoroughly that individual has researched the problem. Also, individuals tend to get into ruts in their thinking. This limits the extent to which they are capable of being creative in generating potential solutions to problems. In a group situation, such a person is exposed to different and perhaps even contrasting points of view and may, as a result, get knocked out of her well-worn ruts.

No decision in politics or government is worth much if it cannot be implemented. If the decision is based on some sort of a group consensus or is, to some extent, a group product, and if the members of the group will play some role in its implementation, then the chances for effective implementation are greatly enhanced. In fact, the task of implementing the decision can be consciously delegated to persons who emerge as the logical implementers as a result of the group process (Drucker 1974, pp. 465–70). Also, if a decision is to be implemented effectively, it must be communicated as accurately as possible. This obviously is easier when the implementers have been privy to the decision-making process. Not only do they have a fuller knowledge of the goals, obstacles, alternatives, and factual information that were taken into consideration in making the decision, but also they do not regard the decision as an essentially arbitrary one reached by superiors via paths unknown.

On the other hand, the social pressures that arise in a group can often make for an undesirable degree of conformity. At its worst such conformity can result in what Janis terms "groupthink," which is "a mode of thinking that people engage in when they are deeply involved in a cohesive in-group, when the members' strivings for unanimity override their motivation to realistically appraise alternative courses of action" (Janis 1972, p. 9). Thus, "majority opinions tend to be accepted regardless of whether or not their objective quality is logically and scientifically sound" (Maier 1980, p. 510).

Also, even in groups in which there is no formal leader and the decision is supposed to be a group product, there is a strong tendency for a dominant individual to emerge and capture a disproportionate share of influence in the decision-making process. No matter how able this individual is (and there is no guaranty of this—sheer persistence may win out), the advantages of group participation will be considerably diluted. Finally, there is a danger that competition within the group will displace the primary goal of solving the problem. As alternative proposals emerge, individual group members may develop personal investment in the adoption of one or another of these solutions. Gradually, their goal becomes that of winning the game rather than of finding the best solution to the problem.

So far we have been dealing with factors that are pretty clearly pros or cons of the group decision-making process. As is usually true, however, everything is not always neat and clear-cut. Some characteristics of group decision making can turn out to be either assets or liabilities, depending on factors such as the skill of the leader. For example, group discussion, if skillfully and dispassionately handled by all concerned, can result in a creative conflict that enhances the chance for a sound and innovative solution. However, if the discussion deteriorates into disagreements leading to personal antagonisms, the quality of the decision may suffer or, at worst, the ability of the group to reach any decision at all may be compromised. Also, it makes a difference if the group develops a tendency to focus on conflicting interests rather than on mutual interests. Then, even if the discussion is amicable, it is difficult to arrive at any group consensus.

Group processes are, by definition, more ponderous than individual decision making. The group is a poor vehicle for reaching decisions under tight deadlines. If a quick decision is needed, individuals usually are more responsive. Even when speed is less imperative, a point is reached where the time consumed is not justified by the value of the outcome. Finally, when too much time is taken in group discussion, many members become subject to the debilitating mental effects of fatigue and boredom. There is a fine balance between taking sufficient time to allow all important aspects of the problem adequate consideration and taking so much time that the quality of the group's decision may suffer.

Finally, in any process of consensus building the people involved usually have to change their views or compromise to some extent. The identity of the individual who decides to change his mind can have a definite impact on the quality of the resulting decision. Also, if a minority or an individual favors the more constructive option, acquiescence to the will of the majority can be undesirable. There is a strong tendency, however, for the pressure of the majority to produce conformity (Asch 1973). The quality of the resulting decision, then, can vary according to whether more merit inheres in the position of the majority or that of the minority.

In cases such as those mentioned above, in which a given factor may have a positive or a negative effect on the quality of the decisions produced by a group, the group leader can exercise influence. A skillful group leader can steer the group toward a focus on mutual rather than conflicting interests. Such a leader can be sensitive to the relationship between the duration of the deliberations and the capacity of the various members of the group to sustain their interest and commitment. Also, a good leader can recognize when the minority has had a sufficient opportunity to persuade the majority, and when a dangerous tendency toward a consensus has not been sufficiently challenged. This is a difficult and demanding task. Maier (1980) sees the ideal leader as one who does not dominate and produce the solution. "Rather, his function is to receive information, facilitate communications between the individuals, relay messages, and integrate the incoming responses to that a single unified response occurs" (ibid., p. 515). To a great extent, any group leader's ability to do this, as well as any group's ability to work constructively toward a good decision, depends on the dynamics of the interpersonal relationships that develop within any task-oriented group.

GROUP DYNAMICS AND DECISION MAKING

The interpersonal dynamics of any small group are affected by its structural characteristics and the way in which it moves through the decision making process. These will be dealt with in this section under the categories: 1) social factors; 2) physical factors; and 3) phases.

Social factors. Any decision making group is, by definition, a task oriented group; the task, of course, is to make a decision or set of related decisions. Interpersonal interaction in such groups can be described or analyzed in terms of three dimensions: 1) the informational; 2) the socioemotional; and 3) the procedural (Kowitz & Knutson 1980, pp. 16–19). The informational dimension refers to the facts, opinions and beliefs the group takes into consideration in dealing with its decision making task. The group collects, analyzes, and integrates information in order to come up with its decision.

The socioemotional dimension reflects the attitudes that the members of the group have toward each other. This includes the characteristics each group member attributes to the others. For example, a group member can see each of his colleagues as being friendly or unfriendly, cooperative or uncooperative, and of high or low status. Beyond this, the group setting affords the opportunity for group members to commit attributional errors (Shaver 1982). For example, group members can assume that everyone else's choices will be identical to their own. Factors such as this affect group cohesiveness and the extent to which the time and energies of the group are directed toward the task, rather than toward working out interpersonal conflicts, tensions, and distrust. Finally, the procedural dimension involves leadership or group guidance. "Common procedurally oriented behaviors include integrating and summarizing group activity, delegating and directing action, introducing and formulating goals, assisting in role and norm development, and in general keeping the group moving toward its goal" (Kowitz & Knutson 1980, p. 17).

Another social factor is the distribution of power within the group. This can range from the situation where a strong leader dominates the group to a situation of group member equality. In political decision making, many factors can influence this dynamic. One is the formal positions held by various group members. It can be difficult not to defer to a president, particularly a president of strong personality and opinions, such as Lyndon Johnson. Influencing the distribution of power in a group is the history of the group. As groups meet again and again, the various members tend to take on roles and images that may in the long run weaken or enhance their power within the group.

Another important factor in political decision making is expertise. If some members of the group have or are perceived to have significantly more knowledge about the topic under discussion, there is a natural tendency for other group members to defer to them. Looking back at the way in which the Bay of Pigs invasion was approved, John F. Kennedy thought that he had made a serious mistake in being "too quick to accept the information and advice of the so-called 'experts'" (Paper 1979, p. 164).

The final social variable to be considered here is group cohesiveness, or the extent to which group members identify with or are loyal to the group (Ridgeway 1983). Some group members will come into the situation perceiving themselves as representatives of some external constituency or interest group. While it is possible for this loyalty to become diluted as the decision making group evolves into a more coherent entity, the degree to which this happens will affect the extent to which group cohesiveness is achieved. The strength of group cohesion will, in turn, influence both the productivity of the group and the satisfaction of its members. High group cohesion does not, however, guarantee that the group will be productive or that its decisions will be wise ones (Janis 1972), but it is very difficult for a group low in cohesiveness to work together in a productive way. In such cases, the group processes may be characterized by "contention, struggle, and the attempt to overpower with superior force" (Mohr 1976, p. 632). This type of conflict contributes little to the quality of the group's decisions. It may even lead to a stalemate in the decision making process. Thus, in a situation such as that of the United Nations, the members of a decision making group would be highly likely to maintain their primary loyalty to their own governments and to regard themselves as representatives of their government's interests. Such an attitude would in turn contribute to a lower potential for group cohesiveness than a situation where the decision-making group was composed of persons selected from the White House staff. The latter, having a common primary loyalty to the president, would possess a much higher potential for developing a cohesive group in which the quality of the group's decision is a primary concern for all group members.

Physical factors.   The first important structural variable we will consider here is group size. Even within the category "small group," there is room for a considerable amount of variation, and this in turn affects the behavior of group members. Generally, as group size increases, interaction among group members becomes more complicated. This is a function of the fact that "the number of potential channels of communication available for interaction increases much more rapidly than the simple arithmetic increase of people to the group" (Kowitz & Knutson 1980, p. 45). One result is that individual group members tend to participate less and less; another is that the more verbally aggressive people tend to dominate (Bales 1951; Gibb 1951). In either case, the group loses the participation of persons who might otherwise make important contributions, and group members tend to be less satisfied with the group. If the group is task-oriented, as decision making groups are supposed to be, five to seven members is a good size (Bormann 1975; Huber 1980, p. 170). The rationale is that this number provides sufficient diversity in the ideas and values the members bring to the decision making process without creating a situation where people are discouraged from making their individual contributions to the group's deliberations.

In addition, the seating arrangement can influence the power of individual group members. For example, people sitting at the head of a rectangular table are in a better position to exercise influence simply because they tend to interact with more group members (Strodbeck and Hook 1961). A round table, on the other hand, tends to encourage equality—at least in the early stages of a group's deliberations.

Phases.   When a group first gathers to begin the decision making process, the group members must go through a phase of getting to know one another. They form impressions regarding the contributions each can make to the information the group needs for accomplishing its task. Here, such factors as the perceived expertise of one or more group members can give them a special role and status in the group. Also, in this phase the interpersonal atmosphere is established. Will the group be a friendly and cooperative one, or are serious conflicts apt to surface? Are some group members good at defusing tense situations with humor? Is there a particularly abrasive group member who will have to be treated carefully? In general, at this stage of the group's life the members tend to proceed somewhat cautiously, watching for others' reactions to their behavior and assessing the behaviors of their colleagues.

Once the group members have gotten to know each other they are in a better position to decide—tacitly or explicitly—how the group will structure itself. Also, they will probably settle on some strategy for moving toward their goal—the making of a decision. One crucial juncture in this process is the emergence of leadership within the group. Usually this process is closely tied to the outcome of the group's efforts to develop a structure and to select a strategy for proceeding. In political contexts, however, the natural process of leadership emergence may be hampered or short-circuited by one or more of the members' holding formal positions of authority, which more or less automatically place them in positions of group leadership. This may lead to a situation in which the group is dominated by one individual to an extent that affects the quality of its deliberations. Conscious of this, President Kennedy sometimes absented himself from meetings of the policy making group during the deliberations on the Cuban missile crisis. Robert Kennedy thought this was important, commenting, "I felt there was less true give-and-take with the president in the room. There was the danger that by indicating his own view and leanings, he would cause others just to fall in line" (Janis 1972, p. 149).

Next, the group usually settles down to work. It begins to bring its informational and analytical resources to bear on the task at hand and to seek additional information as necessary. This tends to be a period of accommodation and coordination in which alternatives are discussed with attention to their pros, cons, and long- and short-term implications. It is at this point that conflict is likely to arise, and that the skills of group members in handling conflict constructively are most crucial. Without a certain amount of conflict it is likely that some viable alternatives will not get adequate consideration. But if conflict gets out of hand, the ability of the group to successfully complete its task may be endangered. Franklin D. Roosevelt was a master at encouraging and benefiting from conflict among his advisers (George 1980, pp. 149–50; Barber 1977, pp. 240–41). He did this "by deliberately fostering among his aides a sense of competition and a clash of wills that led to disarray, heartbreak, and anger but also set off pulses of executive energy and sparks of creativity" (Burns 1978, p. 393).

The final task of a decision-making group is to reach some sort of agreement on the final form and content of its decision proposal. If the decision is to be conveyed in oral form, this stage does not usually present major difficulties. If the group must formalize the decision in written form, there is further opportunity for conflicts and disagreements to arise. There is even the possibility that a painfully erected consensus will fail on a point of word choice.

This whole process assumes that the decision-making group is one that has been formed expressly to complete the task at hand. In political life, however, many decision-making groups tackle a series of tasks and have a life span that goes beyond any single decision-making situation. One example is the president's cabinet, which meets regularly to deal with emerging problems. In such groups, the initial phases are eventually dropped or considerably attenuated, and the group is free to get down quickly to the process of working on the problem at hand. Any change in group membership, however, particularly if it involves a key member, may cause the group to reassess its member relationships as well as its structure and general decision-making strategy.

THE ORGANIZATION AND DECISION MAKING

As we noted earlier, organizational or institutional decision making tends to be derived from the work of smaller decision-making groups. The organizational decision, however, is significantly different from the individual or group decision in at least two basic respects. First, because the decision is being made on behalf of the organization, it becomes much more difficult to establish responsibility for any given decision. When the decision-making process becomes highly diffused among the individuals and groups that make up the organization, there is a tendency toward irresponsibility (Presthus 1978, pp. 39–40). The process can become abstract and impersonal, "the product of an anonymous, fragmented intelligence" (Presthus 1978, p. 39). Second, and related, is the fact that the organization envelops the decision-making situation in a very special type of environment and that this environment significantly shapes and constrains the process. The decision-making task, then, can become the hostage of a multiplicity of organizational imperatives, including bureaucratic politics (Holsti 1976, p. 27).

Among the constraints is the organization's memory. Things have happened in the past that may touch—however lightly—on either the personnel or the issues involved in the current decision-making task (Burns 1978, pp. 379–380). Prior policy commitments and standard operating procedures tend to intrude themselves as further constraints on decision-making flexibility and creativity. The individuals involved in the process tend to bring to it the parochial vested interests of the organizational units or constituencies they represent (Snyder & Diesing 1977, pp. 352–53). Finally, there is sheer organizational inertia (Burns 1978, pp. 381–384). Since decision making frequently involves change, or the consideration of change, just fighting inertia may become a preoccupation of the decision makers. Inertia can also be a powerful impediment to any attempt to implement a decision once it is made, and this possibility can constitute a serious prior restraint on the decision-making process.

Since decision making is, to a great extent, an exercise in information processing, the influence of the organization can perhaps be best studied in terms of some of its effects on information-processing tasks (George 1980, pp. 111–14). First of all, representatives of organizational units tend to attempt to protect or advance the interests of those units. This can take the form of supplying or withholding information that is salient to the decisional process. If unit representatives are directly involved, they may also attempt to influence the direction of the analysis. This is by no means invariably a cynical process. People tend to "believe in" what they do, and their efforts to influence the decision-making process are very likely to be the product of images of the "public interest" which they share with their agency or bureau colleagues.

Some decision makers have a significant advantage over others by virtue of either their position within the organization or their expertise in some aspect of the problem. In the deliberations that preceded the Bay of Pigs fiasco, CIA Chief Allen Dulles and his subordinate, Richard Bissell, had a disproportionate influence on the decision making of the Kennedy administration. First of all, they were top officials in the nation's main intelligence-gathering organization. Second, they were regarded as experts on the problem at hand.

The game of politics is a competitive one. But when the players are associated with each other over long periods of time within some organizational context, they tend to develop methods that soften the harshness of this competition sufficiently to maintain at least a minimal atmosphere of cordiality. It could be argued that without this tendency very little would get done. The prime example is the elaborate system of customs and courtesies that govern the relationships of members of Congress with each other. One outcome of this tendency is the practice of logrolling or compromise (see Chapter 7). The notion that "I'll go along with you now if you go along with me later" can blunt conflict and produce results, but it may not have a good effect on the quality of the decisions made. Also, while many decisions are improved by compromise, many are not.

Finally, playing bureaucratic politics (Snyder & Diesing 1977, pp. 348–61) consumes a great deal of time and energy that might more productively be spent on the decision-making task at hand. Since politics seems to be one of those inevitabilities of organizational life, however, we are probably more realistic to think about mitigating some of its more harmful effects rather than about attempting to eliminate it entirely. Also keep in mind that some of the effects of bureaucratic politics, such as the tendency for participants to be advocates for their agency's concept of the "public interest," may often be instrumental in the making of a well thought-out decision.

THE BAY OF PIGS: A CASE STUDY

At the beginning of this chapter, we asked this question: Why do so many "mistakes" get made? For example, the decision to go ahead with the Bay of Pigs invasion of Cuba, not to mention some of the auxiliary decisions that were made once the operation was underway, is widely acknowledged to have been a "bad" decision. And what's more, it was made by people who would seem to have been uniquely qualified to make "brilliant" decisions. True, the Kennedy administration was new and untried, but the young president had surrounded himself with a group of extraordinarily able men gathered from academia, business, foundations, think-tanks, and even the previous Eisenhower administration. In fact, former President Eisenhower, because of his military expertise, became—in absentia— a member of the inner decision-making circle which decided that a motley group of Cuban refugees should be not only permitted but helped to invade their homeland at a remote stretch of shoreline known as the Bay of Pigs. Afterwards Kennedy asked himself, "How could I have been so stupid . . . ?" (Sorenson 1966, p. 246).

That is not the question to be addressed here. The Bay of Pigs did not happen because Kennedy was a stupid man. Quite the contrary, he was intellectually well endowed, as were those who participated in the decision-making process with him. The answer to why these men (and they were all men) made such a gross mistake is much more complex than mere stupidity. Because the Bay of Pigs was such a fiasco, it has been discussed and analyzed by many, and the interpretations vary over much of the spectrum of factors discussed in this chapter.

To begin with, there is evidence that Kennedy thought that decisions—at least the more important ones—should be made by a process approximating the rational-comprehensive decision-making model (Paper 1979, pp. 126–27). When he was campaigning for president, he sharply criticized the way in which Eisenhower made his decisions. Among other things, he charged that there was inadequate exploration of alternatives by the president and that Eisenhower had been insufficiently open to new and different points of view. He talked of reopening "the channels of communication between the world of thought and the world of power" (*New York Times*, January 15, 1960, p. 14). In short, Kennedy seemed to have a deep conviction that the process of presidential decision making should be as rational, as well-informed, and—in terms of the alternatives considered—as comprehensive as humanly possible. He was "eager to seek the information and ideas which would facilitate the development of optimum solutions" (Paper 1979, p. 136). In the words of Herbert Simon, Kennedy's goal was to "maximize," not merely to "satisfice" (Simon 1961, pp. xxv–xxvi).

For all that, during the deliberations preceding the Bay of Pigs decision, there seems to have been inadequate consideration of the alternatives, as well as premature foreclosure of the decision-making process by Kennedy himself. The former can, in part, be attributed to the imperatives of secrecy. If a country is considering the launching of a surprise invasion of another country, it is obviously desirable to keep the whole matter as secret as possible by limiting the number of persons privy to the deliberations. On the other hand, did it really make sense not to consult with the experts in the intelligence branch of the CIA and the Cuban desk in the State Department (Janis 1972, pp. 32–33)? This makes even less sense when we consider that "every alert newspaper man knew something was afoot" (Schlesinger 1965, p. 248). So a prime source of additional alternatives was totally ignored, the process of decision making was not well-informed, and the chances of even approximating an optimum solution were seriously compromised.

Related to this was the fact that Kennedy seemed to reach a point at which he was simply not interested in exploring any more alternatives. Although he was still withholding final consent for the mission—which indicates a residual ambivalence—Kennedy seems to have ended his search for information and to have exhibited a desire not to be bothered with the matter any more. This could be seen when Leonard Meeker of the State Department was looking for some way to persuade President Kennedy to cancel the operation and was informed by Chester Bowles that "President Kennedy really didn't want to talk about this anymore, but simply wanted to go ahead with it" (Wyden 1979, p. 164). President Kennedy's behavior at this juncture was consistent with Bowles's opinion of his attitude (Wyden 1979, p. 165).

The Bay of Pigs decision was influenced by both individual and group factors. There is no question that Kennedy reserved the final decision to himself and that he accepted responsibility for that decision completely. In the process of reaching his decision, however, he was greatly influenced by a group of advisers, so it is reasonable to ask what influence both his and their personalities had on the outcome.

Using Stoessinger's typology, Kennedy and his advisers tended to be pragmatists rather than crusaders. Mongar describes Kennedy as

> a cool, skeptical, pessimistic realist . . . [who] was chary of ideological discourse, and invariably fastened on the immediate and practical consequences of a problem. His primary test of relevance for a policy was pragmatic: *Can* it be done, can *we* do it, and *how much* will it cost in dollars and power? Feasibility and ease of implementation usually became the primary criteria for adopting value alternatives. [Mongar 1974, p. 350; italics in the original]

This pragmatism and lack of strong ideological commitment also characterized his White House staff and advisers (Paper 1979, p. 145).

Interestingly, however, Kennedy and his advisers seemed to take on some of the characteristics of ideologues when they were contemplating the Bay of Pigs invasion. Specifically, they seem to have developed preconceptions about Castro and about the situation in Cuba that were as much a reflection of their anticommunism as of any hard evidence presented to them or any experience they had had with the relatively new Cuban regime. Also, there was a related, curious reluctance on their part to contemplate the virtues—or lack of same—of the persons who were likely to replace Castro if the invasion was to be successful in overturning the Cuban government. It was sufficient that they would not be communists; whether they would represent a net improvement was an issue that was cavalierly ignored (Wyden 1979, pp. 122–124).

Related to this is the whole matter of cognitive complexity. There is no question that as a general rule Kennedy's thinking, as well as the thinking of his chief advisers, was characterized by a high degree of cognitive complexity (Stuart 1980, p. 14). Given this, it is surprising to note the extent to which they accepted a basically stereotyped view of Castro and the entire Cuban situation. For example, "Castro was regarded as a weak 'hysteric' leader whose army was ready to defect; he was considered so stupid that 'although warned by air strikes, he would do nothing to neutralize the Cuban underground'" (Janis 1972, p. 38). As Janis rightly points out, this is "a stunning example of the classical stereotype of the enemy as weak and ineffectual." It is also indicative of significant attributional errors.

During the halcyon days at the beginning of the Kennedy administration, Kennedy and his advisers shared a common belief system that centered around notions of their power, efficacy, and ability to make a major positive impact on the world. In the words of a person who was privy to that charmed inner circle, "It seemed that, with John Kennedy leading us and with all the talent he had assembled, nothing could stop us" (Guthman 1971, p. 88; Wills 1982, pp. 238–240). When faced with information that they might fail or might make a mistake, they had a strong tendency to ignore it. When Senator Fulbright presented his long negative memorandum to Kennedy, the president read it but did not want to discuss it (Wyden 1979, pp. 122–123, 146–150). Kennedy did allow Fulbright to present the crux of his argument to Kennedy's advisers, but again, the president did not encourage any serious consideration of Fulbright's points. Instead, he actively discouraged it. Faced with something highly at odds with what they already believed, Kennedy and his advisers tended not to take it seriously.

A factor that seems to have been crucial in the Bay of Pigs decision was a form of the machismo syndrome (Etheredge 1978, pp. 1–4, 60). The Kennedy inner circle combined a strong competitiveness with a desire to behave in an appropriately "masculine" way (Wills 1982, pp. 34–35, 236–238). President Kennedy's "thinking was . . . affected by the competitive drive to win whatever there was to win" (Barber 1977, p. 325). Note the machismo overtones of the following:

> Some vehement opposition to the venture developed within the Kennedy administration, but much of it was never allowed to surface to the president's level. When it did, Kennedy discounted it because it came from the thinkers of the Democratic Party, the eggheads, the card-carrying liberals of whom the president liked to say that they, unfortunately, lacked "balls." [Wyden 1979, p. 120]

> The President cut the conversation short. "I know everybody is grabbing their nuts on this," he said. Sorenson inferred that the president thought the project's opponents were chicken. The president was not going to be chicken. And he had heard enough from the doubters. [Wyden 1979, p. 165]

And those around Kennedy, his principal advisers, were similarly afflicted:

> Schlesinger says that when the Cuban invasion plan was being presented to the group, "virile poses" were conveyed in the rhetoric used by the representatives of the CIA and the Joint Chiefs of Staff. He thought the State Department representatives and others responded by becoming anxious to show that they were not softheaded idealists but really were just as tough as the military men . . . [T]he members of Kennedy's in-group may have been concerned about protecting the leader from being embarrassed by their voicing "unvirile" concerns about the high risks of the venture. [Janis 1972, p. 41]

Unfortunately, the men surrounding Kennedy were affected or influenced by strong competitive drives that cancelled out any influence the group might have had in countering and balancing this critical aspect of Kennedy's personality.

When the Bay of Pigs decision is studied as the product of a group process, a slightly different but not incompatible picture emerges. The most influential study of this decision from a group dynamics perspective was done by Irving Janis (1972). He explains the Bay of Pigs mistake in terms of the "groupthink hypothesis." According to Janis, "members of any small cohesive group tend to maintain esprit de corps by unconsciously developing a number of shared illusions and related norms that interfere with critical thinking and reality testing" (Janis 1972, pp. 35–36). The major symptoms he found in the Bay of Pigs decision-making process include:

1. A shared illusion of invulnerability which led to a willingness to take excessive risks.
2. A shared illusion of unanimity based on the reluctance of individual members to voice their doubts and the assumption that this silence implied consent.
3. The related tendency of group members to self-censor their own misgivings and in some cases to discourage others from sharing their concerns with the president.
4. A tendency for Kennedy, acting as a strong group leader, to handle the group's meetings in a way that discouraged discussion of the drawbacks of the emerging plan.

Janis also points out that both Kennedy and his advisers were excessively deferential to the chief architects of the plan, Allen Dulles and Richard Bissell, director and deputy director of the CIA and carryovers from the Eisenhower administration. Another strong influence on the group—in absentia—was President Eisenhower, under whose administration the Bay of Pigs plan had germinated (Wyden 1979, p. 315). Add to this the Joint Chiefs of Staff and you have a situation in which the members of the civilian, new-to-responsibility Kennedy advisory group were dealing with a truly intimidating array of expertise.*

Afterward, Kennedy complained bitterly to his wife and some of his friends that many of these "experts" had fed him faulty information and had exercised poor judgment (Paper 1979, p. 156). He vowed that he would never be so intimidated by expertise again. In this connection, he had McGeorge Bundy set up a system by which Kennedy could get information independent of the federal bureaucracy. He also began a process of expanding the expertise and roles in national security of some of his most trusted advisers. Power became more concentrated in the White House staff, and correspondingly, the representatives of federal departments and agencies found themselves dealing with a much more skeptical president. Also, in meetings with advisers, Kennedy become much more circumspect about revealing his own thoughts: He now understood the danger that he would be told only what others thought he wanted to hear; he became wary of unanimity of opinion. All of this paid off eventually in decision-making processes that are widely acknowledged to have been

---

*For another point of view, see Wills 1982, pp. 230–231.

"good" ones, such as the way in which the Kennedy administration handled several subsequent crises, especially the Cuban missile crisis of 1962.*

SUMMARY

The outcome of any political conflict is normally a decision—even if only a decision to do nothing or to continue the conflict. In analyzing how people do—and perhaps, ought to—go about the process of decision making, scholars have come up with two prototypical models, the rational-comprehensive model and the incremental model. The mixed scanning model and the conflict model represent two different elaborations of the two basic models.

The decision making process is essentially a cognitive one, subject to the regularities people manifest in structuring their cognitive thinking. This fact, in turn, affects the ability of people to engage in decision making under conditions of high complexity and uncertainty—a not uncommon occurrence in political life. The rational-comprehensive approach to decision making emphasizes logical reasoning and the exhaustion of alternatives to be considered. Incremental decision making tries to take into account the limits imposed by human capacities and situational constraints, emphasizing trial and error. Mixed scanning involves combining the other two approaches and using them selectively based on the nature and importance of the decision to be made. Finally, the conflict model emphasizes the psychological state of the decision maker and the ways in which this affects decision making.

Decisions can be made by an individual, a small group, or by an "institution," such as Congress. Individual behavior in the decision making process is influenced by such factors as personality characteristics, either in the form of broad personality configurations or specific personality elements. It is also influenced by the institutional or organizational context, especially with reference to role expectations and the necessity to consult others.

Small-group decision making tends to be the other major approach, since institutional or organizational decisions are usually the product of individual or small-group deliberations. Groups have both advantages and disadvantages. The advantages include the combined knowledge and experience of the group members, the potential for contrasting points of view, and the possibility of facilitating implementation. The disadvantages include the pressure to conform, the tendency for one individual to dominate the process, and the greater ponderousness of group deliberations. Other factors influencing the dynamics of group decision making are size, the distribution of power, the seating arrangement, and member loyalties.

*For another point of view, see Wills, 1982, pp. 264–274.

Decision-making groups are, by definition, task-oriented groups. These tasks can be grouped into three categories: (1) informational, (2) socio-emotional, and (3) procedural. Each category assumes greater or lesser importance depending on the nature of the task and the stage of the deliberations.

Organizational or institutional decisions are significantly different from group decisions though they may, as noted above, derive from group decision making. First, responsibility is more difficult to establish. Second, the original environment shapes and constrains the process. Finally, there is organizational memory, sub-unit loyalty, and organizational inertia to contend with. Change-oriented decisions can be particularly difficult to arrive at and implement. Bureaucratic politics can significantly reduce the time and energy individuals can devote to the actual decision-making task at hand.

Many of these factors came into play in the decision-making process that led to the disastrous attempt of the United States to invade Cuba at the Bay of Pigs. In this case, the sorts of factors that enhance decision-making were overshadowed by personality and situational factors. As a result, the decision makers came to conclusions that resulted in loss of many lives plus significant damage in many of the intangible areas that are important in international relations, such as status and the appearance of informed and measured governmental action.

EVALUATING DECISIONS

Once a political decision has been made and, if necessary, the appropriate actions have been taken to implement it, there remains the task of evaluating it. This does not refer to the formal process of evaluation alone—though it also does not exclude it. It refers to the fact that, formally or informally, those who have an interest in the issue will inevitably come to some conclusion regarding the way the problem was dealt with. If pursued to their logical extreme, such evaluations usually involve some tacit or explicit notion of fairness or justice. Even when purely instrumental considerations seem to be involved, there is usually some prior conclusion that instrumental behavior in that situation is appropriate.

Everything we have dealt with previously has focused on solving a problem or making something happen. Now we will turn to the fact that any solution or outcome that emerges from this process will almost certainly be judged by somebody. As noted in Chapter 1, this evaluation is a critical dynamic in our model of the political process. On the basis of this judgment, the interested parties, the winners and losers, will make a decision about whether to act to reactivate the public resource allocation process, or to go on to other matters. In other words, these evaluations are important because they play a vital part in determining what will be the future preoccupations of authorities and partisans and the nature and activity of the political system itself. We turn, therefore, to a consideration of the types of standards people bring to bear on political outcomes and the implications of the use of such standards.

10

PERCEPTIONS OF JUSTICE: The Driving Force of the Political System

Justice is the first virtue of those who command, and stops the complaints of those who obey. [Diderot, quoted in Edwards 1954, p. 310]

The game of politics inevitably results in winners and losers. This is true in both objective and subjective senses. First, we have cases in which some have clearly won, others have clearly lost, and this evaluation is either a universal one or comes very close to being universal. For example, in 1980 Ronald Reagan won the presidency of the United States and Jimmy Carter lost it. Although some might think the burdens of the office are such that Jimmy Carter was the real winner, most would agree that he lost. Clearly, *he* did not regard it as a victory. Second, we have cases in which the situation is ambiguous and subject to various interpretations. In these cases, whether an individual or a group consider themselves winners or losers is more a matter of perception than of objective or concrete reality. For example, during the second half of the twentieth century, the United States developed the technology for generating energy through controlled nuclear fission. To some, concerned about the finite nature of fossil fuel, this is a blessing that makes the American public winners. To others, the attendant dangers connected with accidents and nuclear waste disposal make the presence of nuclear generating plants in our midst a curse. As long as United States power companies continue to build and operate such facilities, this group would consider the American public losers.

For any political decision there is a range of possibilities. At one extreme is an outcome in which one or more parties are clearly winners and the rest are losers. At the other extreme, all interested parties get something, and their shares can be considered equal, in terms of both the objective situation and their subjective perceptions. Needless to say, the first extreme is far more common than the second in actual political life. Most political payoffs are distributed unequally and are perceived to be distributed unequally by the involved parties. Even in situations in which there is an ideological commitment to equality, some tend to be "more equal" than others.

At the end of any political battle, then, the combatants tend to pause and decide what they think of the outcome.* Are they satisfied or dissatisfied? Did they win or lose? Or alternatively: Did they win more than they lost? Did they get "a fair share" (Wildavsky 1984, pp. 16–18) or what they "deserved"? However expressed, their evaluations tend to center around some notion of justice. This is not surprising, since justice appears to be critical in social relationships. Let us pause to consider why.

Four interlocking perspectives have been suggested by various scholars. First, in Campbell's (1976) evolutionary perspective, a successful society is one in which the people are provided with whatever resources they value. The extent to which a generally acceptable distribution can be decided upon and implemented depends on a certain consensus as to what a just distribution is and the willingness to try to realize this ideal. If the continuation of the society is seen as a value from which its members benefit, they clearly have a stake in the rules of behavior by which it functions—particularly those rules governing the just distribution of valued public resources. In short, it is functional for people to care about the extent to which justice is realized in their society.

Second, Lerner (1975;1977) asks why people in general design their lives so that they can perceive themselves as being entitled to what they get. He suggests that people tend to modify their perceptions of the world so that what is desired and what is received are in rough balance. He sees this tendency as emerging from a fundamental aspect of the socialization process. While growing up, a child usually learns to postpone gratification to some extent. That is, the child learns to give up immediate rewards for alternative ways of behavior that lead to deferred, but potentially greater rewards. For example, all children are taught to regard going to school as necessary, if not always pleasant, so they can earn a living and live comfortably as adults. This inculcation of the idea of deferred gratification causes the child to develop the notion of just rewards based on the agree-

---

*This sort of evaluation may also color their prior anticipation of what the outcome will be (Doob 1983, p. 148).

ment to postpone gratification. Also, they are taught that medical doctors deserve large incomes because medical education is very expensive, difficult, and time-consuming. This personal contract assumes a certain stability in the environment. It assumes that when we defer rewards in the present for rewards in the future, we will indeed be rewarded. If an individual becomes persuaded that he lives in a world in which the assumption might not hold, he will "act as if he lives in a jungle, with all the attendant psychological consequences" (Lerner 1977, p. 6). Thus every individual has a stake in creating or preserving a world where the assumption holds—where his just rewards will be forthcoming.

This notion of a personal contract leads directly to a third perspective on the concern with justice. In some of his early work, Lerner (1965;1970) proposed that there is a generalized "belief in a just world." We are inclined to infer that good things happen to good people and that people who are suffering or deprived deserve their fate. In other words, people believe—or want to believe—that there is a balance between what people get and what they deserve. This idea seems particularly pervasive and widespread in American society. In its cruelest form this belief leads to *blaming the victim*, that is, assigning blame for bad things that happen to a person to the characteristics or behavior of that person (Ryan 1971; Lerner 1980; Peplau & Rubin 1975). For example, there has been a tendency for many people, including police, prosecutors, judges and jurors, to assume that a rape victim must have done something to invite the attack. This allows them to maintain the belief that "nice girls"—themselves or those important to them—are not vulnerable to rape.

A fourth perspective ties concerns for justice more closely into social system dynamics. In this perspective, belief in a just world becomes a way of justifying the status quo of resource distribution. To put it another way, principles of justice can become instruments by which those who control resources can maintain their hold on those resources. Laura Nader, in criticizing the American legal system, maintains that the law is a tool through which "wealthier members of society override and superimpose their views on the poorer, less powerful sectors" (Nader 1975 p. 162). This is similar to the Marxian concept that class interests become institutionalized in those structures—political and legal—which embody conceptions of justice supporting the status quo.

It is also related to Schattschneider's concept of the "mobilization of bias" or Bachrach and Baratz's concept of "nondecisions," in that the explicit or implicit rules of the game embodied in the status quo become instruments for suppressing demands for change (Bachrach & Baratz 1970, pp. 43-51; Schattschneider 1960, p. 71). If people want to believe that the world is arranged in an essentially fair way, it will be easier to persuade them that the inequities perpetuated by any given status quo "deserve" to exist, because both those who benefit and those who are deprived are getting roughly—or perhaps even precisely—that to which they are "entitled."

Three themes emerge from these perspectives. First, concerns for justice arise out of the conditions of our lives and reflect patterns of socialization and adaptation to social reality. If so, the concern for justice will have some close relationship to an individual or system orientation, since the concern for justice will reflect both a concern for system integrity and the pursuit of individual or group goals. Second, justice is not only a label for evaluative standards applied to public resource allocation decisions, but also serves as a tool for justifying those decisions. Finally, we would expect different principles of justice to arise depending upon the nature and the structure of the conflict relationship.

PROCEDURAL AND DISTRIBUTIVE JUSTICE

In deciding whether a particular decision was just, an individual can focus either on the way the decision was made or on its substance. This is the distinction between procedural justice and distributive justice (Mikula 1980; Lerner & Lerner 1982). An assessment on the basis of procedural justice implies that the individual will consider the fairness with which the decision was made. For example, under the American criminal law it is necessary that the proper legal procedures be followed. If they are, we assume that the substantive outcome is just—that the person is, in fact, guilty of the crime as charged. Under normal circumstances, any appeal from the decision of a trial court must be made on procedural rather than substantive grounds. For most practical purposes, then, criminal justice in the United States is procedural. The convicted criminal is assumed to have been treated fairly or justly if she has had her day in court—protestations of innocence notwithstanding.

There is a sense in which procedural justice is easier to establish than distributive justice. If you are setting up a method by which certain important decisions will be made, and if the method proposed does not obviously favor some individuals or groups in inappropriate ways,* then the outputs of the system will be unknown at the time the system is set up. This makes it easier to reach agreement on procedure. Interested parties need only be assured that the procedure will not put them at a significant disadvantage. When setting up standards for distributive justice, however, interested parties can more easily project or predict how they will fare under different standards; therefore, agreement is much more difficult to achieve.

Procedures do have outcomes, however, and the outcomes represent distributive justice for that political issue. If some people are dissatisfied enough about the result to try to do something about it, the result be-

---

*For an example of an appropriate way in which some individuals or groups might be favored, we return to the criminal justice system. The principle "innocent until proven guilty" is designed to make it easier for the accused to prove her innocence if, in fact, she is innocent, than it is for the state to prove her guilty if, in fact, she is guilty.

comes grist for the political mill. When the merits are debated, the dialog tends to be in terms of some notion of distributive justice—unless the parties are trying to change the rules of the game, in which case both procedural and distributive demands or proposals may be made. The political battle usually is not limited to the merits of any particular notion of what constitutes distributive justice. Aside from proposals to change procedures, the argument may also involve attempts to change the persons who made such decisions or the forum in which the conflict and its resolution are played out. Let us take a brief look at each of these.

First, procedural changes need not amount to full-blown revolutionary conflicts. They can range from conflicts over changing the entire set of rules by which the game is played in a political system to conflicts over changing very small details. What interests us here is change that is less than sweeping or all-encompassing. Procedures are not neutral. They may favor one party over the others, and they may make one type of outcome more likely than any others, so a relatively small change in procedure can have a significant impact on outcomes. To return to an example used earlier, the seniority system in Congress has been a target of reform efforts for decades. The opponents of the seniority system have usually wanted to increase the probability that liberal legislation will be passed. Although this effort may have been misguided (Brenner 1983, p. 138), it is a good example of an effort to change procedures in order to realize outcomes that represent a different view of distributive justice.

Another way of making changes in the distributive values of political outcomes is to change the persons who occupy key roles in the system. Like procedures, the people elected or appointed to key political positions are not value neutral. They bring to their job a set of predispositions—perhaps even prejudices—that affect their perception of political problems as well as their consideration of appropriate solutions. For example, from 1981 to 1983, the U.S. Civil Rights Commission tended to have a radically different approach to the achievement of civil rights than did the Reagan Administration. Not only did the commission implement the law in a way antithetical to Reagan's policy preferences, but also members of the commission were openly critical of many administration policies. Finally, after much political maneuvering and acrimony, Reagan succeeded in achieving a reorganization of the commission. As a result, during the first meeting of the newly constituted commission, the members voted 6 to 2 in favor of a resolution repudiating much of what the previous commission had stood for and supporting the approach to civil rights favored by the Reagan administration (*Washington Post*, January 18, 1984, p. A7).

Finally, a change in the probability of certain outcomes sometimes can be effected by changing the forum in which the political conflict is waged. This may represent a significant change in both procedural constraints and personnel. For example, those who support the right of women to have abortions had little luck in state legislatures, where many laws limited the circumstances in which an abortion could be obtained, or forbade them outright. Proponents of the right to choose turned to the forum provided by the court system, and in 1973, in *Roe v. Wade* (410 U.S. 113), the Supreme Court struck down a Texas law that outlawed all abortions except when necessary to save the life of the woman. Because this court decision was based on the constitutional right to privacy, similar laws in other states were also, by implication, void. The proponents of abortion legislation, having lost in the courts, then resorted to an effort to amend the Constitution—thus changing the forum to the halls of the U.S. Congress (Champagne & Dawes 1983, pp. 3–11).

Whatever the outcome, parties to a political dispute are likely to ask: Was it fair? Procedurally? Substantively? In other words, they are concerned with whether it was fair to them or theirs—an individual perspective; or they are concerned with whether it was fair to everyone—a system perspective. By a curious paradox, however, what is fair for individuals (microjustice) does not always turn out to be fair when viewed from a broader perspective (macrojustice).

MICROJUSTICE AND MACROJUSTICE*

Microjustice is the fairness with which valued public resources are distributed to individuals within a political system. *Macrojustice* is the aggregate fairness of the distribution of valued public resources in a political system. The principles of microjustice require that the attributes of individuals be taken into consideration in determining what would be a fair distribution. Does Joan Jones deserve what she is getting? The distribution of valued resources in a political system thus becomes a function of a series of decisions that focus only on individuals within that system. The principles of macrojustice ignore the attributes of individual recipients. Rather, they merely specify a priori what the overall distribution within the political system should be, and they reward individuals without regard to their uniqueness as individuals. For example, it may be determined that no one should have an income falling below one-half of the median income within the society. Under such a rule, anyone who can demonstrate that his income falls below this standard will receive income supplements without reference to any other characteristics he may possess as an individual or any peculiarities which may contribute to his income status. In other words, "[m]icrojustice is concerned with the qualifying attributes of individuals," while "[m]acrojustice is concerned with the appropriate order of society or the goodness of society" (Brickman, et al, 1982, p. 178).

The potential for conflict between these two perspectives on justice

---

*In this and the following sections, we borrow heavily from the work of Brickman, Folger, Goode & Schul 1982.

can be seen in the debate over affirmative action in the United States. The affirmative action program applied what is, in essence, a macrojustice principle. Since certain groups of people, most notably blacks and women, had been systematically excluded from certain professions or jobs *because* they were blacks or women, they were underrepresented compared to their proportion in the population. Affirmative action programs were designed to redress this imbalance by giving the members of underrepresented groups an advantage in the hiring and promotion processes. A black might be hired instead of a white of equal or somewhat higher merit.

Critics of affirmative action invoked the microjustice principle that hiring and promotion should be on the basis of individual qualifications and job performance. But since blacks and women had not had the same advantages as white males both in socialization and in treatment in the educational system, it seemed unlikely that they could—in the short run, at least—compete successfully. Application of the microjustice principle of strict merit hiring and promotion would continue to perpetuate the injustices implied by the principles of macrojustice. The macrojustice principles were applied on the assumption that the availability of jobs in the present and future would cause changes in socialization and education, which would allow the disadvantaged groups to compete more successfully on an individual basis in the long run. This was, however, little comfort to the qualified white male who was passed over for a job or a promotion, since he had not benefited directly from the advantage white males had formerly held in the job market, and he would probably not be at the proper stage in his career to be able to compete equally at that point in the future when affirmative action was no longer necessary.

Affirmative action created a situation in which conflict was not only possible but clearly inevitable. We had a situation in which the given distribution of values (here: desirable jobs and job status) created and perpetuated a situation broadly acknowledged to be unfair and to have spawned practices based on the assumption that the unfairness would continue. Pursuit of the goal of trying to treat each individual exclusively on the basis of personal merit would only perpetuate the status quo, and perhaps even increase the extent to which the overall situation would be unfair in the long run.

Brickman and Stearns (1978) demonstrated this drift toward greater unfairness in an experiment in which subjects were instructed to provide rewards or incentives to hypothetical workers according to the workers' contributions. The result vastly enhanced the differences between the more-able and less-able groups. It seems that "providing greater rewards for those capable of superior performance tends to produce an increasing degree of concentration of resources in the hands of the more talented, or in the hands of those who are believed to be more talented" (Brickman, et al 1982, p. 174).

It is clear that in the short run there is no possibility of dealing with the problem of job inequality in a way that will be perceived as just by all. Disadvantaged groups will invoke macrojustice principles; those who become individually disadvantaged as a result of policies based on macrojustice principles will invoke microjustice principles on their own behalf. Affirmative action programs inevitably create serious inequities in the short run, but abandonment of affirmative action programs will inevitably perpetuate and perhaps even intensify existing inequities. The only question is: Who should pay the price for a situation created by past generations? There is no easy way out. More appropriately, there is no one, just way out. This is a situation in which macrojustice and microjustice principles must certainly clash, and this clash will provide an unending flow of grist for the political mill.

EQUALITY, EQUITY, AND NEED

Although there are many standards for distributive justice, we will limit our discussion here to three that are commonly evoked in political life: equality, equity, and need. Equality is a commonly used macrojustice principle, while equity and need are usually thought of as microjustice principles. Need, however, represents an interesting blend of microjustice and macrojustice because of the way it can be used. More of this later. First, let us turn to equality and equity.

Equality is a form of justice that explicitly tries to eliminate winners and losers by ensuring that everyone is treated the same. This aim arises from the perception of a similarity or belonging together of oneself and the other person. Justice as equality has been a powerful force in shaping much of modern Western political culture. The Declaration of Independence proclaims that "all men are created equal." The French Revolution was infused by the goals of "liberty, equality, fraternity." But equality of opportunity is quite different from equality of outcome. While the fight for equality of opportunity for all persons regardless of race, creed, or origin has been a bitter thread throughout history, that fight has essentially been one to recognize that all human beings share a fundamental equivalence.

The idea that people deserve equality of outcome is more of a problem for political institutions in American society. Since American tradition enshrines equality as a central tenet of political life, why has equality of outcome been resisted as strongly as it has? Two ideas seem relevant. First, equality of outcome has always been threatening to someone, because resources are never distributed equally. Therefore, equality of outcome will require—or be perceived to require—a redistribution of resources. Naturally this will be much less attractive for the "haves" (winners) than it will be for the "have-nots" (losers). Also, the "haves" usually have more resources with which to influence political processes. Moreover, because of the threat equality of outcomes poses to significant soci-

etal groups, authorities will be concerned about the effect this conflict will
have on the integrity of the system. They are likely, therefore, to resist the
principle. Further, to the extent that authorities have come to represent
the partisan interests of the haves, they will be more interested in supporting principles of justice that validate the status quo (Walster &
Walster 1975; Kipnis 1972).

Second, equality of outcome conflicts directly with an equity solution
to public-resource allocation problems. Why? Equity-based justice is derived from a perception of an equivalence of individuals, but also from a
sensitivity to their differences. What really counts are their differences;
equity is a microjustice principle. People are in different positions because
of differences—in their investments, in the costs they incurred in getting
to where they are. Solutions to public-resource allocation problems based
on equity, therefore, speak to the problem of treating people in the same
position equally. In this sense, equity generates immediate winner-loser
problems because it is based on complex computations of a person's merit
balanced against what that person should get. An example should make
this clearer.

If Lauri Bari has earned a Harvard law degree, then she should be
entitled to the same privileges and resources someone with an equivalent
degree has. Of course this does not always happen; some people with
Harvard law degrees may be appointed or elected to high political or
judicial office while others continue to pursue ordinary legal careers. This
does not necessarily lead to anger or hurt on the part of our hypothetical
lawyer, because other factors or "investments" may be taken into account:
Those other Harvard law graduates might be more talented, more highly
motivated, or willing to work harder. Of course, Lauri may feel angry at
individual Harvard law graduates, especially those who got ahead by
"pull" or "luck." In other words, some investments are perceived as legitimate and others are not. This brings out the psychology of equity-based
justice. It requires a continual computation of investments made versus
outcomes received.

In a curious way, then, equity-based justice is fragile; it only works as
long as there is a general agreement on what counts as an investment and
the relationship of these investments to the outcomes received. It also
depends on social comparisons with others in similar and dissimilar situations. Equality of outcome will be seen as eliminating distinctions based on
"meritorious" differences between individuals—a microjustice principle.
This difference is particularly problematical in Western societies in which
the egalitarian aims of the democratic state and the equity aims of the
marketplace clash (Lane 1979).

Here is an interesting research question: Under what conditions will
resource allocation decisions shift from an equity principle toward an
equality of outcome principle? Sampson (1975) has summarized some research on this issue. He notes three factors of importance. First, laboratory
research shows that people prefer an equality principle for dividing up

resources when they are concerned with maintaining or establishing positive interpersonal relationships with other people. This kind of concern may come to the fore particularly when people are affluent, when they perceive enough resources to go around. We might consider the willingness of the U.S. political process to move toward equality of both opportunity and outcome during the 1960s and early 1970s as reflecting a general perception that there was indeed enough to go around. As the U.S. economy soured in the middle of the 1970s, and people began to confront a society and a world of increasingly scarce resources, there arose resistance to resource allocation decisions based on equality of outcome.

Second, some people generally have a cooperative orientation toward others, while other people are generally competitive. That is, by virtue of what we call their personality, some persons may derive gratification from benefiting others as well as the self, while others may feel rewarded by acting to win as much as they can. The interesting question for political psychology then becomes: Under what conditions do one or another of these types find their way into positions of authority?

The third point is related to the second. Equality-oriented behavior is a way of communicating the kind of person you are. It says, "I see you as an equal, as someone with similar characteristics or interests." Equality-oriented behavior also denies the notion of status differences or communicates the desire to relate to others as persons rather than as positions. Numerous studies (Levanthal & Lane 1970; Levanthal & Anderson 1974; Vinacke 1969; Benton 1971) have demonstrated that females tend to prefer an equality-based solution to resource distribution problems. This result is often explained by pointing to training for sex-role behavior in our society. It is suggested that women are trained to be more sensitive to interpersonal feeling and more concerned with the interpersonal situation than with winning. In short, women are socialized to emphasize similarities rather than differences between people.

We come now to perceptions of justice based on identification with the other. Suppose we are watching the television news and we see a report on a subcommittee of Congress that is considering a bill to increase funds for the handicapped. The camera focuses on a painfully handicapped person sitting alone in a wheelchair before the microphone in the hearing room, explaining in distorted and difficult tones the problems of dealing with his handicap. At the end he begins to cry. It would be a hard-hearted person who could resist this plea. The dominant consideration is likely to be the way this person's pain is experienced as our own. It may elicit in us universal feelings of isolation and loneliness. Our political behavior—letters or calls we may make to our representatives urging them to pass the legislation—is based on our sense of the justice of need. To decrease this person's pain is, in some sense, to decrease our own.

This particular example can also be seen in a different light. We may identify not so much with the universal feelings elicited as with this person's position. That is, we may see this person as an innocent victim of forces over which he has no control and to which other members of the society are vulnerable, or could be vulnerable. We may want to urge passage of the legislation because we want to get this person back on his feet, into some new position which will allow him to take greater control of his life. Again, the perception is "this could be me," but in this case it is the me who could one day be crippled, say by an accident, rather than the me who feels within himself the pain of the other.

The difference drawn here has important implications. Identification with the pain or pleasure of others as a psychological process is volatile and difficult to sustain. People have difficulty identifying in this sense with larger groupings or collectivities. The abstract notion of a disadvantaged group is more difficult to empathize with than one obviously disadvantaged person whom we can see and hear.

Position-based identification is based more closely on the personal contract suggested by Lerner. That is, in this form of identification we are concerned that people deserve what they ask for. In the case of the handicapped person, we are concerned that the person's position does not allow him to get what he deserves by virtue of his needs. We perceive a basic violation of his personal contract. Since, if we agree with Lerner, the personal contract is central to the development of our concepts of justice as we experience them through the process of growing up, this form of justice might be more enduring. On the other hand, the belief in a just world may alter the relationship of identification with the other person. This comment leads us to consider the more general question of the relationship between forms of justice.

Need is a standard for distributive justice that is usually thought of as an individualizing or microjustice principle. It is thus viewed because it is usually thought necessary to know each person's situation before a decision can be made as to what they should get—what they need. Need, however, can also be called upon with the implicit goal of leveling out a distribution. That is, it can be used to put disadvantaged persons on a more equal footing with those who are advantaged (Eckhoff 1974):

> In this sense, need is actually a stalking horse for the macrolevel principle of equality, or, at least, the macrolevel principle of some maximum allowable range. Need can be recognized as a disguised version of a macrojustice principle like equality whenever it takes on a self-referential form, or whenever people are held to need Y if they simply have less of Y than others do. The fact that need can often be used to justify what is actually a search for equality, and vice versa, has obscured the extent to which need and equality, like any pair of micro and macrolevel principles, can conflict. A distribution in which the parties actually received resources in strict proportion to their need for these resources would almost certainly be a highly unequal distribution. [Brickman, et al, 1982, pp. 179–180]

To return to our hypothetical handicapped person, individuals with severe disabilities are likely to need more resources than nonhandicapped persons if they are to function satisfactorily in society. The Marxian principle of "from each according to his ability, to each according to his need" does not necessarily imply a general state of equality.

Merit, or equity, can also serve as a stalking horse for a macrojustice principle of inequality. In other words, defending merit as a principle of microjustice can be an implicit defense of inequality, especially in cases in which the existing distribution of resources is perceived as reflecting the existing distribution of merit. In 1984, when the newly constituted U.S. Civil Rights Commission decided to shift away from pursuit of a rough equality of outcome to place more emphasis on equity, it was seen by many as a way for the privileged supporters of Ronald Reagan to defend their status in the society. "It may be a major triumph for egalitarian interests simply to shift the domain of discourse from micro- to macro-concerns, where the question of equality versus inequality can be debated directly rather than by the proxy issues of need and merit" (Brickman, et al 1982, p. 180). When the commission voted 6 to 2 to decline to endorse a report by the old commission "concluding that the federal government need[ed] to increase aid to blacks in some areas of Alabama who [had] lower earnings and less education than whites in the same locale" (*Washington Post*, January 18, 1984, p. A1), it was shifting the emphasis from equality to equity. Egalitarian interests had suffered a significant defeat, but the proponents of the policy of the new commission were able to claim that justice was on their side—microjustice, that is.

To make a distinction between equality of opportunity and equality of outcome is to make a distinction, in part, between procedural and distributive justice. "Equality or inequality of opportunity constrains only the procedures to be followed in allowing individuals to pursue outcomes and is indifferent to the range of outcomes produced" (Brickman, et al 1982, p. 182). Equality of opportunity clears the way for the microjustice principle of equity to operate. On the other hand, equality of outcomes specifies that all will achieve the same level of resources and is indifferent regarding how this is achieved. This is macrojustice.

In Western culture, we distinguish between individual deserving (i.e., need or merit) and majority rule. Under a democratic system the majority decides, usually by voting, what is in the collective interest. This defines what will be considered fair in terms of procedural justice, but it does not extend any protection to minorities against tyranny of the majority. Minority rights are usually protected by need or merit, both of which are microjustice principles in the sense that individuals are perceived to be entitled to what they need or what they can earn.

> The rights of the disadvantaged can also in some measure be protected by the macroprinciple that all people are entitled to some minimum. But this principle does not protect the entitlement of the more advantaged, who have often been in the forefront of the struggles for individual rights and have also been the prime beneficiaries of their existence. Just as principles of macrojustice place limits on what is under individual control, . . . principles of microjustice place limits on what is under collective control. On the

other hand, while macrojustice principles like democracy may threaten microjustice principles of individual deserving, microjustice principles like equity or need threaten democracy every time they dictate a distribution of resources that interferes with the ability of all members of society to exercise their democratic rights (cf. Okun 1975). [Brickman, et al 1982, pp. 183–184].

JUSTICE AND THE STRUCTURE OF CONFLICT

As we discussed earlier, conflict is central to political life. In politics it is difficult to find instances in which the ultimate outcome is not the creation of winners and losers. Equity in some form is more often the standard of justice than is equality. This tends to be true even in political systems such as the Soviet Union or the United States, where equality is firmly entrenched in the reigning political philosophy. If we look at the way these systems actually function, as opposed to the way in which they proclaim that they function, we see clearly that some citizens are more equal than others, and that they think that they "deserve" their extra measure of the good things in life.

Equity expressed in terms of winning and losing becomes an acute problem for any political system. What mechanisms keep losers engaged with the system? How can people be reconciled to being losers? To a large extent, this problem is solved—or more accurately, an attempt is made to solve it—through the way in which conflict is structured in any given political system. The way a conflict is played out to its resolution conditions the way the people perceive that conflict. This is related to several notions we discussed earlier.

First, people will have perceptions regarding the justice of the procedures by which any political conflict is resolved. Previously, we considered the concepts of authority and legitimacy with reference to persons. Processes, however, can also be considered legitimate or authoritative, and if such processes are followed in resolving a conflict, the outcome of the conflict can be assumed to be just by persons who perceive the process as legitimate. Thus, a movement toward greater legitimacy can easily take the form of a movement toward greater structuring of conflict.

Second, there is the role of power expressed as the threat or use of force or sanctions. The ability to use force is seldom, if ever, distributed equally. Winners can be seen as deserving to win simply because they command a superior ability to use force. In fact, this could be regarded as one expression of the equity concept of justice. In many if not all political systems, however, there exists an ingrained notion that might does not create right, except in a fait accompli sense. The assertion of power is likely to be countered by a push toward more rules, making conflict increasingly structured. To the extent that one plays by the rules there is less need for the use of power or naked force.

In any conflict situation, both of these factors affect the attitudes of individuals toward the resulting distribution of resources and the stability of that arrangement. This concern is an outgrowth of a socialization process in which notions of right and wrong are inculcated and, in the United States at least, in which such notions are associated with ideas about procedure (Kohlberg 1978). Most people have a vested interest in the smooth functioning of their societies and political systems. At the very least, such stability increases our ability to make accurate predictions about the future and, as a result, to plan our lives accordingly.

Many rules create conflict situations that approach the state of being fully structured. This reduces the importance of the social comparison calculating process in determining equity by replacing it with a more precise method—determining equity through use of a precise and fully articulated set of rules. Our court system works under the major assumption that the party that wins is the one that deserves to win—and in an adversary system, someone always wins. Put another way, if the proper procedures (as specified by the applicable laws and rules) are followed, we assume that justice has been served. Assuming widespread acceptance of the rules and laws, everyone's calculation of equity is brought into at least rough agreement. Highly structured situations also provide the cues that allow people to govern their behavior in ways that lead both themselves and others to perceive them as entitled to what they get. Finally, notions of justice as equality come into play here also, since strict adherence to a set of rules has the virtue of ensuring equality of treatment as a goal. If there is inequality, it is in terms of rules which have been considered before adoption, legitimized by adoption, and incorporated into people's belief in a just world.*

It is not necessarily desirable for all of the conflict situations in a political system to be fully structured or to approach that state. The more fully structured a situation is, the more rigid it is, eliminating the possibility of adaptive change. Partially structured situations leave more potential for creativity and needed modifications in the status quo. At the same time, however, there is also more room for discretion and arbitrariness. This reduces predictability and leaves much more room for disagreement as to what constitutes justice. The idea of deservingness can then be tied to a respect for wit or skill. Because there are some rules, the potency of this notion of deservingness can be enhanced by the fact that the wit or skill is being exercised within a general framework of rules. Hard work is another relevant criterion of deservingness here. In elections, for example, the winners are seen as deserving to win if it is perceived that they worked hard, made few mistakes, and presented the electorate with timely and attractive policy alternatives.

---

*However, there is another side to increased structure in conflict situations, particularly if the rules guarantee the creation of winners and losers, as is characteristic of the American legal system. Procedures of this sort may increasingly invite perceptions that the procedures themselves are unfair, thus leading to greater polarization, increased alienation from the system of rules, and increased potential for conflict (Peachey & Lerner 1982).

To the extent that we perceive the rules of conflict as legitimate or authoritative, we will accept the outcomes as what ought to be. Accumulated dissatisfactions with outcomes can lead to a challenge to the rules of conflict currently in force. This may result in the establishment of a new, and presumably more justice-promoting, set of rules for the conduct of conflictive processes. In political systems, such a transition can take the form of either reform or revolution.

The success of the management and resolution of conflict over public-resource allocation problems is going to depend in some large measure on the participants' perceptions of justice. It may even be said that political conflict is conflict over which principles of justice will prevail. This point holds whether we view it through the lens of authority, concerned with maintaining the smooth functioning of the system or an orientation toward collective goals, or through the lens of partisans, vying to influence the kinds of decisions that are made.

THE PROCESS OF POLITICS

The phenomena discussed so far in this volume have all been elements in what we conceive to be the process of politics as seen from a conflict perspective. Figure 10-1 shows the relationships among them and identifies certain mediating factors. This section will be devoted to a discussion of the dynamics of the political process, as outlined in Figure 10-1.

The political process, as we conceptualize it, begins with a perception on the part of two or more individuals that a resource allocation problem exists. *Perception* is crucial here. Theoretically, a resource allocation problem may exist as a potentiality but remain dormant with regard to the political process. Such a situation might exist in a case in which the problem was not perceived as needing attention, or not perceived at all, by anyone in a position to activate the political process. Conversely, some authority or partisan could perceive a problem that does not exist in any objective sense, and thereby "create" a problem that would in turn activate the process outlined in Figure 10-1. In short, the crucial point is that a form of perceptual screening takes place, that it takes place within the minds of those able to activate the political process, and that this leads to a tendency for the issues getting attention to be those that filter through the perceptual screens of the authorities and partisans most actively involved.

This process is mediated by the political socialization process in two important ways. First, an individual's socializing experiences with regard to the political system will have a profound influence on whether that individual will be sufficiently interested in politics to become involved in efforts to achieve solutions to public-resource allocation problems. Second, any person who is either involved or receptive to involvement has undergone socializing experiences that have shaped the perceptual screens that mediate those aspects of the political arena of which she is aware, as well as the

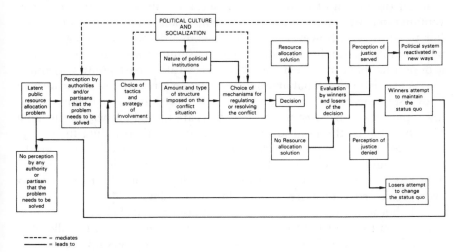

----- = mediates
───── = leads to

FIGURE 10-1 The Process of Politics from a Conflict Perspective

importance she attaches to them. Unless some issue is perceived and is judged to be sufficiently important, why expend the time and energy— not to mention other types of resources—to become involved in an effort to achieve a solution?

Once a problem has been perceived and judged sufficiently important, and a decision to become involved has been made, the individual has a choice as to whether the participation should be change-oriented or status quo-oriented. Here again socialization in the form of the accumulated residue of past experiences plays a role. Authorities—who are likely to have been former winners—will likely emphasize stability and continuity because of their concern with the integrity and maintenance of the system. Partisans—who are less likely to have been winners in the past— will be inclined to emphasize social justice and reform because of their preoccupation with the effects of conflict on the allocation of public resources in which they are interested.

All of the above factors are also mediated by political culture (Rosenbaum 1975, pp. 6–8), which in itself conditions the political socialization process. In fact, political culture and political socialization are inextricably intertwined, since political culture constrains and guides the socialization process, and socialization inculcates and perpetuates political culture.

Once one has become involved in conflict over a public resource problem—either as an authority or as a partisan—it becomes necessary to choose tactics and an overall strategy for carrying out the fight. Every political system has certain approaches that are considered standard or acceptable. They are the rules of the political game for that system. A choice of tactics from this repertoire would involve one in behaviors considered conventional for that particular political system. In most stable political systems most of the time, political activity is carried out by conventional means. There is always the temptation to go outside the rules of fair political play, however, in order to gain a decisive advantage. This is most tempting in political systems that are significantly unstable or among groups that have not been notably successful in past political conflicts.

Various institutional arrangements make it relatively easy or difficult to overstep the boundaries between conventional and unconventional political participation. Most political conflicts are played out within the ambit of only some of the political institutions currently prevailing in that system. The more highly structured the processes governed by these institutions, the less leeway there is for unconventional or ruleless maneuvering. The less structured the processes, the more temptation to stretch—or even break—currently prevailing rules of fair play.

Political institutions also afford a choice of social behaviors or mechanisms that can be used to regulate or resolve conflicts over the allocation of public resources. The major mechanisms are leadership, persuasion, bargaining, and force or the threat of force. In most public-resource allocation conflicts, some combination of these is used. The particular mix can vary with such factors as the nature of the political culture and institutions, the type of problem, and the personalities of the individuals involved. The conflict-regulating and -resolving mechanisms utilized condition the process by which a decision is finally made. This decision may or may not solve the problem. In either case, the participants in the conflict will evaluate the resulting situation and will come to some conclusions as to whether the outcome of the process was just.

If all of the key participants have a perception that justice has been served, at least minimally, they may be inclined to let the matter rest and to turn their attention and energies to other problems. What will happen if some participants see the outcome as unjust? We know that losers may view a decision as unfair and yet do nothing about it. What are the conditions under which such an individual will take action either to reactivate the process or to achieve a fairer outcome? In Chapter 8, we discussed some of the conditions leading to revolution—that is, changing the rules governing conflict. To answer the question about reactivating the political process would require a more ambitious excursion into the psychology of change than is possible here. A few points related to some concepts introduced earlier, however, can be made. In Chapter 3, we discussed the complex ways in which self-esteem, locus of control, personal control, and the sense of political efficacy can lead to political participation. Obviously, one factor influencing any decision to contest an "unfair" outcome will be a set of action-oriented personal characteristics.

But individual qualities are never likely to be enough. Why? Part of the answer lies in the nature of the relationship between winners as a group and losers as a group. Putting aside the situation in which winners employ force or the threat of force to suppress political activity on the part of losers, let us look at some of the psychological dimensions of this relationship. In Chapter 1, we defined a stereotype as a kind of categorization in which we ascribe a certain pattern of characteristics to a set of persons. Stereotypes can have great symbolic power, particularly if the person using the stereotype expects all members of the stereotyped group to behave in the same way. These expectations can have strong effects in creating or inducing the expected behavior (e.g., Rosenthal & Jacobson 1968; Kidder & Stewart 1975). Thus, winners' expectations that losers will behave in ways not related to reactivating the political process can have the effect of suppressing active loser behavior. How does this effect work? If others overtly expect you to behave a certain way, you may find it difficult to resist this pressure (see discussion of *role* in Chapter 1). Thirty years ago in the United States, women were expected to be passive and compliant—and most fulfilled that expectation. Indeed, if a woman did not, she risked rejection. This response came not only from men but from other women who may have felt that it was necessary for all women to conform to these stereotyped expectations.

Notice that implied in these stereotypes is an ethnocentrism. That is, not only did men perceive (and some, to an extent, still do) women as weaker, less assertive, and more conforming than men, but they saw this state of affairs as confirming male superiority. But ethnocentrism can sometimes be reversed in ways that lead to the beginning of political activism. When a group of persons is singled out for stereotyping, the contrast between themselves and the group doing the stereotyping becomes more marked. As a result, the differences between people in the stereotyped group seem smaller in comparison. This leads to great perceptions of similarity among group members (e.g., Byrne 1969) and, therefore, to greater group cohesiveness (see Chapter 9). Consequently, people in the stereotyped group start finding it easier to resist the expectations that result from stereotyping. Either they may come to realize that the characteristics attributed to them are necessarily accurate or they may begin to feel more comfortable acting contrary to those expectations. They may then develop an ethnocentrism of their own, feeling that *their* group is better than the group perpetuating the stereotypes. This in turn increases group cohesiveness. The fact that individuals join together in a group that may provide support for action is also a factor in countering the effects of negative stereotypes.

To summarize, the symbolic power of negative stereotypes may make it difficult for losers to push for reactivation of the political process, even though they may perceive the outcome of a political decision to be unjust. But the feeling of increased cohesiveness that is sometimes a response to negative stereotyping may provide a basis for taking political action (Kidder & Stewart 1975).

This sketchy account only begins to explore this topic. We do not want to leave the reader with the idea that in the post-decision period, winners either become quiescent or spend their time frustrating attempts by losers to reopen the issues. Indeed, it is likely that winning is reinforcing. The taste of victory in a public resource allocation decision may encourage winners to become even more active in prodding the system to make further decisions that increase the winner's share. For example, after Ronald Reagan's successful attempt to cut social programs in the 1982 federal budget, he immediately proposed a further 12 percent cut for most social programs, as well as cuts in general entitlements (*Budgeting for America* 1982). However, in 1982, with the loss of 22 Congressional seats to the Democrats and the prospect of massive deficits, his attempts at further budget cuts were considerably curtailed.

Political conflicts are won and lost, opened and reopened. No matter what the outcome, the political process tends to be self-perpetuating in that it feeds upon itself. Old problems always need to be re-resolved— perhaps many times over as the system proves unable to generate a solution perceived as sufficiently just to allow the losers to accept it gracefully. Further, political conflict is perpetuated by the outcomes of successful solutions—solutions to resource allocation problems that are perceived to be adequately just by both winners and losers.

Why should successful solutions perpetuate political conflict? One reason is that human beings have a decidedly imperfect ability to foresee the consequences of their decisions at the time the decisions are being made. We have a tendency to be satisfied with the hope that implementation of the decision will eliminate the problem that led to the activation of the political process. We have much less of a tendency to consider the new problems that may be generated by the solution at hand. Even when attempts are made, they seem all too often to be flawed or to generate disinterest among the enthusiasts of the new solution.

Let us take an example. The United States Congress traditionally was led by a relatively small number of senators and representatives who had long records of continuous service (Ripley 1983, pp. 130–33). Until quite recently, the resulting seniority and apprenticeship norms and practices generated a leadership almost exclusively representative of the South and of rural areas. These legislators, quite understandably, eased the way for legislation favored by their constituents and to block legislation their constituents opposed. Since the leaders overwhelmingly represented conservative constituencies, this situation was a perpetual source of frustration for liberals and gave rise to perennial attempts at reform. Their frustration reached a zenith during the 1950s and the 1960s when a powerful group of senior senators and representatives battled resolutely against many reforms the liberals thought imperative, most notably Civil Rights legislation. This led to a series of reforms during the first half of the 1970s that eroded the power of the seniority system (Ripley 1983, pp. 179–83, 241–42). The theory behind the reforms was that, among other things, they would make it easier for liberal presidents to get their legislation through Congress (Brenner 1983, p. 138).

The irony of this is that in the early 1980s the liberals found that they had eased the way for a conservative president to get his legislation through Congress. In addition, had the old seniority system been in effect, the leadership would have been liberal rather than conservative (Ornstein & Rohde 1975). Also, Congress lay in disarray and disrepute (*Budgeting for America* 1982) largely because it had no strong leadership. In an attempt to change the balance of power in Congress, to allow the passage of liberal legislation, a weakened and fragmented congressional leadership found it difficult to cope with a conservative president determined to weaken or dispense with much of the liberal legislation that had been passed.

Another example is the Community Action Program which was part of President Lyndon Johnson's "War on Poverty" (Judd 1984, pp. 308–15). It was originally intended to break the poverty cycle by giving the poor a chance to participate in programs that would affect their lives. It was thought that this would change their attitudes about the hopelessness of their condition and galvanize them to strive for better education and better jobs, as well as to lose their defeatist attitudes. The program was strongly supported by congressional representatives, mayors, and other local interests who saw it as a way of getting money to deal with pressing local problems. But the agencies established under this program were given federal funds directly, while existing state and local governments were bypassed. This established new governmental and quasi-governmental bodies that were independent of city hall and local authorities. Soon local authorities who had originally supported the legislation were having second thoughts, and were calling for a change that would allow control of the funds to be given to local officials. This political pressure resulted in a reinterpretation of the legislation that eroded the possibility that these local autonomous agencies could become a political force independent of local political officials and government agencies. The program failed to meet its goals because of the combination of the apathy of the poor and the antipathy of local officials to the possibility of independent actions by the poor.

Another reason why even successful solutions can perpetuate political conflict has to do with the fact that the political process is tied to history. Any solution to a political conflict that is sufficiently satisfactory to allow the issue to become quiescent may become considerably less satisfactory at some point in the future, due to changes in the microenvironment or in the macroenvironment that are independent of the solution itself.

For example, in the late '50s the Tennessee Valley Authority (TVA), the House Appropriations Committee, local congressional leaders, and other local officials cooperated to enact legislation for water resource development. Their objectives included improved navigation, flood control, the generation of electricity, and an infusion of money into the local economy (Yaffee 1982, p. 8). Implementation went along nicely until the explosion of ecological awareness that took place in the 1960s and culminated in the enactment of the Endangered Species Act of 1973. The law mandated the protection of rare species of plants and animals. This in turn meant that the erection of the TVA's Tellico Dam was no longer uncontroversial, even though previously it would have been considered an unobjectionable element in the implementation of the original water resource development objectives. It became controversial because it threatened a tiny fish (the snail darter) with extinction (Yaffee 1982, pp. 13–14). Thus, a program that was doing well what it had originally been intended to do generated further political conflict, not because it had failed or produced serious unforeseen consequences, but because the macroenvironment had changed. The American public, through congressional action, decided to place a high value on the continued existence of obscure species—species which could be extinguished by water resource development projects.

Political systems are marked by the constant interplay of change and stability. The change and stability in the political system is a function of change and stability in the four essential components of any political system: (1) the inner, biological states of the individuals involved, (2) their psychological makeup, (3) the cultural and sociological setting in which their political activity takes place, and (4) the imperatives and limitations imposed by the physical context of the given political system (adapted from Riegel 1978). All of these develop over time, experiencing periods of change and stability. Because this development is never perfectly synchronized, there is a constant potential for change and imbalance. In fact, it must be assumed that change and imbalance are "fully as central to social [and, therefore, political] behavior as stability and balance are" (T. Blank 1982, p. 44).

If we look at political behavior from this perspective, it is clear that there is little reason to expect any resource allocation problem to be solved with finality. The four essential components of any political system have histories, and history is never completed. "At the moment when completion seems to be imminent, questions and doubts arise in the individual and in society" (T. Blank 1982, p. 50). These new questions and doubts give rise to new resource allocation problems and the activity of the political system goes on, bred in conflict and self-perpetuating through the very resolution of conflict.

SUMMARY

People who engage in political conflict also evaluate the outcome of the conflict. This evaluation has objective and subjective aspects. Usually the standards used for evaluation involve some judgment concerning whether the outcome was just, and people tend to design their lives so they can regard the political combatants, themselves included, as deserving what they get. If those just rewards are not forthcoming, people tend to perceive injustice. This can generalize into a more pervasive belief in a just world, in which people who are suffering or disadvantaged are believed to deserve their fate, maintaining an overall balance between what people deserve and what they get. This belief in a just world can, in turn, underpin justifications for the status quo.

The evaluation of a particular decision as just can be based on the way the decision was made (procedural justice) or on the substance of the decision itself (distributive justice). American justice tends to be based strongly on procedural standards—as do most other systems of justice. Changes in procedures will have an effect on distributive outcomes, as may changes in the personnel administering the system or the forum in which a particular political battle is being fought. Finally, what is fair to individuals is not always fair to larger groups. Microjustice is an assessment of the fairness with which valued public goods are distributed to individuals; macrojustice looks toward whether the system-wide distribution is fair, without regard to individual outcomes.

The three standards for distributive justice commonly evoked in political life are equality, equity, and need. Equality is a commonly used macrojustice principle, while equity and need are usually regarded as microjustice principles. Equality can take the form of equality of opportunity or equality of outcome. Equity-based justice is derived from both: It focuses on the equivalence of individuals and on their differences—and it is the differences that count. Also, equity-based justice works only when there is general agreement on what counts as merit and on the relationship of merit to outcomes. Justice based on need is a function of identification with the other. To decrease a person's pain is, in some sense, to decrease our own. The person's position does not allow him to get what he deserves by virtue of his needs. This is a microjustice principle, because one must get to know an individual's situation before need can be determined. Finally, need is related to equality in some important and subtle ways. The distinction between equality of outcome and equality of opportunity is one between distributive justice and procedural justice. Also important to democratic theory is the potential for discrepancy between need or merit and majority rule.

The concept of justice has a significant relationship to the structure of conflict. In politics some form of equity is more often the standard of justice than is equality or need. Because of this, dealing with losers becomes a problem for any political system. One approach is to structure conflict in such a way that the outcomes are perceived as legitimate because of that structure. The standards governing the relationship between structure and perceptions of legitimacy can be inculcated during the socialization process. There must be a balance, however, between too much and too little structuring, since one leads to rigidity and the other to chaos. Revolutions are usually based on the desire to establish more "justice-promoting" rules structuring political conflict.

The process of politics, then, begins with the perception that a public-resource allocation problem needs to be solved. It ends with an evaluation of the justice of the solution. The process of solving the problem can involve any or all of the elements discussed in this book. Persons who perceive themselves as losers are most likely to try to reactivate the political process in order to have the problem dealt with in such a way that they become winners—or at least that they lose less. Winners may try to multiply their successes. This contributes to the self-perpetuating nature of the political process. Also, both winners and losers may contribute by reopening the process when an initially successful result yields unexpected consequences. Thus, political systems are characterized by the constant interplay of change and stability, with change as central to political life as stability is. For these reasons, few political problems are solved with any finality, and the political process is driven by the achievement of conflict management and resolution.

EPILOG:
A Political Psychology of and for the Future

If we've been successful in this book, you should now have a reasonable sense of the sprawling domain we call political psychology. You should know some of the ideas and concepts a psychologist brings to the understanding of political processes. And finally, you have at least one general model for the way politics works, and some sense of how the work of political psychologists fits this model.

But we have not yet discussed the direction in which the study of political psychology is heading. Is there some evolution in the kinds of approaches, problems, perspectives with which political psychologists deal? And perhaps more pointedly, is there some direction in which political psychology *should* go? Taking a deep breath, we will make a few guesses at future directions of political psychology.

Perhaps the safest and simplest prediction we can make is that political psychologists will continue to work on piecing together two or more elements in the framework of person-situation interaction we laid out in the first chapter. That is, we can expect that researchers will try to show how one or more concepts drawn from the *person* realm interact with one or more concepts drawn from the *situation* realm to provide more powerful explanations of political behavior. Two recent studies provide clear examples of this direction. Margaret Hermann, Charles Hermann, and Joe Hagen (1982) have investigated the relationship between beliefs and roles in shaping governments' foreign policy behavior (see also Weinstein

1977). These authors are particularly sensitive to beliefs as they are shared among a regime's leadership. That is, they wish to go beyond those studies that focus on the beliefs of a single powerful leader, as in Weinstein's study of Sukarno's rule in Indonesia, and look at beliefs as they arise from the interaction of various parties in the creation and implementation of foreign policy. Moreover, the authors are very sensitive to the distinction between role conceptions or expectations and actual role behavior. In short, they have a sophisticated sense of both belief and role. Their research attempts to explicate the *decision rules* by which beliefs or *regime orientation* come to be translated into role behavior. For example, they note that "roles may . . . vary according to how strongly the belief is held which the behavior is meant to support" (Hermann, et al, 1982, p. 15). Thus, "the more strongly the belief is held or the more widely it is held, the more likely the regime is to play a hardline role." Further, the authors are almost exquisitely sensitive to the relationship of belief and role behavior to other situational factors. They note, for example, that "which core beliefs are salient at a particular point in time depends on the nature of the problem the policy makers face and how strongly each belief is held. If more than one core belief is triggered by the problem, the belief that is more strongly held will dominate. At some point in time, a core belief may be so strong that the nature of the problem no longer is important in determining regime orientation" (ibid., p. 16).

Stephen Walker and Lawrence Falkowski (1982) have explored the relationship of operational codes to crisis decisions and needs for power, affiliation, and achievement. They suggest that "the individual . . . tends to adopt an operational code that is comparable with this constellation of motives" as developed through socialization, that "the activation of operational code beliefs in crisis situations is likely to arouse needs embedded in the imagery of the belief system," and that "once aroused, these motives contribute to the cognitive rigidity of an individual's beliefs and account for . . . behavioral intransigence during the crisis and its aftermath" (Walker & Falkowski 1982, p. 18). Their works focus on four American presidents and their respective secretaries of state: Truman/Marshall, Eisenhower/Dulles, Kennedy/Rusk, and Johnson/Rusk. For example, they classify Truman as being high in the need for power and low in both the need for achievement and affiliation. They then predict the type of operational code preferred by Truman, the style of decision making he would be likely to prefer; and they look at selected crisis situations in which the outcome was either success or failure (e.g., Berlin airlift or Czechoslovakia). They also envision expanding their sample to incorporate presidential decision making during periods of introversion or extroversion in foreign policy (Klineberg 1979); in this way, they hope to include macrohistorical trends in their analysis. Again, this reflects a strategy of pulling into a grander interaction framework the concepts noted in our first chapter.

Many other examples could be drawn to show how political psychologists are trying to fill out the map of political behavior suggested by

Smith (1968) and enlarged on by us in Chapter 1. The trend in these studies, no matter what their theoretical interest, is toward research in which each element (for example, beliefs and role or beliefs and needs) is part of an equation in which the respective weight of each element, or each element as it interacts with other elements, is assessed. The aim is to account for more and more of the variability in, say, foreign policy behavior, and therefore to be better able to predict future political behavior. But now we would like to suggest that it might be useful to take a further step. At the end of Chapter 1, we pointed out that a truly interactive approach would take into account not only how personal factors and situational factors unite to determine behavior, but also the ways in which that behavior itself, in turn, changes those factors. We pointed out that if "environments influence persons, persons influence environments, and both influence behavior, which in its turn influences persons and environments," then we have a model of political life in which change becomes the central focus of concern. In fact, we might say that stability is a relative term; every change in person, situation, or behavior requires some kind of accommodative change in another aspect. We might say that change and stability exist in a continuing tension. That which exists is continually being disturbed by that which is different.

These ideas take us pretty far in the direction of what is often called a *dialectical perspective* (e.g., Buss 1979; Gergen 1982; Riegel 1978, 1979; Rychlak 1981). While the term *dialectical* is used in a number of different ways, generally it reflects concern with the way in which events, activities, and actions give rise to oppositional forces or tendencies, and the way in which opposition, or antithesis, gives rise to *attempts* at synthesis. Since these attempts are events, activities, and actions, oppositional tendencies arise once again, and so on. At the end of the last chapter, we implied that our model of political life was dialectical in this sense. What we point out here is the importance of *relationships* as key units of analysis. For instance, in a recent critique of a study of the foreign policy behavior of leadership elites, it was suggested that the results obtained could be more fruitfully understood in terms of mutual and reciprocal influences of two nation-states on each other, rather than by simply arraying a set of personal and situational factors into some sort of predictive equation (Rosenwein 1983). In other words, we would have to try to understand how the *relationship* between states moves from relative stability to change and back, and how the relationship itself comes to influence the behavior of nation-states involved. Thus the Hermann, Hermann, and Hagen study, as interesting and exciting as it is, will always be inadequate since it lacks a way of encompassing the relational nature of foreign policy behavior (i.e., that foreign policy behavior is formed in the context of nation-state relationships).

A dialectical perspective (at least in the nonideological sense espoused by the psychologists cited above) requires some interesting changes in mind set. First, it requires us to abandon the notion that resolution, stability, things being "in sync," is a normal, necessary, or optimal state of affairs. In a dialectic perspective, contradiction and conflict are the core of all life; stability becomes either a perceptual point of reference or an ideological stance. Second, this perspective forces us to think in development-historical terms. Opposition, tension, conflict emerge through time, and we are therefore forced to be developmentalists if we want to do justice to political realities.

While a dialectical perspective could be applied to any of the topics with which we have been concerned, nowhere does it seem to be more useful than in the study of political leadership. We have already alluded to this perspective in Chapter 5. For example, Aronson (1982) has developed a typology of leaders based on major Israeli political figures. In commenting on the effects of these people on domestic and foreign political environments, he notes that "such influence might be dialectical in the sense that the leader might succeed, at first in molding his nation, or his public opinion, in the direction in which he wants to lead them. However, his very success might contain the seeds of his future failure, when the changing society—due to his early successes—refuses to follow the same traits and methods which helped him change it, using some of his own goals and values to refuse his leadership." (Aronson 1982, p. 19) In short, leadership activities (as described in chapter 5) give rise to conditions that ultimately lead to resistance, new elements that struggle with leadership activities, ultimately producing some new synthesis (perhaps in the form of new leadership), in turn giving rise to conditions leading to resistance, and so on. The task, then, would be to try to understand precisely how this process works, that is, how one thing gives rise to its opposite, and the ways in which the conflict gives rise to new forms (e.g., political structures, activities). Such an enterprise would, of necessity, be sensitive to history and context, since it requires seeing how elements develop over time within situations.

In terms of a political psychology of the future, we must point to the increasing interest and research in the relationship of biological factors to political behavior. In some cases this simply means looking at biophysical indices of behavior (see Hopple 1980, for a general review). In other instances, however, it means a search for the interaction between genetics, physiology, and psychological-situational factors as they affect (and are affected by) political behavior (see for example, Corning 1983; Davies 1983, 1984; Hines 1982; Masters 1984; Schubert 1983; Wiegele 1979, 1982). While biopolitics is in some sense controversial, and perhaps reflects ideological as well as scientific preoccupations (e.g., Wiegele 1979, pp. 32–35), there is no doubt that increased sophistication about biological functioning and increasing capacity to measure biological factors means we are likely to see some lively attempts to integrate such factors into a broad political psychology.

Finally, surprising as it may seem from our earlier discussion, conflict theory (see Chapter 5) continues to generate interest among political psychologists, as represented by the work of Diamond (1982, 1983) and LaBier (1983). Both of these researchers have developed sophisticated ideas about the linkages between organizational function and personality, focusing on managerial decision making as adaptation to bureaucratic environments (although as we noted in Chapter 5, the growth area in much of political psychology continues to lie with cognitive approaches).

So far we have been discussing a political psychology *of* the future. But what is it that political psychologists can do *for* the future? The world of today confronts us ,with terrible realities. In the face of a shrinking resource base, nations continue to spend over a trillion and a half dollars annually on armaments and armies. The developed countries of the world, with less than a quarter of the world's population, consume 50 to 60 percent of the world's resources. The two most powerful countries in the world *each* have the power to destroy the human species (Schell 1982). Economic and social injustice are present in virtually every human society. The first thing we can say for political psychologists, then, is that they are likely to feel increased pressure to apply their understanding to these problems. Of course, some political psychologists are actively involved in this already. Herbert Kelman's work on the Middle East (1979) and Morton Deutsch's application of social psychological principles of competition and cooperation to the dynamics of the nuclear arms race (1983) are brilliant examples of applied political psychology. But there is a second issue for a political psychology for the future: How do political psychologists make their ideas known to and understood by policy makers? And how, even if communication is successful, do political psychologists have a real impact on public policy? To answer these questions would require another book, of course. Briefly, however, we need to note the resistance people have to psychological knowledge itself. Psychological insights are often uncomfortable, even when translated from the jargon of professional political psychologists into lay language. Coupled with this is the very real threat social science data generally pose to those whose policy positions and ideologies may be threatened by those data.

An important aspect of this issue is the question of *which* policy makers. To what extent can political psychologists—or *should* political psychologists—use their knowledge to further political goals? Actually, we have answered this question in Chapter 2. The separation of the scientist from the citizen, of the scientist from a person with values, is illusory. The nature of the theories and concepts with which political psychologists deal is colored by the kinds of value assumptions that inform political and social attitudes. Nonetheless, to the extent that a political psychologist is also a citizen, decisions need to be made about where knowledge can be most profitably applied. The recent grassroots movement for a nuclear freeze provides an interesting example. Fischoff, Pidgeon, and Fiske (1983) provide a detailed specification of possible actions based on various social psychological principles of persuasion and group dynamics for people working in local nuclear freeze organizations (also see White 1984).

This book is about political psychology as we see it today. We believe that in the future political psychologists will increasingly find their responsibilities as citizens as demanding as their role as scientists. The task will be to see how well political psychologists manage the relationship between these two elements.

APPENDIX A

TWO COMMONSENSE THEORIES OF POLITICAL LEADERSHIP AND THEIR FLAWS

The first view goes like this: If you are a leader, by virtue of your position or by general agreement, then you must possess certain exceptional qualities—that is, qualities that make you special and differentiate you from mere "follower" types. If we want to understand leadership, then we must find out what these characteristics are. This approach, sometimes called the "Great Person" approach to leadership, is an extreme individual-focused approach.

How would we proceed if we thought this approach useful in understanding leadership? We might, for example, compare leaders with followers on certain dimensions of personality or character. Much of the early work in social psychology took this tack (Gibb 1969). Literally dozens of studies were done in which individuals were herded together into small groups, asked to work on a task and to rate others in the group in terms of leadership qualities; these "leaders" were then compared to other group members. The results were disappointing. In a major review of this literature, Mann (1959) found that while six characteristics seemed to distinguish leaders from others in a group—intelligence, extroversion, dominance, self-confidence, degree of participation, and enthusiasm—the differences were slight. Moreover, as you might expect from our earlier discussion, altering the task or some other aspect of the situation changed the nature of the characteristics associated with leaders (Hare 1976, p. 279; Bass 1981, p. 73).

Certainly, we have many examples of political leaders whose extraordinary qualities seem to set them apart. But it is also true that there are many political leaders whose superior qualities are less than obvious (run down a list of your town's mayors over the last fifty years—or American presidents, for that matter). Moreover, while it is undeniably true that many political leaders have been singular individuals, it is also the case that there are many non-leaders who are equally singular (i.e., have the same qualities or characteristics). The principal objection here is that we have confused "leadership" with leaders. The clue is that in this approach, we do not look at what leaders (or followers) do; rather, we focus on the qualities, traits, or characteristics these individuals purportedly *have*. Certainly, we are not concerned with *relationships* between the leader and anyone else.

In contrast, the second commonsense view of leadership is an extreme situation-focused one. It takes two forms, depending on whether we focus on micro- or macroenvironmental factors. The microenvironmental theory would be that the qualities of the leader are variously elicited, valued, and reacted to as a function of differential group settings and their demands (Hollander & Julian 1969). Hemphill states the position well: "There are no absolute leaders, since successful leadership must always take into account the specific requirements imposed by the nature of the group which is to be led, requirements as diverse in nature and degree as are the organizations in which people band together" (1949, p. 225).

At a macroenvironmental level, the individual tends to be dismissed as unimportant; she is seen to be "merely" an agent of larger historical or social forces. Marx, in his later writings—as well as Hegel, Spencer, and other nineteenth-century sociologists and philosophers—took this point of view. Here the word "leader" or "leadership" tends to be less important; words like "power" and "authority" are more relevant. As Donald Searing neatly states,

> Although Hegel, Spencer and Marx each identified different mainsprings within the historical process, they all agree that individual leaders were unable to manipulate the controls. At most no leader was more than a catalyst for events, events which, from deterministic perspectives, would have occurred with or without their heroic personalities. (1972, p. 26)

The extreme situationist approaches have a certain merit. Melvin Seeman has noted that it may be an American tendency to focus on the individual and, therefore, on the "leader"; he questions whether "we may profitably conceive of 'leadership' as a distinct research 'area' separable from more general problems of power . . . or social status" (quoted in Janda 1972, p. 64). In a similar vein, Thibaut and Kelly, two social psychologists, have wondered whether it might not be more profitable to avoid the multiple meanings "encompassed by the term leadership [and direct our efforts toward] clarifying problems of power structure, norms and goals, etc." (1959, p. 290). In short, perhaps we need to disentangle leadership from the structures in which it takes place.

Is the individual unimportant? Can he be safely ignored, or at least treated as engulfed by the situation and its demands? Can one really make the case that if Hitler had not existed, history would have turned out much the same? Of course not. However, this is not the way a "situationist" would phrase the question. The leader's behavior is analyzed in terms of the forces impinging on her and in terms of the interests she might serve (Hollander & Julian 1969, p. 388). The situationist, in short, is likely to raise the question of leadership *to what ends*. As in the "Great Person" approach, there is a lack of emphasis on the relationship between leader and follower.

APPENDIX B

A PRIMER OF
PSYCHOANALYTIC THEORY

Psychoanalytic theory, the general term for the framework that Freud developed, is in fact several interrelated theories: a structural theory (the principal components of personality), a genetic or developmental theory (how personality is formed), and a dynamic theory (how things work in personality). Although the details are complex, the basic assumptions are straightforward. Human beings are driven by powerful motivational forces, notably sex and aggression, which push for expression and immediate gratification (the pleasure principle). Realistically, however, *impulse* expression can be dangerous. The individual must learn to postpone gratification until such time and place as is appropriate (the reality principle). The part of the personality called the *ego* is developed as part of this process. The ego represents all those functions (e.g., memory, perception, thinking) by which the individual learns to adapt to the exigencies of the real world and thereby safely obtain gratification.

There is another element in this equation. We do not obtain gratification of our impulses only when it is safe; we obtain it when it is appropriate. That is, it is not just material reality that thwarts us, but the demands of our society. Over time, humans develop a *superego*, the part of the personality that stands for those standards and values we aspire to (the ego-ideal part of the superego) and those strictures (rules, norms) we must not violate (the conscience part of the superego).

Freud conjectured that a key to this process was the pattern of relationships between father, mother, and child. At some point in male development, the child's close ties to the mother precipitate a sense of rivalry with the father. The child's desire for possession of the mother conflicts with the reality that the child must share the mother with the father (and other siblings). In the pull and tug of fear and attraction the child feels toward both parents, the matter is resolved through the child's becoming like the father by identifying with him. This so-called resolution of the Oedipal conflict is the genesis of the superego. (The situation for females is somewhat confused in Freud's discussion.) Of course, we now believe the situation to be much more complex and sophisticated than Freud suggested. What is interesting here is that this conflict sets a possible pattern for future relations to authority, including political authority.

How do these three parts of the personality (impulse, ego, and superego) work together to produce behavior? The role of emotion is critical. When an impulse struggles to express itself, and when those parts of the ego delegated to monitor reality perceive this to be a danger, alarms go off. The alarms are in the form of *anxiety* (experienced when the person is threatened with external danger) or *guilt* (when the person thinks that impulse expression will violate internalized or superego standards). In order to escape experiencing these painful emotions, the individual will take defensive actions—that is, employ *defense mechanisms.*

There are many different ideas about how many defense mechanisms there are and where they come from, but there is good evidence that they are primarily learned and may be associated with certain kinds of childrearing patterns (e.g., Miller & Swanson 1960). Nonetheless, all defense mechanisms involve distortion of the object toward which the impulse is directed, of the nature of the impulse itself, in the origin of the impulse, or in some combination of these.

For example, *displacement* is a defense in which the impulse is expressed not toward the feared person, but rather toward a safer one. Thus, if one hates but also fears an authority figure, it is safer to displace the anger onto some other less threatening individual or group. Anti-Semitism and other forms of prejudice are often interpreted as displacements. In *projection* something internal is experienced as being external, or "lodged" in some other object. In other words, things that make us feel anxious or guilty are perceived as "belonging" to someone else. It has been suggested that the content of those attitudes we call prejudiced derive from the projection of our own impulses (e.g., "Blacks are overly aggressive; Jews are sneaky and pushy"). A parallel defense mechanism, one that takes on much importance in theories of leadership derived from psychoanalytic theory, is *identification,* in which characteristics of others are taken into the person and become part of her.

If displacement involves distortion of the object, and projection a distortion in the origin of the impulse, *reaction formation* involves a change in the impulse itself. Thus for example, feelings of hatred toward an authority figure are transmuted into feelings of love. One might ask how it is possible to distinguish "true" feelings of love from reaction formation. The answer is that in reaction formation the way the love is expressed is both exaggerated and rigid. The "love" for the authority figure is expressed as idealization (i.e., the authority figure is all good—*never* bad).

Finally, repression and denial involve distortion in object, origin, impulse, and direction. In *repression,* all conscious representations of the disturbing material are made unconscious. In psychoanalytic theory, however, it is assumed that impulses will continue to seek expression and may appear either as symptoms (physical or psychological) or in dreams and fantasies. *Denial* is similar to repression in that it involves invalidating something painful by deliberately ignoring its existence.

Three things should be noted here. First, it is assumed that the human mind works at several levels called conscious, preconscious, and unconscious. It is postulated that defense mechanisms operate at the unconscious level. That is, they become so automatic as mechanisms for relieving us of the pain of anxiety and guilt that we are both unaware of their operation and find it difficult to bring their operation into our consciousness. Second, defenses usually operate in combination. Thus, reaction formation (in the form of the idealization of parental authority) is displaced onto political authority. Repressed hostility is projected onto external enemies (a phenomenon called "scapegoating"). Third, much of what we call "perception of reality" is a mix of reality elements as colored or affected by one's internal dynamics.

Therefore, much of the way we represent the political world is in terms of *fantasy.* This concept becomes particularly important in understanding the dynamics of leadership.

GLOSSARY

Affect   An emotional reaction to some concrete or abstract phenomenon.

Affiliation   Gratification associated with friendly association with others; liking and wanting to be liked.

AGITPROP   The Soviet organization charged with informing the Soviet people about current public policy and with inculcating patriotism and loyalty to the regime and the Soviet system of government.

Anxiety   The emotion of feeling threatened by an external danger that may or may not be specifically identified.

Attitude   An emotional reaction to some conceptual or concrete object about which the individual has certain beliefs.

Attitudinal Factor   An individual's judgment that a contemplated action will be good or bad, that she is in favor of or against performing it.

Authorities   Those in the political system whose decisions about the allocation of valued public resources are binding on others.

Authority   The ability of one person to induce compliance in another, attributable to the perception on the part of the other that the demand is legitimate and should be complied with.

Aversive Stimuli   Forms of punishment.

Bargaining   The actual process of presenting proposals, counterproposals, and concessions in the attempt to reach agreement on particular issues.

Behavior   Observable actions that can be studied in their own right.

Belief   An understanding about ourselves or the environment we regard as "fact."

Civil war, Soviet   The period immediately after the overthrow of the Provisional Government in 1917, during which the supporters of the Bolsheviks fought and eventually defeated their opposition.

Class   A social stratification based on the possession of more or less of something, such as control over economic resources.

Cognition   The realm of understanding and knowing about the world.

Cognitive Development   Changes in a maturing person's ability to make sense of the world and to react appropriately to people, objects, and events.

Cognitive Dissonance   Unpleasant tension within an individual that is caused by conflicts between or among the individual's attitudes, opinions, beliefs, or behaviors.

Communication   The transmission of information that elicits a response; this process is continuous and need not be intentional.

Compliance   The acceptance of political or legal influence in order to gain a reward or escape punishment.

Conation   The process of assessing the potential consequences of overt acts.

Concept   A mental image used to bring together objective and subjective factors that seem to be related or have something in common.

Defense Mechanisms   Actions or beliefs that a person utilizes to escape experiencing painful emotions, such as anxiety or guilt.

Demagogue   A leader who attracts a following with flamboyant behavior and with claims that are often false and appeal to his hearers' prejudices.

Denial   Invalidating something painful by deliberately ignoring its existence.

Dimension   A range of possibilities, usually implying "most to least" of something or "all to none" of something.

Displacement   A defense mechanism in which a forbidden impulse is expressed not toward the feared object, but rather toward a safer one.

Distributive Justice   A judgment regarding fairness that is based on the substance of a decision.

Ego   All those psychological functions a person uses to adapt to the exigencies of the real world and thereby safely obtain gratification.

Ethnocentrism   A pattern of thinking in which the group to which one belongs (the ingroup) is seen in a positive light, while everyone else (the outgroup) is seen in a negative light.

External Locus of Control   The belief that luck, fate, or chance plays a predominant role in life.

Faculties   Skills and abilities related to accomplishing goals.

Group Dynamics   An approach to the analysis of behavior that stresses the pressures toward conformity with group norms that groups exert on their members.

Guilt   The feeling that one has violated important internalized standards or values.

Habits   Patterns of behavior that are characteristic of an individual and established through learning.

Hypervigilance   A state of panic.

Identification   1)The acceptance of the influence of political or governmental officials in order to maintain a satisfying relationship to the political system; 2) the desire to be like another person.

Identity   A personal sense of continuity and coherence through time, coupled with a sense of commitment to the values and standards of one's social groups.

Ideology   An organization of beliefs, attitudes, and values that directs and influences behavior and the evaluation of others' behavior.

Idiosyncrasy Credits   A "credit" or plus that can be earned by doing a desirable thing for someone and that can be drawn on at some later time when the earner's behavior deviates from group norms.

Incremental Model   A model of the decision making process that emphasizes tentativeness and adjustments based on experience.

Internalization   Acceptance of political or governmental influence because it is perceived to be expressive of an accepted value system.

Internal Locus of Control   The belief that an individual can decisively influence the course of his or her own life.

Kinesics   Communication of meaning by means of physical movement or posture.

Legitimacy   The perception that a person has the right to exercise influence over others.

Macrojustice   The fairness with which valued public goods are distributed overall in a political system; individuals are rewarded without regard to their uniqueness as individuals.

Microjustice   The fairness with which valued public goods are distributed to individuals within a political system.

Mixed Scanning Model   A model of the decision making process that advocates the use of both the rational–comprehensive approach and the incremental approach, the choice being based on the situation and type of decisional problem involved.

Myth   A belief shared by a group of people that gives their experiences a particular meaning; it does not have to be empirically based.

Narcissism   An abnormally high interest or investment in the self or one's self-regard.

Negotiations   The whole range of interactions between the parties to a conflict in which the central conflict resolution mechanism is bargaining.

Norm   A formal or informal expectation for behavior.

Normative Factor   An individual's perception of the social pressures on her to perform a given action.

Normative Structure   A pattern of rules or ideas about how people should or should not behave in specific situations.

Operational Code   A group of beliefs about the basic issues of history and politics that serves as a general guide to decision making.

Perception   The way people see and make sense of other people and things in their environment.

Perceptual Screens   Psychological mechanisms that control what we attend to and what we ignore.

Procedural Justice   A judgment regarding fairness that is based on the way a decision was made.

Projection   Something internal to the individual is experienced as being "lodged" in some other person or object.

Propaganda   A form of political persuasion specifically designed to appeal to large numbers of people.

Psychoanalysis   A theory of human development and behavior originated by Sigmund Freud. It is the basis for treatment which attempts to identify the unconscious origins of troublesome behaviors.

Psychodynamics   An approach to psychology that emphasizes humans' emotional reactions to what happens to them in early childhood and the role of their unconscious motivations.

Rational–Comprehensive Model   A model of the decision making process based on logical reasoning.

Reaction Formation   A change in the impulse one is experiencing that distorts it (e.g., feelings of hatred toward an authority figure are transmuted into feelings of love).

Reference Group   A group whose values or standards serve as guides for behavior.

Reification   Treating an abstraction as though it exists in the objective world.

Repression　All conscious representations of some disturbing material are made unconscious.

Role　The behavior or expectations for behavior associated with certain positions in society.

Scapegoating　Projecting repressed hostility onto external enemies.

Self Esteem　The degree to which one does or does not have positive feelings about the self.

Social Comparison　The process of evaluating oneself by comparing the self with others.

Social Learning　A tradition that emphasizes the influence of outside stimuli, imitation, and reinforcement in determining how humans behave.

Social Stratification　The ways in which a society is divided into segments based on various criteria including economic, occupational, and educational status.

Solidarity Group　A group in which the members think in terms of the effects of political decisions on the group and feel in some way personally affected by what happens to that group.

Strategy, Bargaining　A series of organized bargaining tactics to be used throughout a negotiating process.

Subjective Norms　Beliefs about whether an individual's "important others" think that she should or should not perform a given act.

Superego　The part of the personality that represents the standards and values to which we aspire and those limits we must not violate.

Tactic, Bargaining　A specific position to be taken or maneuver to be made at some point in the bargaining sequence.

Testosterone　A steroid of the androgen group which is present in higher levels in males than in females, and which has been associated with a tendency toward aggressive behavior.

Theories　Systematic statements about relationships between two or more concepts and between concepts and observables.

Transactional Leadership　When one person takes the lead in interacting with others in order to exchange valued things.

Transformational Leadership　When a leader induces followers to accept her influence by sensing their needs and responding to them.

Value　A concept that organizes attitudes and associated beliefs in terms of those ends to which all other goals of the individual are directed.

REFERENCES

ABRAHAMSON, D. *Nixon vs. Nixon: An Emotional Tragedy.* New York: NAL, 1978.

ABRAHAMSON, M. *Functionalism.* Englewood Cliffs, NJ: Prentice-Hall, 1978.

ADORNO, T., FRENKEL-BRUNSWIK, E., LEVINSON, D.J., & SANFORD, R. N. *The Authoritarian Personality.* New York: Harper & Row, 1950.

AJZEN, I., & FISHBEIN, M. *Understanding Attitudes and Predicting Social Behavior.* Englewood Cliffs, NJ: Prentice-Hall, 1980.

―――――, TIMKO, C., & WHITE, J. B. Self-monitoring and the attitude-behavior relation. *The Journal of Personality and Social Psychology,* 1982, *42,* 426–35.

ALEXANDER, H. E. *Financing Politics: Money, Elections and Political Reform.* Washington, D.C.: Congressional Quarterly Press, 1976.

ALINSKY, S. D. *Reveille for Radicals.* New York: Vintage, 1969.

ALLAND, A., JR. *The Human Imperative.* New York: Columbia University Press, 1972.

ALLISON, G. T. *Essence of Decision: Explaining the Cuban Missile Crisis.* Boston: Little, Brown, 1971.

ALLPORT, G. W. The historical background of modern social psychology. In G. Lindzay (ed.), *Handbook of Social Psychology* (vol. 1). Reading, MA: Addison-Wesley, 1954.

ALMOND, G. A., & VERBA, S. *The Civic Culture: Political Attitudes and Democracy in Five Nations.* Princeton, NJ: Princeton University Press, 1963.

―――――(eds.). *The Civic Culture Revisited.* Boston: Little, Brown, 1980.

ALTMEYER, B. *Right-Wing Authoritarianism.* Manitoba: University of Manitoba Press, 1981.

APA (American Psychiatric Association). *A Psychiatric Glossary* (vol. 2). Washington, D.C.: American Psychiatric Association, 1964.

ARANGUREN, J. L. *Human Communication.* New York: McGraw-Hill, 1967.

ARISTOTLE. Politics. In William Ebenstein (ed.), *Great Political Thinkers.* New York: Holt, Rinehart & Winston, 1951.

ARONSON, E. *The Social Animal.* San Francisco: Freeman, 1980.

ARONSON, S. Typologies of political leadership. Paper presented at the Meeting of the International Society of Political Psychology, Washington, D.C., 1982.

ASCH, S. E. Forming impressions of personality. *Journal of Abnormal and Social Psychology,* 1946, *41,* 258–92.

————.Opinions and social pressure. In Elliot Aronson (ed.), *Readings About the Social Animal.* San Francisco: Freeman, 1973.

ATKIN, K. Political campaigns: mass communication and persuasion. In E. Roloff and R. Miller (eds.), *Persuasion: New Directions in Theory and Research.* Beverly Hills, CA: Sage Publications, 1980.

ATKINSON, J. W. (ed.). *Motives in Action, Fantasy and Society.* Princeton, NJ: D. Van Nostrand, 1958.

AXELROD, R. (ed.). *Structure of Decision: The Cognitive Map of Political Elites.* Princeton, NJ: Princeton University Press, 1976.

BABBIE, E. R. *The Practice of Social Research.* Belmont, CA: Wadsworth, 1968.

————.*Survey Research Methods.* Belmont, CA: Wadsworth Publishing Co., Inc., 1973.

BAILEY, F. G. *The Tactical Uses of Passion: An Essay on Power, Reason, and Reality.* Ithaca, NY: Cornell University Press, 1983.

BAILEY, K. D. Individual change in childhood political orientations: an analysis of comparative longitudinal samples. Paper presented at the Western Political Science Association Meeting, Los Angeles, CA, 1978.

BALES, R. F. The equilibrium problem in small groups. In T. Parsons, et al. (eds.), *Working Papers in the Theory of Action.* New York: Free Press, 1953.

————.*Interaction Process Analysis.* Reading, MA: Addison-Wesley, 1950.

————.*Personality and Interpersonal Behavior.* New York: Holt, Rinehart & Winston, 1970.

————, & COHEN, S. P. *SYMLOG: A System for Multiple Level Observation of Groups.* New York: Free Press, 1979.

————,& SLATER, P. Role differentiation in small decision-making groups. In T. Parsons et al. (eds.), *Family, Socialization and Interaction Processes.* New York: Free Press, 1955.

————, et al. Channels of communications in small groups. *American Sociological Review,* 1951, *16,* 461–68.

BALL-ROKEACH, S. J. The legitimation of violence. In J. F. Short, Jr. & E. Wolfgang (eds.), *Collective Violence.* Chicago: Aldine-Atherton, 1972.

BANDURA, A., & WALTERS, R. H. *Social Learning and Personality Development.* New York: Holt, Rinehart & Winston, 1963.

————.Social learning theory of identificatory processes. In D. A. Goslin (ed.), *Handbook of Socialization Theory and Research.* Chicago: Rand McNally, 1969.

BARBER, J. D. *The Lawmakers.* New Haven: Yale University Press, 1965.

————.*The Presidential Character: Prediction Performance in the White House,* 2d ed. Englewood Cliffs, NJ: Prentice-Hall, 1977.

_____.*The Pulse of Politics: Electing Presidents in the Media Age.* New York: W. W. Norton, 1980.

BARNER-BARRY, C. An observational study of authority in a preschool peer group. *Political Methodology*, 1977, *4*, 415–49.

_____.Reciprocity, cooperation and modern bureaucracy. In E. White and J. Losco (eds.), *Biology and Bureaucracy* (in preparation).

BARNES, S. H., KAASE, M., et al. *Political Action: Mass Participation in Five Western Democracies.* Beverly Hills, CA: Sage Publications, 1979.

BARRY, D. D., & BARNER-BARRY, C. *Contemporary Soviet Politics* (2nd ed.). Englewood Cliffs, NJ: Prentice-Hall, 1982.

BASS, M. *Leadership, Psychology and Organizational Behavior.* New York: Harper & Row, 1960.

_____.*Stogdill's Handbook of Leadership: A Survey of Theory and Research.* New York: Free Press (rev. ed.), 1981.

BATESON, G. *Steps to an Ecology of Mind.* New York: Ballantine, 1972.

BECK, P. A. The role of agents in political socialization. In S. Renshon (ed.), *Handbook of Political Socialization.* New York: Free Press, 1977.

_____, BRUNER, J. W., & DOBSON, L. D. *Political Socialization Across the Generations.* Washington, D.C.: The American Political Science Association, 1975.

_____, & JENNINGS, M. K. Pathways to participation. *The American Political Science Review*, 1982, *76*, 94–108.

Behavior Today. January 8, 1979, 2–4.

BELL, G. Why Carter failed to gain effective control. *The Baltimore Sunday Sun*, July 18, 1982, K1–K2.

BEM, D. J. *Beliefs, Attitudes, and Human Affairs.* Belmont, CA: Brooks/Cole Publishing Co., 1970.

BENNETT, S. E., OLDENDICK, R., TUCHFARBER, A. J., & BISHOP, G. F. Education and mass belief systems: an extension and some questions. *Political Behavior*, 1979, *1*, 53–72.

BENTON, A. A. Productivity, distributive justice, and bargaining among children. *Journal of Personality and Social Psychology*, 1971, *18*, 68–78.

BERELSON, R., LAZARSFELD, P. F., McPHEE, W. N. *Voting: A Study of Opinion Formation in a Presidential Election.* Chicago: University of Chicago Press, 1954.

BERGER, P. L., & LUCKMANN, T. *The Social Construction of Reality.* New York: Irvington Press, 1966.

BERKOWITZ, L. (ed.). *Roots of Aggression.* New York: Atherton, 1969a.

_____.Simple views of aggression: an easy review. *American Scientist*, 1969b, *57*, 372–83.

_____.*A Survey of Social Psychology.* Hinsdale, IL: Dryden Press, 1975.

BESCHLOSS, M. R. *Kennedy and Roosevelt: The Uneasy Alliance.* New York: Norton, 1980.

BETTINGHAUS, E. P. *Persuasive Communication* (2nd ed.). New York: Holt, Rinehart & Winston, 1973.

BIDDLE, B. J., & THOMAS, E. J. (eds.). *Role Theory: Concepts and Research.* New York: John Wiley, 1966.

BINFORD. S. Apes and original sin. *Human Behavior*, 1972, *1*, 64–71.

BION, W. R. *Experiences in Groups.* New York: Basic Books, 1959.

BITZER, L. F. Political rhetoric. In D. D. Nimmo & K. R. Sanders (eds.), *Handbook of Political Communication.* Beverly Hills, CA: Sage Publications, 1981.

BLANK, B. *The Political Implications of Human Genetic Technology.* Boulder, Colo.: Westview Press, 1982.

BLANK, T. *A Social Psychology of Developing Adults.* New York: John Wiley, 1982.

BONHAM, M., & SHAPIRO, M. Explanation of the unexpected: the Syrian intervention in Jordan in 1970. In R. Axlerod (ed.), *The Structure of Decision.* Princeton, NJ: Princeton University Press, 1976.

BORMANN, A. G. *Discussion and Group Methods: Theory and Practice* (2nd ed.). New York: Harper & Row, 1975.

BRADLEY, C. P. *The Camp David Peace Process: A Study of Carter Administration Policies.* Grantham, NH: Tompson & Rutter, 1981.

BREHM, J. W., & COHEN, R. *Explorations in Cognitive Dissonance.* New York: John Wiley, 1962.

BRENNER, P. *The Limits and Possibilities of Congress.* New York: St. Martin's Press, 1983.

BRICKMAN, P. *Social Conflict: Readings in Rule Structures and Conflict Relationships.* Lexington, MA: D. C. Heath, 1974.

————.Preference for inequality. *Sociometry,* 1977, *40,* 303–10.

————, et al. Microjustice and macrojustice. In M. J. Lerner & S. C. Lerner (eds.), *The Justice Motive in Social Behavior: Adapting to Times of Scarcity and Change.* New York: Plenum, 1982.

————& STEARNS, A. Help that is not called help. *Personality and Social Psychology Bulletin,* 1978, *4,* 314–17.

BRONFENBRENNER, U. Freudian theories of identification and their derivatives. *Child Development,* 1960, *31,* 15–40.

BROWN, B. Face-saving and face-restoration in negotiation. In D. Druckman (ed.), *Negotiations: Social-Psychological Perspectives.* Beverly Hills, CA: Sage Publications, 1977.

BROWN, B. R. The effects of need to maintain face on interpersonal bargaining. *Journal of Experimental Social Psychology,* 1968, *4,* 107–22.

BROWN, R. *Social Psychology.* New York: Free Press, 1965.

BROWNING, R. P. The interaction of personality and political system in decisions to run for office: some data and a simulation technique. *Journal of Social Issues,* 1968, *24,* 93–109.

BRUNER, J., & TAGIURI, R. The perception of people. In G. Lindzay (ed.), *Handbook of Social Psychology.* Cambridge, vol. 1. Addison-Wesley, 1954.

Budgeting for America. Washington, DC: Congressional Quarterly, 1982.

BUNCE, V. *Do New Leaders Make a Difference?* Princeton, NJ: Princeton University Press, 1981.

BURGOON, M., & BETTINGHAUS, E. P. Persuasive message strategies. In M. E. Roloff & G. R. Miller (eds.), *Persuasion: New Directions in Theory and Research.* Beverly Hills, CA: Sage Publications, 1980.

BURKE, P. J. Role differentiation and the legitimation of task activity. *Sociometry,* 1968, *31,* 404–11.

BURNS, J. M. *Leadership.* New York: Harper & Row, 1978.

BUSS, A. R. *A Dialectical Psychology.* New York: Irvington, 1979.

CAMPBELL, B. A. *The American Electorate: Attitudes and Action.* New York: Holt, Rinehart & Winston, 1979.

CAMPBELL, D. T. On the conflicts between biological and social evolution and between psychology and moral tradition. *American Psychologist,* 1976, *30,* 1103–1126.

_____Social attitudes and other acquired behavioral dispositions. In S. Koch (ed.), *Psychology: A Study of a Science* (vol. 6). New York: McGraw-Hill, 1963.

CARO, R. *The Years of Lyndon Johnson.* New York: Knopf, 1982.

CARTER, J. *Keeping Faith,* New York: Knopf, 1981.

CARY, C. D. Patterns of emphasis upon Marxist-Leninist ideology: a computer content analysis of Soviet school history, geography, and social science textbooks. *Comparative Education Review.* 1976, *20,* 11–19.

_____.Peer groups in the political socialization of Soviet school children. *Social Science Quarterly,* 1974, *54,* 451–61.

CASPER, J. D. *American Criminal Justice: The Defendant's Perspective.* Englewood Cliffs, NJ: Prentice-Hall, 1972.

CHAFFEE, S. H. The diffusion of political information. In S. H. Chaffee (ed.), *Political Communication: Issues and Strategies for Research.* Beverly Hills, CA: Sage Publications, 1975.

_____.Mass communication in political socialization. In S. A. Renshon (ed.), *Handbook of Political Socialization.* New York: Free Press, 1977.

CHAMBLISS, W. J. *On the Take.* Bloomington: Indiana University Press, 1978.

_____, & SEIDMAN, R. *Law, Order and Power.* Reading, MA: Addison-Wesley, 1982.

CHAMPAGNE, A., & DAWES, R. H. *Courts and Modern Medicine.* Springfield, IL: Charles C. Thomas, 1983.

CHRISTIE, R. Authoritarianism re-examined. In R. Christie and M. Jahoda (eds.), *Studies in the Scope and Method of the "Authoritarian Personality."* New York: Free Press, 1954.

_____, & GEIS, F. L. Some consequences of taking Machiavelli seriously. In E. F. Borgatta & W. W. Lambert (eds.), *Handbook of Personality Theory and Research.* Chicago: Rand-McNally, 1968.

_____(eds.). *Studies in Machiavellianism.* New York: Academic Press, 1970.

CHURCH, R. M. The varied effects of punishment on behavior. *Psychological Review,* 1963, *70,* 369–402.

CLARK, K. The pathos of power: a psychological perspective. *American Psychologist,* 1971, *26,* 1047–1057.

COHEN, A. R. *Attitude Change and Social Influence.* New York: Basic Books, 1964.

COHEN, M. D., MARCH, J. G., & OLSEN, J. P. A garbage can model of organizational choice. *Administrative Science Quarterly,* 1972, *17,* 1–25.

Committee on Public Information. *A Psychiatric Glossary.* Washington, DC: American Psychiatric Association, 1964.

Committee on the Judiciary. House of Representatives, Ninety-Third Congress, Second Session. Political Matters Memoranda: August 13, 1971–September 18, 1972 (statement of information: appendix 4). Washington, DC: U.S. Government Printing Office, 1974.

CONNELL, R. W. *The Child's Construction of Politics.* Carlton, Victoria: Melbourne University Press, 1971.

CONROY, R., & SUNDSTROM, E. Territorial dominance in a dyadic conversation as a function of similarity of opinion. *Journal of Personality and Social Psychology,* 1977, *35,* 570–76.

CONVERSE, P. E. Information flow and the stability of partisan attitudes. *Public Opinion Quarterly,* 1962, *26,* 578–99.

_____.New dimensions of meaning for cross-section sample surveys in politics. *International Social Science Journal,* 1964, *16,* 19–34.

CONWAY, M., AHERN, D., & SYCKOFF, M. L. Media uses and gratifications and adolescents' attitudes, knowledge, and participation during an election year. Paper presented at the Meeting of the International Society of Political Psychology, Washington, D.C., 1979.

COOPER, S., & PETERSON, C. Machiavellianism and spontaneous cheating in competition. *Journal of Research in Personality,* 1980, *14,* 20–25.

CORNING, P. A. *The Synergism Hypothesis: A Theory of Progressive Evolution.* New York: McGraw-Hill, 1983.

CRAIN, W. C. *Theories of Development: Concepts and Approaches.* Englewood Cliffs, NJ: Prentice-Hall, 1980.

CROSS, J. G. *The Economics of Bargaining.* New York: Basic Books, 1969.

CROW, J., & NOEL, C. An experiment in simulated historical decision making. In M. G. Hermann & T. Milburn (eds.). *A Psychological Examination of Political Leaders.* New York: Free Press, 1977.

CULBERTSON, F. M. Modification of an emotionally held attitude through role-playing. *Journal of Abnormal and Social Psychology,* 1957, *54,* 230–34.

DAHL, R. A. *Modern Political Analysis* (3rd ed.). Englewood Cliffs, NJ: Prentice-Hall, 1976.

DAHRENDORF, R. *Class and Class Conflict in Industrial Society.* Stanford: Stanford University Press, 1959.

DALTON, R. J. Reassessing parental socialization: indicator unreliability versus generational transfer. *American Political Science Review,* 1980, *74,* 421–31.

DANSEREAU, F., & DUMAS, M. Pratfalls and pitfalls in drawing inferences about leader behavior in organizations. In J. G. Hunt & L. L. Larson (eds.), *Leadership: The Cutting Edge.* Carbondale: Southern Illinois Press, 1977.

DAVIES, J. C. Aggression, violence, revolution, and war. In J. N. Knutson (ed.), *Handbook of Political Psychology.* San Francisco: Jossey-Bass, 1973.

————.The J-curve of rising and declining satisfaction as a cause of some great revolutions and a constrained rebellion. In Graham, H. D. & T. R. Gurr (eds.), *Violence in America: Historical and Comparative Perspectives.* Washington, DC: National Commission on the Causes and Prevention of Violence, 1969.

————.The Physiology of Aggression. Paper presented at the Conference on Ethological Contributions to Research in Political Science, Tutzing, Federal Republic of Germany, 1984.

————.Political socialization: from womb to childhood. In S. A. Renshon (ed.), *Handbook of Political Socialization: Theory and Research.* New York: Free Press, 1977.

————.The proper biological study of politics. *Political Psychology,* 1983, *4* (4), 731–43.

————.Toward a theory of revolution. *American Sociological Review,* February 1962, *27,* 5–19.

DAWSON, R. E., PREWITT, K., & DAWSON, K. S. *Political Socialization* (2nd ed.). Boston: Little, Brown, 1977.

DELGADO, J. *Physical Control of the Mind.* New York: Harper's, 1969.

DEUTSCH, M. Bargaining, threat and communication: some experimental studies. In K. Archibald (ed.), *Strategic Interaction and Conflict: Original Papers and Discussion.* Berkeley, CA: Institute of International Studies, 1966.

————.Conflicts: productive and destructive. *Journal of Social Issues,* 1969, *25,* 7–41.

————.Equity, equality and need: what determines which value will be used as a basis for distributive justice? *Journal of Social Issues,* 1975, *31,* 137–50.

_____.Justice in "the crunch." In M. J. Lerner and S. C. Lerner (eds.), *The Justice Motive in Social Behavior: Adapting to Times of Scarcity and Change*. New York: Plenum, 1982.

_____.The prevention of World War III: a psychological perspective. *Political Psychology*, 1983, *4*, 3–42.

_____.*The Resolution of Conflict: Constructive and Destructive Processes*. New Haven: Yale University Press, 1973.

_____.Trust and suspicion. *Journal of Conflict Resolution*, 1958, *2*, 265–79.

_____, & KRAUSS, R. M. Studies of interpersonal bargaining. *Journal of Conflict Resolution*, 1962, *6*, 52–76.

DEUTSCHER, I. S. *The Prophet Unarmed: Trotsky: 1921–1929*. New York: Vintage, 1959.

DEUTSCHER, I. R.*What We Say/What We Do: Sentiments and Acts*. Glenview, IL: Scott, Foresman, 1973.

DIAMOND, M. Anxiety, psychological defensiveness, and personal responsibility: an action model of dilemma in modern bureaucracy. Paper presented at the Meeting of the International Society of Political Psychology, Oxford, England, 1983.

_____.Bureaucracy as externalized self-system: a view from the psychological interior. Paper presented at the Meeting of the International Society of Political Psychology, Washington, DC, 1982.

DION, L., BARON, R. S., & MILLER, N. Why do groups make riskier decisions than individuals? In L. Berkowitz (ed.), *Advances in Experimental Social Psychology* (vol. 5). New York: Academic Press, 1970.

DIPALMA, G. *Apathy and Participation: Mass Politics in Western Societies*. New York: Free Press, 1970.

DOLLARD, J., et al. *Frustration and Aggression*. New Haven, Conn.: Yale University Press, 1939.

DOMHOFF, G. W. *The Powers that Be*. New York: Random House, 1978.

_____.*Who Rules America?* Englewood Cliffs, NJ: Prentice-Hall, 1967.

DONLEY, R. E., & WINTER, D. G. Measuring the motives of public officials at a distance: an exploratory study of American Presidents. *Behavioral Science*, 1970, *15*, 227–36.

DOOB, L. W. *Personality, Power, and Authority: A View from the Behavioral Sciences*. Westport, CT: Greenwood Press, 1983.

DREW, E. Politics and money—parts I and II. *The New Yorker*, Dec. 6, 1982, and Dec. 13, 1982.

DRIVER, M. J. Individual differences as determinants of aggression in the inter-nation simulation. In M. G. Hermann & T. Milburn (eds.). *A Psychological Examination of Political Leaders*. New York: Free Press, 1977.

DRUCKER, P. F. *Management: Tasks, Responsibilities, Practices*. New York: Harper & Row, 1974.

DRUCKMAN, D. Dogmatism, prenegotiation experience, and simulated group representation as determinants of dyadic behavior in a bargaining situation. *Journal of Personality and Social Psychology*, 1967, *6*, 279–90.

_____.Ethnocentrism in the inter-nation simulation. *Journal of Conflict Resolution*, 1968, *12*, 45–68.

_____.*Negotiations: Social-Psychological Perspectives*. Beverly Hills, CA: Sage Publications, 1977.

_____.Social-psychological approaches to the study of negotiation. In D. Druckman (ed.), *Negotiations: Social-Psychological Approaches*. Beverly Hills, CA: Sage Publications, 1971, 15–44.

DYSON-HUDSON, & SMITH, E. Human territoriality: an ecological reassessment. *American Anthropologist*, 1978, *80*, 21–41.

EASTON, D. *The Political System: An Inquiry into the State of Political Science.* New York: Alfred A. Knopf, 1953 (2nd ed., 1971).

_____.*A Systems Analysis of Political Life.* New York: John Wiley, 1965.

ECKHOFF, T. *Justice: Its Determinants in Social Interaction.* Rotterdam: Rotterdam University Press, 1974.

ECKSTEIN, H. On the etiology of internal wars. In I. K. Feierabend, R. L. Feierabend & T. R. Gurr, *Anger, Violence and Politics, Theories and Research.* Englewood Cliffs, NJ: Prentice-Hall, 1972.

_____, & GURR, T. R. *Patterns of Authority: A Structural Basis for Political Inquiry.* New York: John Wiley, 1975.

EDELMAN, M. *Political Language: Words that Succeed and Policies that Fail.* New York: Academic Press, 1977.

_____.*Politics as Symbolic Action: Mass Arousal and Quiescence.* New York: Academic Press, 1971.

EDINGER, L. J. Political science and political biography (II): reflections on the study of leadership. *Journal of Politics,* 1964, *26*, 648–76.

EDNEY, J. Territoriality and control: a field experiment. *Journal of Personality and Social Psychology,* 1975, *31*, 1118–1125.

EDWARDS, M. Affective development and political education: children's reactions to group differences. Paper presented at the Meeting of the American Political Science Association, Washington, DC, 1972.

EDWARDS, T., CATREVAS, C. N. & EDWARDS, J. *The New Dictionary of Thoughts.* New York: Standard Book Company, 1954.

ELDRIDGE, A. F. *Images of Conflict.* New York: St. Martin's, 1979.

ELLUL, J. *Propaganda: The Formation of Men's Attitudes.* New York: Vintage, 1973.

ELMS, A. C. *Personality in Politics.* New York: Harcourt Brace Jovanovich, 1976.

ERIKSON, E. *Childhood and Society.* New York: Norton, 1950.

_____.*Gandhi's Truth: On the Origins of Militant Nonviolence.* New York: Norton, 1969.

_____.Identity and the life cycle. *Psychological Issues,* 1959, *1*, Monograph, No. 1.

_____.On the nature of psychohistorical evidence in search of Gandhi. In F. Greenstein & M. Lerner (eds.), *A Source Book for the Study of Personality and Politics.* Chicago: Markham, 1971.

ESTES, W. K. An experimental study of punishment. *Psychological Monographs,* 1944, *57*.

ETHEREDGE, L. Hardball politics: a model. *Political Psychology,* 1979, *1*, 3–26.

_____.*A World of Men: The Private Sources of American Foreign Policy.* Cambridge, MA: MIT Press, 1978.

ETZIONI, A. Mixed scanning: a "third" approach to decision making. *Public Administration Review,* 1967a, *27*, 385–92.

_____.The Kennedy experiment. *Western Political Quarterly,* 1967b, *20*, 361–80.

EYSENCK, H. J. (ed.). *Encyclopedia of Psychology.* New York: Herder & Herder, 1972.

FAINSOD, M. Terror as a system of power. In S. Hendel (ed.), *The Soviet Crucible: The Soviet System in Theory and Practice,* North Scituate, MA: Duxbury Press, 1980.

FALKOWSKI, L. (ed.), *Psychological Models in International Politics.* Boulder, CO: Westview, 1979.

FAYOL, H. *General and Industrial Management.* London: Pittman, 1930.

FAZIO, R. H., & ZANNA, M. P. On the predictive validity of attitudes: the roles of direct experience and confidence. *Journal of Personality,* 1978, *46,* 228–43.

FEIERABEND, I. K., & FEIERABEND, R. L. Aggressive behaviors within polities, 1948–1962: a cross-national study. *Journal of Conflict Resolution,* 1966, *10,* 249–71.

FESTINGER, L. *A Theory of Cognitive Dissonance.* Stanford, CA: Stanford University Press, 1957.

———.A theory of social comparison processes. *Human Relations,* 1954, *7,* 117–40.

FIEDLER, F. E. The contingency model and the dynamics of the leadership process. In L. Berkowitz (ed.), *Advances in Experimental Social Psychology.* New York: Academic Press, 1978.

———.What triggers the person-situation interaction in leadership. In D. Magnusson & N. S. Endler (eds.), *Personality at the Crossroads: Current Issues in International Psychology.* Hillsdale, NJ: Erlbaum, 1977, 151–64.

FINIFTER, A. W. Dimensions of political alienation. *American Political Science Review,* 1970, *64,* 389–410.

FISCHHOFF, B., PIDGEON, N., & FISKE, S. T. Social science and the politics of the arms race. *Journal of Social Issues,* 1983, *39,* 161–80.

FISHBEIN, M., & AJZEN, I. *Belief, Attitude, Intention and Behavior: An Introduction to Theory and Research.* Reading, MA: Addison-Wesley, 1975.

FISHER, R. J. Fractionating conflict. In R. Fisher (ed.), *International Conflict and Behavioral Science: The Craigville Papers.* New York: John Wiley, 1964.

———.Third party consultation: a method for the study and resolution of conflict. *Journal of Conflict Resolution,* 1974, *16,* 67–94.

———.Third party consultation as a method of intergroup conflict resolution. *Journal of Conflict Resolution,* 1983, *27,* 301–34.

FLACKS, R. The liberated generation: an exploration of the roots of student unrest. *Journal of Social Issues,* 1967, *23,* 35–61.

FLEMING, D. F. *The Cold War and its Origins, 1917–1960.* London: Allen and Unwin, 1961.

FLETCHER, J. F., & TERRY, J. C. Psychic costs and benefits of political participation. Paper presented at the Meeting of the International Society of Political Psychology, Boston, MA, 1980.

FOA, U. G., & FOA, E. B. Resource exchange: toward a structural theory of interpersonal communication. In A. W. Siegman & B. Pope (eds.), *Studies in Dyadic Communication.* New York: Pergamon, 1971.

FOLLETT, M. P. *Creative Experience.* Gloucester, MA: Peter Smith, 1951.

FONTES, N. E., & BUNDENS, R. W. Persuasion during the trial process. In M. E. Roloff & G. R. Miller (eds.), *Persuasion: New Directions in Theory and Research.* Beverly Hills, CA: Sage Publications, 1980.

FREEDMAN, A. E., & FREEDMAN, P. E. *The Psychology of Political Control.* New York: St. Martin's, 1975.

FREUD, S. *Beyond the Pleasure Principle.* New York: Bantam Books, 1959.

———.*Group Psychology and the Analysis of the Ego.* London: International Psychoanalytical Press, 1922.

FROMM, E. *Escape from Freedom.* New York: Farrar & Rinehart, 1941.

_____.*The Sane Society.* Greenwich, CT: Fawcett, 1955.

FRIED, M. L., & DEFAZIO, V. J. Territoriality and boundary conflicts in the subway. *Psychiatry*, 1947, *37*, 47–59.

FRIEDGUT, T. H. *Political Participation in the USSR.* Princeton, NJ: Princeton University Press, 1979.

GAMSON, W. A. Experiments in coalition formation. In L. Berkowitz (ed.), *Advances in Experimental Social Psychology.* New York: Academic Press, 1964, 81–110.

_____.*Power and Discontent.* Homewood, IL: Dorsey Press, 1968.

_____.*The Strategy of Social Protest.* Homewood, IL: Dorsey Press, 1975.

_____, FIREMAN, B., & RYTINA, S. *Encounters with Unjust Authority.* Homewood, IL: Dorsey Press, 1982.

GEORGE, A. L. The "operational code": a neglected approach to the study of political leaders and decision-making. *International Studies Quarterly*, 1969, *13*, 190–222.

_____.*Presidential Decision-Making in Foreign Policy: The Effective Use of Information and Advice.* Boulder, CO: Westview, 1980.

_____, & GEORGE, J. L. *Woodrow Wilson and Colonel House: A Personality Study.* New York: John Day, 1956.

GERGEN, K. J. Social psychology as history. *Journal of Personality and Social Psychology*, 1973, *26*, 309–20.

_____.*Toward Transformation in Social Knowledge.* New York: Springer-Verlag, 1982.

GERTH, H., & MILLS, C. W. (eds.). *Max Weber: Essays in Sociology.* New York: Oxford University Press, 1958.

GESCHWENDER, J. A. Social structure and the Negro revolt: an examination of some hypotheses. *Social Forces*, 1964, *42*, 248–56.

GEWIRTZ, J. L. Mechanisms of social learning: some roles of stimulation and behavior in early human development. In D. A. Goslin (ed.), *Handbook of Socialization Theory and Research.* Chicago: Rand McNally, 1969.

GIBB, C. A. The effects of group size and the threat reduction upon creativity in a problem-solving situation. *American Psychologist*, 1951, *6*, 324.

_____.An interactional view of leadership. *Australian Journal of Psychology*, 1958, *10*, 101–10.

_____.Leadership. In G. Lindzay & E. Aronson (eds.), *The Handbook of Social Psychology* (2nd ed., vol. 4). Reading, MA: Addison-Wesley, 1969.

GIBSON, J. L. Attitudes, role perceptions, and criminal court decision making. Paper delivered at the Meeting of the American Political Science Association, 1978.

GILMORE, R. S., & Lamb, R. B. *Political Alienation in Contemporary America.* New York: St. Martin's, 1975.

GLAD, B. Contributions of psychobiography. In J. N. Knutson (ed.), *Handbook of Political Psychology.* San Francisco: Jossey-Bass, 1973.

GLUCKMAN, M. *Custom and Conflict in Africa.* Oxford: Basil Blackwell, Ltd., 1956.

GOEL, M. L. Conventional political participation. In D. H. Smith, J. Macaulay & Associates. *Participation in Social and Political Activities.* San Francisco: Jossey-Bass, 1980.

_____, & SMITH, D. H. Political activities. In D. H. Smith, J. Macaulay & Associates. *Participation in Social and Political Activities.* San Francisco: Jossey-Bass, 1980.

GOFFMAN, E. On face-work: an analysis of ritual elements in social interaction. *Psychiatry*, 1955, *18*, 213–31.

————.*Presentation of Self in Everyday Life*. Garden City, NY: Anchor Books, 1959.

GOLDSTEIN, J. H. *Aggression and Crimes of Violence*. New York: Oxford University Press, 1975.

GOLEMBIEWSKI, R. T., & MILLER, G. J. Small groups in political science: perspectives on significance and stuckness. In S. L. Long (ed.), *The Handbook of Political Behavior* (vol. 2). New York: Plenum Press, 1981.

GORDON, M. *Human Nature, Class, and Ethnicity*. New York: Oxford Press, 1978.

GORE, P. & ROTTER, J. B. A personality correlate of social action. *Journal of Personality*, 1963, *31*, 58–64.

GOULDNER, A. W. Anti-minotaur: the myth of a value-free sociology. In M. Stein & A. Vidich (eds.), *Sociology on Trial*. Englewood Cliffs, NJ: Prentice-Hall, 1963.

GRABER, D. A. *Mass Media and American Politics*. Washington, DC: Congressional Quarterly Press, 1980.

————.Political languages. In D. D. Nimmo & K. R. Sanders (eds.), *Handbook of Political Communication*. Beverly Hills, CA: Sage Publications, 1981.

————.*Verbal Behavior and Politics*. Urbana: University of Illinois Press, 1976.

GRAEN, G. Role making processes within complex organizations. In M. D. Dunnette (ed.), *Handbook of Industrial and Organizational Psychology*. Chicago: Rand McNally, 1976.

GREENSTEIN, F. I. *Children and Politics*. New Haven: Yale University Press, 1965.

————.*Personality and Politics*. New York: Norton, 1969.

GULICK, L., & URWICK, L. (eds.). *Papers on the Science of Administration*. New York: Institute of Public Administration, 1937.

GULLIVER, P. H. *Disputes and Negotiations: A Cross-Cultural Perspective*. New York: Academic Press, 1979.

GURR, T. R. Psychological factors in civil violence. In I. K. Feierabend, R. L. Feierabend, & T. R. Gurr (eds.), *Anger, Violence, and Politics: Theories and Research*. Englewood Cliffs, NJ: Prentice-Hall, 1972.

————.*Why Men Rebel*. Princeton, NJ: Princeton University Press, 1970.

————, & BISHOP, V. F. Violent nations and others. *Journal of Conflict Resolution*, 1976, *20*, 79–110.

GUTHMAN, E. W. *We Band of Brothers*. New York: Harper & Row, 1971.

HAAS, J. E., & DRABEK, T. E. *Complex Organizations : A Sociological Perspective*. New York: Macmillan Co., 1973.

HAMNER, W. C., & YUKL, G. A. The effectiveness of different offer strategies in bargaining. In D. Druckman (ed.), *Negotiations: Social-Psychological Perspectives*. Beverly Hills, CA: Sage Publications, 1977.

HARE, A. P. *Handbook of Small Group Research*. New York: Free Press, 1976.

HARRELL, W. A., & HARTNAGEL, T. The impact of Machiavellianism and the trustfulness of the victim on laboratory theft. *Sociometry*, 1976. *39*, 157–65.

HARSANYI, J. C. Bargaining in ignorance of the opponent's utility function. *Journal of Conflict Resolution*, 1962, *7*, 67–80.

————.Some social-science implications of a new approach to game theory. In K. Archibald (ed.), *Strategic Interaction and Conflict: Original Papers and Discussion*. Berkeley, CA: Institute of International Studies, 1966.

HARTLE, T. W., & HELPERIN, M. J. Rational and incremental decision making: an exposition and critique with illustrations. In M. J. White, et al. (eds.), *Managing Public Systems: Analytic Techniques for Public Administration*. North Scituate, MA: Duxbury Press, 1980.

HARTMAN, J. Carter and the utopian group-fantasy. *The Journal of Psychohistory*, 1977, *5*, 239–58.

————, & GIBBARD, G. Anxiety, boundary evolution and social change. In G. S. Gibbard, J. J. Hartman & R. D. Mann (eds.), *Analysis of Groups*. San Francisco: Jossey-Bass, 1974.

HAWLEY, W. D. *The Implicit Civics Curriculum: Teacher Behavior and Political Learning*. Durham, NC: Duke University, Center for Policy Analysis, 1976.

HEATH, R. G. Electrical self-stimulation of the brain in man. *American Journal of Psychiatry*, 1963, *120*, 571–77.

HEIDER, F. *The Psychology of Interpersonal Relations*. New York: John Wiley, 1958.

HEMPHILL, J. K. The leader and his group. *Journal of Educational Research*, 1949, *28*, 225–29.

HENDEL, S. (ed.). *The Soviet Crucible: The Soviet System in Theory and Practice* (5th ed.). North Scituate, MA: Duxbury Press, 1980.

HENLEY, N. M. *Body Politics: Power, Sex, and Nonverbal Communication*. Englewood Cliffs, NJ: Prentice-Hall, 1977.

HERADSTVEIT, D. *The Arab-Israeli Conflict: Psychological Obstacles to Peace*. Oslo, Norway: Universitetsforlaget, 1979.

————.The dynamics of favorable and unfavorable attributions. Paper presented to the Meeting of the International Society for Political Psychology, Washington, DC, 1982.

HERMANN, C. F. The effects of decision structures and processes on foreign policy behaviors. Paper presented at the meeting of the International Society of Political Psychology, Washington, DC, 1979.

HERMANN, M. G. Assessing the personalities of Politburo members at a distance. Paper presented at the symposium on "Methods of assessing political leaders' personality at a distance," American Psychological Association Convention, Toronto, 1978.

————.Explaining foreign policy behavior using personal characteristics of political leaders. *International Studies Quarterly*, 1980, *24*, 7–46.

————.Leadership and nation building. Paper presented at the Meeting of the International Society of Political Psychology, Oxford, England, 1983.

————.Some personal characteristics related to foreign aid voting of congressmen. In M. G. Hermann & T. Milburn (eds.), *A Psychological Examination of Political Leaders*. New York: Free Press, 1977.

————.Who becomes a political leader? In L. Falkowski (ed.), *Psychological Models in International Politics*. Boulder, CO: Westview, 1979.

————, & CANTOR, R. A. Counterattack or delay: characteristics influencing decision makers' responses to the simulation of an unidentified attack. *Journal of Conflict Resolution*, 1974, *18*, 75–106.

————, HERMANN, C. F., & HAGEN, J. D. The relationship between beliefs and roles in shaping governments' foreign policy behavior. Paper presented at the Meeting of the International Society of Political Psychology, Washington, DC, 1982a.

————, & HERMANN, C. F. A look inside the "Black Box": building on a decade of research. In G. W. Hopple and L. S. Falkowski (eds.), *Biopolitics, Political Psychology and International Politics: Toward a New Discipline*. New York: Frances Printer Publishers, 1982b.

HERSEY, P., & BLANCHARD, K. H. *Management of Organizational Behavior* (2nd ed.). Englewood Cliffs, NJ: Prentice-Hall, 1972.

HERSH, S. M. *The Price of Power: Kissinger in the Nixon White House.* New York: Summit Books, 1983.

HESS, R. D., & TORNEY, J. V. *The Development of Political Attitudes in Children.* Garden City, NY: Anchor Books, 1968.

HILL, B. J. An analysis of conflict resolution techniques. *Journal of Conflict Resolution,* 1982, *26,* 109–38.

HINES, S. M. Politics and the evolution of inquiry in political science. *Politics and the Life Sciences,* 1982, 1, 5–16.

HIRSCH, F. *Social Limits to Growth.* London: Routledge & Kegan Paul, 1977.

HOFSTETTER, C., & BUSS, T. Politics and last-minute political television. *Western Political Quarterly,* 1980, *33,* 24–37.

HOFSTETTER, C. R., ZUKIN, C., & BUSS, T. F. Political imagery and information in an age of television. *Journalism Quarterly,* 1978, *55,* 562–69.

HOLLANDER, E. P. Competence and conformity in the acceptance of influence. *Journal of Abnormal and Social Psychology,* 1960, *61,* 365–69.

————.Conformity, status, and idiosyncrasy credit. *Psychological Review,* 1958, *65,* 117–27.

————.Some effects of perceived status on responses to innovative behavior. *Journal of Abnormal and Social Psychology,* 1961, *63,* 247–50.

————, & JULIAN, J. W. Contemporary trends in the analysis of leadership processes. *Psychological Bulletin,* 1969, *71,* 387–97.

HOLSTI, O. Foreign policy formation viewed cognitively. In R. Axelrod (ed.), *Structure of Decision: The Cognitive Maps of Political Elites.* Princeton, NJ: Princeton University Press, 1976.

HOMANS, G. C. *Social Behavior: Its Elementary Forms.* New York: Harcourt, Brace, & World, 1961.

HOOK, E. B. Behavioral implications of the human XYY genotype. *Science,* 1973. *179,* 139–50.

HOPPLE, G. W. *Political Psychology and Biopolitics: Assessing and Predicting Elite Behavior in Foreign Policy Crises.* Boulder, CO: Westview, 1980.

HOROWITZ, I. Paradigms of political psychology. *Political Psychology,* 1979, *1,* 99–103.

HOVLAND, C. I., JANIS, I. L., & KELLEY, H. H. *Communication and Persuasion.* New Haven, Yale University Press, 1953.

HOWARD, J. H. Person-situation interaction models. *Personality and Social Psychology Bulletin,* 1979, *5,* 191–95.

HUBER, G. P. *Managerial Decision Making.* Glenview, IL: Scott, Foresman, 1980.

HUNT, R. W., & GOEL, M. L. Unconventional political participation. In D. H. Smith, J. Macaulay & Associates. *Participation in Social and Political Activities.* San Francisco: Jossey-Bass, 1980.

HUNTER, J. E., GERBING, D. W., & BOSTER, F. J. Machiavellian beliefs and personality: construct invalidity of the Machiavellian dimension. *Journal of Personality and Social Psychology.* 1982, *43,* 1293–1305.

HUTT, S. J., & HUTT, C. *Direct Observation and Measurement of Behavior.* Springfield, IL: Charles C. Thomas, 1974.

HYMAN, H. *Political Socialization.* New York: Free Press, 1959.

HYMAN, H. H., & SHEATSLEY, P. B. The authoritarian personality—a methodological critique. In R. Christie & M. Jahoda (eds.), *Studies in the Scope and Method of the Authoritarian Personality.* New York: Free Press, 1954.

IKLÉ, F. *How Nations Negotiate.* New York: Harper & Row, 1964.

IRISH, M. D. Advance of the discipline? In M. D. Irish (ed.), *Political Science: Advance of the Discipline.* Englewood Cliffs, NJ: Prentice-Hall, 1968.

ISAAK, A. C. *Scope and Methods of Political Science: An Introduction to the Methodology of Political Inquiry.* Homewood, IL: Dorsey Press, 1969.

IVANCEVICH, J. M., & MATTESON, M. T. *Stress and Work: A Managerial Perspective.* Glenview, IL: Scott, Foresman, 1980.

JACKMAN, M. D., & JACKMAN, R. W. *Class Awareness in the United States.* Berkeley: University of California Press, 1983.

JACOBS, P., BRUNTON, M., & MELVILLE, M. Aggressive behavior, mental subnormality and the XYY male. *Nature,* 1965, *208,* 1351–1352.

JACQUES, E. Social systems as a defense against persecutory and depressive anxiety. In M. Klein, P. Heimann, & R. E. Money-Kyrle (eds.), *New Directions in Psychoanalysis.* New York: Basic Books, 1955.

JANDA, K. Toward the explication of the concept of leadership in terms of the concept of power. In G. D. Paige (ed.), *Political Leadership: Readings for an Emerging Field.* New York: Free Press, 1972.

JANIS, I. L., & MANN, L. *Decision Making: A Psychological Analysis of Conflict, Choice, and Commitment.* New York: Free Press, 1977.

JANIS, L. *Victims of Groupthink: A Psychological Study of Foreign-Policy Decisions and Fiascoes.* Boston: Houghton Mifflin, 1972.

JAROS, D. *Socialization to Politics.* New York: Praeger, 1973.

JARVIK, L. F., KLODIN, V., & MATSUYAMA, S. S. Human aggression and the extra Y chromosome. *American Psychologist,* 1973, *28,* 674–82.

JENNINGS, M. K., & NIEMI, R. G. The division of political labor between mothers and fathers. *American Political Science Review,* 1971, *65,* 69–82.

_____.*The Political Character of Adolescence: The Influence of Families and Schools.* Princeton, NJ: Princeton University Press, 1974.

_____.The transmission of political values from parent to child. *American Political Science Review,* 1968, *62,* 169–84.

JERVIS, R. How decision-makers think: applying cognitive psychology to international relations. *CSS Newsletter* (Columbia University), 1981, *2,* 1–3.

_____.Perception and misperception: an updating of the analysis. Paper presented at the Meeting of the International Society of Political Psychology, Washington, DC, 1982.

_____.*Perception and Misperception in International Relations.* Princeton, NJ: Princeton University Press, 1976.

_____.Political decision making: recent contributions. *Political Psychology,* 1980, *2,* 86–101.

JOHNSON, C. *Revolutionary Change.* Boston: Little, Brown, 1966.

JOHNSON, L. Operational code and the prediction of leadership behavior: Senator Frank Church at mid-career. In M. G. Hermann & T. Milburn (eds.), *A Psychological Examination of Political Leaders.* New York: Free Press, 1977.

JONES, E. E. The strategic control of attributions in international relations. Paper presented at the Meeting of the International Society for Political Psychology. Washington, DC, 1982.

JÖNSSON, C. *Soviet Bargaining Behavior: The Nuclear Test Ban Case.* New York: Columbia University Press, 1979.

JUDD, D. R. *The Politics of American Cities: Private Power and Public Policy* (2nd ed.). Boston: Little, Brown, 1984.

KAASE, M., & MARSH, A. Political action repertory: changes over time and a new typology. In S. H. Barnes, M. Kaase, et al., *Political Action: Mass Participation in Five Western Democracies.* Beverly Hills, CA: Sage, 1979.

KAID, L. L. Political Advertising. In D. D. Nimmo & K. R. Sanders (eds.), *Handbook of Political Communication.* Beverly Hills, CA: Sage Publications, 1981.

KAPLAN, M. A. *Alienation and Identification.* New York: Free Press, 1976.

KATZ, D. Attitude formation and public opinion. In D. D. Nimmo & C. M. Bonjean (eds.), *Political Attitudes and Public Opinion.* New York: David McKay, 1972.

_____.The functional approach to the study of attitudes. In W. J. Crotty (ed.), *Public Opinion and Politics: A Reader.* New York: Holt, Rinehart & Winston, 1970.

_____.Patterns of leadership. In J. N. Knutson (ed.), *Handbook of Political Psychology.* San Francisco: Jossey-Bass, 1973, 203–33.

_____, & KAHN, R. L. *The Social Psychology of Organizations* (2nd ed.). New York: John Wiley, 1978.

KAUFMANN, H. *Aggression and Altruism.* New York: Holt, Rinehart & Winston, 1970.

KELLERMAN, B. Is there life after adolescence and if so, should political scientists care? Paper presented at the Meeting of the American Political Science Association, Washington, DC, 1979.

_____ (ed.). *Leadership: Multidisciplinary Perspectives.* Englewood Cliffs, NJ: Prentice-Hall, 1984.

KELLEY, H. H. A classroom study of the dilemmas in interpersonal negotiations. In K. Archibald (ed.), *Strategic Interaction and Conflict: Original Papers and Discussion.* Berkeley, CA: Institute of International Studies, 1966.

KELMAN, H. C. Compliance, identification and internalization: three processes of attitude change. *Journal of Conflict Resolution,* 1958, *2,* 51–60.

_____. An interactional approach to conflict resolution and its application to Israeli-Palestinian relations. *International Interactions,* 1979, *6,* 99–122.

_____. The problem-solving workshop in conflict resolution. In R. L. Merritt (ed.), *Communication in International Politics.* Urbana, IL: University of Illinois Press, 1972.

_____. The problem-solving workshop: a social-psychological contribution to the resolution of international conflicts. *Journal of Peace Research,* 1976, *13,* 79–90.

_____. Remarks on "ethical imperatives and social responsibility in the practice of political psychology." *Political Psychology,* 1979, *1,* 100–2.

KENISTON, K. *Radicals and Militants.* Lexington, MA: Heath, 1973.

KERNBERG, O. *Borderline Conditions and Pathological Narcissism,* New York: Aronson, 1975.

KERR, C. Industrial conflict and its mediation. *American Journal of Sociology,* 1954, *60,* 230–45.

KEY, V. O., JR. *Politics, Parties and Pressure Groups* (vol. 4). New York: Thomas Y. Crowell, 1958.

KHRUSHCHEV, N. S. Stalin and the cult of the individual. In S. Hendel (ed.), *The Soviet Crucible: The Soviet System in Theory and Practice,* North Scituate, MA: Duxbury Press, 1980, *5,* 144–55.

KIDDER, L. A. & STEWART, V. M. *The Psychology of Intergroup Relations: Conflict and Consciousness.* New York: McGraw-Hill, 1975.

KINGDON, J. W. *Agendas, Alternatives, and Public Policies.* Boston: Little, Brown, 1984.

KIPNIS, D. Does power corrupt? *Journal of Personality and Social Psychology*, 1972, *24*, 33–41.

KIRSCHT, J. P., LODAHL, T. M., & HAIRE, M. Some factors in the selection of leaders by members of small groups. *Journal of Abnormal and Social Psychology*, 1959, *58*, 406–8.

KLEIN, M. *The Psychoanalysis of Children*. London: Hogarth Press, 1932.

KLINEBERG, F. Cyclical trends in American foreign policy models and their policy implications. In C. Kegley, Jr. & P. McGowan (eds.), *Challenges to America*. Beverly Hills, CA: Sage Publications, 1979.

KNAPP, M. *Interpersonal Communication and Human Relationships*. Newton, Mass.: Allyn & Bacon, 1984.

KNUTSON, J. N. (ed.). *Handbook of Political Psychology*. San Francisco: Jossey-Bass, 1973.

————. *The Human Basis of the Policy*. Chicago: Aldine, 1972.

————. Personality in the study of politics. In J. Knutson (ed.), *Handbook of Political Psychology*. San Francisco: Jossey-Bass, 1973b.

————. *Victimization and Political Violence: The Spectre of Our Times*. Los Angeles: Unpublished, 1981.

KOHLBERG, L. Revisions in the theory and practice of moral development. *New Directions for Child Development*, 1978, *2*, 83–87.

————. Stage and sequence: the cognitive-developmental approach to socialization. In D. A. Goslin (ed.), *Handbook of Socialization Theory and Research*. Chicago: Rand McNally, 1969.

KOHUT, H. Forms and transformations of narcissism. *Journal of the American Psychoanalytical Association*, 1966, *14*, 243–72.

KOMORITA, S. S., & MECHLING, J. Betrayal and reconciliation in a two-person game. *Journal of Personality and Social Psychology*, 1967, *6*, 349–53.

KOWITZ, A. C., & KNUTSON, T. J. *Decision Making in Small Groups: The Search for Alternatives*. Boston: Allyn & Bacon, 1980.

KOZHOKAR', N.SH., & MARKIMAN, S. N. Vozrastanie Obshchestvenno-Politicheskoi Aktivnosti Mass v Sovremennykh Usloviiakh. In *Formirovanie Novogo Cheloveka-Stroitelia Kommunizma*. Kishinev: Izdatel'stvo "Shtiintza," 1973.

KRAMER-BADONI, T., & WAKEHUT, R. Theoretical and methodological considerations on Kohlberg's moral judgement approach to the study of political socialization. Paper presented at the Meeting of the International Society for Political Psychology, Washington, DC, 1979.

KRAUS, S., & DAVIS, K. Political debates. In D. Nimmo & K. R. Sanders (eds.), *Handbook of Political Communication*. Beverly Hills, CA: Sage Publications, 1981.

LABAW, R., & RAPPEPORT, M. *Alienation: policy vs. structure*. Princeton, NJ: Opinion Research Corporation, 1975.

LABIER, D. Bureaucracy and psychopathology. *Political Psychology*, 1983, *4*, 223–44.

LANE, E. Motives for liberty, equality, fraternity: the effects of market and state. *Political Psychology*, 1979, *1*, 3–20.

LANGER, W. C. *The Mind of Adolf Hitler*. New York: New American Library, 1972.

LANGTON, K. P. *Political Participation and Learning*. North Quincy, MA: Christopher Publishing House, 1980.

————. *Political Socialization*. New York: Oxford University Press, 1969.

LAPALOMBARA, J. *Politics Within Nations*. Englewood Cliffs, NJ: Prentice-Hall, 1974.

LAPIERE, R. T. Attitudes vs. actions. *Social Forces*, Oct. 1934–May 1935, *13*, 230–37.

LAQUER, W. *Terrorism.* Boston: Little, Brown, 1977.

LARSEN, K. S. *Aggression: Myths and Models.* Chicago: Nelson-Hall, 1976.

LASCH, C. *The Culture of Narcissism.* New York: Norton, 1978.

LASSWELL, H. D. *Politics: Who Gets What, When How.* Cleveland: World Publishing Co., 1958.

_____. *Politics: Who Gets What, When, How.* New York: Whittlesey House, 1936.

_____. *Power and Personality.* New York: Norton, 1948.

_____. *Psychopathology and Politics.* Chicago: University of Chicago Press, 1930.

_____. The selective effects of personality on political participation. In R. Christie & M. Jahoda (eds.), *Studies in the Scope and Methods of the Authoritarian Personality.* Glencoe, IL: Free Press, 1954.

_____, & KAPLAN, A. *Power and Society: A Framework for Political Inquiry.* New Haven: Yale University Press, 1950.

LATHAM, E. The group basis of politics: notes for a theory. In H. Eulau, J. Eldersfeld & M. Janowitz (eds.), *Political Behavior.* Glencoe, IL: Free Press, 1956.

LAVE, C. A., & MARCH, J. G. *An Introduction to Models in the Social Sciences.* New York: Harper & Row, 1975.

LEARY, T. *Interpersonal Diagnosis of Personality.* New York: Academic Press, 1958.

LEITES, N. *The Operational Code of the Politboro.* New York: McGraw-Hill, 1951.

LEMERT, J. B. *Does Mass Communication Change Public Opinion After All?* Chicago: Nelson-Hall, 1981.

LERNER, M. J. The desire for justice and reactions to victims. In J. Macaulay & L. Berkowitz (eds.), *Altruism and Helping Behavior.* New York: Academic Press, 1970.

_____. Evaluation of performance as a function of performer's reward and attractiveness. *Journal of Personality and Social Psychology,* 1965, *1,* 355–60.

_____. The justice motive in social behavior: introduction. *Journal of Social Issues,* 1975, *31,* 1–19.

_____. The justice motive: some hypotheses as to its origins and forms. *Journal of Personality,* 1977, *45,* 1–54.

_____. The law as a social trap. *Culture Learning Institute Report.* August, 1976.

_____, & LERNER, S. C. (eds.). *The Justice Motive in Social Behavior: Adapting to Times of Scarcity and Change.* New York: Plenum, 1982.

_____, & WHITEHEAD, L. A. Procedural justice viewed in the context of justice motive theory. In G. Mikula (ed.), *Justice and Social Interaction.* New York: Springer-Verlag, 1980.

LEUCHTENBURG, W. E. *Franklin Roosevelt and the New Deal.* New York: Harper & Row, 1963.

LEVENTHAL, G. S. & ANDERSON, D. Self-interest and the maintenance of equity. *Journal of Personality and Social Psychology,* 1970, *15,* 57–62.

LEVENTHAL, G. S. & LANE, D. W. Sex, age, and equity behavior. *Journal of Personality and Social Psychology,* 1970, *15,* 312–16.

LEVENTHAL, H. Findings and theory in the study of fear communication. In L. Berkowitz (ed.), *Advances in Experimental Social Psychology.* New York: Academic Press, 1970.

LEVINE, R. A., & CAMPBELL, D. T. *Ethnocentrism: Theories of Conflict, Ethnic Attitudes and Group Behavior.* New York: John Wiley, 1972.

LEVINE, S., & CONNER, R. Endocrine aspects of violence. An unpublished staff report to the National Commission on the Causes and Prevention of Violence, December 1969.

LEVINSON, D. J. Role, personality, and social structure in the organizational setting. *Journal of Abnormal and Social Psychology*, 1969, *58*, 170–80.

_____. *The Seasons of a Man's Life*. New York: Knopf, 1978.

LEVY, S. G. Political violence: a critical evaluation. In S. L. Long (ed.), *The Handbook of Political Behavior*. New York: Plenum, 1981.

LEWIN, K. Group decision and social change. In T. M. Newton & E. L. Hartley (eds.), *Reading in Social Psychology*. New York: Holt, 1947.

_____, LIPPITT, R., & WHITE, R. K. Patterns of aggressive behavior in experimentally created "social climates." *Journal of Social Psychology*. 1939, *10*, 271–99.

LICHTER, R. S., & ROTHMAN, S. Jewish ethnicity and radical culture: a social psychological study of political activity. *Political Psychology*, 1981, *3*, 116–57.

LIEBMAN, M. *The Russian Revolution*. New York: Random House, 1970.

LIFTON, R. J. *History and Human Survival*. New York: Vintage, 1971.

LINDBLOM, C. The science of muddling through. *Public Administration Review*, 1959, *19*, 79–88.

LITTLE, G. Leaders and followers: a psychosocial prospectus. *Melbourne Journal of Politics*, 1980, *12*, 3–29.

LORENZ, K. *On Aggression*. New York: Harcourt, Brace & World, 1966.

LUCE, R. D., & RAIFFA, H. *Games and Decisions: Introduction and Critical Survey*. New York: John Wiley, 1957.

MADDI, S. R. *Personality Theories: A Comparative Analysis*. Homewood, IL: Dorsey Press, 1968.

MADDOX, W. S., & HANDBERG, R. Motivational factors in media usage. Paper presented at the Meeting of the International Society of Political Psychology. Washington, DC, 1979.

MAIER, N. R. Assets and liabilities in group problem solving: the need for an integrative function. In D. Mankin, R. E. Ames, Jr. & M. A. Grodsky (eds.), *Classics of Industrial and Organizational Psychology*. Oak Park, IL: Moor Publishing Co., 1980.

_____. *Frustration: The Study of Behavior Without a Goal*. New York: McGraw-Hill, 1949.

MANHEIM, J. B. *The Politics Within: A Primer in Political Attitudes and Behavior*. Englewood Cliffs, NJ: Prentice-Hall, Inc., 1975 (2nd ed.: Longman, 1982).

MANN, L., & JANIS, I. L. A follow-up study on the long-term effects of emotional role-playing. *Journal of Personality and Social Psychology*, 1968, *8*, 339–42.

MANN, R. D. A review of the relationships between personality and performance in small groups. *Psychological Bulletin*, 1959, *56*, 241–70.

MARCH, J. G., & SIMON, H. A. *Organizations*. New York: John Wiley, 1958.

MARK, V. H., & ERVIN, F. R. *Violence and the Brain*. New York: Harper & Row, 1970.

MARTINDALE, D. A. Territorial dominance behavior in dyadic verbal interactions. *Proceedings of the 79th Annual Convention of the American Psychological Association*, 1971, *6*, 305–6.

MASER, W. *Hitler: Legend, Myth and Reality*. New York: Harper & Row, 1971.

MASLOW, A. *Motivation and Personality*. New York: Harper & Bros., 1954.

MASTERS, R. D. Human nature and political theory: can biology contribute to the study of politics? *Politics and the Life Sciences*, 1984, *2*, 120–27.

_____. Nice guys don't finish last: aggressive and appeasement gestures in media images of politicians. Paper delivered at the Meeting of the American Association for the Advancement of Science, Washington, DC, 1982.

McCAULEY, M. *The Soviet Union Since 1917.* New York: Longman, 1981.

McCLELLAND, D. C. *The Achieving Society.* New York: Irvington, 1961.

_____. *Power: The Inner Experience.* New York: Irvington, 1975.

McGUIRE, W. J. The concept of attitudes and their relations to behaviors. In H. W. Sinaiko & L. A. Broedling (eds.), *Perspectives on Attitude Assessment: Surveys and Their Alternatives.* Champaign, IL: Pendleton, 1976.

McGUIRE, W. J. Inducing resistence to persuasion. In L. Berkowitz (ed.), *Advances in Experimental Social Psychology* (vol. 1). Reading, MA: Addison-Wesley, 1969.

_____. The nature of attitudes and attitude change. In G. Lindzey & E. Aronson (eds.), *The Handbook of Social Psychology* (vol. 3, 2nd ed.), Reading, MA: Addison-Wesley, 1969.

_____. Personality and susceptibility to social influence. In E. Borgatta & W. Lambert (eds.), *Handbook of Personality Theory and Research.* Chicago: Rand McNally, 1968.

MEEHL, P. E. The selfish voter paradox and the thrown-away vote argument. *The American Political Science Review,* 1977, *71,* 11–30.

MENDELSOHN, H. Some reasons why information campaigns can succeed. *Public Opinion Quarterly,* 1973, *37,* 50–61.

MERTON, R. K. *Social Theory and Social Structure* (rev. ed.). Glencoe, IL: Free Press, 1957.

MIKULA, G. (ed.). *Justice and Social Interaction.* New York: Springer-Verlag, 1980.

_____. On the role of justice in allocation decisions. In G. Mikula (ed.), *Justice and Social Interaction.* New York: Springer-Verlag, 1980.

MILBRATH, L. W. *Political Participation: How and Why Do People Get Involved in Politics?* Chicago: Rand McNally, 1965.

_____, & GOEL, M. L. *Political Participation: How and Why Do People Get Involved in Politics?* (2nd ed). Chicago: Rand McNally, 1977.

_____. Political participation. In S. L. Long (ed.), *The Handbook of Political Behavior* (vol. 4). New York: Plenum, 1981.

MILGRAM, S. *Obedience to Authority.* New York: Harper Colophon, 1974.

MILIBAND, R. *The State in Capitalist Society.* New York: Basic Books, 1969.

MILLER, D. R. Psychoanalytic theory of development: a re-evaluation. In D. A. Goslin (ed.), *Handbook of Socialization Theory and Research.* Chicago: Rand McNally, 1969.

MILLER, D. R. & SWANSON, G. *Inner Conflict and Defense.* New York: Holt, Rinehart & Winston, 1960.

MILLER, M. *Lyndon: An Oral Biography.* New York: Ballantine, 1980.

MILLER, N. E. The frustration-aggression hypothesis. *Psychological Review,* 1941, *38,* 337–42.

MILLS, C. *The Power Elite.* New York: Oxford University Press, 1959.

MILLS, T. *The Sociology of Small Groups.* Englewood Cliffs, NJ: Prentice-Hall, 1967.

MITCHELL, C. R. *The Structure of International Conflict.* New York: St. Martin's, 1981.

MOHR, L. B. Organizations, decisions, and courts. *Law and Society Review,* 1976, *10,* 621–42.

MOLLENKOPF, J. Theories of the state and power structure research. *Insurgent Sociologist,* 1975, *5,* 245–64.

MONGAR, M. Personality and decision-making: John F. Kennedy in four crisis decisions. In G. J. DiRenzo (ed.), *Personality and Politics.* Garden City, NY: Anchor, 1974.

MONTAGU, M. F. Chromosomes and crime. *Psychology Today.* October 1968, 42–49.

————. The new litany of "innate depravity," or original sin revisited. In M.F. Montagu (ed.), *Man and Aggression.* New York: Oxford University Press, 1968.

MUELLER, C. *The Politics of Communication.* New York: Oxford University Press, 1973.

MURPHY, W. T., Jr., & Schneier, E. *Vote Power: How to Work for the Person You Want Elected.* Garden City, NY: Anchor Press/Doubleday, 1974.

MURRAY, H. A. *Explorations in Personality.* London: Oxford University Press, 1938.

MUSSEN, P. H., & WARREN, A. B. Personality and political participation. In R. S. Sigel (ed.), *Learning About Politics: A Reader in Political Socialization.* New York: Random House, 1970.

NADER, L. Forums for justice: a cross-cultural perspective. *Journal of Social Issues,* 1975, *31,* 151–70..

NEISSER, U. *Cognition and Reality.* San Francisco: Freeman, 1976.

NEUSTADT, R. E. *Presidential Power: The Politics of Leadership from F.D.R. to Carter.* New York: John Wiley, 1980.

NEWHOUSE, J. *Cold Dawn: The Story of SALT.* New York: Holt, Rinehart & Winston, 1972.

News Roundup. *Behavior Today,* June 18, 1979, 8.

NEWTON, J. W., & MANN, L. Crowd size as a factor in the persuasion process: a study of religious crusade meetings. *Journal of Personality and Social Psychology,* 1980, *39,* 874–83.

NIE, N. H., & VERBA, S. Political participation. In F. I. Greenstein & N. W. Polsby (eds.), *Handbook of Political Science* (vol. 4). Reading, MA: Addison-Wesley, 1975.

NIEMI, R. G. Political socialization. In J. N. Knutson (ed.), *Handbook of Political Psychology.* San Francisco: Jossey-Bass, 1973.

NIMMO, D. D. *Political Communication and Public Opinion in America.* Santa Monica, CA: Goodyear, 1978.

————. *Popular Images of Politics: A Taxonomy.* Englewood Cliffs, NJ: Prentice-Hall, 1974.

————, & COMBS, J. E. *Subliminal Politics: Myths and Mythmakers in America.* Englewood Cliffs, NJ: Prentice-Hall, 1980.

———— & SAVAGE, R. L. *Candidates and Their Images: Concepts, Methods and Findings.* Santa Monica, CA: Goodyear, 1976.

———— & UNGS, T. *Political Patterns in America: Conflict Representation and Resolution.* San Francisco: Freeman, 1979.

NIXON, R. M. *The Real War.* New York: Warner, 1981.

NUTTIN, J. R. A conceptual frame of personality-world interaction: a relational theory. In D. Magnusson & N. S. Endler (eds.), *Personality at the Crossroads: Current Issues in Interactional Psychology.* Hillsdale, NJ: Erlbaum, 1977.

NYE, R. *Conflict Among Humans: Some Basic Psychological and Social-Psychological Considerations.* New York: Springer, 1973.

OFFE, C. Political authority and class structure: an analysis of late capitalistic societies. *International Journal of Social Sciences,* 1974, *2,* 73–108.

OKUN, A. *Equality and Efficiency: The Big Trade-Off.* Washington, DC: Brookings Institute, 1975.

ORNSTEIN, N. J., & ROHDE, D. W. Seniority and future power in congress. In N. J. Ornstein (ed.), *Congress in Change.* New York: Praeger, 1975.

OSGOOD, C. *An Alternative to War or Surrender.* Urbana: University of Illinois Press, 1962.

OSHEROW, N. Making sense of the nonsensical: an analysis of Jonestown. In E. Aronson (ed.), *Readings about the Social Animal* (3rd ed.). San Francisco: Freeman, 1981.

OSKAMP, S. *Attitudes and Opinions.* Englewood Cliffs, NJ: Prentice-Hall, 1977.

PADGETT, V. R., & Jorgenson, D. O. Superstition and economic threat: Germany, 1918–1940. *Personality and Social Psychology Bulletin,* 1982, *8,* 736–41.

PAIGE, G. D. *The Scientific Study of Political Leadership.* New York: Free Press, 1977.

PAPER, L. J. *John F. Kennedy: The Promise and the Performance.* New York: DaCapo Press, 1979.

PARSONS, T., BALES, R. F., & SHILS, E. *Working Papers in the Theory of Action.* New York: Free Press, 1955.

PATEMAN, C. The civic culture: a philosophic critique. In Almond & Verba (eds.), *The Civic Culture Revisited.* Boston, MA: Little, Brown, 1980.

_____. *Participation and Democratic Theory.* Cambridge: Cambridge University Press, 1970.

PATTERSON, T. E., & McCLURE, R. D. *The Unseeing Eye: The Myth of Television Power in National Politics.* New York: Putnam, 1976.

PEACHEY, D. E., & LERNER, M. J. Law as a social trap: problems and possibilities for the future. In M. J. Lerner & S. C. Lerner (eds.), *The Justice Motive in Social Behavior: Adapting to Times of Scarcity and Change.* New York: Plenum, 1982.

PEPLAU, L. A., & RUBIN, Z. Who believes in a just world? *Journal of Social Issues,* 1975, *31,* 65–90.

PETERSON, S. A. Biology and political socialization: a cognitive development link? *Political Psychology,* 1983, *4,* 265–88.

_____. Sociology and ideas-become-real; case study and assessment. *Journal of Social and Biological Structures,* 1981, *4,* 125–43.

PETROCIK, J. R. The limits of individual variables: electoral participation, attitudes, and party systems. May 1980.

PHARES, E. J. *Locus of Control: A Personality Determinant of Behavior.* Morristown, NJ: General Learning Press, 1973.

_____. Internal-external control as a determinant of amount of social influence exerted. *Journal of Personality and Social Psychology,* 1965, *36,* 642–47.

PIAGET, J., & WEIL, A. The development in children of the idea of the homeland and relations with other countries. *International Social Science Bulletin,* 1951, *3,* 561–78.

PIRAGES, D. *Managing Political Conflict.* New York: Praeger, 1976.

PIVEN, F. F., & CLOWARD, R. A. *The New Class War: Reagan's Attack on the Welfare State and its Consequences.* New York: Pantheon, 1981.

PLATT, J. Social traps. *American Psychologist,* 1973, *28,* 641–51.

POOL, I., FREY, F. W., SCHRAMM, W., MACCOBY, N., & PARKER, E. B. *Handbook of Communication.* Chicago: Rand McNally, 1973.

POST, J. M. The seasons of a leader's life: influence of the life cycle on political behavior. *Political Psychology,* 1980, *2,* 35–49.

POULANTZAS, N. The problem of the capitalist state. *New Left Review,* 1969, *58,* 67–78.

PRESTHUS, R. *The Organizational Society* (rev. ed.). New York: St. Martin's, 1978.

PRUITT, D. B. Methods for resolving differences of interest: a theoretical analysis. *Journal of Social Issues*, 1972, *28*, 133–54.

————. *Negotiation Behavior*. New York: Academic Press, 1981.

————, & LEWIS, S. The psychology of integrative bargaining. In D. Druckman (ed.), *Negotiations: Social-Psychological Perspectives*. Beverly Hills, CA: Sage Publications, 1977.

RAMBERG, B. Tactical advantages of opening positioning strategies. *Journal of Conflict Resolution*, 1977, *21*, 685–700.

RAPOPORT, A. *Fights, Games and Debates*. Ann Arbor: University of Michigan Press, 1960.

————. Prospects for experimental games. *Journal of Conflict Resolution*, 1968, *12*, 461–470.

RAUSH, H. Pardox, levels, and junctures in person-situation systems. In D. Magnusson & N. S. Endler (eds.), *Personality at the Crossroads: Current Issues in Interactional Psychology*. Hillsdale, NJ: Erlbaum, 1977.

REARDON, K. K. *Persuasion: Theory and Context*. Beverly Hills, CA: Sage Publications, 1981.

REDL, F. Group emotion and leadership. *Psychiatry*, 1942, *5*, 573–96.

REILLY, T. A., & SIGALL, M. W. *Political Bargaining: An Introduction to Modern Politics*. San Francisco: Freeman, 1976.

REJAI, M. *The Comparative Study of Revolutionary Strategy*. New York: David McKay, 1977.

RENSHON, S. A. (ed.). *Handbook of Political Socialization: Theory and Research*. New York: Free Press, 1977.

————. Personality and family dynamics in the political socialization process. Paper delivered at the Meeting of the American Political Science Association, New Orleans, LA, 1973.

————. *Psychological Needs and Political Behavior*. New York: Free Press, 1974.

————. The role of personality development in political socialization. In D. C. Schwartz & K. Schwartz (eds.), *New Directions in Political Socialization*. New York: Free Press, 1975.

RIDGEWAY, C. L. *The Dynamics of Small Groups*, New York: St. Martin's, 1983.

RIEGEL, K. *Foundations of a Dialectical Psychology*. New York: Academic Press, 1979.

————. *Psychology, Mon Amour*. Boston: Houghton-Mifflin, 1978.

RINGWALD, B. Some political ramifications of the literature of social psychology: a conceptual and empirical study. Unpublished doctoral dissertation, University of Michigan, 1974.

RIPLEY, R. B. *Congress: Process and Policy*, 3rd ed. New York: Norton, 1983.

ROHTER, I. S. A social-learning approach to political socialization. In D. C. Schwartz & S. K. Schwartz (eds.), *New Directions in Political Socialization*. New York: Free Press, 1975.

ROKEACH, M. *Beliefs, Attitudes and Values: A Theory of Organization and Change*. San Francisco: Jossey-Bass, 1968.

————. *The Open and Closed Mind*. New York: Basic Books, 1960.

———— (ed.) *Understanding Human Values: Individual and Societal*. New York: Free Press, 1979.

ROLOFF, M. E. Self-awareness and the persuasion process. In M. E. Roloff & G. R. Miller (eds.), *Persuasion: New Directions in Theory and Research*. Beverly Hills, CA: Sage Publications, 1980.

ROMMETWEIT, R. *Social Norms and Roles: Explorations in the Psychology of Enduring Pressures.* Minneapolis: Univ. of Minnesota Press, 1955.

ROSENAU, N. The sources of children's political concepts: an application of Piaget's theory. In C. Schwartz & S. K. Schwartz (eds.), *New Directions in Political Socialization.* New York: Free Press, 1975.

ROSENBAUM, A. *Political Culture.* New York: Praeger, 1975.

ROSENBERG, S. W. Forms of thought and types of social reasoning: the structural bases of social cognition. Paper presented at the 1982 Annual Meeting of the American Psychological Association, Washington, D.C., 1982.

————. The structural developmental analysis of political cognition. Paper presented at the Meeting of the American Political Science Association, Chicago, Illinois, 1983.

————, NELSON, C., & VIVEKANANTHAN, P. S. A multidimensional approach to the structure of personality impressions. *Journal of Personality and Social Psychology,* 1968, *9,* 258–90.

ROSENTHAL, R., & JACOBSON, L. *Pygmalion in the Classroom: Teachers' Expectations and Pupils' Intellectual Development.* New York: Holt, Rinehart and Winston, 1968.

ROSENWEIN, R. Whiter interaction? A review of "political psychology and biopolitics." *Politics and the Life Sciences,* 1983, *1,* 161–63.

ROSS, M. H. Explaining differences in political participation cross-culturally: socioeconomic development, political structure, and personality dispositions. Paper presented at the Meeting of the International Society of Political Psychology, Boston, MA, 1980.

ROSS, M. Salience of reward and intrinsic motivation. *Journal of Personality and Social Psychology,* 1975, *25,* 245–54.

ROTHMAN, S., & LICHTER, S. R. *Radical Christians, Radical Jews.* New York: Oxford University Press, 1981.

ROTHSCHILD, M. L. On the use of multiple methods and multiple situations in political communications research. In Steven H. Chaffee (ed.), *Political Communication: Issues and Strategies for Research.* Beverly Hills, CA: Sage Publications, 1975.

————, & RAY, M. L. Involvement and political advertising effect: an exploratory experiment. *Communication Research,* 1974, *1,* 264–85.

ROTTER, J. B. Generalized expectancies for internal versus external control of reinforcement. *Psychological Monographs,* 1966, *80* (no. 609).

RUBIN, J. Z. (ed.), *Dynamics of Third-Party Intervention: Kissinger in the Middle East.* New York: Praeger, 1981.

————, & BROWN, B. R. *The Social Psychology of Bargaining and Negotiation.* New York: Academic Press, 1975.

RYAN, W. *Blaming the Victim.* New York: Pantheon, 1971.

RYCHLAK, J. F. The case for a modest revolution in modern psychological science. In R. A. Kasschau & C. N. Cofer (eds.), *Psychology's Second Century.* New York: Praeger, 1981.

SALES, S. M. Threat as a factor in authoritarianism: an analysis of archival data. *Journal of Personality and Social Psychology,* 1973, *28,* 44–57.

SAMPSON, E. E. On justice as equality. *Journal of Social Issues,* 1975, *31,* 21–44.

SANFORD, N. *Self and Society: Social Change and Individual Development.* New York: Atherton, 1966.

SARNOFF, I., & KATZ, D. The motivational bases of attitude change. *Journal of Abnormal and Social Psychology,* 1954, *49,* 115–24.

SCHATTSCHNEIDER, E. E. *The Semi-Sovereign People.* New York: Holt, Rinehart & Winston, 1960.

SCHEFLEN, A. E. *Body Language and Social Order: Communication as Behavior Control.* Englewood Cliffs, NJ: Prentice-Hall, 1972.

————, & ASHCRAFT, N. *Human Territories: How We Behave in Space-Time.* Englewood Cliffs, NJ: Prentice-Hall, 1976.

SCHELL, J. *The Fate of the Earth.* New York: Knopf, 1982.

SCHELLING, T. C. *The Strategy of Conflict.* New York: Oxford University Press, 1963.

SCHLESSINGER, A. M., Jr. *A Thousand Days.* Boston: Houghton Mifflin, 1965.

SCHNEIRLA, T. C. Instinct and aggression. In M. F. A. Montagu (ed.), *Man and Aggression.* New York: Oxford University Press, 1968.

SCHRODER, H. M., & SUEDFELD, P. *Personality Theory and Information Processing.* New York: Ronald Press, 1971.

SCHUBERT, G. The evolution of political science: paradigms of physics, biology, and politics. *Politics and the Life Sciences,* 1983, *1,* 97–110.

SCHULTZ, D. E. Political participation in communist systems: the conceptual frontier. In D. E. Schultz & J. S. Adams (eds.), *Political Participation in Communist Systems.* New York: Pergamon, 1981.

SCHUTZ, W. *FIRO: Fundamental Interpersonal Relations Orientation.* New York: Holt, Rinehart and Winston, 1958.

SCHWARTZ, D. C. *Political Alienation and Political Behavior.* Chicago: Aldine, 1973.

————.Political alienation: the psychology of revolution's first stage. In I. K. Feierabend, R. Feierabend & T. R. Gurr (eds.), *Anger, Violence, and Politics: Theories and Research.* Englewood Cliffs, NJ: Prentice-Hall, 1972.

————, & SCHWARTZ, S. K. (eds.). *New Directions in Political Socialization.* New York: Free Press, 1975.

SCHWARTZ, M. *Soviet Perceptions of the United States.* Berkeley: University of California Press, 1978.

SCHWARTZ, S. The justice of need and the activation of humanitarian norms. *Journal of Social Issues,* 1975, *31,* 111–36.

SCHWINGER, T. Just allocation of goods: decisions among three principles. In G. Mikula (ed.), *Justice and Social Interaction.* New York: Springer-Verlag, 1980.

SCIOLI, F. P., & COOK, J. Political socialization research in the United States: a review. In D. D. Nimmo & C. M. Bonjean (eds.), *Political Attitudes and Public Opinion.* New York: David McKay, 1972.

SCOTT, J. P. That old-time aggression. In M. F. A. Montagu (ed.), *Man and Aggression.* New York: Oxford University Press, 1968.

SEARING, D. G. Models and images of man and society in leadership theory. In G. D. Paige (ed.), *Political Leadership: Readings for an Emerging Field.* New York: Free Press, 1972.

SEARS, D. O., & WHITNEY, R. E. Political Persuasion. In I. Pool et al. (eds.), *Handbook of Communication,* Chicago: Rand McNally, 1973.

SELIGMAN, M. E. *Helplessness.* San Francisco: Freeman, 1975.

SHAVER, K. Attributional error and policy formation: how do we know our own position? Paper presented at the Meeting of the International Society of Political Psychology. Washington, DC, 1982.

SHAW, D. L., & McCOMBS, M. E. (eds.), *The Emergence of American Political Issues.* St Paul, MN: West Publishing Co., 1977.

SHINGLES, R. D. Black consciousness and political participation: the missing link. *The American Political Science Review*, March 1981, 76–91.

SILBIGER, S. L. Peers and political socialization. In S. A. Renshon (ed.), *Handbook of Political Socialization: Theory and Research*. New York: Free Press, 1977.

SIMON, H. A. *Administrative Behavior*. New York: Macmillan, 1961.

————. On the concept of organizational goal. *Administrative Science Quarterly*, 1964, *9*, 1–22.

SIUNE, K., & BORRE, O. Setting the agenda for a Danish election. *Journal of Communication*, 1975, *25*, 65–73.

SIUNE, K., & KLEIN, F. G. Communication, mass political behavior, and mass society. In S. H. Chaffee (ed.), *Political Communication: Issues and Strategies for Research*. Beverly Hills, CA: Sage Publications, 1975.

SKINNER, B. F. *Beyond Freedom and Dignity*. New York: Knopf, 1971.

SKOLNICK, J. H. *The Politics of Protest*. New York: Simon & Schuster, 1969.

SLOAN, A. T., & WHICKER, M. L. A hierarchy of government goals and the interface of ranked government goals with Maslow's hierarchy of needs. Paper presented at the Meeting of the American Political Science Association, Chicago, IL, 1983.

SMITH, D. H., & MACAULAY, J. and ASSOCIATES. *Participation in Social and Political Activities*. San Francisco: Jossey-Bass, 1980.

SMITH, G. *Doubletalk: The Story of the First Strategic Arms Limitation Talks*. Garden City, NY: 1980.

SMITH, M. B. A map for the analysis of personality and politics. *Journal of Social Issues*, 1968, *24*, 15–28.

————, BRUNER, J. S., & WHITE, R. W. *Opinions and Personality*. New York: John Wiley, 1956.

SNIDERMAN, P. M. *Personality and Democratic Politics*. Berkeley: University of California Press, 1975.

SNYDER, G. H., & DIESING, P. *Conflict among Nations: Bargaining, Decision Making, and System Structure in International Crises*, Princeton, NJ: Princeton University Press, 1977.

SNYDER, M., & KENZIERSKI, D. Acting on one's attitudes: procedures for linking attitude and behavior. *Journal of Experimental Psychology*, 1982, *18*, 165–83.

SOMMER, R. Further studies of small group ecology. *Sociometry*, 1965, *28*, 337–48.

SORENSON, C. *Kennedy*. New York: Harper & Row, Bantam ed., 1966.

SPECTOR, B. I. Negotiations as a psychological process. *Journal of Conflict Resolution*, 1977, *2*, 607–18.

STARR, H. *Henry Kissinger: Perceptions of International Politics*. Lexington: University of Kentucky Press, 1984.

STEINBRUNER, J. D. *The Cybernetic Theory of Decision: New Dimensions of Political Analysis*. Princeton, NJ: Princeton University Press, 1974.

STEPHENSON, W. *The Play Theory of Mass Communication*. Chicago: University of Chicago Press, 1967.

STODGILL, R. M. *Handbook of Leadership*. New York: Free Press, 1974.

————. Leadership, membership and organization. *Psychological Bulletin*, 1950, *47*, 1–14.

STOESSINGER, J. G. *Crusaders and Pragmatists: Movers of Modern American Foreign Policy*. New York: W. W. Norton, 1979.

STONE, W. F. The myth of left-wing authoritarianism. *Political Psychology*, 1980, *2*, 3–19.

_____. Political psychology: a Whig history. In S. Long (ed.), *The Handbook of Political Behavior.* New York: Plenum, 1981.

_____. *The Psychology of Politics.* New York: Free Press, 1974.

STORR, A. *Human Aggression.* New York: Atheneum, 1968.

STRICKLAND, B. R. The prediction of social action from a dimension of internal-external control. *Journal of Social Psychology,* 1965, *66,* 353–58.

STRODBECK, F. L., & HOOK, L. H. The social dimensions of a twelve man jury table. *Sociometry,* 1961, *24,* 397–415.

STUART, D. T. The link between general and situation-specific beliefs: JFK, the missile crisis, and the Bay of Pigs. Paper presented at the Meeting of the International Society of Political Psychology, Boston, MA, 1980.

SUMNER, W. G. Folkways. New York: Ginn, 1906.

SWENSON, C. H. *Introduction to Interpersonal Relations.* Glenview, IL: Scott, Foresman, 1978.

SZAMUELY, T. Five years after Khrushchev. *Survey,* 1969, *72,* 56–90.

TALBOTT, S. *Endgame: The Inside Story of SALT II.* New York: Harper & Row, 1979.

TAYLOR, F. W. *The Principles of Scientific Management.* New York: Harper & Brothers, 1911.

TAYLOR, L. *Born to Crime: The Genetic Causes of Criminal Behavior,* Westport, CT: Greenwood, 1984.

TEDIN, K. L. The influence of parents on the political attitudes of adolescents. *American Political Science Review,* 1974, *68,* 1579–1592.

TEICH, A. M., & THORNTON, R. (eds.). *Science, Technology, and the Issues of the Eighties.* Boulder, CO: Westview, 1982.

THIBAUT, J. W. The development of contractual norms in bargaining: replication and variation. *Journal of Conflict Resolution,* 1968, *12,* 102–12.

_____, & KELLY, H. H. *The Social Psychology of Groups.* New York: John Wiley, 1959.

TINBERGEN, N. On war and peace in animals and man. *Science,* 1968, *160,* 1411–1418.

TOLAND, J. *Adolf Hitler.* New York: Ballantine, 1976.

TRUMAN, D. B. *The Governmental Process.* New York: Alfred A. Knopf, Inc., 1951, 1971.

TUCKER, R. C. The Georges' Wilson reexamined: an essay on psychobiography. *The American Political Science Review,* 1977, *71,* 606–18.

_____. *Politics as Leadership.* Columbia: University of Missouri Press, 1981.

_____. *Stalin as Revolutionary, 1879–1929: A Study in History and Personality.* New York: W. W. Norton, 1973.

U.S. Department of State, bulletin. (vol. 47, no. 1220), November 12, 1962, 741–43.

VAN MAANEN, J. Breaking in: socialization to work. In R. Dubin (ed.), *Handbook of Work, Organization and Society.* Chicago: Rand-McNally, 1976, 67–130.

VEN DEN BERGHE, L. Territorial behavior in a natural human group. *Social Science Information,* 1977, *16,* 419–31.

VERBA, S. *Small Groups and Political Behavior.* Princeton, NJ: Princeton University Press, 1961.

_____, & NIE, N. H. *Participation in America: Political and Social Equality.* New York: Harper & Row, 1972.

_____, NIE, H., & KIM, J. *Participation and Political Equality: A Seven-Nation Comparison.* New York: Cambridge University Press, 1978.

VEROFF, J. Development and validation of a projective measure of power motivation. *Journal of Abnormal and Social Psychology*, 1957, *54*, 1–8.

VINACKE, W. E. Sex roles in a three-person game. *Sociometry*, 1959, *22*, 343–60.

VOLKAN, V. D. Narcissistic personality organization and "reparative" leadership. *The International Journal of Group Psychotherapy*, 1980, *30*, 131–52.

VONNEGUT, K. *Mother Night*. New York: Avon Books, 1966.

VROOM, V. H. A new look at managerial decision making. In D. Mankin, R. E. Ames, Jr. & M. A. Grodsky (eds.), *Classics of Industrial and Organizational Psychology*. Oak Park, IL: Moore, 1980.

WAHLKE, J. C. Pre-behavioralism in political science. *American Political Science Review*, 1979, *73*, 9–31.

WALKER, G., & FALKOWSKI, L. S. The operational codes of U.S. Presidents and Secretaries of State: motivational foundations and behavioral consequences. Paper presented at the Meeting of the International Society of Political Psychology, Washington, DC, 1982.

WALKER, S. The interface between beliefs and behavior: Henry Kissinger's operational code and the Vietnam War. *Journal of Conflict Resolution*, 1977, *21*, 129–68.

WALLACE, A. E. *Culture and Personality* (2nd ed.). New York: Random House, 1971.

WALLACH, M. A., KOGAN, N., & BEM, D. J. Group influence on individual risk taking. *Journal of Abnormal and Social Psychology*, 1962, *65*, 75–86.

————, & KOGAN, N. The roles of information, discussion and consensus in group risk taking. *Journal of Experimental and Social Psychology*, 1965, *1*, 1–19.

WALSTER, E., & WALSTER, G. Equity and social justice. *The Journal of Social Issues*, 1975, *31*, 21–44.

WALTON, R. E., & McKERSIE, R. B. *A Behavioral Theory of Labor Negotiations: An Analysis of a Social Interaction System*. New York: McGraw-Hill, 1965.

WEGNER, D., & VALLACHER, R. *Implicit Psychology: An Introduction to Social Cognition*. New York: Oxford University Press, 1977.

WEINSTEIN, D., ANDERSON, J. W., & LINK, A. S. Woodrow Wilson's political personality: a reappraisal. *Political Science Quarterly*, 1978, *93*, 585–98.

WEINSTEIN, F. B. *Indonesian Foreign Policy and the Dilemma of Independence*. Boston: Houghton-Mifflin, 1977.

WEISSBERG, R. Adolescent experiences with political authorities. *Journal of Politics*, 1972, *34*, 797–824.

WERTENBAKER, M. The law of the sea treaty—parts I and II. *The New Yorker*, July 16, 1983 and July 23, 1983.

WHITE, R. K. *Preventing Nuclear War: A Psychological Perspective*. New York: Free Press, 1984.

WICKER, T. *JFK and LBJ: The Influence of Personality upon Politics*. New York: Penguin, 1968.

WIEBE, G. Two psychological factors in media audience behavior. *Public Opinion Quarterly*, 1969–1970, *22*, 523–36.

WIEGELE, T. C. (ed.). *Biology and the Social Sciences: An Emerging Revolution*. Boulder, CO: Westview, 1982.

————. *Biopolitics: Search for a More Human Political Science*. Boulder, CO: Westview, 1979.

WILDAVSKY, A. *The Politics of the Budgetary Process* (4th ed.). Boston: Little, Brown, 1984.

WILLOUGHBY, W. F. *Principles of Public Administration.* Washington, DC: Brookings Institution, 1927.

WILLS, G. *The Kennedy Imprisonment: A Meditation on Power.* Boston: Little, Brown, 1982.

WILSON, E. O. *Sociobiology.* Cambridge, MA: Harvard University Press, 1975.

WILSON, J. Q. *Varieties of Police Behavior.* Cambridge, MA: Harvard University Press, 1968.

WINTER, D. G. An exploratory study of the motives of Southern African political leaders measured at a distance. *Political Psychology,* 1980, *2,* 75–85.

_____. Power motivation in thought and action. Harvard University, Department of Social Relations, unpublished Ph.D. dissertation, 1967.

_____. *The Power Motive.* New York: Free Press, 1973.

WOLFE, B. D. *Three Who Made a Revolution.* New York: Dell, 1964.

Women on Words and Images. *Dick and Jane as Victims: Sex Stereotyping in Children's Readers.* Princeton, NJ: Women on Words and Images, 1972.

WRIGHTSMAN, L. The social psychology of U.S. presidential effectiveness. Unpublished paper, 1982.

WYDEN, P. *The Bay of Pigs: The Untold Story.* New York: Simon & Schuster, 1979.

YAFFEE, S. L. *Prohibitive Policy: Implementing the Federal Endangered Species Act.* Cambridge, MA: MIT Press, 1982.

YINGER, J. M. Anomie, alienation, and political behavior. In J. N. Knutson (ed.), *Handbook of Political Psychology.* San Francisco: Jossey-Bass, 1973.

ZALD, N., & ASH, R. Social movements of organizations: growth, decay, and change. *Social Forces,* 1966, *44,* 327–39.

ZARTMAN, W. The political analysis of negotiations. *World Politics,* 1974, *26,* 385–99.

_____. Negotiations: theory and reality. *Journal of International Affairs,* 1975, *9,* 69–77.

ZIMBARDO, P. G., & EBBESEN, E. B. *Influencing Attitudes and Changing Behavior.* Reading, MA: Addison-Wesley, 1970.

_____, EBBESEN, E. B., & MASLACH, C. *Influencing Attitudes and Changing Behavior.* Reading, MA: Addison-Wesley, 1977.

INDEX